It's another Quality Book from CGP

This book is for anyone doing Edexcel Modular
GCSE Mathematics at Foundation Level.

Whatever subject you're doing it's the same
old story — there are lots of facts and you've just got
to learn them. KS4 Maths is no different.

Happily this CGP book gives you all that important
information as clearly and concisely as possible.

It's also got some daft bits in to try and make the whole
experience at least vaguely entertaining for you.

What CGP is all about

Our sole aim here at CGP is to produce the highest quality books
— carefully written, immaculately presented and dangerously
close to being funny.

Then we work our socks off to get them out to you
— at the cheapest possible prices.

Contents

Unit Two

Probability *1*
Relative Frequency *3*
Tables, Charts and Graphs *4*
Pie Charts *7*
Mean, Median, Mode and Range *8*
Grouped Frequency Tables *9*
Revision Test for Unit Two *12*

Unit Three

Big Numbers *13*
Multiplying by 10, 100, 1000, etc *14*
Dividing by 10, 100, 1000, etc *15*
Multiplying without a Calculator *16*
Dividing without a Calculator *17*
Rounding Off *18*
Accuracy and Estimating *20*
Special Number Sequences *22*
Prime Numbers *23*
Multiples, Factors and Prime Factors *24*
LCM and HCF *25*
Fractions *26*
Fractions, Decimals and Percentages *27*
Powers *28*
Square Roots and Cube Roots *29*
Standard Index Form *30*
Calculator Buttons *32*
Negative Numbers and Letters *34*
Basic Algebra *35*
Number Patterns and Sequences *37*
Metric and Imperial Units *39*
Rounding Off Measurements *40*
Conversion Factors *41*
Clock Time Questions *43*
Formula Triangles *44*
Density and Speed *45*
The Shapes You Need to Know *46*
Perimeters *47*
Areas *48*
Circles *50*
Solids and Nets *51*
Volume or Capacity *52*

Contents

Lines and Angles 53
Measuring Angles with Protractors 54
Compass Directions and Bearings 55
Six Angle Rules 56
Parallel Lines 57
X, Y and Z Coordinates 58
Midpoint of a Line Segment 59
Straight Line Graphs 60
Drawing Graphs from Equations 61
Revision Test for Unit Three 62

Unit Four

Ratio in the Home 64
Ratio — Rat 'n' Toad Pie 65
The Best Buy 66
More Fractions 67
Percentages 68
Making Formulas from Words 71
Substituting Values into Formulas 72
Solving Equations 73
Trial and Improvement 75
Inequalities 76
Straight Line Graphs — Gradients 77
Straight Line Graphs — "y = mx + c" 78
Simultaneous Equations with Graphs 79
Quadratic Graphs 80
Typical Graph Questions 81
Travel and Conversion Graphs 82
Regular Polygons 83
Projections, Congruence and Similarity 84
Pythagoras' Theorem 85
Circle Questions 86
Constructing Triangles 87
Loci and Constructions 88
Symmetry 90
The Four Transformations 92
Combinations of Transformations 94
Enlargement — Scale Factors 95
Length, Area and Volume 97
3D-Shapes and Converting Measures 98
Maps and Map Scales 99
Revision Test for Unit Four 101

Answers 103
Index 107

Published by Coordination Group Publications Ltd.

Written By Richard Parsons

Updated by: Simon Little and Alison Palin

With thanks to Charley Darbishire and Janet Dickinson for the proofreading.

ISBN: 978 1 84146 547 0

Groovy website: www.cgpbooks.co.uk
Printed by Elanders Hindson Ltd, Newcastle upon Tyne

Text, design, layout and original illustrations © Richard Parsons 2006
All rights reserved.

UNIT TWO

Probability

Probability definitely seems a bit of a "Black Art" to most people. It's not as bad as you think, but YOU MUST LEARN THE BASIC FACTS, which is what we have on these 3 pages.

All Probabilities are between 0 and 1

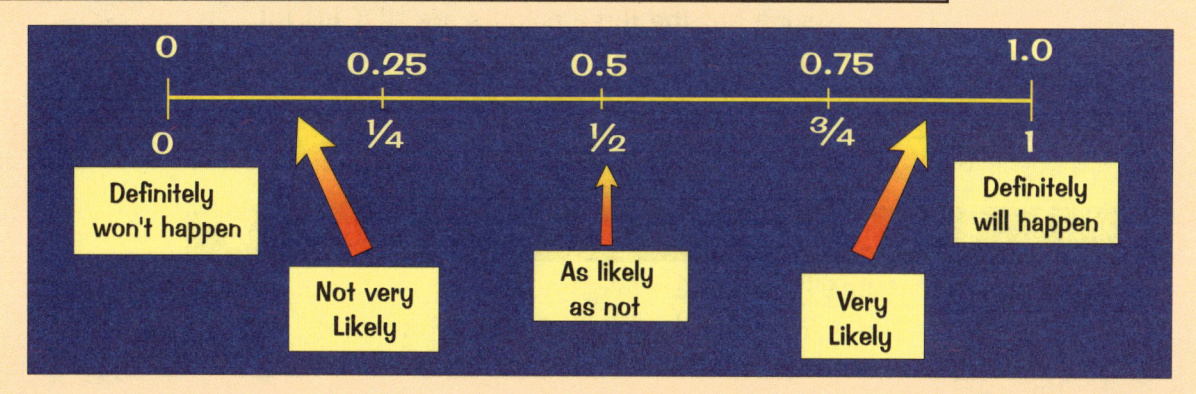

0	0.25	0.5	0.75	1.0
0	¼	½	¾	1

- 0: Definitely won't happen
- ¼: Not very Likely
- ½: As likely as not
- ¾: Very Likely
- 1: Definitely will happen

Probabilities can only have values from 0 to 1 (including those values). You should be able to put the probability of any event happening on this scale of 0 to 1.

Remember you can give probabilities using
FRACTIONS, DECIMALS or PERCENTAGES.

Equal Probabilities

When the different results all have the same chance of happening, then the probabilities will be EQUAL. These are the two cases which usually come up in Exams:

1) **TOSSING A COIN**: Equal chance of getting a head or a tail (probability = ½)

2) **THROWING A DICE**: Equal chance of getting any of the numbers (probability = ⅙)

Probability

Unequal Probabilities

These make for more interesting questions. (Which means you'll get them in the Exam.)

EXAMPLE 1: "A bag contains 6 blue balls, 5 red balls and 9 green balls. Find the probability of picking out a green ball."

ANSWER: The chances of picking out the three colours are NOT EQUAL. The probability of picking a green is simply:

$$\frac{\text{NUMBER OF GREENS}}{\text{TOTAL NUMBER OF BALLS}} = \frac{9}{20}$$

EXAMPLE 2: "What is the probability of winning £45 on this spinner?"

ANSWER:
The pointer has the same chance of stopping on every sector...
... and since there are 2 out of 8 which are £45
then it's a 2 out of 8 chance of getting £45.

BUT REMEMBER ... you have to say this as a FRACTION or a DECIMAL or a PERCENTAGE:

2 out of 8 is 2 ÷ 8 which is 0.25 (as a decimal)
or ¼ (as a fraction) or 25% (as a percentage)

The Probability of the OPPOSITE happening is just the rest of the probability that's left over

This is simple enough AS LONG AS YOU REMEMBER IT.
If the probability of something happening is, say, 0.3 then the chance of it NOT HAPPENING is 1 − 0.3 (= 0.7), i.e. it's what's left when you subtract it from 1.

Example: A loaded dice has a 0.25 chance of coming up TWO. What is the chance of it not coming up TWO?

Answer: 1 − 0.25 = 0.75
So, the chance of the dice not coming up TWO is 0.75

Listing All Outcomes: 2 Coins, Dice, Spinners

A simple question you might get is to list all the possible results from tossing two coins or two spinners or a dice and a spinner, etc. Whatever it is, it'll be very similar to these, so LEARN THEM:

The possible outcomes from TOSSING TWO COINS are:

Head	Head	H	H
Head	Tail	H	T
Tail	Head	T	H
Tail	Tail	T	T

From TWO SPINNERS with 3 sides:

BLUE, 1   RED, 1   GREEN, 1
BLUE, 2   RED, 2   GREEN, 2
BLUE, 3   RED, 3   GREEN, 3

Try and list the possible outcomes METHODICALLY
— to make sure you get them ALL.

UNIT TWO

Relative Frequency

This isn't the number of times your granny comes to visit. It's a way of working out probabilities.

Fair or Biased?

The probability of rolling a three on a dice is $1/6$ — you know that each of the 6 numbers on a dice is equally likely to be rolled, and there's only 1 three.

BUT this only works if it's a fair dice. If the dice is a bit wonky (the technical term is "biased") then each number won't have an equal chance of being rolled. That's where Relative Frequency comes in — you can use it to work out probabilities when things might be wonky.

Do the Experiment Again and Again and Again and Again

You need to do an experiment over and over again and then do a quick calculation. (Remember, an experiment could just mean rolling a dice.)
Usually the results of these experiments will be written in a table.

The Formula for Relative Frequency

$$\text{Probability of something happening} = \frac{\text{Number of times it has happened}}{\text{Number of times you tried}}$$

You can work out the relative frequency as a fraction but usually decimals are best.

The important thing to remember is: **The more times you do the experiment, the more accurate the probability will be.**

Example:

So, back to the wonky dice. **What is the probability of rolling a three?**

Number of Times the dice was rolled	10	20	50	100
Number of threes rolled	3	9	19	36
Relative frequency	$\frac{3}{10}=0.3$	$\frac{9}{20}=0.45$	$\frac{19}{50}=0.38$	$\frac{36}{100}=0.36$

So, what's the probability? We've got 4 possible answers, but the best is the one worked out using the highest number of dice rolls.
This makes the probability of rolling a three on this dice 0.36.

And since for a fair, unbiased dice, the probability of rolling a three is $1/6$ (about 0.17), then our dice is probably biased.

The Acid Test

1) What is the probability of picking from a shuffled deck of cards (no jokers)
   a) an Ace of any suit   b) a number less than 7   c) a red picture card

2) A 3-sided spinner is spun 100 times – it lands on red 43 times, blue 24 times and green the other times. Calculate the relative frequency of each outcome.

Unit Two

Tables, Charts and Graphs

Make sure you know all the different types of charts, tables and graphs that you can use to represent your data. Here they all are, in all their glory. Enjoy.

1) Frequency Tables

You've seen these before. Nothing too complicated.

Groups here:

Length l (m)	Frequency
$20 \leq l < 30$	12
$30 \leq l < 40$	21
$40 \leq l < 50$	18
$50 \leq l < 60$	10

Number of things in each group here:

2) Line Graphs and Frequency Polygons

A line graph is just a set of points joined with straight lines.

A frequency polygon looks similar and is used to show the information from a frequency table like the one above.

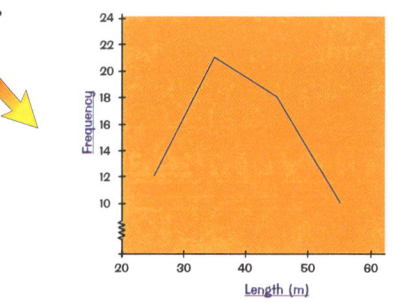

3) Two-Way Tables

Two-way tables are a bit like frequency tables, but they show two different things:

EXAMPLE:

"Use this table to work out how many
(a) right-handed people and
(b) left-handed women there were in this survey."

	Women	Men	TOTAL
Left-handed		27	63
Right-handed	164	173	
TOTAL	200	200	400

ANSWER:

(a) Either: (i) add up the number of right-handed women and the number of right-handed men. So that's 164 + 173 = <u>337 right-handed people</u>.

Or: (ii) take away the total number of left-handed people from the total number of people. So that's 400 − 63 = <u>337 right-handed people</u>.

(b) Either: (i) take away the number of right-handed women from the total number of women. That's 200 − 164 = <u>36 left-handed women</u>.

Or: (ii) take away the left-handed men from the total number of left-handed people. Which would be 63 − 27 = <u>36 left-handed women</u>.

The Acid Test

Sketch examples of the three things on this page. Then copy out the two-way table, turn over the page and fill in the blanks yourself.

UNIT TWO

Tables, Charts and Graphs

4) Pictograms — these use pictures instead of numbers.

EXAMPLE: The pictogram opposite shows the number of talking cats used in ridiculous TV adverts in a 3-month period:

🐈 = 500 talking cats

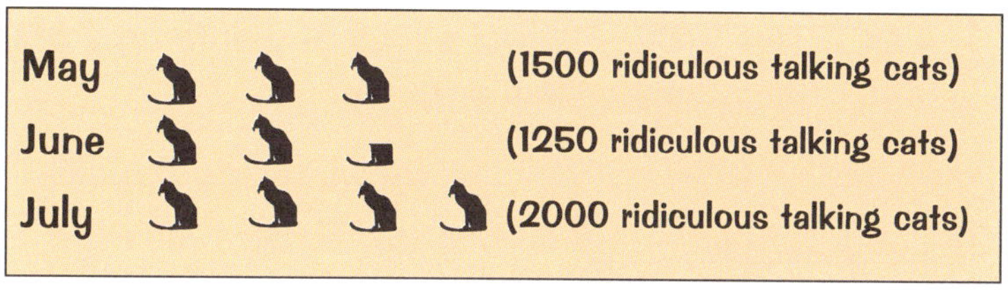

May	🐈 🐈 🐈	(1500 ridiculous talking cats)
June	🐈 🐈 🐈	(1250 ridiculous talking cats)
July	🐈 🐈 🐈 🐈	(2000 ridiculous talking cats)

In a PICTOGRAM each picture or symbol represents a certain number of items.

5) Bar Charts
Just watch out for when the bars should touch or not touch:

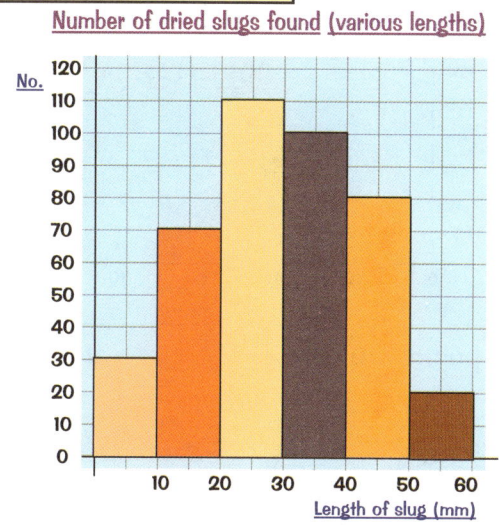

Number of dried slugs found (various lengths)

Popular Choices at the School Canteen

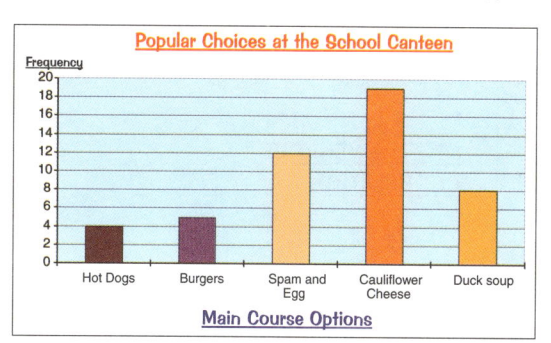

This bar chart compares <u>totally separate items</u> so the bars are <u>separate</u>.

ALL the bars in this chart are for **LENGTHS** and you must <u>put every possible length into one bar or the next</u> so there mustn't be any spaces.

A **BAR-LINE GRAPH** is just like a bar chart except you draw thin lines instead of bars.

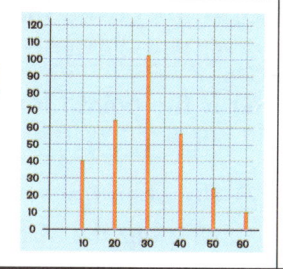

6) Stem and Leaf Diagrams

Stem and leaf diagrams are a bit like bar charts, but more confusing. They're supposed to be easy to read, but they're not. So **LEARN** this example.

EXAMPLE: This diagram shows the ages of my school teachers.
a) How many of the teachers are in their forties?
b) How old is the oldest teacher?

```
3 | 5
4 | 0 5 7 8
5 | 1 4 9
6 | 1 3
```
Key: 5 | 4 means 54

ANSWER:

Step 1: Write down all the ages of the teachers, using the key.

35,
40, 45, 47, 48,
51, 54, 59,
61, (63)

Step 2: Answer the question.
a) four
b) 63

The key tells you how to read the diagram. A 5 in the stem and a 4 in the leaf means 54.

UNIT TWO

Tables, Charts and Graphs

7) Scatter Graphs

1) A SCATTER GRAPH is just a load of points on a graph that end up in a bit of a mess rather than in a nice line or curve.

2) There is a posh word to say how much of a mess they are in — it's CORRELATION.

3) Good Correlation (or Strong Correlation) means the points form quite a nice line, and it means the two things are closely related to each other. When this is the case, you can draw a line of best fit roughly through the middle of the scatter of points.

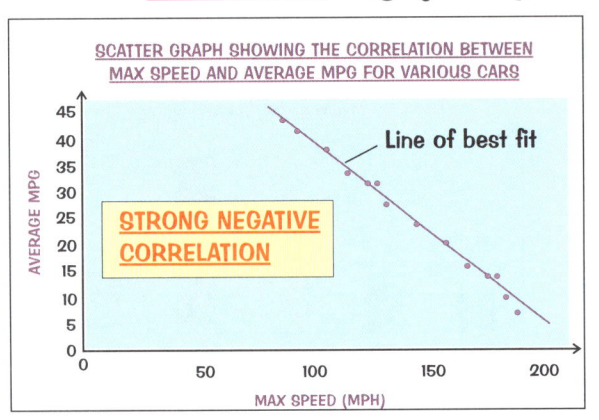

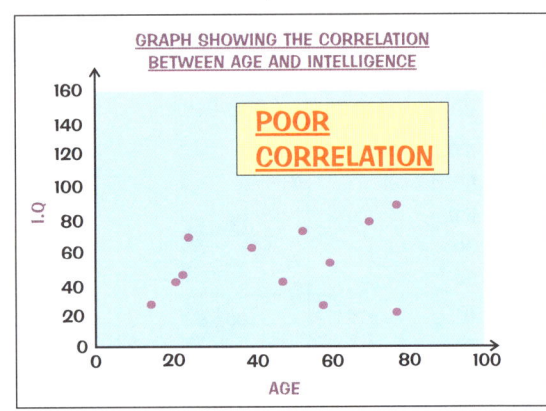

SCATTER GRAPH SHOWING THE CORRELATION BETWEEN MAX SPEED AND AVERAGE MPG FOR VARIOUS CARS — Line of best fit — STRONG NEGATIVE CORRELATION

GRAPH SHOWING THE CORRELATION BETWEEN AGE AND INTELLIGENCE — POOR CORRELATION

4) Poor Correlation (or Weak Correlation) means the points are all over the place and so there is very little relation between the two things.

5) If the points form a line sloping UPHILL from left to right, then there is POSITIVE CORRELATION, which just means that both things increase or decrease together.

6) If the points form a line sloping DOWNHILL from left to right, then there is NEGATIVE CORRELATION, which just means that as one thing increases the other decreases.

7) So when you're describing a scatter graph you have to mention both things, i.e. whether it's strong/weak/moderate correlation and whether it's positive/negative.

SCATTER GRAPH SHOWING THE RELATIONSHIP BETWEEN AGE AND BALDNESS IN MEN — MODERATE POSITIVE CORRELATION

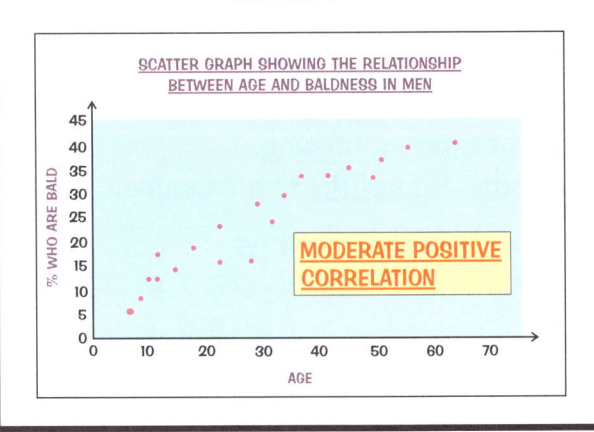

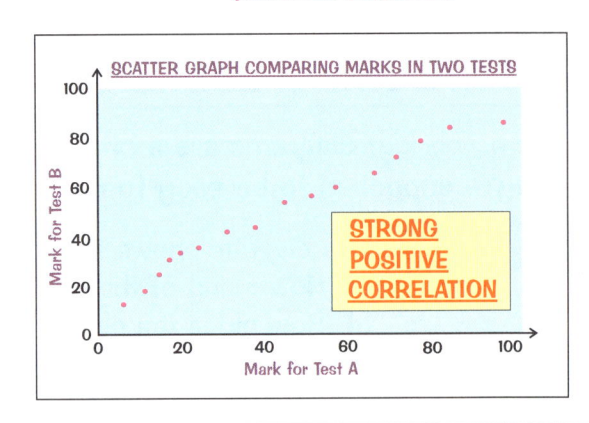

SCATTER GRAPH COMPARING MARKS IN TWO TESTS — STRONG POSITIVE CORRELATION

The Acid Test — LEARN ALL THE CHARTS on these two pages

1) Turn over the page and draw an example of each type of chart or graph.
2) If the points on a scatter graph are all over the place, what does it tell you about the two things that the scatter graph is comparing?

UNIT TWO

Pie Charts

They can make Pie Charts into quite tricky Exam questions.
So learn the Golden Rule for Pie Charts:

The TOTAL of Everything = 360°

Remember that 360° is the trick for dealing with most Pie Charts

1) Relating Angles to Fractions

These five simplest ones you should just know straight off:

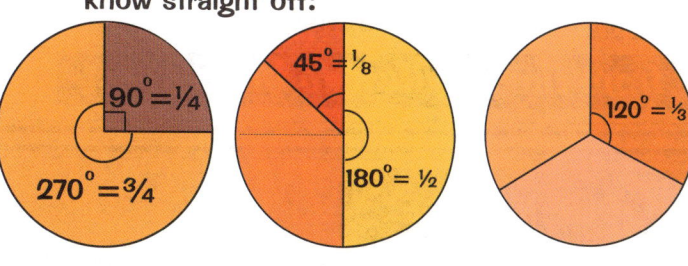

90° = ¼
270° = ¾
45° = 1/8
180° = ½
120° = 1/3

For any angle the formula is:

Fraction = Angle / 360°

And then cancel it down with your calculator (see P.32)

If you have to measure an angle, you should expect it to be a nice round number like 90° or 180° or 120°, so don't go writing 89° or 181° or anything silly like that.

2) Relating Angles to Numbers of Other Things

Creature	Stick insects	Hamsters	Guinea Pigs	Rabbits	Ducks	Total
Number	12	20	17	15	26	90

×4 ×4 ×4 ×4 ×4 ×4

Angle	48°	80°	68°	60°	104°	360°

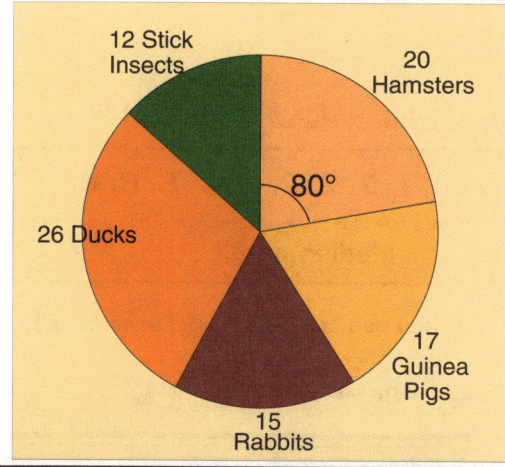

1) Add up all the numbers in each sector to get the TOTAL (90 for this one)

2) Then find the MULTIPLIER (or divider) that you need to turn your total into 360°:
For 90 → 360 as above, the MULTIPLIER is 4

3) Now MULTIPLY EVERY NUMBER BY 4 to get the angle for each sector. E.g. the angle for hamsters will be
20 × 4 = 80°

The Acid Test

Display this data in a Pie Chart:

Football Team	Wigan A.	Luton	Man.Utd.	Others
No. of Fans	53	15	30	22

UNIT TWO

Mean, Median, Mode and Range

If you don't manage to learn the 4 basic definitions then you'll be passing up on some of the easiest marks in the whole Exam. It can't be that difficult can it?

1) MODE	= MOST common

Mode = most (emphasise the 'o' in each when you say them)

2) MEDIAN	= MIDDLE value

Median = mid (emphasise the m*d in each when you say them)

3) MEAN	= TOTAL of items ÷ NUMBER of items

Mean is just the average, "but it's mean 'cos you have to work it out"

4) RANGE	= How far from the smallest to the biggest

THE GOLDEN RULE:

Mean, median, mode and range should be easy marks but even people who've gone to the incredible extent of learning them still manage to lose marks in the Exam because they don't do this one vital step:

Always REARRANGE the data in ASCENDING ORDER

(and then check you have the same number of entries!)

Example:
"Find the mean, median, mode and range of these numbers:"

2, 5, 3, 2, 6, -4, 0, 9, -3, 1, 6, 3, -2, 3   (14)

1) FIRST... rearrange them: -4, -3, -2, 0, 1, 2, 2, 3, 3, 3, 5, 6, 6, 9   (✓14)

2) MEAN = $\frac{total}{number}$ = $\frac{-4-3-2+0+1+2+2+3+3+3+5+6+6+9}{14}$

= 31 ÷ 14 = **2.21**

3) MEDIAN = the middle value (only when they're arranged in order of size, that is!).

When there are two middle numbers, as in this case, then the median is halfway between the two middle numbers.

-4, -3, -2, 0, 1, 2, 2, 3, 3, 3, 5, 6, 6, 9
← seven numbers this side ↑ seven numbers this side →
Median = **2.5**

4) MODE = most common value, which is simply **3**. (Or you can say "The modal value is 3")

5) RANGE = distance from lowest to highest value, i.e. from -4 up to 9, = **13**

The Acid Test: LEARN The Four Definitions and THE GOLDEN RULE...

..then cover this page and write them down from memory.

1) Apply all that you have learnt to find the mean, median, mode and range for this set of data: 1, 3, 14, -5, 6, -12, 18, 7, 23, 10, -5, -14, 0, 25, 8

UNIT TWO

Grouped Frequency Tables

Frequency tables are used to sort large amounts of data into groups, making the data easier to understand. Frequency tells you "how many" so a frequency table is just a "HOW MANY IN EACH GROUP" table. It's always best to do a tally first — you'll make less mistakes that way.

Example:

The marks of 28 students in a test (out of 80) were:

63, 45, 44, 52, 58, 49, 48, 22, 37, 34, 44, 49, 66, 73, 69, 32, 49, 29, 55, 57, 30, 72, 59, 46, 70, 39, 27, 40

The data can be grouped together and put into the table below:
The tally has been done for the first 12 numbers. Once the tally column is completed, just add up each tally to get the frequency.

Marks	Tally	Frequency
$0 \leq x \leq 10$		
$11 \leq x \leq 20$		
$21 \leq x \leq 30$			
$31 \leq x \leq 40$	||	
$41 \leq x \leq 50$	||||		
$51 \leq x \leq 60$	||	
$61 \leq x \leq 70$			
$71 \leq x \leq 80$		
		Total

You get the bottom value of an interval by adding 1 to the highest value of the previous interval.

The notation $41 \leq x \leq 50$ means $41 \leq x$ and $x \leq 50$, so it says x is greater than or equal to 41 and less than or equal to 50. So it's basically the same as saying "41 to 50". (x represents the number of marks).

The intervals in the table above only work for whole number data (try putting 50.2 into it...). Data like this that can only have certain values (only whole numbers in this case) is called discrete data.

The Acid Test

Complete the tally/frequency table above and make sure your total is 28.
If not, do the whole thing again.

UNIT TWO

Grouped Frequency Tables

Example:

The weights (in kg) of a bunch of 20 school kids are shown below.

67.3, 45.6, 47.7, 65.0, 54.2, 76.5, 44.6, 34.3, 69.8, 53.9, 32.3, 54.5, 78.9, 59.8, 57.4, 30.0, 79.1, 46.2, 66.0, 51.6

Weight w (kg)	Tally	Frequency
$30 \leq w < 40$	|||	3
$40 \leq w < 50$	||||	4
$50 \leq w < 60$	||||		6
$60 \leq w < 70$	||||	4
$70 \leq w < 80$	|||	3

We don't have nice whole numbers this time which means we need to use different intervals to group the data. Look at the first interval "$30 \leq w < 40$":

1) the $\leq$ symbol means w can be greater than or equal to 30

2) the < symbol means w must be less than 40 (but not equal to it)

So a value of 30 will go in this group, but a value of 40 will have to go in the next group up: $40 \leq w < 50$.

Intervals like this are used when you have continuous data — data that can take any value, not just whole numbers, within the range you're looking at. Weight and height are both continuous measurements — you can never measure them exactly, only as accurately as the scales you're using.

Mid-Interval Values

The mid-interval value is exactly what you'd expect — the number exactly in the middle of the interval. You do need to be a little careful when working them out though.

1) For simple ones like $10 \leq x < 20$, it's pretty obvious — 15 is the mid-interval value.

2) For something like $11 \leq x \leq 20$, it's a bit more awkward.

   Use this simple method: work out the difference, half it, then add this to the bottom number. Here, the difference is 9, half that is 4.5.

   So the mid-interval value is 11 + 4.5 = 15.5

The Acid Test

1) Say if the following are continuous or discrete data and design a data table for each one:

   a) shoe size of 20 adults b) height of 30 adults

UNIT TWO

Grouped Frequency Tables

Estimating The Mean For Grouped Data

You need to be able to estimate the mean for data in a grouped frequency table. Note you can only estimate the mean because you don't know the actual values.

The method is a bit fiddly at first, but it's easy once you've learnt it:

> 1) Add a 3rd row and enter MID-INTERVAL VALUES for each group.
> 2) Add a 4th row and multiply FREQUENCY × MID-INTERVAL VALUE for each group.
> 3) Work out the TOTALS of rows 2 and 4.
> 4) Get the mean by dividing ROW 4 TOTAL by ROW 2 TOTAL.

Note — if your table is arranged like the one on the previous page, you'll need to add extra columns rather than rows...

Example:

The table below shows the distribution of weights for 60 children.
Find the modal group and use the data in the table to estimate the mean.

Weight (kg)	30 ≤ w < 40	40 ≤ w < 50	50 ≤ w < 60	60 ≤ w < 70	70 ≤ w < 80
Frequency	8	16	18	12	6

The modal group is just the one with the highest frequency: 50 ≤ w < 60 kg

To find the mean, add two rows to the table as described above:

Weight (kg)	30 ≤ w < 40	40 ≤ w < 50	50 ≤ w < 60	60 ≤ w < 70	70 ≤ w < 80	TOTALS
Frequency	8	16	18	12	6	60
Mid-Interval Value	35	45	55	65	75	—
Frequency × Mid-Interval Value	280	720	990	780	450	3220

Now, just divide the totals to get an estimate of the mean:

$$\text{Mean} = \frac{\text{Overall Total (Final Row)}}{\text{Frequency Total (2nd Row)}} = \frac{3220}{60} = \underline{53.7}$$

The Acid Test:
LEARN all the details on this page, then turn over and write down everything you've learned. Good, clean fun.

1) Estimate the mean for this table:
2) State the modal group.

Length L (cm)	15.5 ≤ L < 16.5	16.5 ≤ L < 17.5	17.5 ≤ L < 18.5	18.5 ≤ L < 19.5
Frequency	12	18	23	8

UNIT TWO

Revision Test for Unit Two

Now it's time to put all of the methods of unit 2 into practice.... some of these questions may be a bit tricky, but they're the very best revision you can do.

1) A bag contains 3 red balls, 5 green balls and 7 black balls. Find the probability of picking out a black ball.

2) If I toss 2 coins, list all the possible outcomes. Since all these outcomes are equally likely, what is the chance of getting two heads?

3) If I toss a coin and throw a dice, list all the possible outcomes and say what the probability is of me getting a HEAD and a SIX.

4) The probability of a biased dice giving a SIX is 0.2. What is the chance of it NOT giving a six?

5) What is this diagram called? How many angry customers were there on Thursday?

6) What is the diagram on the right called? How good is the CORRELATION between Result A and Result B?

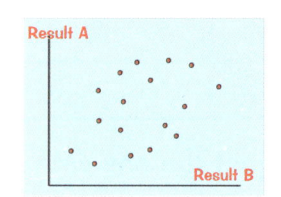

7) Complete this table and then put the information into a PIE CHART.

Colour	Blue	Red	Yellow	White	Totals:
Number of Cars	12	15	4	9	40
Angle on Pie Chart					360 degrees

8) For this set of numbers: 2, 6, 7, 12, 3, 7, 4, 15

   a) Find the MODE
   b) Find the MEDIAN
   c) Find the MEAN
   d) Find the RANGE

9) In a frequency table what does $50 \leq w < 60$ mean? Would you put 50 in this group? What about 60, would it go in this group or the next one up, $60 \leq w < 70$?

10) The times of all 1000 runners in the Skelly Crag half-marathon are recorded in the table below. State the modal group and estimate the mean time.

Time (min)	$60 < t \leq 90$	$90 < t \leq 120$	$120 < t \leq 150$	$150 < t \leq 180$	$180 < t \leq 210$	$210 < t \leq 240$
Frequency	15	60	351	285	206	83

Unit Two

Unit Three

Big Numbers

You need to know how to:

1) <u>Read big numbers</u>   E.g. how would you say 1,734,564?
2) <u>Write them down</u>   E.g. write "<u>Thirty-two thousand and three</u>" as a number.

Groups of Three

Always look at big numbers in <u>groups of three</u>.

2,351,243

So many MILLION   So many THOUSAND   And the rest
(i.e. 2 *million*, 351 *thousand*, 243)   or written fully in words:
Two *million*, three hundred and fifty-one *thousand*, two hundred and forty-three)

1) Always start from the extreme <u>right-hand side</u> of the number →
2) Moving <u>left</u>, ←, put a comma in <u>every 3 digits</u> to break it up into <u>groups of 3</u>.
3) Now going <u>right</u>, →, <u>read each group of three</u> as a separate number and add "million" and "thousand" on for the first two groups (assuming 3 groups in all).

Putting Numbers in Order of Size

<u>Example</u>:   12   84   623   32   486   4,563   75   2,143

① It may not be exactly difficult, but it's still best to do it in two steps.
First put them into groups, the ones with fewest digits first:

(all the <u>2-digit</u> ones,   then all the <u>3-digit</u> ones,   then all the <u>4-digit</u> ones etc.)
12 84 32 75   623 486   4,563 2,143

② Then just put each separate group in order of size:

12 32 75 84   486 623   2,143 4,563

For decimals, do the whole-number bit first before looking at what's after the point. With numbers between 0 and 1, first group them by the number of 0s at the start. The group with the most 0s at the start comes first, just like this:

(those with <u>2 initial 0s</u>,   then those with <u>1 initial 0</u>,   then those with <u>no initial 0s</u>.)
0.0026 0.007   0.03 0.098   0.14 0.531 0.7

Once they're in groups, just order them by comparing the first <u>non-zero</u> digits.
(If the first digits are the same, look at the next digit along instead.)

The Acid Test

1) Write these numbers fully in words:
   a) 1,234,531   b) 23,456   c) 2,415   d) 3,402   e) 203,412
2) Write this down as a number: Fifty-six thousand, four hundred and twenty-one
3) Put these numbers in order of size: 23 493 87 1,029 3,004 345 9
4) Write these numbers in ascending order: 0.37 0.008 0.307 0.1 0.09 0.2

Multiplying by 10, 100, 1000, etc.

You really should know this because
a) it's <u>very simple</u>, and   b) they're likely to <u>test you on it</u> in the Exam.

1) TO MULTIPLY ANY NUMBER BY 10

Move the Decimal Point ONE place BIGGER and if it's needed, ADD A ZERO on the end.

Examples:
23.6 × 10 = <u>236</u>
345 × 10 = <u>3450</u>
45.678 × 10 = <u>456.78</u>

2) TO MULTIPLY ANY NUMBER BY 100

Move the Decimal Point TWO places BIGGER and ADD ZEROS if necessary.

Examples:
296.5 × 100 = <u>29650</u>
34 × 100 = <u>3400</u>
2.543 × 100 = <u>254.3</u>

3) TO MULTIPLY BY 1000, OR 10,000, the same rule applies:

Move the Decimal Point so many places BIGGER and ADD ZEROS if necessary.

Examples:
341 × 1000 = <u>341000</u>
2.3542 × 10,000 = <u>23542</u>

You always move the DECIMAL POINT this much:
<u>1 place for 10</u>,   <u>2 places for 100</u>,
<u>3 places for 1000</u>,   <u>4 for 10,000</u>   etc.

4) TO MULTIPLY BY NUMBERS LIKE 20, 300, 8000 ETC.

Multiply by 2 or 3 or 8 etc. FIRST, then move the Decimal Point so many places BIGGER according to how many noughts there are.

Example:
To find 234 × 200, <u>first multiply by 2</u>   234 × 2 = 468,
then <u>move the DP 2 places</u>   = <u>46800</u>

The Acid Test

1) Work out   a) 12.3 × 100   b) 345 × 10   c) 9.65 × 1000
2) Work out   a) 2.4 × 20   b) 1.5 × 300   c) 60 × 3000

UNIT THREE

Dividing by 10, 100, 1000, etc.

This is pretty easy too. Just make sure you know it — that's all.

1) TO DIVIDE ANY NUMBER BY 10

Move the Decimal Point one place SMALLER and if it's needed, REMOVE ZEROS after the decimal point.

Examples:
23.6 ÷ 10 = 2.36
340 ÷ 10 = 34
45.678 ÷ 10 = 4.5678

2) TO DIVIDE ANY NUMBER BY 100

Move the Decimal Point 2 places SMALLER and REMOVE ZEROS after the decimal point.

Examples:
296.5 ÷ 100 = 2.965
340 ÷ 100 = 3.4
2543 ÷ 100 = 25.43

3) TO DIVIDE BY 1000, OR 10,000, the same rule applies:

Move the Decimal Point so many places SMALLER and REMOVE ZEROS after the decimal point.

Examples:
341 ÷ 1000 = 0.341
23500 ÷ 10,000 = 2.35

You always move the DECIMAL POINT this much:
1 place for 10,   2 places for 100,
3 places for 1000,   4 for 10,000   etc.

4) DIVIDING BY 40, 300, 7000 ETC.

DIVIDE BY 4 or 3 or 7 etc. FIRST and then move the Decimal Point so many places SMALLER (i.e. to the left).

Example:
To find 960 ÷ 300, first divide by 3   960 ÷ 3 = 320,
then move the DP 2 places smaller   = 3.2

The Acid Test

1) Work out   a) 2.45 ÷ 10   b) 654.2 ÷ 100   c) 3.08 ÷ 1000
2) Work out   a) 32 ÷ 20   b) 360 ÷ 30   c) 4000 ÷ 800

UNIT THREE

Multiplying Without a Calculator

You need to be really happy doing multiplications without a calculator — you'll definitely need to do it in your exam. So make sure you learn the methods on this page...

Multiplying Whole Numbers

There are lots of methods you can use for this. Two of the popular ones are shown below. Just make sure you can do it using whichever method you prefer...

The Traditional Method:

Split it into separate multiplications, and then add up the results in columns (right to left).

```
    4 6
  × 2 7
  ─────
  3 2 2    — This is 7 × 46
  9 2 0    — This is 20 × 46
  ─────
  1 2 4 2
```

The 'Gelosia' Method:

Arrange the calculation like below and do 4 easy multiplications to fill up the grid...

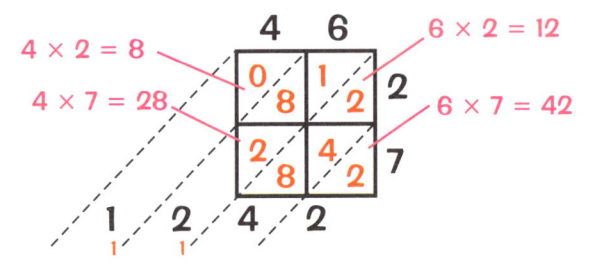

$4 \times 2 = 8$
$4 \times 7 = 28$
$6 \times 2 = 12$
$6 \times 7 = 42$

Then just add up along the diagonals (going right to left) to get the answer.

Answer in both cases: 46 × 27 = 1242

Multiplying Decimals

OK, this is a little more tricky — so you'll just have to make sure you learn it.

1) To start with, forget about the decimal points and do the multiplication using whole numbers.
   (E.g. for 1.2 × 3.45 you'd do 12 × 345.)

2) Now count the total number of digits after the decimal points in the original numbers.
   (E.g. 1.2 and 3.45 — so that's 3 digits after the decimal point.)

3) Make the answer have the same number of decimal places.

Example: "Work out 4.6 × 2.7"

1) We know that 46 × 27 = 1242 ('cos we've just worked it out)
2) 4.6 × 2.7 has 2 digits after the decimal points
3) so the answer is 12.42

UNIT THREE

Dividing Without a Calculator

OK, time for dividing now. Just remember, if you don't learn these basic methods, you'll find yourself in real trouble in the exam...

Dividing Whole Numbers

Example "What is 896 ÷ 8?"

```
    1              11            112
8)896          8)89⁶6         8)89⁶6
```

8 into 8 goes once.   8 into 9 goes once, carry the remainder of 1.   8 into 16 goes twice, so 896 ÷ 8 = 112.

Dividing with Decimals

Example "What is 52.8 ÷ 3?"

Just set it out like the one we've just done but put the decimal point in the answer right above the one in the question...

```
    1              17.           17.6
3)5²2.8         3)5²2.¹8        3)5²2.¹8
```

3 into 5 goes once, carry the remainder of 2.   3 into 22 goes 7 times, carry the remainder of 1.   3 into 18 goes 6 times exactly. So 52.8 ÷ 3 = 17.6.

Example "What is 83.6 ÷ 0.4?"

The trick with ones like this is to remember it's a fraction: $\frac{83.6}{0.4}$

Now you can get rid of the decimals by multiplying the top and bottom by 10 (turning it into an equivalent fraction): $\frac{83.6}{0.4} = \frac{836}{4}$

It's now a lovely decimal-free division that you know how to solve:

```
    2              20            209
4)836           4)83³6         4)83³6
```

4 into 8 goes twice.   4 into 3 won't go so carry 3.   4 into 36 goes 9 times so 83.6 ÷ 0.4 = 209.

The Acid Test

Time to test what you've learnt. Try all of these <u>without</u> a calculator:

1) 28 × 12   2) 56 × 11   3) 104 × 8
4) 96 ÷ 8   5) 242 ÷ 2   6) 84 ÷ 7
7) 3.2 × 56   8) 0.6 × 10.2   9) 5.5 × 10.2
10) 33.6 ÷ 0.6   11) 69 ÷ 1.5   12) 43.2 ÷ 3.6

UNIT THREE

Rounding Off

When you have DECIMAL NUMBERS you might have to round them off to the nearest whole number. The trouble is, they could also ask you to round them off to either ONE DECIMAL PLACE (or possibly TWO decimal places). This isn't too bad but you do have to learn some rules for it:

Basic Method

1) Identify the position of the LAST DIGIT.

2) Then look at the next digit to the right – called the DECIDER.

3) If the DECIDER is 5 or more, then ROUND-UP the LAST DIGIT.
   If the DECIDER is 4 or less, then leave the LAST DIGIT as it is.

EXAMPLE: What is 7.35 to 1 Decimal Place?

7.35   =   7.4

LAST DIGIT to be written (because we're rounding to 1 Decimal Place)
DECIDER
The LAST DIGIT ROUNDS UP to 4 because the DECIDER is 5 or more

Decimal Places (D. P.)

1) To round off to ONE DECIMAL PLACE, the LAST DIGIT will be the one just after the decimal point.

2) There must be NO MORE DIGITS after the LAST DIGIT (not even zeros).

EXAMPLES
Round off 2.34 to 1 decimal place.   ANSWER: 2.3
Round off 4.57 to 1 decimal place.   ANSWER: 4.6
Round off 2.08 to 1 decimal place.   ANSWER: 2.1
Round off 2.346 to 2 decimal places   ANSWER: 2.35

The Acid Test

1) LEARN the 3 Steps of the Basic Method and the 2 Extra Rules for Decimal Places.
2) Round these numbers off to 1 decimal place:
   a) 3.24   b) 1.78   c) 2.31   d) 0.46   e) 9.76
3) Round these off to the nearest whole number:
   a) 3.4   b) 5.2   c) 1.84   d) 6.9   e) 3.26

UNIT THREE

Rounding Off

Rounding *Whole Numbers*

The easiest ways to round off a number are:
1) "To the nearest WHOLE NUMBER"
2) "To the nearest TEN"
3) "To the nearest HUNDRED".
4) "To the nearest THOUSAND"

This isn't difficult so long as you remember the 2 RULES:

> 1) The number always lies between 2 POSSIBLE ANSWERS. Just choose the one it's NEAREST TO.
>
> 2) If the number is exactly in the MIDDLE, then ROUND IT UP.

EXAMPLES:

1) Give 231 to the nearest TEN.
ANSWER: 231 is between 230 and 240, but it is nearer to 230

2) Give 145 to the nearest HUNDRED.
ANSWER: 145 is between 100 and 200, but it is nearer to 100

3) Round 45.7 to the nearest WHOLE NUMBER.
ANSWER: 45.7 is between 45 and 46, but it is nearer to 46

4) Round 4500 to the nearest THOUSAND.
ANSWER: 4500 is between 4000 and 5000. In fact it is exactly halfway between them. So we ROUND IT UP (see Rule 2 above) to 5000

Significant Figures

> 1) The MORE SIGNIFICANT FIGURES a number has, the MORE ACCURATE it is.
> 2) The NUMBER OF SIGNIFICANT FIGURES is just HOW MANY DIGITS the number has at the front THAT ARE NOT ZERO.

EXAMPLES:

234 has 3 significant figures	230 has 2 sig fig	900 has 1 sig fig
9810 has 3 sig fig.	4000 has 1 sig fig	2.8 has 2 sig fig

The Acid Test

1) Round these off to the nearest 10:
 a) 453 b) 682 c) 46.2 d) 98 e) 14
2) Round these numbers to the stated no. of significant figures:
 a) 352 to 2 s.f. b) 465 to 1 s.f. c) 12.38 to 3 s.f. d) 0.03567 to 2 s.f.
3) Round these numbers off to the nearest hundred: a) 2865 b) 450 c) 123

UNIT THREE

Accuracy and Estimating

Appropriate Accuracy

In the Exam you may well get a question asking for "an appropriate degree of accuracy" for a certain measurement. So how do you decide what is appropriate accuracy? The key to this is the number of significant figures (See P.19) that you give it to:

1) For fairly casual measurements, 2 SIGNIFICANT FIGURES is most appropriate.

E.g. COOKING — 250 g (2 sig. fig.) of sugar, not 253 g (3 S.F.), or 300 g (1 S.F.))
DISTANCE OF A JOURNEY — 450 miles or 25 miles or 3500 miles (All 2 S F)
AREA OF A GARDEN OR FLOOR — 330 m² or 15 m²

2) For MORE IMPORTANT OR TECHNICAL THINGS, 3 SIGNIFICANT FIGURES is essential.

E.g. A LENGTH that will be CUT TO FIT,
e.g. you'd measure a shelf as 25.6cm long (not 26cm or 25.63cm)
A TECHNICAL FIGURE, e.g. 34.2 miles per gallon, (rather than 34 mpg)
Any ACCURATE measurement with a ruler: e.g. 67.5cm, (not 70cm or 67.54cm)

3) Only for REALLY SCIENTIFIC WORK would you have more than 3 SIG FIG.

For example, only someone really keen would want to know the length of a piece of string to the nearest tenth of a mm — like 34.46cm, for example. (Get a life!)

Estimating Calculations

As long as you realise what's expected, this is VERY EASY. People get confused because they over-complicate it. To estimate something this is all you do:

> 1) ROUND EVERYTHING OFF to nice easy CONVENIENT NUMBERS.
> 2) Then WORK OUT THE ANSWER using those nice easy numbers — and that's it!

You don't worry about the answer being "wrong", because we're only trying to get a rough idea of the size of the proper answer, e.g. is it about 20 or about 200?
Don't forget though, in the Exam you'll need to show all the steps you've done, to prove you didn't just use a calculator.

Example: ESTIMATE the value of $\frac{127 + 49}{56.5}$ showing all your working.

ANSWER:

$$\frac{127 + 49}{56.5} \approx \frac{130 + 50}{60} = \frac{180}{60} = 3$$

("≈" means "roughly equal to")

UNIT THREE

Accuracy and Estimating

Estimating Areas and Volumes

This isn't bad either — so long as you LEARN the TWO STEPS of the method:

1) Draw or imagine a RECTANGLE OR CUBOID of similar size to the object in question.
2) Round off all lengths to the NEAREST WHOLE, and work it out — easy.

EXAMPLES:

a) Estimate the area of this splodge:

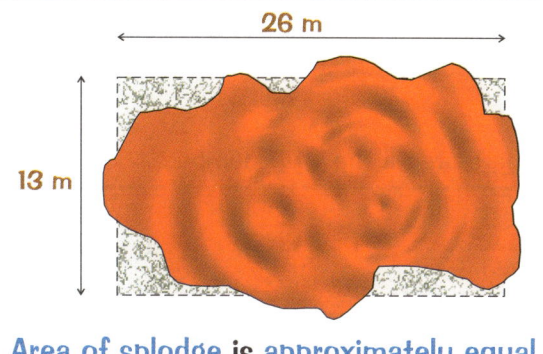

26 m
13 m

Area of splodge is approximately equal to area of dashed rectangle:
i.e. 26m × 13m = 338m²
(or, without a calculator:
30 × 10 = 300m²)

b) Estimate the volume of the bottle:

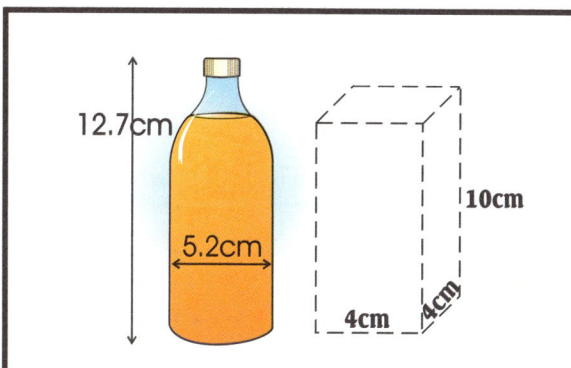

12.7cm
5.2cm
10cm
4cm
4cm

Volume of bottle is approximately equal to volume of dashed cuboid
= 4 × 4 × 10
= 160cm³

Estimating Square Roots

Looks horrible — but it's OK if you know your square numbers (page 22).

1) Find the TWO SQUARE NUMBERS EITHER SIDE of the number in question.
2) Find the SQUARE ROOTS and pick a SENSIBLE NUMBER IN BETWEEN.

EXAMPLE: "Estimate $\sqrt{85}$ without using a calculator."

① The square numbers either side of 85 are 81 and 100.

② The square roots are 9 and 10, so $\sqrt{85}$ must be between 9 and 10. But 85 is much nearer 81 than 100, so $\sqrt{85}$ must be much nearer 9 than 10. So pick 9.1, 9.2 or 9.3.
(The answer's actually 9.2195... if you're interested.)

The Acid Test:

LEARN the 3 RULES about Appropriate Accuracy and the 4 RULES for Estimating.
Then cover the page and write them all down from memory.

THEN TRY THESE:
1) Decide which category of accuracy these should belong in and round them off accordingly: a) A jar of jam weighs 34.56g b) A car has a max speed of 134.25mph c) A cake needs 852.3g of flour d) A table is 76.24cm high.
2) Estimate: a) the area of the UK in square miles, b) the volume of a tin of beans in cm³.
3) Estimate: a) $\sqrt{34}$ b) $\sqrt{5}$ c) $\sqrt{61}$ d) $\sqrt{22}$

UNIT THREE

Special Number Sequences

1) EVEN NUMBERS ...all Divide by 2

2 4 6 8 10 12 14 16 18 20 ...

All EVEN numbers END in 0, 2, 4, 6 or 8

e.g. 200, 342, 576, 94

2) ODD NUMBERS ...DON'T divide by 2

1 3 5 7 9 11 13 15 17 19 21 ...

All ODD numbers END in 1, 3, 5, 7 or 9

e.g. 301, 95, 807, 43

3) SQUARE NUMBERS:

They're called SQUARE NUMBERS because they're like the areas of this pattern of squares:

$1 \times 1 = 1$, $2 \times 2 = 4$, $3 \times 3 = 9$, $4 \times 4 = 16$

(1×1) (2×2) (3×3) (4×4) (5×5) (6×6) (7×7) (8×8) (9×9) (10×10) (11×11) (12×12) (13×13) (14×14) (15×15)

1 4 9 16 25 36 49 64 81 100 121 144 169 196 225...

3 5 7 9 11 13 15 17 19 21 23 25 27 29

Note that the DIFFERENCES between the square numbers are all the ODD numbers.

4) CUBE NUMBERS:

They're called CUBE NUMBERS because they're like the volumes of this pattern of cubes.

$1 \times 1 \times 1 = 1$, $2 \times 2 \times 2 = 8$, $3 \times 3 \times 3 = 27$, $4 \times 4 \times 4 = 64$

(1×1×1) (2×2×2) (3×3×3) (4×4×4) (5×5×5) (6×6×6) (7×7×7) (8×8×8) (9×9×9) (10×10×10)...

1 8 27 64 125 216 343 512 729 1000...

Admit it, you never knew maths could be this exciting did you!

5) POWERS:

Powers are "numbers multiplied by themselves so many times".

"Two to the power three" = $2^3 = 2 \times 2 \times 2 = 8$

Here's the first few POWERS OF 2:

2 4 8 16 32...

$2^1 = 2$ $2^2 = 4$ $2^3 = 8$ $2^4 = 16$ etc...

... and the first POWERS OF 10 (even easier):

10 100 1000 10 000 100 000...

$10^1 = 10$ $10^2 = 100$ $10^3 = 1000$ etc...

6) TRIANGLE NUMBERS:

To remember the triangle numbers you have to picture in your mind this increasing pattern of triangles, where each new row has one more blob than the previous row.

1 3 6 10 15 21 28 36 45 55 ....

2 3 4 5 6 7 8 9 10 11 12

It's definitely worth learning this simple pattern of differences, as well as the formula for the nth term (see P.38) which is:

n^{th} term = $\frac{1}{2} n(n+1)$

The Acid Test:

LEARN the first 10 NUMBERS in all seven sequences above.

1) Cover up the page and then write down the first 15 numbers in all seven sequences.
2) From this list of numbers: 23, 45, 56, 81, 25, 97, 134, 156, 125, 36, 1, 64
   write down: a) all the even numbers b) all the odd numbers c) all the square numbers
   d) all the cube numbers e) all the powers of 2 and 10. f) all the triangle numbers.

UNIT THREE

Prime Numbers

1) Basically, PRIME Numbers don't divide by anything

And that's the best way to think of them.
So Prime Numbers are all the numbers that DON'T come up in Times Tables:

> 2   3   5   7   11   13   17   19   23   29   31   37   ...

As you can see, they're an awkward-looking bunch (that's because they don't divide by anything!).   For example:

> The only numbers that multiply to give 7 are   1 × 7
> The only numbers that multiply to give 31 are   1 × 31

In fact the only way to get ANY PRIME NUMBER is   1 × ITSELF

2) They All End in 1, 3, 7 or 9

1) 1 is NOT a prime number.
2) The first four prime numbers are 2, 3, 5 and 7.
3) Prime numbers end in 1, 3, 7 or 9
   (2 and 5 are the only exceptions to this rule).
4) But NOT ALL numbers ending in 1, 3, 7 or 9
   are primes, as shown here:
      (Only the circled ones are primes)

(2) (3) (5) (7)
(11) (13) (17) (19)
21 (23) 27 (29)
(31) 33 (37) 39
(41) (43) (47) 49
51 (53) 57 (59)
(61) 63 (67) 69

3) HOW TO FIND PRIME NUMBERS — a very simple method

1) Since all primes (above 5) end in 1, 3, 7, or 9, then to find a prime number between say, 70 and 80, the only possibilities are: 71, 73, 77 and 79

2) Now, to find which of them ACTUALLY ARE primes you only need to divide each one by 3 and 7. If it doesn't divide exactly by either 3 or 7 then it's a prime.
     (This simple rule using just 3 and 7 is true for checking primes up to 120)

So, to find the primes between 70 and 80, just try dividing 71, 73, 77 and 79 by 3 and 7:

71 ÷ 3 = 23.667,   71 ÷ 7 = 10.143   so 71 IS a prime number
                                       (because it ends in 1, 3, 7 or 9 and it doesn't divide by 3 or 7)

73 ÷ 3 = 24.333,   73 ÷ 7 = 10.429   so 73 IS a prime number

79 ÷ 3 = 26.333   79 ÷ 7 = 11.286   so 79 IS a prime number

77 ÷ 3 = 25.667   BUT: 77 ÷ 7 = 11 — 11 is a whole number (or 'integer'),
                       so 77 is NOT a prime, because it will divide by 7 (7 × 11 = 77)

The Acid Test: LEARN the main points in ALL 3 SECTIONS above.

Now cover the page and write down everything you've just learned.
1) Write down the first 15 prime numbers (*without* looking them up).
2) Using the above method, find all the prime numbers between 90 and 110.

Multiples, Factors and Prime Factors

Multiples

The MULTIPLES of a number are simply its TIMES TABLE:

E.g. the multiples of 13 are   13   26   39   52   65   78   91   104 ...

Factors

The FACTORS of a number are all the numbers that DIVIDE INTO IT. There's a special way to find them:

Example 1: "Find ALL the factors of 24".

Start off with 1 × the number itself, then try 2×, then 3× and so on, listing the pairs in rows like this. Try each one in turn and put a dash if it doesn't divide exactly. Eventually, when you get a number repeated, you stop.

```
1 × 24
2 × 12
3 × 8
4 × 6
5 × –
6 × 4
```
(Increasing by 1 each time)

So the FACTORS OF 24 are 1,2,3,4,6,8,12,24

This method guarantees you find them ALL — but don't forget 1 and 24!

Factors   Example 2: "Find the factors of 64".

```
1 × 64
2 × 32
3 × –
4 × 16
5 × –
6 × –
7 × –
8 × 8
```

Check each one in turn, to see if it divides or not. Use your calculator when you can, if you're not totally confident.

So the FACTORS of 64 are 1,2,4,8,16,32,64

The 8 has repeated so stop here.

Finding Prime Factors — The Factor Tree

Any number can be broken down into a string of PRIME NUMBERS all multiplied together — this is called "Expressing it as a product of prime factors", and to be honest it's pretty tedious – but it's in the Exam, and it's not difficult so long as you know what it is.

The mildly entertaining "Factor Tree" method is best, where you start at the top and split your number off into factors as shown. Each time you get a prime, you ring it and you finally end up with all the prime factors, which you can then arrange in order.

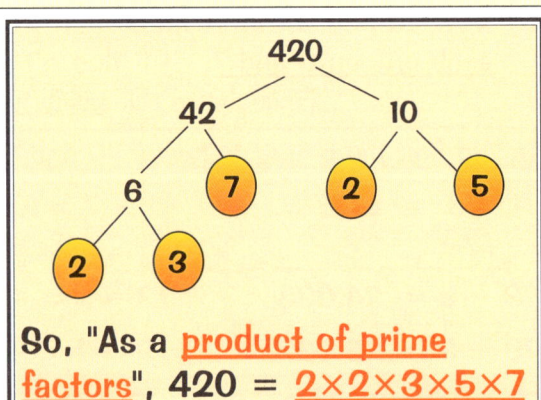

```
        420
       /   \
      42    10
     /  \  / \
     6  7  2  5
    / \
    2  3
```

So, "As a product of prime factors", 420 = 2×2×3×5×7

The Acid Test:

LEARN what Multiples, Factors and Prime Factors are, AND HOW TO FIND THEM. Turn over and write it down.

Then try these without the notes:
1) List the first 10 multiples of 7, and the first 10 multiples of 9.
2) List all the factors of 36 and all the factors of 84.
3) Express as a product of prime factors: a) 990   b) 160.

LCM and HCF

Two big fancy names but don't be put off — they're both really easy.

LCM — "Lowest Common Multiple"

"Lowest Common Multiple" — sure, it sounds kind of complicated but all it means is this:

The SMALLEST number that will DIVIDE BY ALL the numbers in question.

Method
1) LIST the MULTIPLES of ALL the numbers.
2) Find the SMALLEST one that's in ALL the lists.
3) Easy peasy innit.

Example Find the lowest common multiple (LCM) of 6 and 7
Answer Multiples of 6 are: 6, 12, 18, 24, 30, 36, (42,) 48, 54, 60, 66, ...
Multiples of 7 are: 7, 14, 21, 28, 35, (42,) 49, 56, 63, 70, 77, ...

So the lowest common multiple (LCM) of 6 and 7 is 42.
Told you it was easy.

HCF — "Highest Common Factor"

"Highest Common Factor" — all it means is this:

The BIGGEST number that will DIVIDE INTO ALL the numbers in question.

Method
1) LIST the FACTORS of all the numbers.
2) Find the BIGGEST one that's in ALL the lists.
3) Easy peasy innit.

Example Find the highest common factor (HCF) of 36, 54, and 72
Answer Factors of 36 are: 1, 2, 3, 4, 6, 9, 12, (18,) 36
Factors of 54 are: 1, 2, 3, 6, 9, (18,) 27, 54
Factors of 72 are: 1, 2, 3, 4, 6, 8, 9, 12, (18,) 24, 36, 72

So the highest common factor (HCF) of 36, 54 and 72 is 18.
Told you it was easy.

Just take care listing the factors — make sure you use the proper method (as shown on the previous page) or you'll miss one and blow the whole thing out of the water.

The Acid Test:
LEARN what LCM and HCF are, AND HOW TO FIND THEM. Turn over and write it all down.

1) List the first 10 multiples of 8, and the first 10 multiples of 9. What's their LCM?
2) List all the factors of 56 and all the factors of 104. What's their HCF?
3) What's the Lowest Common Multiple of 7 and 9?
4) What's the Highest Common Factor of 36 and 84?

UNIT THREE

Fractions

This page covers some really important basic concepts of fractions. If you don't know it all already, then just make jolly sure you learn it now...

Equivalent Fractions

Equivalent fractions are fractions that are equal in value, even though they look different. Starting with any fraction you like, you can make up a list of equivalent fractions by simply MULTIPLYING top and bottom by the SAME NUMBER each time:

$$\frac{1}{2} \xrightarrow{\times 3} \frac{3}{6} \qquad \frac{3}{4} \xrightarrow{\times 5} \frac{15}{20} \qquad \frac{1}{5} \xrightarrow{\times 100} \frac{100}{500}$$

Cancelling Down

Going the other way, you will sometimes need to simplify a fraction by "cancelling down" — which only means DIVIDING top and bottom by the SAME NUMBER:

$$\frac{3}{15} \xrightarrow{\div 3} \frac{1}{5} \qquad \frac{22}{33} \xrightarrow{\div 11} \frac{2}{3}$$

Ordering Fractions

— Put them over the Same No.

E.g. Put these fractions in ascending order of size: $\frac{8}{3}, \frac{6}{4}, \frac{12}{5}$

① First, to find the new denominator, just find the LCM (see p25) of the denominators: LCM of 3, 4 and 5 is 60

② Then change each fraction so it's over the new number: $\frac{8}{3} = \frac{160}{60}, \frac{6}{4} = \frac{90}{60}, \frac{12}{5} = \frac{144}{60}$

③ Now they're easy to write in order: $\frac{90}{60}, \frac{144}{60}, \frac{160}{60}$ or $\frac{6}{4}, \frac{12}{5}, \frac{8}{3}$.

The Acid Test: Learn how to CANCEL DOWN and ORDER FRACTIONS — and no cheating with a calculator.

1) Reduce these fractions to their simplest form: a) 30/36 b) 18/27 c) 45/66
2) Order the following fractions: 11/15, 3/5, 2/3

UNIT THREE

Fractions, Decimals And Percentages

The one word that could describe all these three is PROPORTION. Fractions, decimals and percentages are simply three different ways of expressing a proportion of something — and it's pretty important you should see them as closely related and completely interchangeable with each other. This table shows the really common conversions which you should know straight off without having to work them out:

Fraction	Decimal	Percentage
1/2	0.5	50%
1/4	0.25	25%
3/4	0.75	75%
1/3	0.333333... or $0.\dot{3}$	33⅓%
2/3	0.666666.... or $0.\dot{6}$	66⅔%
1/10	0.1	10%
2/10	0.2	20%
X/10	0.X	X0%
1/5	0.2	20%
2/5	0.4	40%

⅓ and ⅔ have what're known as 'recurring' decimals — the same pattern of numbers carries on repeating itself forever. (Except here, the pattern's just a single 3 or a single 6. You could have, for instance: 0.143143143...)

The more of those conversions you learn, the better — but for those that you don't know, you must also learn how to convert between the three types. These are the methods:

Fraction —Divide (use your calculator if you can)→ Decimal —× by 100→ Percentage
e.g. ½ is 1÷2   = 0.5   e.g. 0.5 × 100   = 50%

Fraction ←The tricky one— Decimal ←÷ by 100— Percentage

Converting decimals to fractions is only possible for exact decimals that haven't been rounded off. It's simple enough, but it's best illustrated by examples — see below. You should be able to work out what the simple rule is.

0.6 = ⁶/₁₀   0.3 = ³/₁₀   0.7 = ⁷/₁₀   0.X = ˣ/₁₀, etc.

0.12 = ¹²/₁₀₀   0.78 = ⁷⁸/₁₀₀   0.45 = ⁴⁵/₁₀₀   0.05 = ⁵/₁₀₀, etc.

0.345 = ³⁴⁵/₁₀₀₀   0.908 = ⁹⁰⁸/₁₀₀₀   0.024 = ²⁴/₁₀₀₀   0.XYZ = ˣʸᶻ/₁₀₀₀, etc.

These can then be cancelled down.

Recurring decimals like 0.3333... are all actually just exact fractions in disguise. But don't worry, you don't need to know how to convert them back into fractions.

The Acid Test:

LEARN the whole of the top table and the 4 conversion processes for FDP.

Turn the following decimals into fractions and reduce to their simplest form.
a) 0.6   b) 0.02   c) 0.77   d) 0.555   e) 5.6

Unit Three

Powers

Powers are a very useful shorthand:

$2\times2\times2\times2\times2\times2\times2 = 2^7$ ("two to the power 7")
$7\times7 = 7^2$ ("7 squared")
$6\times6\times6\times6\times6 = 6^5$ ("Six to the power 5")
$4\times4\times4 = 4^3$ ("four cubed")

That bit is easy to remember. Unfortunately, there are SIX SPECIAL RULES for powers that are not quite so easy, but you do need to know them for the Exam:

The Six Rules

The first two only work for powers of the SAME NUMBER.

1) When MULTIPLYING, you ADD the powers.

e.g. $3^4 \times 3^6 = 3^{4+6} = 3^{10}$ $8^3 \times 8^5 = 8^{3+5} = 8^8$

2) When DIVIDING, you SUBTRACT the powers.

e.g. $5^4 \div 5^2 = 5^{4-2} = 5^2$ $12^8/12^3 = 12^{8-3} = 12^5$

3) When RAISING one power to another, you MULTIPLY the powers.

e.g. $(3^2)^4 = 3^{2\times4} = 3^8$, $(5^4)^6 = 5^{24}$

4) $X^1 = X$, ANYTHING TO THE POWER 1 is just ITSELF

e.g. $3^1 = 3$, $6 \times 6^3 = 6^4$, $4^3 \div 4^2 = 4^{3-2} = 4^1 = 4$

5) $X^0 = 1$, ANYTHING TO THE POWER 0 is just 1

e.g. $5^0 = 1$ $67^0 = 1$ $3^4/3^4 = 3^{4-4} = 3^0 = 1$

6) $1^x = 1$, 1 TO ANY POWER is still just 1

e.g. $1^{23} = 1$ $1^{89} = 1$ $1^2 = 1$ $1^{1012} = 1$

The Acid Test:

LEARN the Six Rules for Powers. Then turn over and write it all down. Keep trying until you can do it!

Then cover the page and apply the rules to SIMPLIFY these:
1) a) $3^2 \times 3^6$ b) $4^3 \div 4^2$ c) $(8^3)^4$ d) $(3^2 \times 3^3 \times 1^6) / 3^5$ e) $7^3 \times 7 \times 7^2$
2) a) $5^2 \times 5^7 \times 5^3$ b) $1^3 \times 5^0 \times 6^2$ c) $(2^5 \times 2 \times 2^6) \div (2^3 \times 2^4)$

UNIT THREE

Square Roots and Cube Roots

Square Roots

"Squared" means "times by itself": $P^2 = P \times P$
— SQUARE ROOT is the reverse process.

The best way to think of it is this:

> "Square Root" means
> "What Number Times by Itself gives..."

Example: "Find the square root of 49" (i.e. "Find $\sqrt{49}$")
To do this you should say "what number times by itself gives... 49?"
And the answer of course is 7.

Square Roots can be Positive or Negative

When you take the square root of a number, the answer can actually be positive or negative... you always have a positive and negative version of the same number.

E.g. $x^2 = 4$ gives $x = \pm\sqrt{4} = +2$ or -2

To understand why, look at what happens when you work backwards by squaring the answers: $2^2 = 2 \times 2 = 4$ but also $(-2)^2 = (-2) \times (-2) = 4$

> On your calculator, it's easy to find the positive square root using the SQUARE ROOT BUTTON: Press $\sqrt{}$ 49 = = 7

Cube Roots

"Cubed" means "times by itself three times": $T^3 = T \times T \times T$
— CUBE ROOT is the reverse process.

> "Cube Root" means "What Number
> Times by Itself THREE TIMES gives..."

Well, strictly there are only two × signs, but you know what I mean.

Example: "Find the cube root of 64" (i.e "Find $\sqrt[3]{64}$")

You should say "What number times by itself three times gives... 64?"
And after a few guesses, the answer is 4.

> Or on your calculator just use the cube root button:
> Press $\sqrt[3]{}$ 64 = = 4

The Acid Test:

LEARN the 2 statements in the blue boxes and the methods for finding roots. Then turn the page and write it all down.

1) Use your calculator to find to 2 d.p. a) $\sqrt{200}$ b) $\sqrt[3]{8000}$
   For a) what is the other value that your calculator didn't give?
2) a) If $g^2 = 36$, find g.   b) If $b^3 = 64$, find b.   c) If $4 \times r^2 = 36$, find r.

UNIT THREE

Standard Index Form

Standard Form and **Standard Index Form** are the **same thing**.
So remember both of these names as well as what it actually is:

Ordinary Number: 4,300,000   **In Standard Form:** 4.3×10^6

Standard form is really useful for writing <u>very big</u> or <u>very small</u> numbers in a more convenient way, e.g.

56,000,000,000 would be 5.6×10^{10} in standard form.
0.000 000 003 45 would be 3.45×10^{-9} in standard form.

but <u>ANY NUMBER</u> can be written in standard form and you need to know how to do it:

What it Actually is:

A number written in standard form must <u>ALWAYS</u> be in <u>EXACTLY</u> this form:

$$A \times 10^n$$

This <u>number</u> must <u>always</u> be <u>BETWEEN 1 AND 10</u>.
(The fancy way of saying this is:
"$1 \leqslant A < 10$" — they sometimes write that in Exam questions — don't let it put you off, just remember what it means).

This number is just the <u>NUMBER OF PLACES</u> <u>the Decimal Point moves</u>.

Learn The Three Rules:

1) The <u>front number</u> must always be <u>BETWEEN 1 AND 10</u>

2) The power of 10, n, is purely: <u>HOW FAR THE D.P. MOVES</u>

3) n is <u>+ve for BIG numbers</u>,   n is <u>−ve for SMALL numbers</u>
(This is much better than rules based on which way the D.P. moves.)

Examples:

1) "Express 35 600 in standard form".

METHOD:
1) Move the D.P. until 35 600 becomes 3.56 ("$1 \leqslant A < 10$")
2) The D.P. has moved 4 places so n=4, giving: 10^4
3) 35600 is a BIG number so n is +4, not −4

ANSWER:
$3.5600. = 3.56 \times 10^4$

2) "Express 8.14×10^{-3} as an ordinary number".

METHOD:
1) 10^{-3}, tells us that the D.P. must move 3 places...
2) ...and the "−" sign tells us to move the D.P. to make it a SMALL number. (i.e. 0.00814, rather than 8140)

ANSWER:
$8.14 = 0.00814$

UNIT THREE

Standard Index Form

Standard Form and The Calculator

People usually manage all that stuff about moving the decimal point OK (apart from always forgetting that FOR A BIG NUMBER it's "ten to the power +ve something" and FOR A SMALL NUMBER it's "ten to the power –ve something"), but when it comes to doing standard form on a calculator it's often a sorry saga of confusion and mistakes...

But it's not so bad really — you just have to learn it, that's all.....

1) Entering Standard Form Numbers [EXP]

The button you MUST USE to put standard form numbers into the calculator is the [EXP] (or [EE]) button — but DON'T go pressing [X] [10] as well, like a lot of people do, because that makes it WRONG

EXAMPLE: "Enter 2.67×10^{15} into the calculator"

Just press: [2.67] [EXP] [15] [=]   and the display will be $2.67^{\ 15}$

Note that you ONLY PRESS the [EXP] (or [EE]) button — you DON'T press [X] or [10] at all.

2) Reading Standard Form Numbers:

The big thing you have to remember when you write any standard form number from the calculator display is to put the "×10" in yourself. DON'T just write down what it says on the display.

EXAMPLE: "Write down the number $7.986^{\ 05}$ as a finished answer."

As a finished answer this must be written as 7.986×10^5.

It is NOT 7.986^5 so DON'T write it down like that — YOU have to put the $\times 10^n$ in yourself, even though it isn't shown in the display at all. That's the bit people forget.

The Acid Test:

LEARN the Three Rules and the Two Calculator Methods, then turn over and write them down.

Now cover up these 2 pages and answer these:
1) What are the Three Rules for standard form?
2) Express 958,000 in standard index form.   3) And the same for 0.00018
4) Express 4.56×10^3 as an ordinary number.
5) Work this out using your calculator: $3.2 \times 10^{12} \div 1.6 \times 10^{-9}$, and write down the answer, first in standard form and then as an ordinary number.

UNIT THREE

Calculator Buttons

In the parts of your Exam where you're allowed to use a calculator, you really need to make the most of it. It would be a disaster if you ended up throwing away easy marks simply because you pressed the wrong button.

The FRACTION BUTTON [a b/c]

You do need to know how to deal with fractions without your calculator.
But when you're allowed to use it, you definitely should do...

1) **TO ENTER A NORMAL FRACTION like ¼**

   Just press: [1] [a b/c] [4]

2) **TO ENTER A MIXED FRACTION like 1 ³⁄₅**

   Just press: [1] [a b/c] [3] [a b/c] [5]

3) **TO DO A REGULAR CALCULATION such as ⅕ × ¾**

   Just press: [1] [a b/c] [5] [X] [3] [a b/c] [4] [=]

4) **TO REDUCE A FRACTION TO ITS LOWEST TERMS**

   Just enter it and then press [=],

   e.g. ⁹⁄₁₂ , [9] [a b/c] [12] [=]   [3 ⌐ 4] = ¾

5) **TO CONVERT BETWEEN MIXED AND TOP HEAVY FRACTIONS**

   Just press [SHIFT] [a b/c]   e.g. to give 2 ⅜ as a top heavy fraction:

   Press: [2] [a b/c] [3] [a b/c] [8] [=] [SHIFT] [a b/c]   which gives an answer of ¹⁹⁄₈

The MEMORY BUTTONS ([STO] Store, [RCL] Recall)

These are really useful for keeping a number you've just calculated,
so you can use it again shortly afterwards.

EXAMPLE: Find $\frac{840}{15+5^3}$ — just work out the bottom line first and stick it in the memory.

So press [15] [+] [5] [x³] [=] and then [STO] [M] to keep the result of the bottom line in the memory. Then you simply press [840] [÷] [RCL] [M] [=], and the answer is **6**.

(Note — memory buttons work differently on different calculators.
You must learn exactly how the memory buttons work on your calculator.)

UNIT THREE

Calculator Buttons

Bodmas and the Brackets Buttons

The BRACKETS BUTTONS are (and).

One of the biggest problems people have with their calculators is not realising that the calculator always works things out IN A CERTAIN ORDER, which is summarised by the word BODMAS, which stands for:

Brackets, Other, Division, Multiplication, Addition, Subtraction

This is really important when you want to work out even a simple thing like $\frac{23+45}{64\times 3}$

You can't just press [23] [+] [45] [÷] [64] [×] [3] [=] — it will be completely wrong.

The calculator will think you mean $23+\frac{45}{64}\times 3$ because the calculator will do the division and multiplication BEFORE it does the addition.

The secret is to OVERRIDE the automatic BODMAS order of operations using the BRACKETS BUTTONS. Brackets are the ultimate priority in BODMAS, which means anything in brackets is worked out before anything else happens to it.

> So all you have to do is:
> 1) Write a couple of pairs of brackets into the expression: $\frac{(23+45)}{(64\times 3)}$
> 2) Then just type it as it's written:
>
> [(] [23] [+] [45] [)] [÷] [(] [64] [×] [3] [)] [=]

You might think it's difficult to know where to put the brackets in.
It's not that difficult, you just put them in pairs around each group of numbers.
It's OK to have brackets within other brackets too, e.g. (4 + (5÷2))
As a rule, you can't cause trouble by putting too many brackets in,

SO LONG AS THEY ALWAYS GO IN PAIRS.

The Powers Button   [xʸ] or [^]   (See P.28 for more on powers)

It's used for working out powers of numbers quickly. For example to find 7^5, instead of pressing 7×7×7×7×7 you should just press [7] [xʸ] [5] [=].

The Acid Test: Learn everything on these two pages, then practise doing it on YOUR CALCULATOR.

Use your calculator to work out the following:
1) Convert these into top-heavy fractions: a) 2 ¾ b) 16 ½ c) 8 ¼
2) Calculate the following to 2 d.p. using the brackets or memory buttons:
   a) $\frac{15+5^6}{21^3-4^3}$ b) $\frac{74^2-10^3}{\sqrt{49}\times 2^4}$

UNIT THREE

Negative Numbers and Letters

Everyone knows RULE 1, but sometimes RULE 2 applies instead, so make sure you know BOTH rules AND when to use them.

Rule 1

+	+	makes	+
+	−	makes	−
−	+	makes	−
−	−	makes	+

Only to be used when:

1) Multiplying or dividing

e.g. $-2 \times 3 = -6$, $-8 \div -2 = +4$ $-4p \times -2 = +8p$

2) Two signs appear next to each other

e.g. $5 - -4 = 5 + 4 = 9$ $4 + -6 - -7 = 4 - 6 + 7 = 5$

Rule 2

Use the NUMBER LINE for ADDING OR SUBTRACTING:

E.g. "Simplify $4X - 8X - 3X + 6X$"

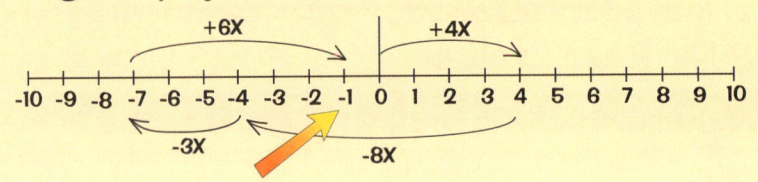

So $4X - 8X - 3X + 6X = \underline{-1X}$

Letters Multiplied Together

This is the super-slick notation they like to use in algebra which just ends up making life difficult for folks like you. You've got to remember these five rules:

1) "abc" means "a×b×c"   The ×'s are often left out to make it clearer.
2) "gn^2" means "g×n×n"   Note that only the n is squared, not the g as well.
3) "$(gn)^2$" means "g×g×n×n"   The brackets mean that BOTH letters are squared.
4) "$p(q-r)^3$" means "p×(q−r)×(q−r)×(q−r)"   Only the brackets get cubed.
5) "-3^2" is too ambiguous.   It should either be written $(-3)^2 = 9$, or $-(3^2) = -9$.

The Acid Test:
LEARN the Two Rules for negative numbers and the 5 special cases of Letters Multiplied Together.

Then turn over and write down what you've learned.
1) For each of a) to d), decide where Rule 1 and Rule 2 apply, and then work them out.
   a) -4×-3 b) $-4 + -5 + 3$ c) $(3X + -2X - 4X) \div (2+ -5)$ d) $120 \div -40$
2) If $m=2$ and $n=-3$, work out: a) mn^2 b) $(mn)^3$ c) $m(4+n)^2$ d) n^3 e) $3m^2n^3 + 2mn$

UNIT THREE

Basic Algebra

Algebra really terrifies so many people. But honestly, it's not that bad. You've just got to make sure you *understand and learn* these *basic rules* for dealing with algebraic expressions. After that, all it needs is practice, practice, practice... and a little love.

1) Terms

Before you can do anything else, you **MUST** understand what a **TERM** is:

1) **A TERM IS A COLLECTION OF NUMBERS, LETTERS AND BRACKETS, ALL MULTIPLIED/DIVIDED TOGETHER.**
2) Terms are **SEPARATED BY + AND − SIGNS**   e.g. $4x^2 - 3py - 5 + 3p$
3) Terms always have a + or − **ATTACHED TO THE FRONT OF THEM**
4) e.g. $-4xy$ $+5x^2$ $-2y$ $+6y^2$ $+4$

Invisible + sign   "xy" term   "x²" term   "y" term   "y²" term   "number" term

2) Simplifying — "Collecting Like Terms"

EXAMPLE: "Simplify $2x - 4 + 5x + 6$"

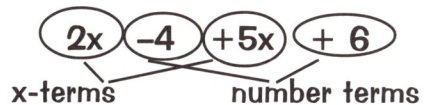

$(2x)(-4)(+5x)(+6)$ = $(+2x)(+5x)(-4)(+6)$
x-terms   number terms   = $7x$ $+2$ = $7x + 2$

1) <u>Put bubbles round each term</u>, — be sure you <u>capture the +/− sign IN FRONT of each</u>.
2) Then you can <u>move the bubbles into the best order</u> so that **LIKE TERMS are together**.
3) "<u>LIKE TERMS</u>" have exactly the same combination of letters, e.g. "x-terms" or "xy-terms".
4) <u>Combine LIKE TERMS</u> using the <u>NUMBER LINE</u> (not the other rule for negative numbers).

3) Multiplying out Brackets

1) The thing **OUTSIDE** the brackets <u>multiplies each separate term INSIDE the brackets</u>.
2) When letters are <u>multiplied together</u>, they are just <u>written next to each other</u>, e.g. pq
3) Remember, $R \times R = R^2$, and TY^2 means $T \times Y \times Y$, whilst $(TY)^2$ means $T \times T \times Y \times Y$.
4) Remember <u>a minus outside the bracket REVERSES ALL THE SIGNS when you multiply</u>.

EXAMPLE: 1) $3(2x + 5) = 6x + 15$ 2) $4p(3r - 2t) = 12pr - 8pt$
                3) $-4(3p^2 - 7q^3) = -12p^2 + 28q^3$ —— (note both signs have been <u>reversed</u> — Rule 4)

The Acid Test:

LEARN all the <u>key algebra facts</u> on this page, then have a go at these questions to see how well you've got it.

1) Simplify: a) $5x + 3y - 4 - 2y - x$ b) $3x + 2 + 5xy + 6x - 7$
               c) $2x + 3x^2 + 5y^2 + 3x$ d) $3y - 6xy + 3y + 2yx$

2) Expand: a) $2(x - 2)$ b) $x(5 + x)$ c) $y(y + x)$ d) $3y(2x - 6)$

UNIT THREE

Basic Algebra

4) Expanding and Simplifying

a) DOUBLE BRACKETS

You get 4 terms after multiplying and usually 2 of them combine to leave 3 terms:

$(2P - 4)(3P + 1) = (2P \times 3P) + (2P \times 1) + (-4 \times 3P) + (-4 \times 1)$
$= 6P^2 + 2P - 12P - 4$
$= 6P^2 - 10P - 4$ (these 2 combine together)

b) SQUARED BRACKETS: e.g. $(3x + 5)^2$

The trick is to always write these out as two brackets: $(3d + 5)(3d + 5)$
and then you can work them out like above.

$(3x + 5)^2 = (3x + 5)(3x + 5)$
$= 9x^2 + 15x + 15x + 25 = 9x^2 + 30x + 25$

(The usual WRONG ANSWER, by the way, is $(3d + 5)^2 = 9d^2 + 25$ — eeek!)

5) Factorising   — putting brackets in

This is the exact reverse of multiplying-out brackets. Here's the method to follow:

1) Take out the biggest NUMBER that goes into all the terms.
2) For each letter in turn, take out the highest power (e.g. x, x^2 etc) that will go into EVERY term.
3) Open the brackets and fill in all the bits needed to reproduce each term.

EXAMPLE: Factorise $15x^4y + 20x^2y^3z - 35x^3yz^2$

ANSWER: $5x^2y(3x^2 + 4y^2z - 7xz^2)$

- Biggest number that'll divide into 15, 20 and 35
- Highest powers of x and y that will go into all three terms
- z wasn't in ALL terms so it can't come out as a common factor

REMEMBER: 1) The bits taken out and put at the front are the common factors.
2) The bits inside the brackets are what's needed to get back to the original terms if you were to multiply the brackets out again.

The Acid Test:
LEARN all the details about expanding brackets and factorising, then try the questions below.

1) Expand: a) $(x + 1)(x + 2)$ b) $(y - 3)(y + 4)$ c) $(x + 5)^2$
d) $(3x - 1)(x - 4)$ e) $(2x + 1)(x + 2)$ f) $(2x - 1)^2$

2) Factorise: a) $5xy + 15x$ b) $5a - 7ab$ c) $12xy + 6y - 36y^2$

Number Patterns and Sequences

There are five different types of number sequences they could give you.
They're not difficult — AS LONG AS YOU WRITE WHAT'S HAPPENING IN EACH GAP.

1) "Add or Subtract the Same Number"

The SECRET is to write the differences in the gaps between each pair of numbers:

E.g.   2   5   8   11   14 ...   30   24   18   12 ...
      +3 +3 +3   +3   +3   -6   -6   -6   -6

The RULE: "Add 3 to the previous term"   "Subtract 6 from the previous term"

2) "Add or Subtract a Changing Number"

Again, WRITE THE CHANGE IN THE GAPS, as shown here:

E.g.   8   11   15   20   26 ...   or   53   43   34   26   19 ...
      +3 +4   +5   +6   +7   -10 -9   -8   -7   -6

The RULE: "Add 1 extra each time to the previous term"   "Subtract 1 extra from the previous term"

3) Multiply by the Same Number each Time

This type have a common MULTIPLIER linking each pair of numbers:

E.g.   5   10   20   40 ...   2   6   18   54 ...
      ×2   ×2   ×2 ×2   ×3 ×3   ×3   ×3

The RULE: "Multiply the previous term by 2"   "Multiply the previous term by 3"

4) A Divide by the Same Number each Time

This type have the same DIVIDER between each pair of numbers:

E.g.   400   200   100   50 ...   40 000   4000   400   40 ...
       ÷2   ÷2   ÷2   ÷2   ÷10   ÷10   ÷10 ÷10

The RULE: "Divide the previous term by 2"   "Divide the previous term by 10"

5) Add the Previous Two Terms

This type of sequence works by adding the last two numbers to get the next one.

E.g.   1   1   2   3   5   8   13 ...   2   4   6   10   16 ...
          1+1 1+2 2+3 3+5 5+8 8+13   2+4 4+6 6+10 10+16

The RULE: "Add the previous two terms"

UNIT THREE

Number Patterns and Sequences

"State the rule for extending the pattern"

This is what a lot of Exam questions end up asking for and it's easy enough so long as you remember this:

ALWAYS say what you do to the PREVIOUS TERM to get the next term.

All the number sequences on the previous page have the rule for extending the pattern written in the box underneath them. Notice that they all refer to the previous term.

Finding the nth number:

You could be asked in the Exam to "give an expression for the nth number in the sequence." You'll only have to do this for a "type 1" sequence (where the same number is added or subtracted). It's not that difficult because there's a simple formula:

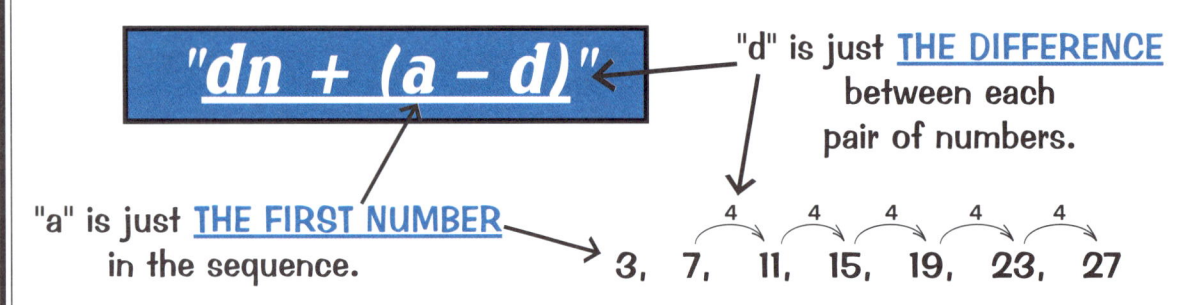

$$dn + (a - d)$$

"d" is just THE DIFFERENCE between each pair of numbers.

"a" is just THE FIRST NUMBER in the sequence.

3, 7, 11, 15, 19, 23, 27 (differences of 4)

To get the nth term, you just find the values of "a" and "d" from the sequence and stick them in the formula. You don't replace n though — that wants to stay as n. Of course you have to learn the formula, but life is like that.

Example:
"Find the nth number of this sequence: 5, 8, 11, 14 ...."

ANS:
1) The formula is dn + (a – d)
2) The first number is 5, so a = 5.   The differences are 3 so d = 3
3) Putting these in the formula gives: 3n + (5 – 3) = 3n + 2

So the nth number for this sequence is given by: "3n + 2"

The Acid Test
LEARN the 5 types of number patterns and the formula for finding the nth number.

1) Find the next two numbers in each of these sequences, and say in words what the rule is for extending each one:
   a) 2, 5, 9, 14 ....   b) 2, 20, 200 ....   c) 64, 32, 16, 8 ...
2) Find the expression for the nth number in this sequence: 7, 9, 11, 13

UNIT THREE

Metric and Imperial Units

This topic is Easy Marks — make sure you get them.

Metric Units

1) **Length** mm, cm, m, km
2) **Area** mm², cm², m², km²,
3) **Volume** mm³, cm³, m³,

MEMORISE THESE KEY FACTS:

1cm = 10mm   1 tonne = 1000kg
1m = 100cm   1 litre = 1000ml

4) **Weight** ounces, pounds, stones, tons
5) **Speed** mph

1 Pound = 16 Ounces (Oz)

Metric-Imperial Conversions

YOU NEED TO LEARN THESE — they **DON'T** promise to give you these in the Exam and if they're feeling mean (as they often are), they won't.

Approximate Conversions

1 kg = 2 ¼ lbs   1 gallon = 4.5 litres
1m = 1 yard (+ 10%)   1 foot = 30cm
1 litre = 1¾ Pints   1 metric tonne = 1 imperial ton
1 Inch = 2.5 cm   1 mile = 1.6km
                         or 5 miles = 8 km

The Acid Test

In the shaded boxes above, there are 21 Conversions. LEARN THEM, then turn the page over and write them down.

1) a) How many cm is 2 metres?   b) How many mm is 6.5cm?
2) a) How many kg is 2500g?   b) How many litres is 1500 cm³?
3) A rod is 46 inches long. What is this in feet and inches?
4) a) Roughly how many yards is 200m?   b) How many cm is 6 feet 3 inches?

UNIT THREE

Rounding off Measurements

A lot of things you measure have a value which you can never know exactly, no matter how carefully you try and measure them.
Take this slimy black slug for example:

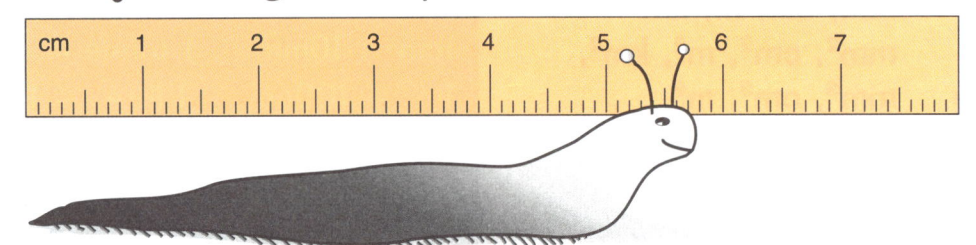

It has a length somewhere between 5cm and 6cm and if you look closer you can even say it's somewhere between 5.7cm and 5.8cm, but you can't really tell any more accurately than that.

So really we only know its length to within 0.1cm. (But let's face it, who needs to know the length of a slimy black slug more accurately than that?)

The thing is though that whenever you measure such things as lengths, weights, speeds etc, you always have to take your answer to a certain level of accuracy because you can never get the exact answer.

The simple rule is:

> You always round off to the number that it's NEAREST TO

If we take our slimy slug, then to the nearest cm his length is 6cm (rather than 5cm) and to the nearest 0.1cm it's 5.8cm (rather than 5.7)

Postage Rates

All this about rounding off to the nearest number is all well and good, but in the Exam they can cheerfully spring a question on you about how much it costs to send a parcel and then the rules are completely different.

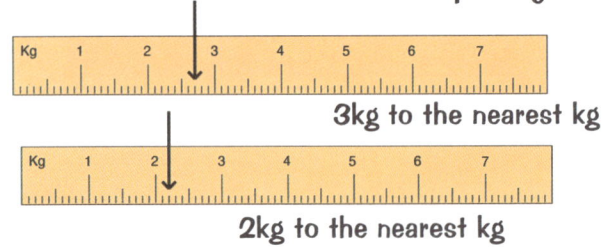

3kg to the nearest kg

2kg to the nearest kg

POSTAGE RATES	
Weight not over:	Price
1kg	£2.70
2kg	£3.30
3kg	£4.10

One reading would round off to 3kg and the other to 2kg but the postage rate is set by "WEIGHT NOT OVER.." so both of these would cost the same (£4.10) because they are both more than 2kg but less than 3kg. It's tricky, so watch out for questions like that.

UNIT THREE

Conversion Factors

Conversion Factors are a really good way of dealing with all sorts of questions and the method is dead easy.

Method

1) Find the Conversion Factor   (always easy)

2) Multiply AND divide by it

3) Choose the common sense answer

Example 1

"A Giant Sea-slug called Kevin was washed up near Grange-Over-Sands. He was over 5.75m in length. How long is this in cm?"

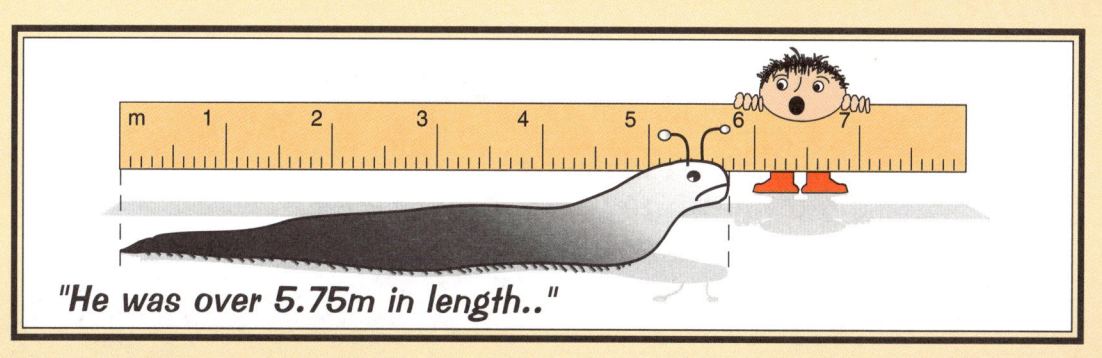

"He was over 5.75m in length.."

Convert 5.75m into cm.

Step 1) Find the CONVERSION FACTOR

In this question the Conversion factor = 100
— simply because 1m = 100 cm

Step 2) MULTIPLY AND DIVIDE by the conversion factor:

5.75m × 100 = 575 cm (makes sense)
5.75 m ÷ 100 = 0.0575 cm (ridiculous)

Step 3) Choose the COMMON SENSE answer:

Obviously the answer is that 5.75m = 575 cm

UNIT THREE

Conversion Factors

Example 2

"If £1 is equal to 1.7 US Dollars, how much is 63 US Dollars in £s?"

Step 1) **Find the CONVERSION FACTOR**

In this question the Conversion Factor is obviously 1.7
(When you're changing foreign money it's called the "Exchange Rate")

Step 2) **MULTIPLY AND DIVIDE by the conversion factor**:

63 × 1.7 = 107.1 = £107.10
63 ÷ 1.7 = 37.06 = £37.06

Step 3) **Choose the COMMON SENSE answer**:

Not quite so obvious this time, but since 1.7 US Dollars = £1, you're clearly going to have less pounds than you had Dollars (roughly half).
In other words, the answer has to be less than 63, so it's £37.06

Example 3

"A popular item at our local Supplies is "Froggatt's Lumpy Sprout Ketchup" (not available in all areas). The Farmhouse Economy Size is the most popular and weighs 2400g. How much is this in kg?"

Step 1) Conversion Factor = 1000 (simply because 1kg = 1000g)

Step 2) 2400 × 1000 = 2,400,000 kg (Uulp..)
2400 ÷ 1000 = 2.4 kg (that's more like it)

Step 3) So the answer must be that 2400 g = **2.4 kg**

The Acid Test

LEARN the 3 steps of the Conversion Factor method. Then turn over and write them down.

1) Kevin the Sea-slug was found to weigh 0.16 tonnes. What is this in kg?
2) Froggatt's also do a nice line in thick-sliced custard. How many pints is 2½ gallons?

UNIT THREE

Clock Time Questions

Since every video recorder in the country uses the 24 hour clock you must know how to read it by now. The only thing you might need reminding about is "am" and "pm" in the 12 hour clock:

1) am and pm

"am" means "Morning"
"pm" means "Afternoon and Evening"

"am" runs from 12 midnight to 12 noon
"pm" runs from 12 noon to 12 midnight
(but you must know that already, surely)

2) Conversions

You'll definitely need to know these very important facts:

1 day = 24 hours
1 hour = 60 minutes
1 minute = 60 seconds

3) Exam questions involving "time"

There are lots of different questions they can ask involving time but the same GOOD OLD RELIABLE DEPENDABLE METHOD will work wonders on all of them.

"And what is this good old reliable dependable method?", I hear you cry. Well, it's this:

Take your time, write it down, and split it up into SHORT EASY STAGES

EXAMPLE: Find the time taken by a train which sets off at 1325 and arrives at 1910.

WHAT YOU DON'T DO is try to work it all out in your head in one go — this ridiculous method fails nearly every time. Instead, do this:

"Take your time, write it down, and split it up into SHORT EASY STAGES"

1325 → 1400 → 1900 → 1910
   35 mins   5 hours   10 mins

This is a nice safe way of finding the total time from 1325 to 1910:
5 hours + 35 mins + 10 mins = 5 hours 45 mins.

4) If you use your Calculator, BEWARE...

Try to avoid using the calculator with time measurements — it's a pain in the neck. You'll get answers in decimals, and you have to convert them into hours and minutes.

So learn this example:

2.5 hours = 2½ hours = 2 hours and 30 minutes

That sound right? Of course it does.

SO DON'T GO WRITING ANYTHING STUPID, like: **2.5 hours = 2 hours 50 minutes** ← WRONG WRONG WRONG WRONG!!

The Acid Test

1) What is 1715 in 12 hour clock? (don't forget am/pm)
2) A plane sets off at 10.15 am. The flight lasts 5 hrs 50 mins. What is the arrival time?
3) How many minutes are there in a day? And how many seconds are there in a day?
4) What is 3.5 hours in hours and minutes? What is 5¾ hours in hours and minutes?

UNIT THREE

Formula Triangles

You may have already come across these in physics, but whether you have or you haven't, the fact remains that they're extremely potent tools for quite a number of tricky maths problems — so make sure you know how to use them.
They're very easy to use and very easy to remember. Watch:

If 3 things are related by a formula that looks either

like this: $A = B \times C$ or like this: $B = \dfrac{A}{C}$

then you can put them into a FORMULA TRIANGLE like this:

1) First decide where the letters go:

1) If there are TWO LETTERS MULTIPLIED TOGETHER in the formula then they must go ON THE BOTTOM of the Formula Triangle (and so the other one must go on the top).

   For example the formula "$F = m \times a$" fits into a formula triangle like this →

2) If there's ONE THING DIVIDED BY ANOTHER in the formula then the one ON TOP OF THE DIVISION goes ON TOP IN THE FORMULA TRIANGLE (and so the other two must go on the bottom — it doesn't matter which way round).

   So the formula "Speed = Distance / Time" fits into a formula triangle like this ↑.

2) Using the Formula Triangle:

Once you've got the formula triangle sorted out, the rest is easy:

1) COVER UP the thing you want to find and just WRITE DOWN what's left showing.
2) PUT IN THE VALUES for the other two things and just WORK IT OUT.

EXAMPLE:

"Using $F = m \times a$, find the value of 'a' when F = 20 and m = 50"

ANSWER: Using the formula triangle, we want to find "a" so we cover "a" up, and that leaves "F/m" showing (i.e. F ÷ m).
So "a = F/m", and putting the numbers in we get: a = 20/50 = 0.4

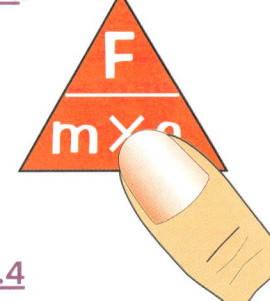

The Acid Test: LEARN THIS WHOLE PAGE then turn over and write down all the important details including the examples.

UNIT THREE

Perimeters

Perimeter is the distance **all the way around the outside of a 2D shape**.

Perimeters of complicated shapes

To find a PERIMETER, you ADD UP THE LENGTHS OF ALL THE SIDES, but....THE ONLY RELIABLE WAY to make sure you get all the sides is this:

> 1) **PUT A BIG BLOB AT ONE CORNER** and then go around the shape
>
> 2) **WRITE DOWN THE LENGTH OF EVERY SIDE AS YOU GO ALONG**
>
> 3) **EVEN SIDES THAT SEEM TO HAVE NO LENGTH GIVEN**
>   — you must work them out
>
> 4) Keep going until you get back to the **BIG BLOB**.

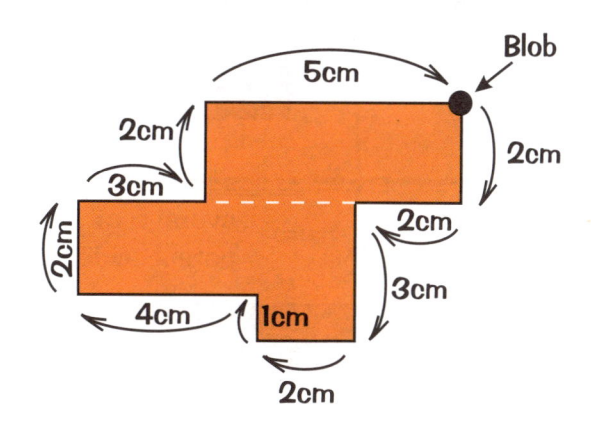

E.g. 2+2+3+2+1+4+2+3+2+5 = **26cm**

Yes, I know you think it's yet another fussy method, but believe me, it's so easy to miss a side. You must use good reliable methods for everything — or you'll lose marks willy nilly.

The Acid Test

LEARN THE RULES for finding the perimeter of complicated shapes.

1) Turn over and write down what you have learnt.
2) Find the perimeter of the shape shown here:

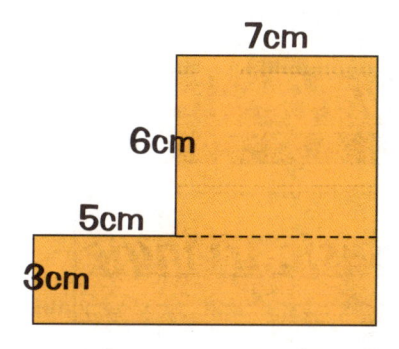

UNIT THREE

Areas

First things first — below are four basic area formulas. You simply must learn these unless you're planning on tipping bucketloads of easy exam marks down the toilet.

YOU MUST LEARN THESE FORMULAS:

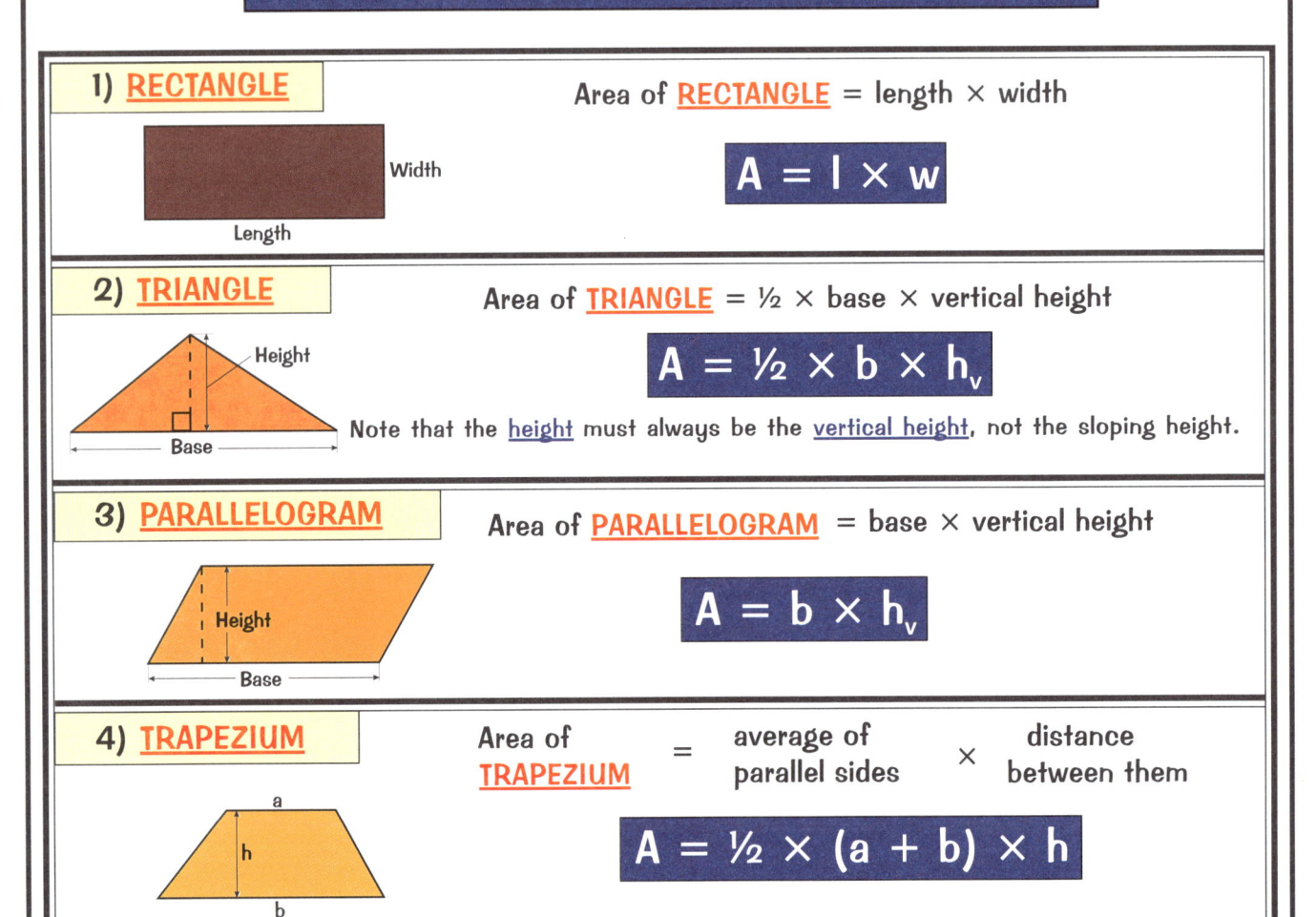

1) RECTANGLE

Area of RECTANGLE = length × width

$$A = l \times w$$

2) TRIANGLE

Area of TRIANGLE = ½ × base × vertical height

$$A = \tfrac{1}{2} \times b \times h_v$$

Note that the height must always be the vertical height, not the sloping height.

3) PARALLELOGRAM

Area of PARALLELOGRAM = base × vertical height

$$A = b \times h_v$$

4) TRAPEZIUM

Area of TRAPEZIUM = average of parallel sides × distance between them

$$A = \tfrac{1}{2} \times (a + b) \times h$$

Areas of more complicated shapes

You often have to find the area of strange looking shapes in exam questions. What you always find with these questions is that you can break the shape up into simpler ones that you can deal with.

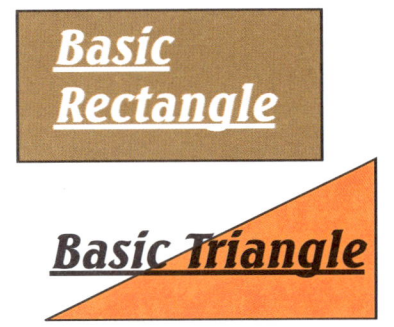

Basic Rectangle

Basic Triangle

1) **SPLIT THEM UP** into the two basic shapes: **RECTANGLE** and **TRIANGLE**
2) Work out the area of each bit **SEPARATELY**
3) Then **ADD THEM ALL TOGETHER**

See next page for a lovely example...

UNIT THREE

Areas

EXAMPLE: Work out the area of the shape shown:

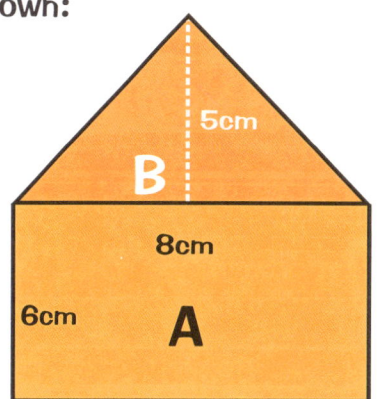

ANSWER:

Shape A is a <u>rectangle</u>:
Area = L × W
    = 8 × 6
    = <u>48cm^2</u>

Shape B is a <u>triangle</u>:
Area = ½ × b × h
     = ½ × 8 × 5
     = <u>20cm^2</u>

TOTAL AREA = 48 + 20 = <u>68cm^2</u>

Don't Reach Straight for the Calculator

You might be <u>kidding yourself</u> that it "<u>takes too long</u>" to write down your working out — but what's so great about getting <u>ZERO MARKS for an easy question</u>?

Compare these two answers for finding the area of the triangle opposite:

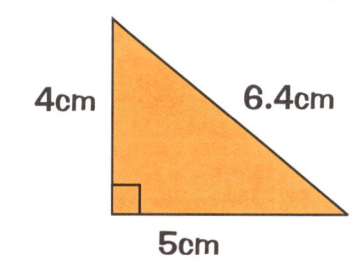

ANSWER 1:   20   ✗

<u>ANSWER 1</u> gets <u>NO MARKS AT ALL</u> — 20 is the wrong answer and there's nothing else to give any marks for.

ANSWER 2:
A = ½ × B × H ✓
  = ½ × 5 × 4 ✓
  = <u>10 cm^2</u> ✓

<u>ANSWER 2</u> has <u>3 bits that all get marks</u>, — so even if the answer was wrong it would still get most of the marks!

The thing is though, when you <u>write it down step by step</u>, you can see what you're doing <u>and you won't get it wrong in the first place</u> — try it next time, go on... just for the wild experience.

The Acid Test:
MEMORISE THE AREA FORMULAS AND LEARN THE RULES FOR DEALING WITH COMPLICATED SHAPES.

Then find the areas of these 4 shapes...

1) 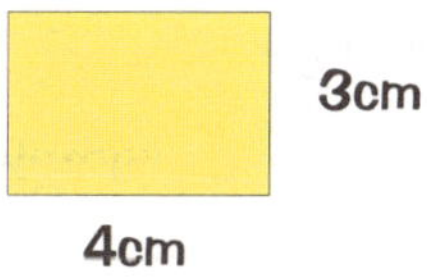 3cm, 4cm
2) 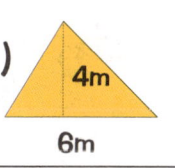 4m, 6m
3) 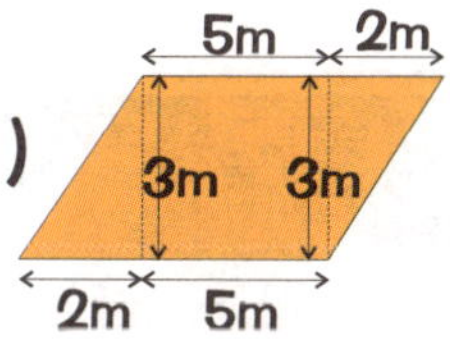 5m, 2m, 3m, 3m, 2m, 5m
4) 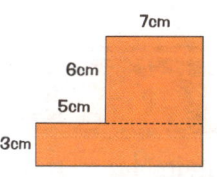 7cm, 6cm, 5cm, 3cm

UNIT THREE

Circles

There's a surprising number of terms you need to know related to circles. Don't get them mixed up...

1) Radius and Diameter

The DIAMETER goes right across the circle

The RADIUS only goes halfway across

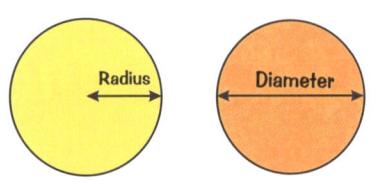

Remember: the DIAMETER IS EXACTLY DOUBLE THE RADIUS

Examples: If the radius is 4cm, the diameter is 8cm,
If the diameter is 24m, the radius is 12m.

2) Area, Circumference and π

The CIRCUMFERENCE is the distance round the outside of the circle.
You should know the formulas for area and circumference...

AREA of CIRCLE = π × (radius)²

$$A = \pi \times r^2$$

e.g. if the radius is 4cm, then
A = 3.14×(4×4)
= 50.24cm²

π = 3.141592....
= 3.14 (approx)

CIRCUMFERENCE = π × Diameter

$$C = \pi \times D$$

The big thing to remember is that π (called "pi") is just an ordinary number (3.14159...) which is usually rounded off to either 3.1 or 3.14.

3) Tangents, Chords, Arcs and the rest...

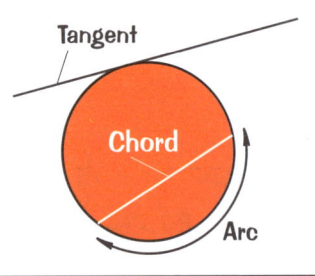

A TANGENT is a straight line that just touches the outside of the circle.

A CHORD is a line drawn across the inside of a circle.

AN ARC is just part of the circumference of the circle.

A SECTOR is a WEDGE SHAPED AREA (like a piece of cake) cut right from the centre.

SEGMENTS are the areas you get when you cut the circle with a chord.

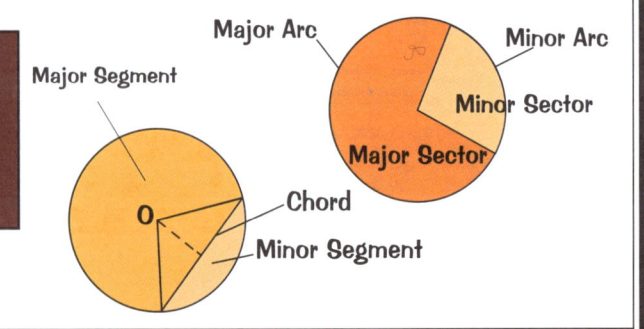

The Acid Test:

Once again, learn it all, turn over and scribble it down. Then see what you missed.

UNIT THREE

Solids and Nets

You need to know what <u>Face</u>, <u>Edge</u> and <u>Vertex</u> mean:

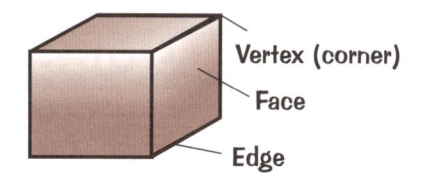

Vertex (corner)
Face
Edge

Surface Area and Nets

1) <u>SURFACE AREA</u> only applies to solid 3-D objects, and it's simply <u>the total area of all the outer surfaces added together</u>. If you were painting it, it's all the bits you'd paint!

2) There is <u>never a simple formula</u> for surface area — <u>you have to work out each side in turn and then ADD THEM ALL TOGETHER</u>.

3) <u>A NET</u> is just <u>A SOLID SHAPE FOLDED OUT FLAT</u>.

4) So obviously: <u>SURFACE AREA OF SOLID = AREA OF NET</u>.

There are 4 nets that you need to know really well for the Exam, and they're shown below. They may well ask you to draw one of these nets and then work out its area.

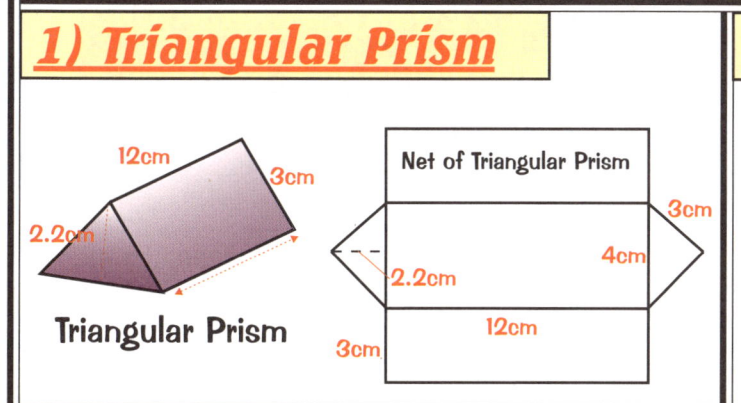

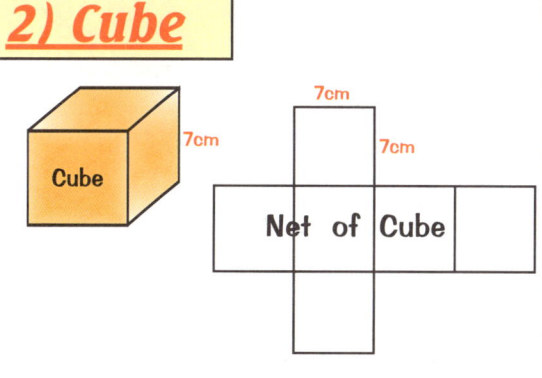

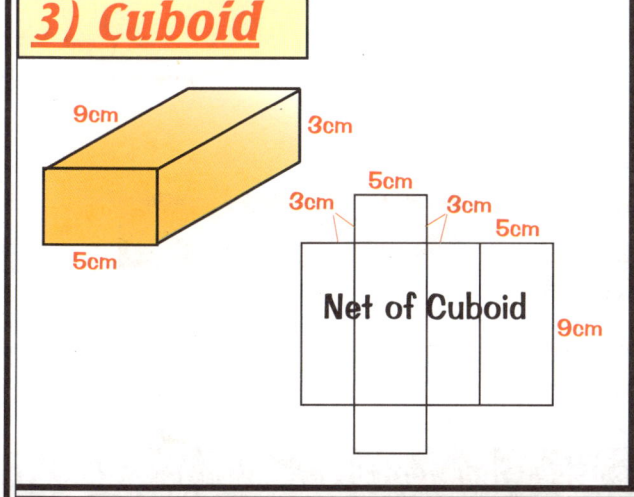

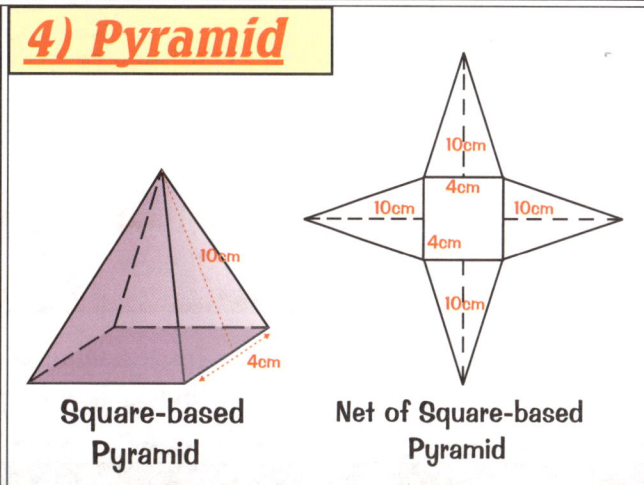

1) Triangular Prism

12cm, 3cm, 2.2cm

Triangular Prism

Net of Triangular Prism
3cm, 2.2cm, 4cm, 12cm, 3cm

2) Cube

7cm

Cube

7cm, 7cm

Net of Cube

3) Cuboid

9cm, 3cm, 5cm

3cm, 5cm, 3cm, 5cm

Net of Cuboid
9cm

4) Pyramid

10cm, 4cm

Square-based Pyramid

10cm, 4cm, 10cm, 4cm, 10cm, 10cm

Net of Square-based Pyramid

The Acid Test:

<u>LEARN</u> the <u>4 details on surface area and nets</u> and the <u>FOUR NETS</u> on this page, and also the little <u>diagram</u> at the top of the page.

Now cover the page and write down everything you've learnt.
1) Work out the area of all four nets shown above.

UNIT THREE

Volume or Capacity

VOLUMES — YOU MUST LEARN THESE TOO!

1) Cuboid (rectangular block)

(This is also known as a '*rectangular prism*' — see below to understand why)

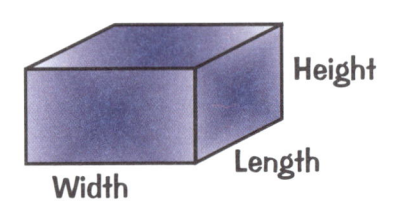

Volume of Cuboid = length × width × height

$$V = l \times w \times h$$

(The other word for volume is CAPACITY)

2) Prism

A PRISM is a solid (3-D) object which has a **CONSTANT AREA OF CROSS-SECTION** — i.e. it's the same shape all the way through.

Now, for some reason, not a lot of people know what a prism is, but they come up all the time in Exams, so make sure YOU know.

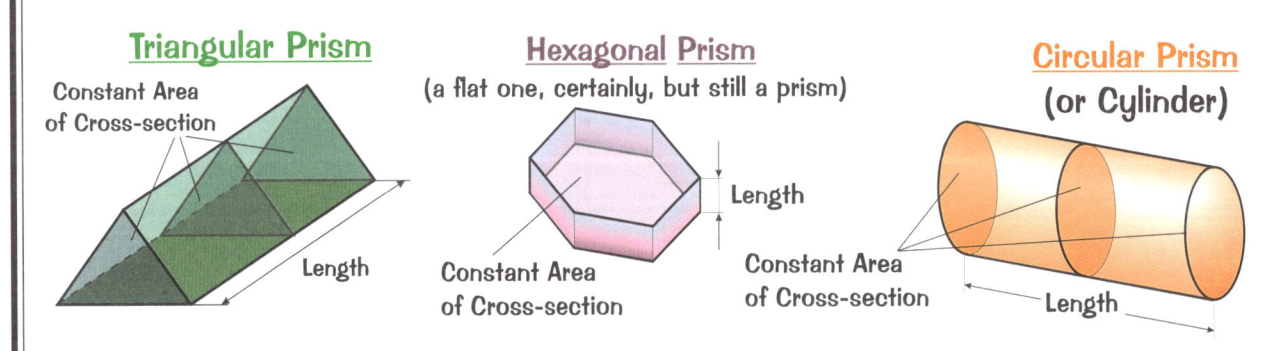

Triangular Prism
Constant Area of Cross-section
Length

Hexagonal Prism
(a flat one, certainly, but still a prism)
Length
Constant Area of Cross-section

Circular Prism
(or Cylinder)
Constant Area of Cross-section
Length

Volume of prism = Cross-sectional Area × length

$$V = A \times l$$

As you can see, the formula for the volume of a prism is *very simple*. The *difficult* part, usually, is *finding the area of the cross-section*.

The Acid Test:

LEARN this page. Then turn over and try to write it all down. Keep trying until you can do it.

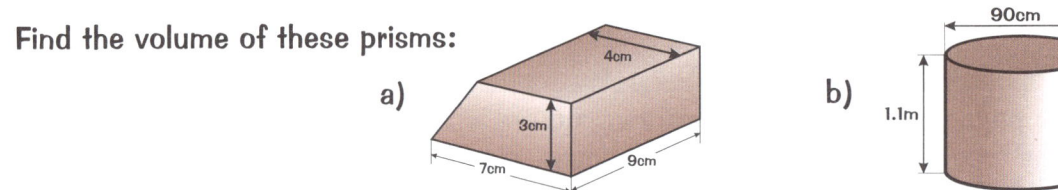

Find the volume of these prisms:

a) 7cm, 9cm, 3cm, 4cm

b) 90cm, 1.1m

UNIT THREE

Lines and Angles

Angles aren't that bad — you just have to learn them, that's all!

1) Estimating Angles

The secret here is to **KNOW THESE FOUR SPECIAL ANGLES** as reference points. Then you can COMPARE any other angle to them.

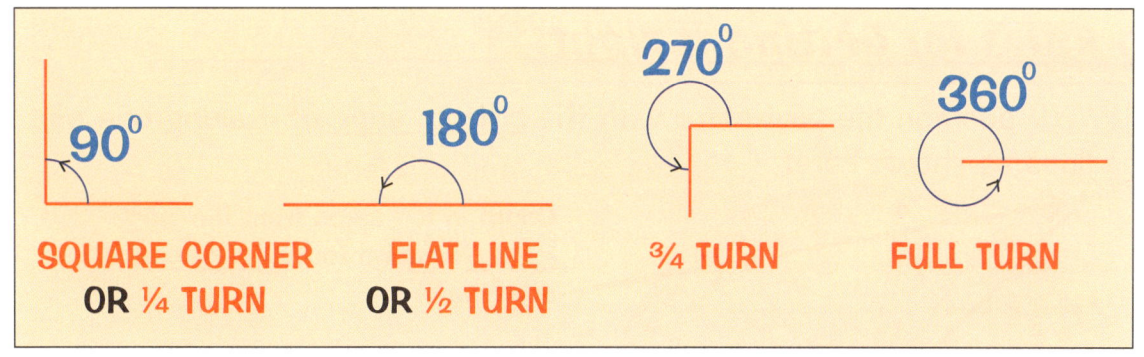

90° — SQUARE CORNER OR ¼ TURN
180° — FLAT LINE OR ½ TURN
270° — ¾ TURN
360° — FULL TURN

When two lines meet at 90° they are said to be **PERPENDICULAR** to each other.

Example: Estimate the size of these three angles A, B and C:

If you compare each angle to the reference angles of 90°, 180° and 270° you can easily estimate that:
A = 70°, B = 110°, C = 260°

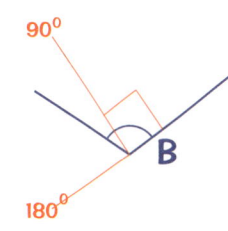

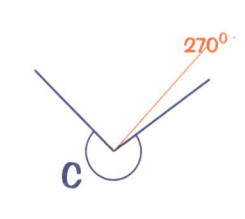

2) Three Letter Angle Notation

The best way to say which angle you're talking about in a diagram is by using **THREE letters**.

For example in the diagram, angle ACB = 25°.

angle ACD = 20°

1) The **MIDDLE LETTER** is where the angle is.
2) The **OTHER TWO LETTERS** tell you **WHICH TWO LINES** enclose the angle.

The Acid Test: LEARN the four main reference angles.

1) Estimate these angles:

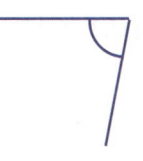

a)   b)   c)   d)

UNIT THREE

Measuring Angles with Protractors

The 2 big mistakes that people make with PROTRACTORS:

1) Not putting the 0° line at the start position
2) Reading from the WRONG SCALE.

Two Rules for Getting it right!

1) ALWAYS position the protractor with the bottom edge of it along one of the lines as shown here:

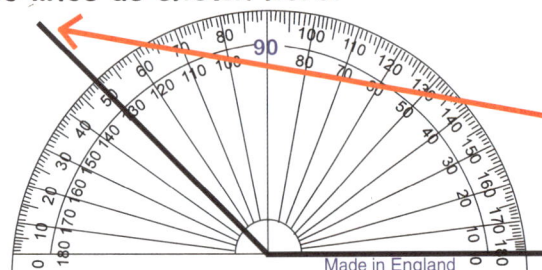

Count in 10° steps from the start line right round to the other one over there.

← Start line

2) COUNT THE ANGLE IN 10° STEPS from the start line right round to the other one.

DON'T JUST READ A NUMBER OFF THE SCALE – it will probably be the WRONG ONE because there are TWO scales to choose from.
The answer here is 130° – NOT 50°! – which you will only get right if you start counting 10°, 20°, 30°, 40° etc. from the start line until you reach the other line. You should also estimate it as a check.

Acute Angles
SHARP POINTY ONES
(less than 90°)

Obtuse Angles
FLATTER-LOOKING ONES
(between 90° and 180°)

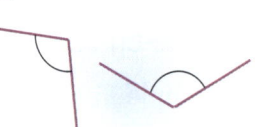

Reflex Angles
ONES THAT BEND BACK ON THEMSELVES
(more than 180°)

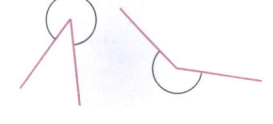

Right Angles
SQUARE CORNERS
(exactly 90°)

The Acid Test

1) LEARN 2 rules for using protractors.
2) LEARN what ACUTE, OBTUSE, REFLEX and RIGHT ANGLES are.
   Draw one example of each.
3) Use a protractor to accurately draw these angles: a) 35° b) 150° c) 80°

UNIT THREE

Compass Directions and Bearings

The Eight Points Of the Compass

Make sure you know all these
8 DIRECTIONS ON THE COMPASS.

For other directions (i.e. not exactly North or South or South-East, etc), you have to use BEARINGS.

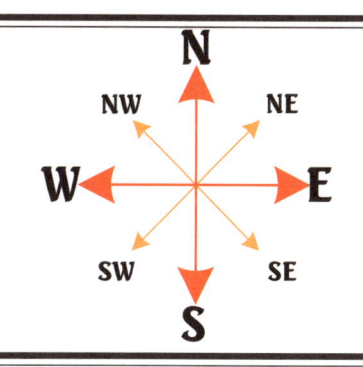

Bearings

1) A bearing is just a DIRECTION given as an ANGLE in degrees.
2) All bearings are measured CLOCKWISE from the NORTHLINE.
3) All bearings are given as 3 figures: e.g. 060° rather than just 60°, 020° rather than 20° etc.

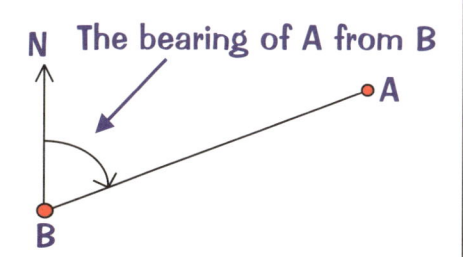

The bearing of A from B

The 3 Key Words

Only learn this if you want to get bearings RIGHT

1) "FROM"

Find the word "FROM" in the question, and put your pencil on the diagram at the point you are going "from".

2) NORTHLINE

At the point you are going "FROM", draw in a NORTHLINE.

3) CLOCKWISE

Now draw in the angle CLOCKWISE from the northline to the line joining the two points. This angle is the BEARING.

EXAMPLE:

Find the bearing of Q from P:

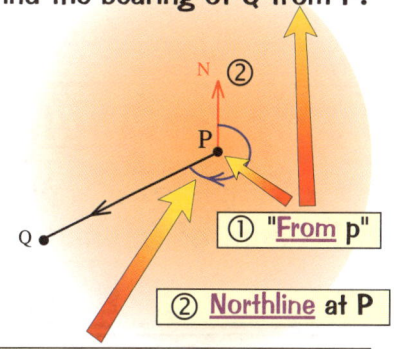

① "From p"
② Northline at P
③ Clockwise, from the N-line.

This angle is the bearing of Q from P and is 245°.

The Acid Test

1) LEARN the Eight points of the Compass, then turn over and DRAW IT OUT AGAIN.
2) LEARN the 3 KEY WORDS for BEARINGS, then turn over and write them down.
3) Draw a blob on a piece of paper to represent home, and then draw 2 lines, one going out in a South-Westerly direction and the other on a bearing of 080°.

UNIT THREE

Six Angle Rules

6 Simple Rules — that's all:

If you know them ALL — THOROUGHLY, you at least have a fighting chance of working out problems with lines and angles. If you don't — you've no chance.

1) Angles in a triangle

Add up to 180°.

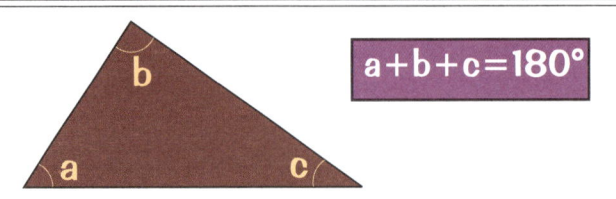

a+b+c=180°

2) Angles on a straight line

Add up to 180°.

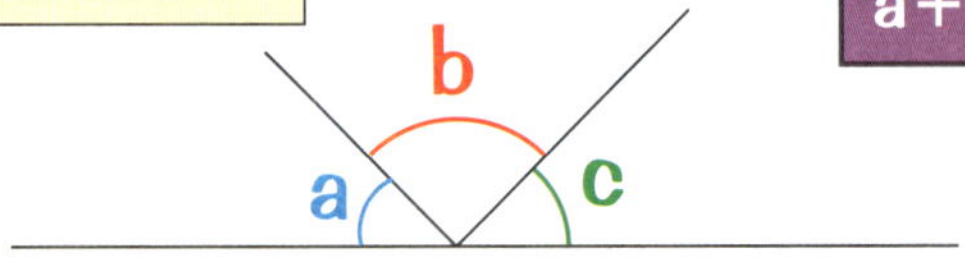

a+b+c=180°

3) Angles in a 4-sided shape

(a "Quadrilateral")

Add up to 360°.

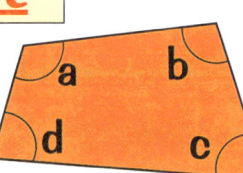

a+b+c+d=360°

4) Angles round a point

Add up to 360°.

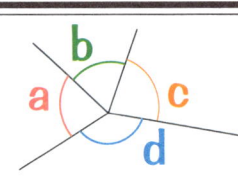

a+b+c+d=360°

5) Exterior Angle of Triangle

Exterior Angle of triangle
= sum of Opposite Interior angles

i.e. a+b=d

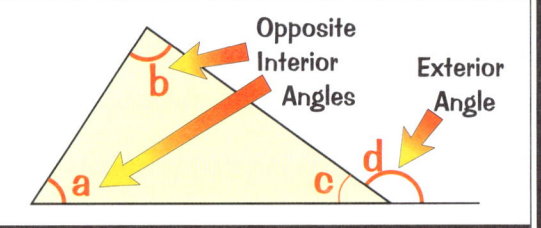

Opposite Interior Angles

Exterior Angle

6) Isosceles triangles

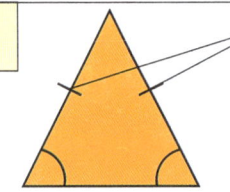

These dashes indicate two sides the same length

2 sides the same
2 angles the same

In an isosceles triangle, YOU ONLY NEED TO KNOW ONE ANGLE to be able to find the other two, which is very useful IF YOU REMEMBER IT.

a)

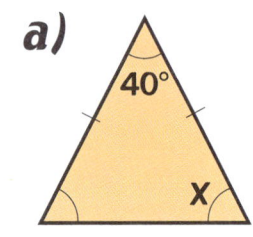

180° − 40° = 140°
The two bottom angles are both the same and they must add up to 140°, so each one must be half of 140° (= 70°). So X = 70°.

b)

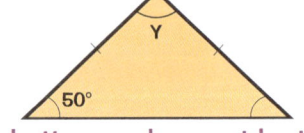

The two bottom angles must be the same, so 50° + 50° = 100°.
All the angles add up to 180° so Y = 180° − 100° = 80°.

UNIT THREE

# Parallel lines

Whenever one line goes across <u>2 parallel lines</u>, then the two <u>bunches of angles</u> are the <u>same</u>, as shown below:

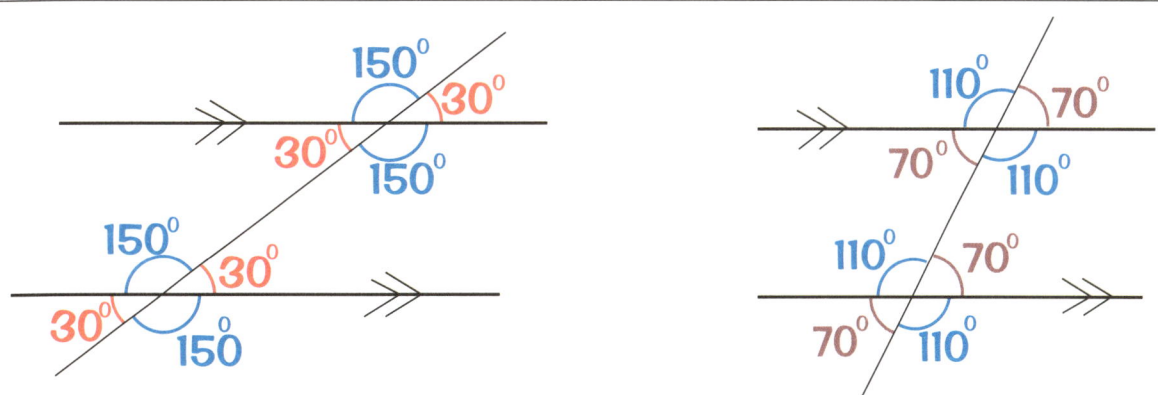

(The arrows mean those 2 lines are parallel)

Whenever you have TWO PARALLEL LINES....

1) there are <u>only two different angles</u>:

    <u>A SMALL ONE</u> and <u>A BIG ONE</u>

2) and they <u>ALWAYS ADD UP TO 180°</u>.
    E.g.   30° and 150°   or   70° and 110°

The trickiest bit about parallel lines is <u>SPOTTING THEM IN THE FIRST PLACE</u>

— watch out for these "Z", "C", "U" and "F" shapes popping up
They're a dead giveaway that you've got a pair of parallel lines.

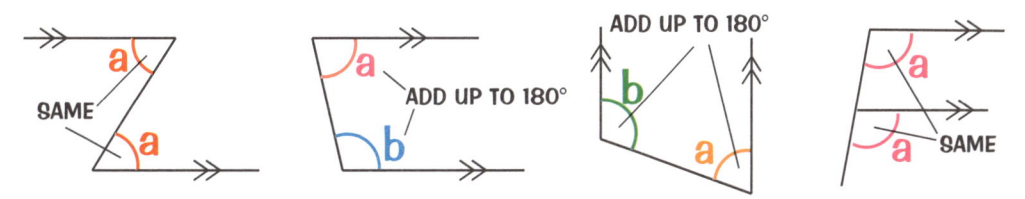

In a <u>Z-shape</u> they're called
"<u>ALTERNATE ANGLES</u>"

If they add up to 180° they're called
"<u>SUPPLEMENTARY ANGLES</u>"

In an F-shape they're called
"<u>CORRESPONDING ANGLES</u>"

Alas you're expected to learn these three silly names too!

The Acid Test

The diagram shown here has one angle given as 60°.
Find all the other 7 angles.

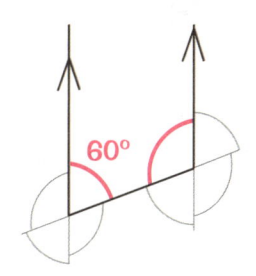

UNIT THREE

X, Y and Z Coordinates

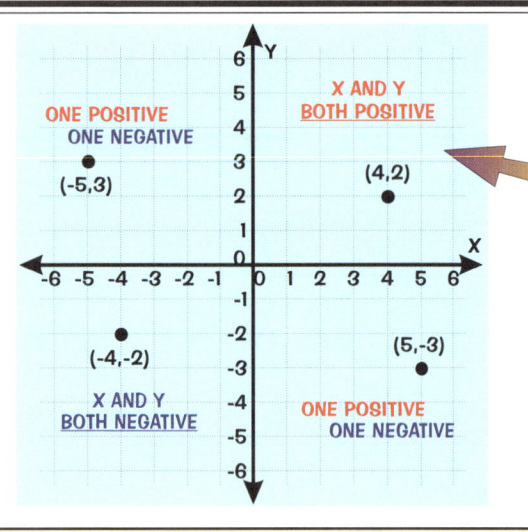

A graph has four different regions where the X- and Y- coordinates are either positive or negative.

This is the easiest region by far because here ALL THE COORDINATES ARE POSITIVE.

You have to be dead careful in the OTHER REGIONS though, because the X- and Y- coordinates could be negative, and that always makes life much more difficult.

X, Y Coordinates — getting them in the right order

You must always give COORDINATES in brackets like this: (x,y)

(x , y)

And you always have to be real careful to get them the right way round, X first, then Y. Here are THREE POINTS to help you remember:

1) The two coordinates are always in ALPHABETICAL ORDER, X then Y.

2) X is always the flat axis going ACROSS the page.
   In other words " X is a..cross "   Get it! - x is a "×".   (Hilarious isn't it)

3) Remember it's always IN THE HOUSE (→) and then UP THE STAIRS (↑),
   so it's ALONG first and then UP, i.e. X-coordinate first, and then Y-coordinate.

Z Coordinates are for 3-D space

1) All z-coordinates do is extend the normal x-y coordinates into a third direction, z, so that all positions then have 3 coordinates: (x,y,z)

2) This means you can give the coordinates of the corners of a box or any other 3-D SHAPE.

   For example in this drawing, the coordinates of B and F are   B(7,4,0)   F(7,4,2)

The Acid Test:

OH – AND DON'T FORGET:
3 COORDINATES = 3-D SPACE
2 COORDINATES = 2-D SPACE

LEARN the 3 Rules for getting X and Y the right way round.
Then turn over and write it all down.

Write down the coordinates of the letters A to H on this graph:

UNIT THREE

Density and Speed

You might think this is physics, but density is specifically mentioned in the maths syllabus, and it's very likely to come up in your Exam. The standard formula for density is:

Density = Mass ÷ Volume

so we can put it in a FORMULA TRIANGLE like this:

One way or another you must remember this formula for density, because they won't give it to you and without it you'll be pretty stuck. The best method by far is to remember the order of the letters in the formula triangle as D^MV or DiMoV (The Russian Agent!).

EXAMPLE: Find the volume of an object which has a mass of 40 g and a density of 6.4 g/cm³

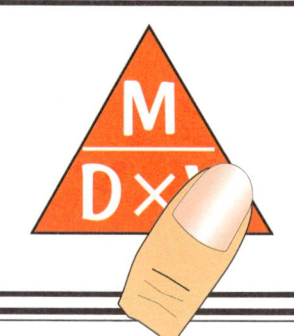

ANSWER: To find volume, cover up V in the formula triangle. This leaves M/D showing, so V = M ÷ D
= 40 ÷ 6.4
= 6.25 cm³

Speed = Distance ÷ Time

This is very common. In fact it probably comes up every single year — and they never give you the formula! Either learn it beforehand or wave goodbye to lots of easy marks. Life isn't all bad though — there's an easy FORMULA TRIANGLE:

Of course you still have to remember the order of the letters in the triangle (S^DT) — but this time we have the word SoDiT to help you.

So if it's a question on speed, distance and time just say: **SOD IT**.

EXAMPLE: "A car travels 90 miles at 36 miles per hour. How long does it take?"

ANSWER: We want to find the TIME, so cover up T in the triangle which leaves D/S,
so T = D/S = Distance ÷ speed = 90 ÷ 36 = 2.5 hours

LEARN THE FORMULA TRIANGLE, AND YOU'LL FIND QUESTIONS ON SPEED, DISTANCE AND TIME VERY EASY.

The Acid Test:
LEARN the formulas for DENSITY and SPEED — and also the two Formula triangles.

1) What's the formula for Density?
2) A metal object has a volume of 45 cm³ and a mass of 743 g. What is its density?
3) Another piece of the same metal has a volume of 36.5 cm³. What is its mass?
4) What's the formula for speed, distance and time?
5) Find the time taken, for a person walking at 3.2 km/h to cover 24 km.
   Also, find how far she'll walk in 3 hrs 30 mins.

UNIT THREE

The Shapes You Need to Know

These are easy marks in the Exam — make sure you know them all.

Three-sided Shapes — Triangles
(just in case you didn't know...)

1) EQUILATERAL Triangle
3 lines of symmetry.
Rotational symmetry order 3

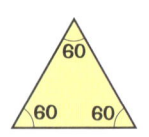

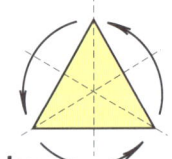

2) RIGHT-ANGLED Triangle
No symmetry unless the angles are 45°

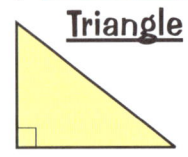

3) ISOSCELES Triangle
2 sides equal
2 angles equal 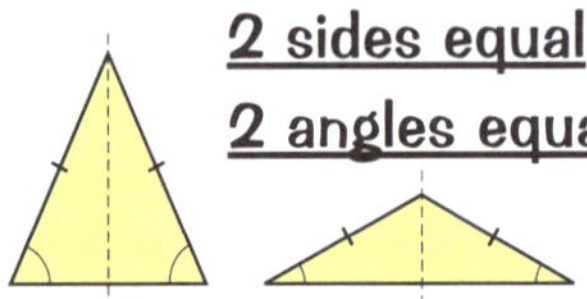
1 line of symmetry.
No rotational symmetry

Four-sided Shapes — Quadrilaterals

1) SQUARE
4 lines of symmetry.
Rotational symmetry order 4

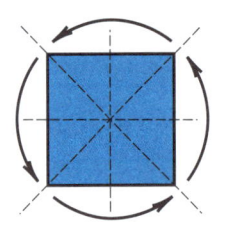

2) RECTANGLE
2 lines of symmetry.
Rotational symmetry order 2

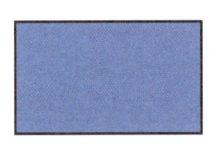

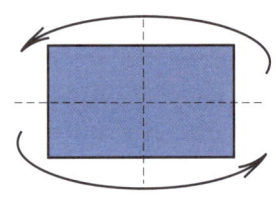

3) RHOMBUS (A square pushed over) (It's also a diamond)
2 lines of symmetry.
Rotational symmetry order 2

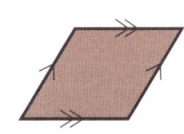

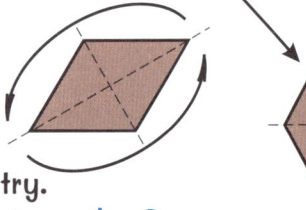

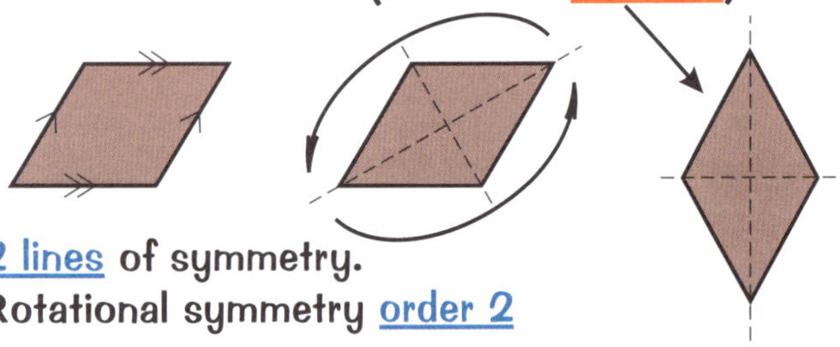

4) PARALLELOGRAM (A rectangle pushed over — two pairs of parallel sides)
NO lines of symmetry.
Rotational symmetry order 2

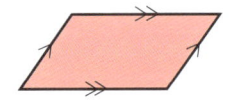

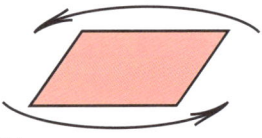

5) TRAPEZIUM (One pair of parallel sides)
Only the isosceles trapezium has a line of symmetry.
None have rotational symmetry

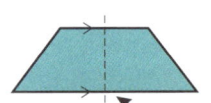

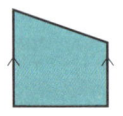

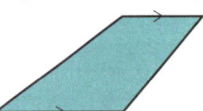

6) KITE
1 line of symmetry.
No rotational symmetry

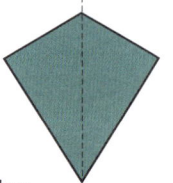

The Acid Test: LEARN everything on this page.
Then turn over and write down all the details that you can remember. Then try again.

UNIT THREE

Midpoint of a Line Segment

The "Midpoint" is just the Middle of the Line

The "MIDPOINT OF A LINE SEGMENT" is the POINT THAT'S BANG IN THE MIDDLE of it.

(Not exactly rocket science, is it...)

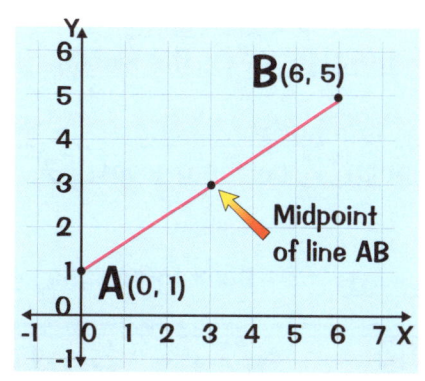

Find the Coordinates of a Midpoint

The only thing you really need to know about midpoints is how to find the coordinates of one.

And it's pretty easy. The x-coordinate of the midpoint is the average of the x-coordinates of the end points — and the same goes for the y-coordinates.

EXAMPLE: "A and B have coordinates (2,1) and (6,3). Find the midpoint of the line AB."

ALWAYS START BY DRAWING A GRAPH

Then follow these THREE EASY STEPS...

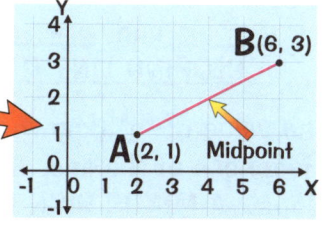

1) Find the AVERAGE of the X-COORDINATES of the two points. → Average of x-coordinates = (2+6) ÷ 2 = **4**

2) Find the AVERAGE of the Y-COORDINATES of the two points. → Average of y-coordinates = (1+3) ÷ 2 = **2**

3) Plonk them IN BRACKETS. → Plonk them in brackets (x-coordinate first): **(4, 2)**

The Acid Test:

Learn the 3 easy steps for finding midpoints. Close the book and write them down.

Plot these points on some graph paper: A(1,4), B(5,6), C(3,2), D(7,0).
1) Draw a line between points A and B and find the midpoint of the line AB.
2) Draw a line between points C and D and find the midpoint of line CD.

UNIT THREE

Straight Lines Graphs

Any straight line graph can be described by a simple equation.
You should be able to recognise a lot of graphs just from their equations.

1) Horizontal and Vertical lines: "x = a" and "y = b"

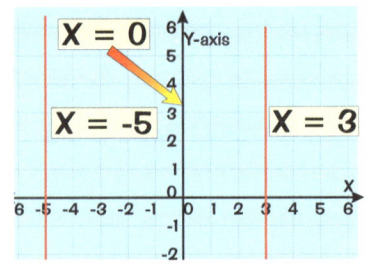

x = a is a vertical line through "a" on the x-axis

y = a is a horizontal line through "a" on the y-axis

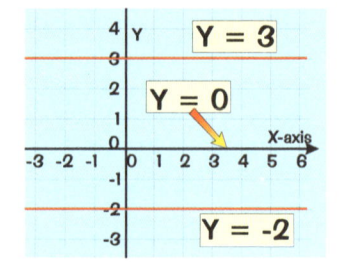

Don't forget: the y-axis is also the line x = 0

Don't forget: the x-axis is also the line y = 0

2) The Main Diagonals: "y = x" and "y = −x"

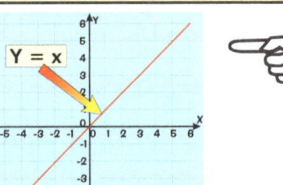

"y = x" is the main diagonal that goes UPHILL from left to right.

"y = −x" is the main diagonal that goes DOWNHILL from left to right.

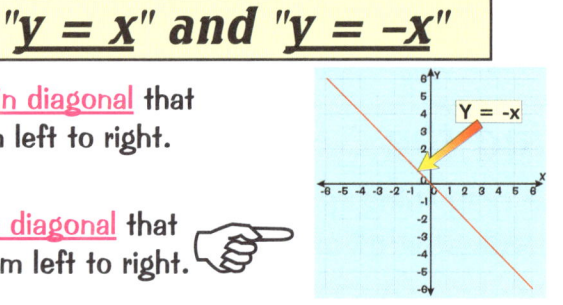

3) Other Sloping Lines Through the origin: "y = ax" and "y = −ax"

y = ax and y = -ax are the equations for A SLOPING LINE THROUGH THE ORIGIN.

The value of "a" (known as the gradient) tells you the steepness of the line. The bigger "a" is, the steeper the slope. A MINUS SIGN tells you it slopes DOWNHILL.

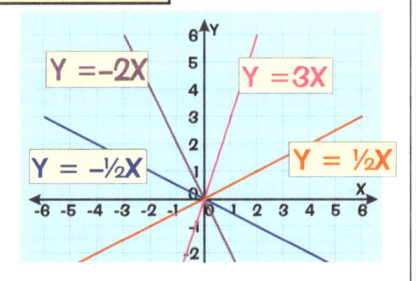

All Other Straight Lines

Other straight-line equations are a little more complicated. The next page shows you how to draw them, but the first step is identifying them in the first place. Remember:

All straight line equations just contain "something x, something y, and a number".

Straight lines:		NOT straight lines:	
x − y = 0	y = 2 + 3x	y = x³ + 3	2y − 1/x = 7
2y − 4x = 7	4x − 3 = 5y	1/y + 1/x = 2	x(3 − 2y) = 3
3y + 3x = 12	6y − x − 7 = 0	x² = 4 − y	xy + 3 = 0

The Acid Test:

LEARN all the specific graphs on this page and also how to identify straight line equations.

Now turn over the page and write down everything you've learned.

UNIT THREE

Drawing Graphs from Equations

OK, so you should now be able to recognise a straight-line graph from its equations. The next step is to learn how to draw them...

1) Doing the Table Of Values

1) What you're likely to get in the Exam is an equation such as "y = x + 3", or "y = 3x + 2"   and a half-finished table of values:

Example: "Complete this table of values, using the equation y = 2x – 7"

x	-2	0	2	4	6
y	-11		-3		

2) Put each x-value into the equation and work out the corresponding y-values.

E.g. For x = 0   y = 2x – 7 = (2 × 0) – 7 = 0 – 7 = -7, etc...

...until you get this:

x	-2	0	2	4	6
y	-11	-7	-3	1	5

2) Plotting The Points and Drawing The Graph

1) **PLOT EACH PAIR** of x- and y- values from the table as a point on the graph.
2) Do it very **CAREFULLY** — and don't mix up the x- and y-values (See P.58)
3) The points will always form **A DEAD STRAIGHT LINE**.

   NEVER let one point drag your line off in some ridiculous direction. You never get **SPIKES** – only **MISTAKES**.

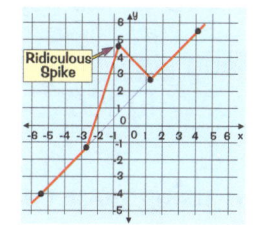

4) If one point does look a bit wacky, check 2 things:
   – the y-value you worked out in the table
   – that you've plotted it properly!

Continuing the Example from part 1):

"Use your table of values to plot the graph of y = 2x – 7"

Simple — plot each point carefully, then you should be able to draw a nice **STRAIGHT LINE** through all the points.

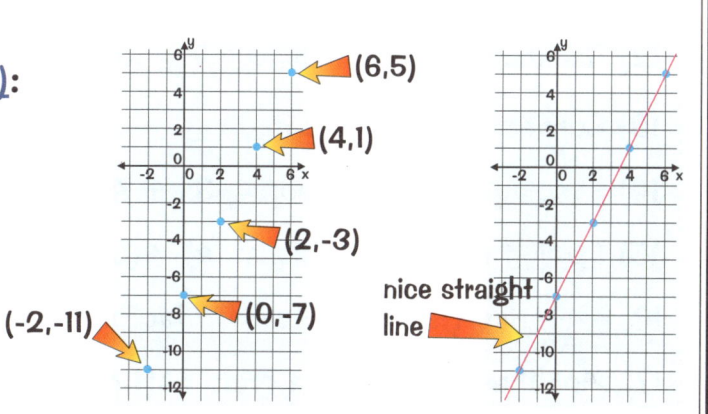

Points: (6,5), (4,1), (2,-3), (0,-7), (-2,-11) — nice straight line

The Acid Test

x	-4	-2	-1	0	1	2	4
y		-6		-2			

1) **LEARN** all the important details on this page.
2) Then use them to complete this table of values for the equation: y = x – 2
3) Then plot the points on graph paper and draw the graph.

UNIT THREE

Revision Test for Unit Three

OK, so there's lots of questions here, but just keep reminding yourself that they're the very best revision you can do. It's really important to keep practising these as often as you can.

1) Write this number out in words: 21,306,515

2) Put these numbers in order of size:
   a) 23   6,534   123   2,200   2   132   789   45
   b) -2,   4,   0,   -7,   -6,   10,   8,   5

3) Work out: a) -3 × -2   b) -4 × 8   c) 12 ÷ -4   d) -20 ÷ -4

4) Find the highest common factor of 42 and 28.

5) Find the lowest common multiple of 8 and 10.

6) Find all the prime numbers between 40 and 60 (there are 5 of them).

7) Express as a product of prime factors: a) 210   b) 1050

8) Round these numbers off to 1 decimal place: a) 5.32 b) 3.46   c) 6.15

9) a) Give 246 to the nearest 10   b) Give 860 to the nearest 100

10) How many significant figures have these numbers got?
    a) 12   b) 150   c) 2000   d) 23.4   e) 8,500

11) Without using your calculator, estimate the answer to $\dfrac{390}{28 + 12.3}$

12) Use the [a b/c] button to reduce $^{12}/_{15}$ to its simplest form.

13) Convert 0.645 into a fraction.

14) Simplify the expression: 3x + 4y + 2x − 4y

15) Expand these expressions: a) 4(3g + 5h − 1)   b) (x+2)(x−6)

16) Factorise (take out common factors) this expression: 2x + 6xy.

17) Plot these points on a grid: A(1,4), B(-4,2), C(-3,-5), D(5,-6), E(5,0)

18) Estimate these angles and then measure them, and make sure your two answers are similar for each angle:
    a)   b)   c)   d)

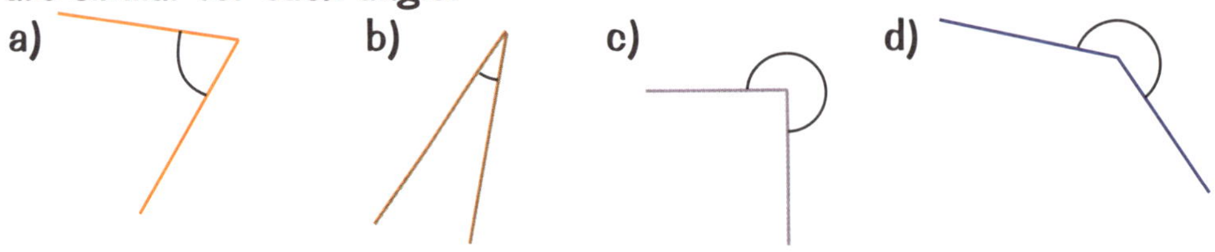

Revision Test for Unit Three

19) Draw these 7 shapes with all their lines of symmetry:

   a) Parallelogram   b) Rhombus   c) Trapezium   d) Kite
   e) Isosceles Triangle   f) Equilateral Triangle   g) Right-angled Triangle

20) What are cube numbers? Write down the first ten of them.

21) Without a calculator, find all possible answers of a) $\sqrt{256}$ b) $\sqrt[3]{216}$.

22) Work out the value of: a) 6^4 b) 7^5 c) 4 squared
   d) 12^5 e) $5^3 \times 4^7$ f) 8 cubed

23) Write 35600000000 in standard form.

24) Work out the expression for the nth number in this sequence: 1, 5, 9, 13, ...

25) For the diagram shown, work out angles BDE, AED and BDC.

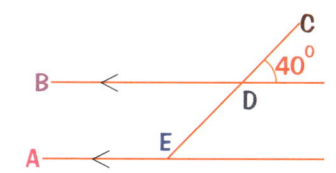

26) What is a perimeter?   Find the perimeter and area of this shape:

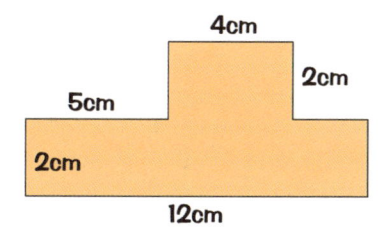

27) Work out the volumes of the two objects below.

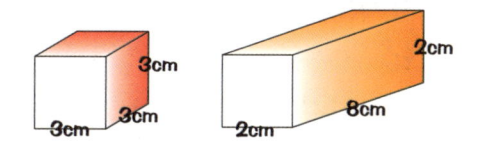

28) Complete the table of values below for the equation $y = x + 3$ and draw the graph.

x	-5	-3	-1	0	1	2	4	6
y	-2				4			

29) A bar is 30 inches long. How long is this in feet and inches?

Ratio in The Home

There are lots of Exam questions which at first sight seem completely different but in fact they can all be done using the GOLDEN RULE...

DIVIDE FOR ONE, THEN TIMES FOR ALL

Example 1:
"5 pints of Milk cost £1.30. How much will 3 pints cost?"

The GOLDEN RULE says:

DIVIDE FOR ONE, THEN TIMES FOR ALL

which means:

Divide the price by 5 to find how much FOR ONE PINT, then multiply by 3 to find how much FOR 3 PINTS.

So..... £1.30 ÷ 5 = 0.26 = 26p (for 1 pint)
×3 = 78p (for 3 pints)

Example 2:
"Divide £400 in the ratio 5:3"

The GOLDEN RULE says:

DIVIDE FOR ONE, THEN TIMES FOR ALL

The trick with this type of question is to add together the numbers in the RATIO to find how many PARTS there are: 5 + 3 = 8 parts. Now use The Golden Rule:

Divide the £400 by 8 to find how much it is for ONE PART
then multiply by 5 and by 3 to find how much 5 PARTS ARE
and how much 3 PARTS ARE.

So... £400 ÷ 8 = £50   (for 1 part)
×5 = £250 (for 5 parts)   and ×3 = £150   (for 3 parts)

So £400 split in the ratio 5:3 is   £250 : £150

The Acid Test

1) If seven pencils cost 98p, how much will 4 pencils cost?
2) Divide £2400 in the ratio 5:7.

Ratio — Rat 'n' Toad Pie

Example 3 — The Recipe:

The following recipe is for "Froggatt's Homespun Rat 'n' Toad Pie" and serves 4 people.

- 4 Freshly-caught Rats
- 2 Slimy Brown Toads
- 5 Ounces of "Froggatt's Lumpy Sprout Ketchup"
- 8 Freshly-dug Potatoes
- A big wodge of pastry

"Change these amounts so there's enough for SIX people."

ANSWER: The GOLDEN RULE says:

DIVIDE FOR ONE, THEN TIMES FOR ALL

which means:

DIVIDE each amount to get enough for one person, then TIMES to get enough for SIX.

Since the recipe is for 4 people then DIVIDE EACH AMOUNT BY 4 to find the amount for 1 person — then MULTIPLY THAT BY 6 to find how much for 6 people — simple enough:

4 Rats ÷ 4 = 1 Rat   (for one person)   ×6 = 6 Rats   (For 6 people)

2 Toads ÷ 4 = 0.5 Toad   (for one person)   ×6 = 3 Toads   (For 6 people)

5 Ounces of "Froggatt's Lumpy Sprout Ketchup" ÷ 4 = 1.25 Oz   (for one person)   ×6 = 7.5 Oz   (For 6 people)

8 'taties ÷ 4 = 2 'taties (per person)   ×6 = 12 'taties   (For 6 people)

A big wodge of pastry ÷ 4 then ×6 = A wodge of pastry half as big again.

In fact, all the amounts are just HALF AS MUCH AGAIN, if you notice.

The Acid Test

Work out the amount of each ingredient needed to make enough Rat 'n' Toad pie for 9 people.

Unit Four

The Best Buy

A favourite type of question they like to ask you in Exams is comparing the "value for money" of 2 or 3 similar items. Always follow the GOLDEN RULE...

Divide by the PRICE in pence (to get the amount per penny)

Example: The local "Supplies 'n' Vittals" stocks three sizes of Jamaican Gooseberry Jam. The question is: Which of these represents "THE BEST VALUE FOR MONEY"?

500g at £1.08    350g at 80p    100g at 42p

ANSWER: the GOLDEN RULE says:

DIVIDE BY THE PRICE IN PENCE TO GET THE AMOUNT PER PENNY

So we shall:
500g ÷ 108p = 4.6g PER PENNY
350g ÷ 80p = 4.4g PER PENNY
100g ÷ 42p = 2.4g PER PENNY

So we can now see straight away that THE 500g JAR is the best value for money because you get MORE JAM PER PENNY (As you should expect, it being the big jar).

With any question comparing "value for money", DIVIDE BY THE PRICE (in pence) and it will always be the BIGGEST ANSWER is the BEST VALUE FOR MONEY.

The Acid Test

Froggatt's "Slugtail Soup" comes in three different sizes:

The 150g tin at 87p, the 250g tin at £1.37 and the Farmhouse Size, 750g at £3.95.

Work out which one is the best value for money.   (And don't just guess!)

Unit Four

More Fractions

This page shows you how to cope with fraction calculations without your <u>beloved calculator</u>. But before you get stuck into this stuff, have a flick back to pages 26-27 and make sure you know all of the <u>basics</u> covered on those pages.

1) Multiplying — easy

Multiply top and bottom separately:

$$\frac{3}{5} \times \frac{4}{7} = \frac{3 \times 4}{5 \times 7} = \frac{12}{35}$$

2) Dividing — quite easy

Turn the 2nd fraction <u>UPSIDE DOWN</u> and then <u>multiply</u>:

$$\frac{3}{4} \div \frac{1}{3} = \frac{3}{4} \times \frac{3}{1} = \frac{3 \times 3}{4 \times 1} = \frac{9}{4}$$

3) Adding, subtracting — fraught

Add or subtract <u>TOP LINES ONLY</u> <u>but only if</u> the bottom numbers are the same. (If they're not, you have to make them the same – see p26.)

$$\frac{2}{6} + \frac{1}{6} = \frac{3}{6}$$

$$\frac{5}{7} - \frac{3}{7} = \frac{2}{7}$$

4) Cancelling down — easy

<u>Divide top and bottom by the same number</u>, till they won't go any further:

$$\frac{18}{24} \xrightarrow{\div 3} \frac{6}{8} \xrightarrow{\div 2} \frac{3}{4}$$

5) Finding a fraction of something — just multiply

<u>Multiply</u> the 'something' by the <u>TOP</u> of the fraction, then <u>divide</u> it by the <u>BOTTOM</u>:

$$\frac{9}{20} \text{ of } £360 = \{(9) \times £360\} \div (20) = \frac{£3240}{20} = £162$$

or: $\frac{9}{20}$ of £360 = $\frac{9}{1} \times £360 \times \frac{1}{20}$ = £162

6) Dealing with Mixed Numbers

There's only one way to deal with calculations involving <u>mixed numbers</u> (that's things like $3\frac{1}{3}$):

1) change them to 'normal' fractions
2) then you can do them as usual.

<u>Don't</u> try to do them <u>any other way</u>, or you'll definitely get it wrong.

$$3\frac{2}{3} \times 7\frac{3}{4} = \frac{11}{3} \times \frac{31}{4}$$
$$2 + (3 \times 3)$$
$$3 + (7 \times 4)$$
$$= \frac{341}{12}$$

The Acid Test

Try all of the following <u>without</u> a calculator.

1) a) $\frac{3}{8} \times \frac{5}{12}$ b) $\frac{4}{5} \div \frac{7}{8}$ c) $\frac{3}{4} + \frac{2}{5}$ d) $\frac{2}{5} - \frac{3}{8}$ e) $4\frac{1}{9} + 2\frac{2}{27}$

2) a) Find $\frac{2}{5}$ of 550.   b) What's $\frac{7}{8}$ of £2?

UNIT FOUR

Percentages

Discounts, VAT, Interest, Increase, etc.

MOST percentage questions are like this:

> Work out "something %" of "something else"

E.g. Find 20% of £60

This is the method to use:

1) WRITE IT DOWN: Find   20%   of   £60
                             ↓   ↓   ↓
2) TRANSLATE IT INTO MATHS: $\frac{20}{100}$ ×   60

3) WORK IT OUT: 20 ÷ 100 × 60 = £12

Two Important Details:

Make sure you remember them!

1) "Per cent" means "out of 100"
so 20% means "20 out of 100" = 20 ÷ 100 = $\frac{20}{100}$

(That's how you work it out in the method shown above)

2) "OF" means "×"

In maths, the word "of" can always be replaced with "×" for working out the answer
(as shown in the above method)

UNIT FOUR

Percentages

Important Example No. 1

1) A radio is priced at £8.50 but there is a discount of 20% available. FIND THE REDUCED PRICE OF THE RADIO.

Answer:
First find 20% of £8.50 using the method from the last page:

1) 20% of £8.50
2) $\frac{20}{100}$ × 8.5
3) [20] [÷] [100] [×] [8.5] [=]   1.7 = **£1.70**   ← It's money, so 1.7 on the calculator display is £1.70.

This is the DISCOUNT so we take it away to get the final answer:
£8.50 − £1.70 = **£6.80**

Important Example No. 2

2) A plumber's bill for fixing a small leak is £98 + VAT. The VAT is charged at 17.5%. WORK OUT THE TOTAL BILL.

Answer: First find 17.5% of £98 using the standard method:

1) 17.5% of £98
2) $\frac{17.5}{100}$ × 98
3) [17.5] [÷] [100] [×] [98] [=]   17.15 = **£17.15**

This £17.15 is the VAT which then has to be ADDED to the £98 to give the FINAL BILL:
£98 + £17.15 = **£115.15**

UNIT FOUR

Percentages

Comparing Numbers using Percentages

This is the other common type of percentage question.

Give "one number" AS A PERCENTAGE OF "another number"

For example, "Express £2 _as a percentage of_ £20." This is the method to use:

The FDP Method:

Fraction → Decimal → Percentage

$\frac{2}{20}$ →(2 ÷ 20)→ 0.1 →(× 100)→ 10%

First make a FRACTION out of the 2 numbers, always with the smaller number on top.

DIVIDE them to get a DECIMAL.

Then multiply by 100 to get a PERCENTAGE.

Two Important Examples

1) A shopkeeper buys pens at 8p each and sells them for 10p each. What is his profit AS A PERCENTAGE?

   Answer: The two numbers we want to compare are the PROFIT (which is 2p) with the ORIGINAL cost (which is 8p). We then apply the FDP method:

   Fraction → Decimal → Percentage:
   $\frac{2}{8}$ → 0.25 → 25%

   so the shopkeeper makes a 25% profit on the pens.

2) "In a sale, a tennis racket is reduced in price from £60 to £48. What PERCENTAGE REDUCTION is this?"

   Answer: The two numbers we want to compare are the REDUCTION (which is £12) and the ORIGINAL VALUE (which is £60). We then apply the FDP method:

   Fraction → Decimal → Percentage:
   $\frac{12}{60}$ → 0.2 → 20%

The Acid Test

1) A bank charges interest at 12% per year. If £1000 is borrowed for one year, how much interest will be charged?
2) A house increases in value from £140,000 to £182,000. What is the increase in value of the house as a percentage?

UNIT FOUR

Making Formulas From Words

These can seem a bit confusing but they're not as bad as they look once you know the "tricks of the trade", as it were. There are two main types.

Type 1

In this type there are <u>instructions about what to do with a number</u> and you have to write it as a <u>formula</u>. The only things they're likely to want you to do in the formula are:

1) Multiply x   2) Divide x   3) Square x (x^2)   4) Add or subtract a number

EXAMPLE 1: " To find y, multiply x by three and then subtract four"

ANSWER: Start with x   →   3x   →   3x – 4   so $\underline{y = 3x - 4}$
                     Times it by 3   Subtract 4   (not too gruelling, is it?)

EXAMPLE 2: This is the most difficult you'd ever get:

"To find y, square x, divide this by three and then subtract seven. Write a formula for y."

ANSWER: Start with x   → x^2 → $\dfrac{x^2}{3}$ → $\dfrac{x^2}{3} - 7$
                     Square it   Divide it by 3   Subtract 7

They're not that bad, are they? $Y = \dfrac{x^2}{3} - 7$

Type 2

This is a bit harder. <u>You have to make up a formula</u> by putting in letters like "C" for "<u>cost</u>" or "n" for "<u>number of something-or-others</u>". Although it may look confusing the formulas always turn out to be <u>REALLY SIMPLE</u>, so make sure you give it a go.

EXAMPLE: Froggatt's deep-fry "CHOCCO-BURGERS" (chocolate-covered beef burgers — not available in all areas) cost 58 pence each. Write a formula for the total cost, T, of buying n "CHOCCO-BURGERS" at 58p each.

Answer: T stands for the total cost
n stands for the number of "CHOCCO-BURGERS"

In words the formula is: Total Cost = Number of "CHOCCO-BURGERS" × 58p

Putting the letters in: T = n × 58   or to write it better: $\underline{T = 58n}$

The Acid Test

1) The value of y is found by taking x, multiplying it by five and then subtracting three. Write down a formula for y in terms of x.

2) One of Froggatt's main competitors are "Hobnails", who produce a vast range of products including their widely-acclaimed "Hobnail Soup" which costs 95p a tin. Write a formula for the total cost C pence of buying n tins of Hobnail Soup.

Unit Four

Substituting Values into Formulas

This topic is a lot easier than you think! $F = \frac{9}{5}C + 32$

Generally speaking, algebra is a pretty grim subject, but you should realise that some bits of it are VERY easy, and this is definitely the easiest bit of all, so whatever you do, don't pass up on these easy Exam marks.

Method

If you don't follow this STRICT METHOD you'll just keep getting them wrong — it's as simple as that.

1) **Write out the Formula**   e.g $F = \frac{9}{5}C + 32$

2) **Write it again**, directly underneath, but substituting numbers for letters on the RHS. $F = \frac{9}{5}15 + 32$
(Right Hand Side)

3) Work it out **IN STAGES**. $F = 27 + 32$
Use **BODMAS** to work things out **IN THE RIGHT ORDER**. $= 59$
WRITE DOWN values for each bit as you go along. $F = 59°$

4) **DO NOT** attempt to do it all in one go on your calculator. That ridiculous method fails at least 50% of the time!

BODMAS

Brackets, Other, Division, Multiplication, Addition, Subtraction

BODMAS tells you the ORDER in which these operations should be done: Work out Brackets first, then Other things like squaring, then Divide / Multiply groups of numbers before Adding or Subtracting them. This set of rules works really well for simple cases, so remember the word BODMAS.

EXAMPLE: A mysterious quantity T, is given by: $T = (P - 7)^2 + 4R/Q$
Find the value of T when P = 4, Q = -2 and R = 3

ANSWER:
1) Write down the formula: $T = (P - 7)^2 + 4R/Q$
2) Put the numbers in: $T = (4 - 7)^2 + 4 \times 3/-2$
3) Then work it out in stages : $= (-3)^2 + 12/-2$
   $= 9 + -6$
   $= 9 - 6 = 3$

Note BODMAS in operation:

Brackets worked out first, then squared. Multiplications and divisions done before finally adding and subtracting.

The Acid Test:

LEARN the 4 Steps of the Substitution Method and the full meaning of BODMAS. Then turn over.....

... and write it all down from memory.   1) Practise the above example until you can do it easily without help.   2) If $C = \frac{5}{9}(F - 32)$, find the value of C when F = 77.

UNIT FOUR

Solving Equations

The "proper" way to solve equations is shown on P.74. In practice the "proper way" can be pretty difficult so there's a lot to be said for the much easier methods shown below.

The drawback with these is that you can't always use them on very complicated equations. In most Exam questions though, they do just fine.

1) The "Common Sense" Approach

The trick here is to realise that the unknown quantity "x" is after all just a number and the "equation" is just a cryptic clue to help you find it

Example: "Solve this equation: 3x + 4 = 46"
(i.e. find what number x is)

Answer: This is what you should say to yourself:

> "Something + 4 = 46" hmm, so that "something" must be 42.
>
> So that means 3x = 42, which means "3 times something = 42"
>
> So it must be 42 ÷ 3 which is 14   so x = 14 "

In other words don't think of it as algebra, but as "Find the mystery number".

2) The Trial and Error Method

This is a perfectly good method, and although it won't work every time, it usually does, especially if the answer is a whole number.

The big secret of trial and error methods is to find TWO OPPOSITE CASES and keep taking values IN BETWEEN them.

In other words, find a number that makes the Right Hand Side bigger, and then one that makes the Left Hand Side bigger, and then try values in between them.

Example: "Solve for x: 3x + 5 = 21 − 5x"
(i.e. find the number x)

Answer:

> Try x=1:   3+5 = 21 − 5,   8 = 16 — no good, RHS too big
>
> Try x=3:   9 + 5 = 21 − 15,   14 = 6 — no good, now LHS too big

SO TRY IN BETWEEN: x = 2: 6 + 5 = 21 − 10, 11 = 11,   YES, so x = 2.

The Acid Test:
LEARN these two methods until you can turn the page and write them down with an example for each.

1) Solve: 4x − 12 = 20   2) Solve: 3x + 5 = 5x − 9

UNIT FOUR

Solving Equations

The "proper" way of solving equations isn't hard, it just needs lots of practice.

3) The "Proper" Way

Golden Rules
1) Always do the SAME thing to both sides of the equation.
2) To get rid of something, do the opposite.
   The opposite of + is − and the opposite of − is +.
   The opposite of × is ÷ and the opposite of ÷ is ×.
3) Keep going until you have a letter on its own.

EXAMPLE 1: Solve $5x = 15$

$5x = 15$
$x = 3$

5x means $5 \times x$, so do the opposite — divide both sides by 5.

EXAMPLE 2: Solve $p/3 = 2$

$p/3 = 2$
$p = 6$

$p/3$ means $p \div 3$, so do the opposite — multiply both sides by 3.

EXAMPLE 3: Solve $4y - 3 = 17$

$4y - 3 = 17$
$4y = 20$
$y = 5$

The opposite of −3 is +3 so add 3 to both sides.
The opposite of ×4 is ÷4 so divide both sides by 4.

EXAMPLE 4: Solve $2(x + 3) = 11$

$2(x + 3) = 11$
$x + 3 = 5.5$
$x = 2.5$

The opposite of ×2 is ÷2 so divide both sides by 2.
The opposite of +3 is −3 so subtract 3 from both sides.

EXAMPLE 5: Solve $3x + 5 = 5x + 1$

there are x's on both sides, so subtract 3x from both sides.
the opposite of +1 is −1, so subtract 1 from each side.
the opposite of ×2 is ÷2, so divide each side by 2.

$3x + 5 = 5x + 1$
$5 = 2x + 1$
$4 = 2x$
$2 = x$

4) Rearranging Formulas

You do this in exactly the same way that you solve equations — watch...

EXAMPLE 6: Rearrange the formula $q = 3p + 4$ to make p the subject:

The opposite of +4 is −4 so take 4 from both sides.
The opposite of ×3 is ÷3 so divide both sides by 3.

$q = 3p + 4$
$q - 4 = 3p$
$\frac{q - 4}{3} = p$

The Acid Test

1) Solve these equations: a) $3x + 1 = 13$ b) $q/4 = 8$ c) $5y + 4 = 2y - 2$
2) Rearrange this formula to make b the subject: $2(b - 3) = a$

UNIT FOUR

Trial and Improvement

This is a good method for finding approximate answers to equations that don't have simple whole number answers. Although it basically boils down to trial and error, there is a clear method which you must learn if you want to get it right...

Method

1) **SUBSTITUTE TWO INITIAL VALUES** into the equation that give **OPPOSITE CASES**.

Opposite cases means one answer too big, one too small. If they don't give opposite cases try again.

2) Choose your next value **IN BETWEEN** the previous two, and **PUT IT** into the equation.

Continue the process, choosing new values between the two closest opposite cases, (and preferably nearer to the one which is closest to the answer you want).

3) After only 3 or 4 steps you should have **2 NUMBERS** which are to the right degree of accuracy but **DIFFER BY 1 IN THE LAST DIGIT**.

E.g. if you had to get your answer to 2 DP, you'd eventually end up with say 5.43 and 5.44, with these giving OPPOSITE cases.

4) Now take the **EXACT MIDDLE VALUE** to decide which is the answer you want.

E.g. for 5.43 and 5.44, you'd try 5.435 to see if the real answer was between 5.43 and 5.435 or between 5.435 and 5.44.

Example

"The equation $x^3 + x = 40$ has a solution between 3 and 3.5. Find this solution to 1 DP"

| Try $x = 3$ | $3^3 + 3 = 30$ | (Too small) |
| Try $x = 3.5$ | $3.5^3 + 3.5 = 46.375$ | (Too big) |

← (2 opposite cases)

40 is what we want and it's closer to 46.375 than it is to 30 so we'll choose our next value for x closer to 3.5 than 3.

| Try $x = 3.3$ | $3.3^3 + 3.3 = 39.237$ | (Too small) |

Good, this is very close, but we need to see if 3.4 is still too big or too small:

| Try $x = 3.4$ | $3.4^3 + 3.4 = 42.704$ | (Too big) |

Good, now we know that the answer must be between 3.3 and 3.4.
To find out which one it's nearest to, we have to try the **EXACT MIDDLE VALUE**: 3.35

| Try $x = 3.35$ | $3.35^3 + 3.35 = 40.945$ (Too big) |

This tells us with certainty that the solution must be between 3.3 (too small) and 3.35 (too big), and so to 1 DP it must round down to 3.3. ANSWER = 3.3

The Acid Test:

"LEARN and TURN" — if you don't actually commit it to memory, then you've wasted your time even reading it.

To succeed with this method you must **LEARN the 4 steps above**. Do it now, and practise until you can write them down without having to look back at them. It's not as difficult as you think.

The equation $x^3 - 2x = 1$ has a solution between 1 and 2. Find it to 1 DP.

Unit Four

Inequalities

This is basically quite difficult, but it's still worth learning the easy bits in case they ask a very easy question on it, as well they might. Here are the easy bits:

The 4 Inequality Symbols:

> means "Greater than"   ≥ means "Greater than or equal to"
< means "Less than"   ≤ means "Less than or equal to"

REMEMBER, the one at the BIG end is BIGGEST

so "x > 4" and "4 < x" BOTH say: "x is greater than 4"

Algebra With Inequalities — this is generally a bit tricky

The thing to remember here is that inequalities are just like regular equations:

$$5x < x + 2$$
$$5x = x + 2$$

in the sense that all the normal rules for solving equations (See P.74) apply...

...BUT WITH ONE BIG EXCEPTION:

Whenever you MULTIPLY OR DIVIDE BY A NEGATIVE NUMBER, you must FLIP THE INEQUALITY SIGN.

Example: "Solve   5x < 6x + 2"

ANS: Subtract 6x from both sides: $5x - 6x < 2$

         combining the x-terms gives: $-x < 2$

To get rid of the "−" in front of x you need to divide both sides by -1 — but remember that means the "<" has to be flipped as well, which gives:

   $x > -2$ i.e. "x is greater than -2" is the answer

(The < has flipped around into a >, because we divided by a −ve number)

This answer, $x > -2$, can be displayed as a shaded region on a number line like this:

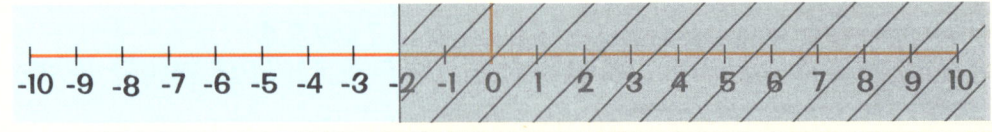

The main thing you should realise, is that MOST OF THE TIME you just treat the "<" or ">" as though it was an "=" and do all the usual algebra that you would for a regular equation. The "Big Exception" doesn't actually come up very often at all.

The Acid Test: LEARN: The 4 Inequality Signs, the similarity with EQUATIONS and the One Big Exception.

Now turn over and write down what you've learned.
1) Solve this inequality: $4x + 3 \leq 6x + 7$.
2) Solve the inequalities and find the values of x: $2x + 9 \geq 1$ and $4x < 6 + x$

UNIT FOUR

Straight Line Graphs — Gradients

Remember that the gradient measures the slope of a graph. Working out the gradient of a straight line is a slightly involved business, and there are quite a few things that can go wrong. So follow the method very carefully...

Strict Method For Finding the Gradient

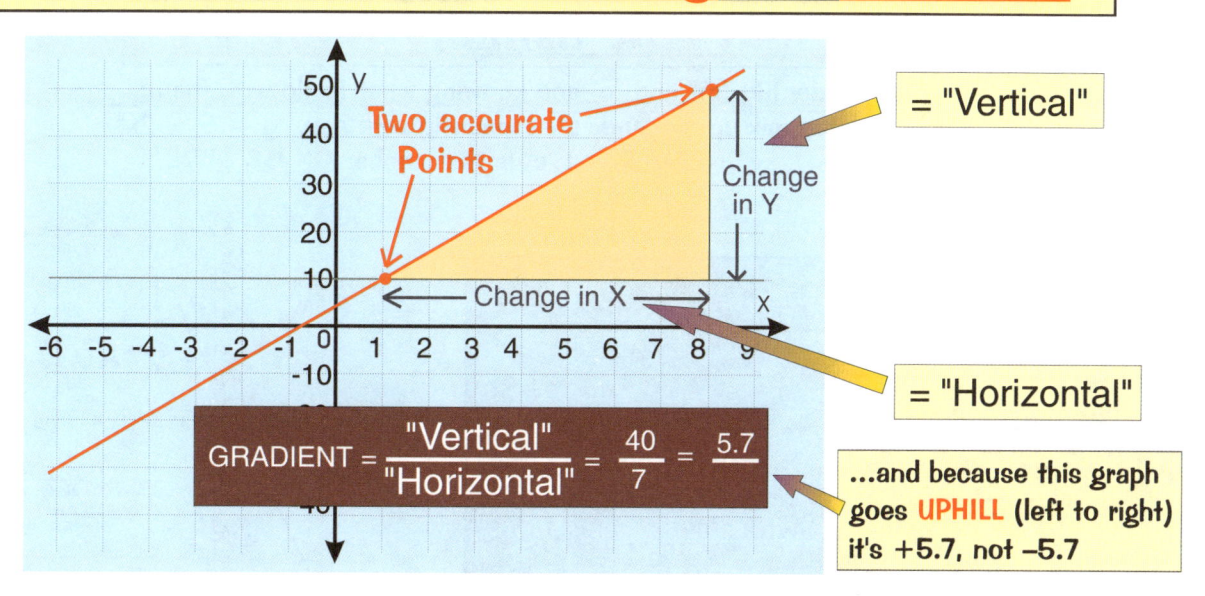

= "Vertical"

Two accurate Points

Change in Y

Change in X

= "Horizontal"

GRADIENT = "Vertical" / "Horizontal" = 40/7 = 5.7

...and because this graph goes UPHILL (left to right) it's +5.7, not −5.7

1) Find two accurate points, reasonably far apart

Both in the upper right quadrant if possible, (to keep all the numbers positive and so reduce the chance of errors).

2) Complete the triangle as shown

3) Find the change in y and the change in x

Make sure you do this using the SCALES on the y- and x- axes, not by counting cm! (So in the example shown, the Change in y is 40 units off the y-axis.)

4) Learn this formula, and use it:

GRADIENT = VERTICAL / HORIZONTAL

Make sure you get it the right way up too! Remember it's
VERy HOt — VERtical over HOrizontal

5) Finally, is the gradient POSITIVE or NEGATIVE?

If it slopes UPHILL left → right (⁄) then it's +ve
If it slopes DOWNHILL left → right (\ ) then it's −ve   (so put a minus(−) in front of it)

The Acid Test:

LEARN the FIVE STEPS for finding a gradient then turn over and WRITE THEM DOWN from memory.

Plot these 3 points on a graph: (0,3) (2,0) (5,-4.5) and then join them up with a straight line. Now carefully apply the FIVE STEPS to find the gradient of the line.

UNIT FOUR

Straight Line Graphs: "y = mx + c"

$y = mx + c$ is the general equation for a straight line graph, and you need to remember:

"m" is equal to the GRADIENT of the graph
"c" is the value WHERE IT CROSSES THE Y-AXIS and is called the Y-INTERCEPT.

1) Drawing a Straight Line using "y = mx + c"

The main thing is being able to identify "m" and "c" and knowing what to do with them:
BUT WATCH OUT — people often mix up "m" and "c", especially with say, "y = 5 + 2x"
REMEMBER: "m" is the number IN FRONT OF X and "c" is the number ON ITS OWN.

Method

1) Get the equation into the form "y = mx + c".
2) IDENTIFY "m" and "c" CAREFULLY.
3) PUT A DOT ON THE Y-AXIS at the value of c.
4) Then go ALONG ONE UNIT and up or down by the value of m and make another dot.
5) Repeat the same "step" in both directions as shown:
6) Finally CHECK that the gradient LOOKS RIGHT.

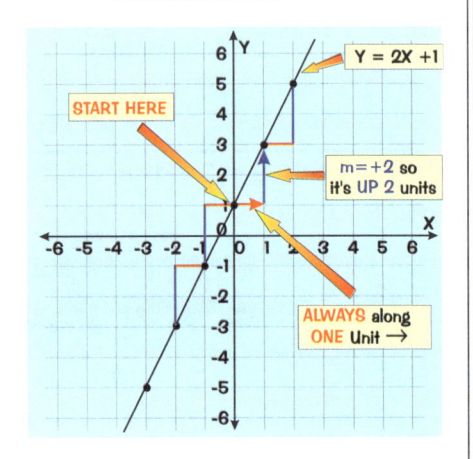

The graph shows the process for the equation "y = 2x + 1":
1) "c" = 1, so put a first dot at y = 1 on the y-axis.
2) Go along 1 unit → and then up by 2 because "m" = +2.
3) Repeat the same step, 1→ 2↑ in both directions. (i.e. 1 ← 2 ↓ the other way)
4) CHECK: a gradient of +2 should be quite steep and uphill left to right — which it is.

2) Finding the Equation Of a Straight Line Graph

THIS IS EASY:
1) Find where the graph CROSSES THE Y-AXIS. This is the value of "c".
2) Find the value of the GRADIENT (see P.77). This is the value of "m"
3) Now just put these values for "m" and "c" into "y = mx + c" — and there you have it!

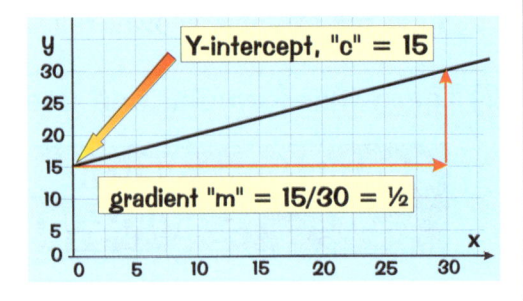

For the graph shown here, m = ½ and c = 15 so "y = mx + c" becomes "y = ½x + 15"

The Acid Test:

LEARN THE DETAILS of the two methods for "y = mx + c". Then TURN OVER and WRITE IT ALL DOWN.

1) Using "y = mx + c" draw the graphs of y = x − 3 and y = 4 − 2x.
2) Using "y = mx + c" find the equations of these 3 graphs →

UNIT FOUR

Simultaneous Equations With Graphs

Simultaneous equations are two equations with two unknowns (e.g. x and y).

For example $y = x + 3$ and $x + y = 6$.

You solve them by finding a value for x and for y for which both equations are true. The easiest way by far to solve them (avoiding any nasty algebra) is with graphs...

Solving Simultaneous Equations Using Graphs

The solution of two simultaneous equations is simply the x and y values where their graphs cross

Three Step Method

1) Do a "TABLE OF VALUES" for both equations.

2) Draw the two GRAPHS.

3) Find the x- and y-values WHERE THEY CROSS.

Easy Peasy.

Example

"Draw the graphs for "$y = 2x + 3$" and "$y = 6 - 4x$" and then use your graphs to solve these simultaneous equations."

1) TABLE OF VALUES
   for both equations:

X	0	1	2
Y	6	2	-2

X	-2	0	2
Y	-1	3	7

2) DRAW THE GRAPHS:

3) WHERE THEY CROSS, $x = ½$, $y = 4$.

   And that's the answer: $x = ½$ and $y = 4$

   (You can stick these values back into the original equations to prove they're right.)

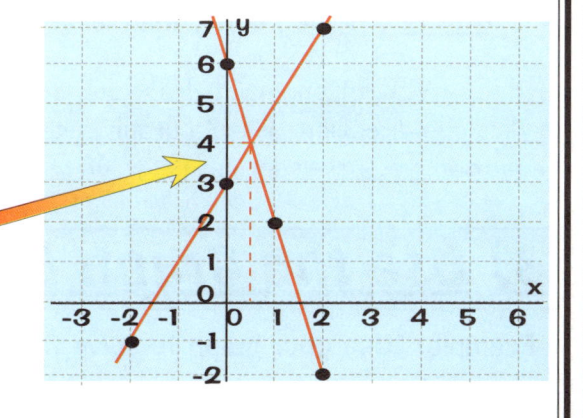

The Acid Test:

LEARN the Simple Rule and the 3 step method for solving simultaneous equations using GRAPHS.

1) Cover the page and write down the Simple Rule and the 3 step method.
2) Use graphs to find the solutions to these pairs of equations:
   a) $y = 4x - 4$ and $y = 6 - x$
   b) $y = 2x$ and $y = 6 - 2x$

UNIT FOUR

Quadratic Graphs

Equations with an x² term in them are called quadratic equations. The graphs of these equations always have the same SYMMETRICAL bucket shape.

If the x² bit is positive (i.e. +x²) the bucket is the normal way up, but if the x² bit has a "minus" in front of it (i.e. −x²) then the bucket is upside down.

The graphs get steeper and steeper but never vertical — remember this when you're drawing them.

Most questions follow a set pattern...

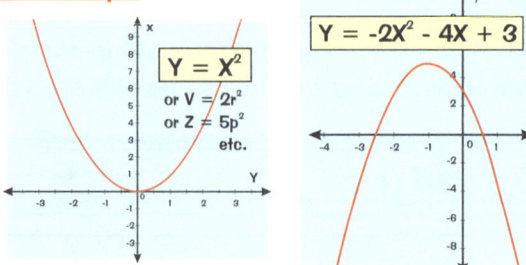

1) Fill in the Table of Values

Example: "Fill in the table of values for the equation $y = x^2 + 2x - 3$ and draw the graph."

x	-5	-4	-3	-2	-1	0	1	2	3
y		5		-3	-4	-3	0		

Work out each point very carefully, writing down all your working. Don't just plug it all straight in your calculator — you'll make mistakes. To check you're doing it right, make sure you can reproduce the y-values they've already given you.

2) Draw the Curve

1) PLOT THE POINTS CAREFULLY, and don't mix up the x and y values.

2) The points should form a COMPLETELY SMOOTH CURVE. If they don't, they're wrong.

NEVER EVER let one point drag your line off in some ridiculous direction. When a graph is generated from an equation, you never get spikes or lumps — only MISTAKES.

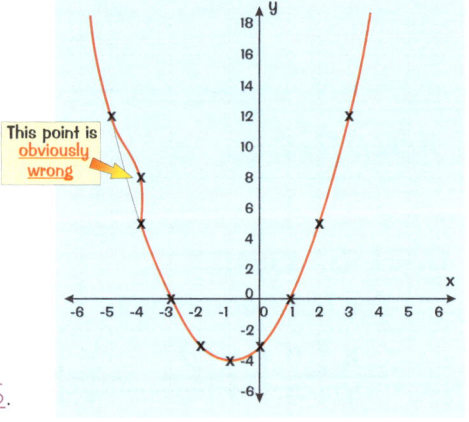

3) Use the Graph to Answer a Question

Example: "Use your graph to solve the equation $x^2 + 2x - 3 = 0$."

1) Look — the equation you've been asked to solve is what you get when you put y=0 into the graph's equation, $y = x^2 + 2x - 3$.

2) To solve the equation, all you do is read the x-values where y = 0, i.e. where it crosses the x-axis.

3) So the solutions are $x = -3$ and $x = +1$. (Quadratic eqns usually have 2 solutions.)

The Acid Test: LEARN THE DETAILS of the method above for DRAWING QUADRATIC GRAPHS and SOLVING THE EQUATION.

Plot the graph of $y = x^2 - x - 6$ (use x-values from -4 to 5).
Use your graph to solve the equation $x^2 - x - 6 = 0$.

UNIT FOUR

Typical Graph Questions

Getting Answers from Your Graph

1) **FOR A SINGLE CURVE OR LINE**, you **ALWAYS** get the answer by drawing a straight line to the graph from one axis, and then down or across to the other axis, as shown here:

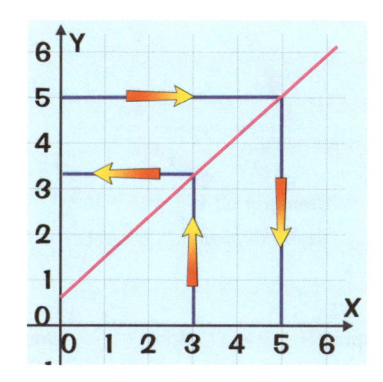

You should be fully expecting this to happen so that even if you don't understand the question, you can still have a pretty good stab at it:

If the question said "Find the value of y when x is equal to 3", **ALL YOU DO IS THIS**: start at 3 on the x-axis, go straight up to the graph, then straight over to the y-axis and read off the value, which in this case is y = 3.3 (as shown opposite).

2) **IF TWO LINES CROSS.....**

you can bet your very last fruitcake the answer to one of the questions will simply be: **THE VALUES OF X AND Y WHERE THEY CROSS** and you should be expecting that before they even ask it! (See Simultaneous Eqns. P.79).

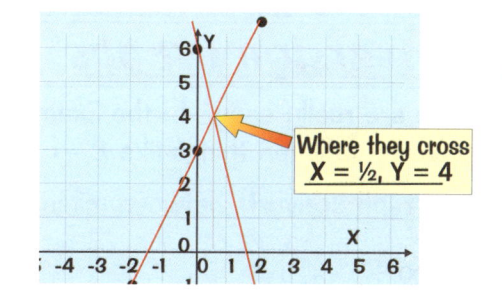

Where they cross X = ½, Y = 4

What The Gradient of a Graph MEANS

No matter what the graph, **THE MEANING OF THE GRADIENT** is always simply:

(Y-axis UNITS) PER (X-axis UNITS)

EXAMPLES:

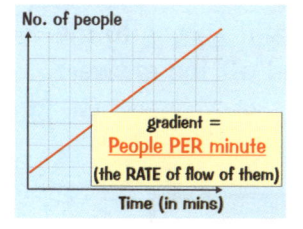

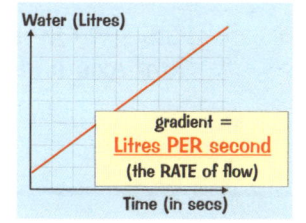

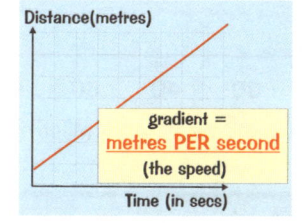

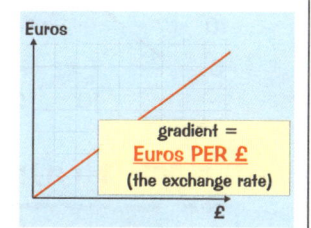

gradient = People PER minute (the RATE of flow of them)

gradient = Litres PER second (the RATE of flow)

gradient = metres PER second (the speed)

gradient = Euros PER £ (the exchange rate)

Some gradients have special names like Exchange Rate or Speed, but once you've written down "something PER something" using the Y-axis and X-axis UNITS, it's then pretty easy to work out what the gradient represents.

The Acid Test:

LEARN the 2 simple Rules for getting answers, and the meaning of gradient. Then turn over... bla bla bla ... you know what to do...

UNIT FOUR

Travel and Conversion Graphs

Travel Graphs

1) A **TRAVEL GRAPH** is always **DISTANCE** (↑) against **TIME** (→)
2) **FLAT SECTIONS** are where it's **STOPPED**.
3) The **STEEPER** the graph the **FASTER** it's going.
4) The graph **GOING UP** means it's travelling **AWAY**. The graph **COMING DOWN** means it's **COMING BACK AGAIN**.

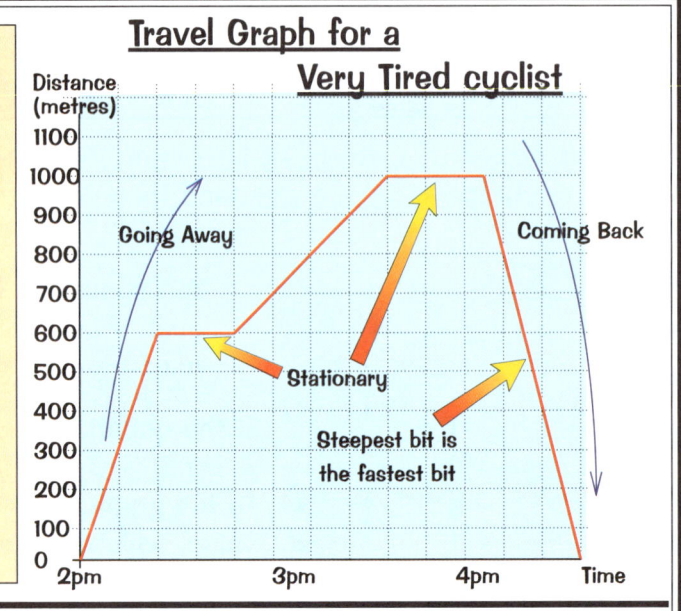

Travel Graph for a Very Tired cyclist

Going Away — *Stationary* — *Steepest bit is the fastest bit* — *Coming Back*

(Distance in metres vs Time from 2pm to 4pm)

Conversion Graphs

These are really easy. In the Exam you're likely to get a Conversion Graph question which converts between things like £ → Dollars or mph → km/h, etc.

This graph converts between miles and kilometres

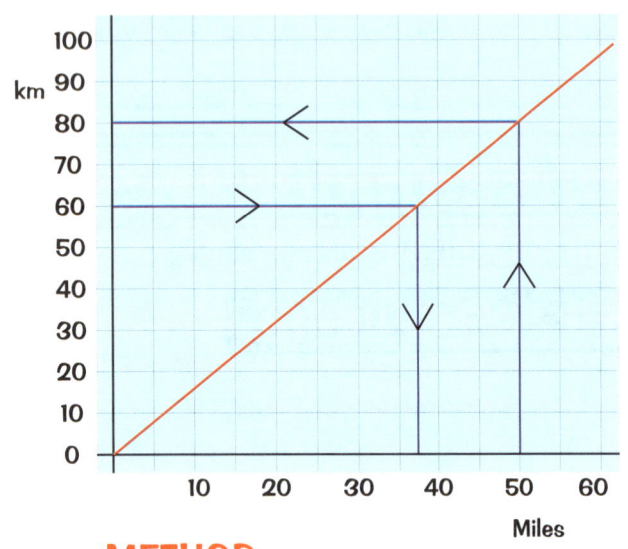

2 very typical questions:

1) How many miles is 60 km?

ANS: Draw a line straight across from "60" on the "km" axis 'til it hits the line, then go straight down to the "miles" axis and read off the answer:
37.5 miles

2) How many km is 50 miles?

ANS: Draw a line straight up from "50" on the "miles" axis 'til it hits the line, then go straight across to the "km" axis and read off the answer:
80 km

METHOD:

1) Draw a line from the value on one axis.
2) Keep going 'til you hit the LINE.
3) Then change direction and go straight to the other axis.
4) Read off the new value from the axis. That's the answer.

If you remember those 4 simple steps you really can't go wrong
— let's face it, Conversion Graphs are a doddle.

UNIT FOUR

Regular Polygons

A _polygon_ is a _many-sided shape_. A _regular_ polygon is one where all the _sides_ and _angles_ are the same. The regular polygons are a never-ending series of shapes with some fancy features. They're very easy to learn. Here are the first few but they don't stop — you can have one with 12 sides or 25, etc.

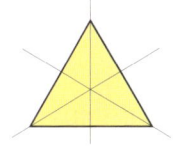

EQUILATERAL TRIANGLE
3 sides
3 lines of symmetry
Rot^{nl} symm. order 3

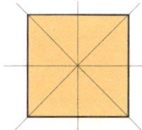

SQUARE
4 sides
4 lines of symmetry
Rot^{nl} symm. order 4

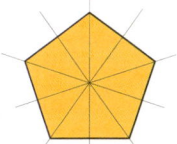

REGULAR PENTAGON
5 sides
5 lines of symmetry
Rot^{nl} symm. order 5

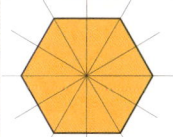

REGULAR HEXAGON
6 sides
6 lines of symmetry
Rot^{nl} symm. order 6

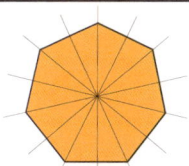

REGULAR HEPTAGON
7 sides
7 lines of symmetry
Rot^{nl} symm. order 7
(A 50p piece is like a heptagon)

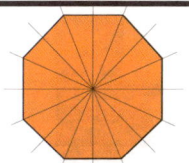

REGULAR OCTAGON
8 sides
8 lines of symmetry
Rot^{nl} symm. order 8

Interior And Exterior Angles

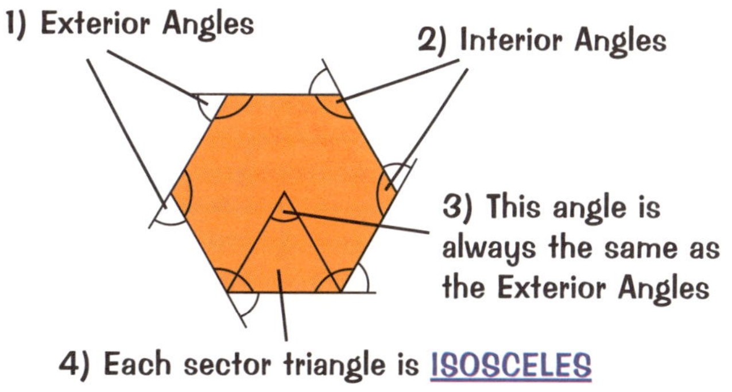

1) Exterior Angles
2) Interior Angles
3) This angle is always the same as the Exterior Angles
4) Each sector triangle is ISOSCELES

There are 4 formulas to learn:

$$\text{EXTERIOR ANGLE} = \frac{360°}{n}$$

$$\text{INTERIOR ANGLE} = 180° - \text{EXTERIOR ANGLE}$$

$$\text{SUM OF EXTERIOR ANGLES} = 360°$$

$$\text{SUM OF INTERIOR ANGLES} = (n - 2) \times 180°$$

(n is the number of sides)

Note — the two SUM formulas above work for **any** polygons, not just regular ones.

You also need to know the next two, but I'm not drawing them for you. Learn their names:

REGULAR NONEGON
9 sides, etc. etc.

REGULAR DECAGON
10 sides, etc. etc.

REGULAR POLYGONS HAVE LOADS OF SYMMETRY

1) The pentagon shown here has only 3 different angles in the whole diagram.
2) This is typical of regular polygons. They display an amazing amount of symmetry.
3) With a regular polygon, if two angles look the same, they will be. That's not a rule you should normally apply in geometry, and anyway you'll need to prove they're equal.

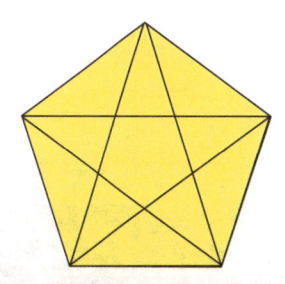

The Acid Test:
LEARN THIS PAGE.
Then cover it up and answer these little jokers:

1) What is a Regular Polygon?   2) Name the first six of them.
3) Draw a regular pentagon and a regular hexagon and put in all their lines of symmetry.
4) Work out the two key angles for a regular pentagon   5) And for a 12-sided regular polygon.

UNIT FOUR

Projections, Congruence and Similarity

Projections show Different Views of a Shape

A 'projection' shows the relative size and shape of an object from either the front, side or back — they're usually known as 'elevations'. A 'plan' shows the view from above. They're always drawn to scale.

Take this church (naff picture, I know) — you can represent it like this:

FRONT Elevation — the view you'd see if you looked from directly in front:

SIDE Elevation — the view you'd see if you looked from directly to one side:

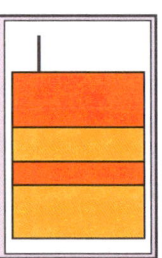

PLAN — the view you'd see if you looked from directly above:

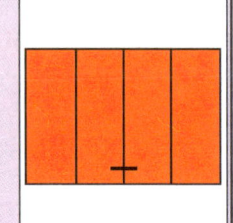

If they're feeling really mean (and they often are), you might get a question on:

This one's a bit trickier, so you might want to spend a little longer practising it — just to get your head round it.

ISOMETRIC Projection — this is where the shape is drawn (again, to scale) from a view at equal angles to all three axes (x, y and z). Or more simply, it's a drawing like this:

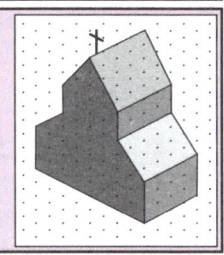

Congruence and Similarity

Congruence is another ridiculous maths word which sounds really complicated when it's not: If two shapes are CONGRUENT, they're simply the same — the same size and the same shape.

CONGRUENT
— same size, same shape A, B, and C are CONGRUENT (with each other).
Note – you can have mirror images.

SIMILAR
— same shape, but can be different size
D and E are SIMILAR, (but not congruent)

Remember: when you have similar shapes the angles are always the same.

The Acid Test:
Learn ALL FOUR TYPES OF PROJECTION, and what "SIMILAR" and "CONGRUENT" mean.

Now cover the page and write down what you've learned. Then REMEMBER it forever!
1) Draw a plan, front and side elevations and an isometric projection of your own house.
2) a) Which of these four shapes are similar?
   b) Which are congruent?
   i) ii) iii) iv)

UNIT FOUR

Pythagoras' Theorem

PYTHAGORAS' THEOREM is a handy little formula for RIGHT-ANGLED TRIANGLES. What it does is let you find the length of the third side when you know two of them.

The formula for Pythagoras' theorem is: $a^2 + b^2 = h^2$

where a and b are the short sides and h is the long side of the triangle (called the hypotenuse)

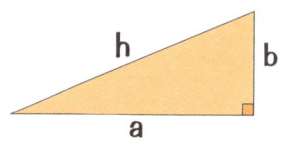

Remember that Pythagoras can only be used on RIGHT-ANGLED TRIANGLES.

The trouble is, the formula can be quite difficult to use. Instead, it's a lot better to just remember these three simple steps, which work every time:

1) Square Them
SQUARE THE TWO NUMBERS that you are given, (use the x^2 button if you've got your calculator.)

2) Add or Subtract
To find the longest side, ADD the two squared numbers.
To find a shorter side, SUBTRACT the smaller one from the larger.

3) Square Root
Once you've got your answer, take the SQUARE ROOT. (use the √ button on your calculator).

EXAMPLE 1: "Find the missing side in the triangle shown."

1. Square them: $5^2 = 25$, $3^2 = 9$
2. You want to find a shorter side, so SUBTRACT: $25 - 9 = 16$
3. Square root: $\sqrt{16} = 4$

   So the missing side = 4m

(You should always ask yourself: "Is it a sensible answer?" — in this case you can say "YES, because it's shorter than 5m, as it should be since 5m is the longest side, but not too much shorter")

EXAMPLE 2: "Find the length of the line segment shown."

1. Work out how far across and up it is from A to B
2. Treat this exactly like a normal triangle...
3. Square them: $3^2 = 9$, $4^2 = 16$
4. You want to find the longest side (the hypotenuse), so ADD: $9 + 16 = 25$
5. Square root: $\sqrt{25} = 5$

   So the length of the line segment = 5 units

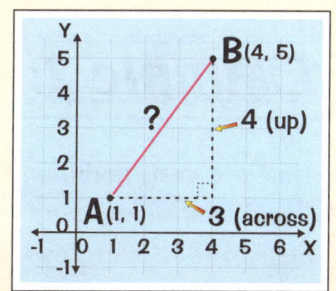

The Acid Test:
LEARN the 3 steps of the Pythag. method.

Now turn over and write down what you've learned.
1) Then apply the above method to find the missing side BC:
2) Another triangle has sides of 5 m, 12 m and 13 m. Is it a right-angled triangle? How do you know?

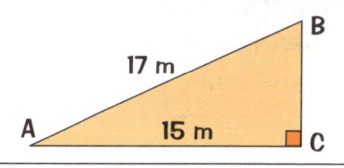

UNIT FOUR

Circle Questions

The Big Decision:

"Which circle formula do I use?"

1) If the question asks for "the area of the circle", YOU MUST use the FORMULA FOR AREA:

$$A = \pi \times r^2$$

2) If the question asks for "circumference" (the distance around the circle) YOU MUST use the FORMULA FOR CIRCUMFERENCE:

$$C = \pi \times D$$

And remember, it makes no difference at all whether the question gives you the radius or the diameter, because whichever one they give you, it's DEAD EASY to work out the other one — the diameter is always DOUBLE the radius.

Example 1:

"Find the circumference and the area of the circle shown below."

ANSWER:

The radius=5cm, so the Diameter=10cm (easy huh?)

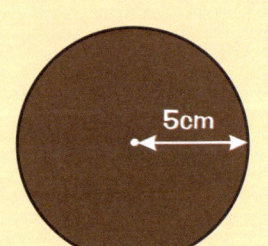

Formula for circumference is:
$C = \pi \times D$, so
$C = 3.14 \times 10$
= 31.4cm

Formula for AREA is:
$A = \pi \times r^2$
$= 3.14 \times (5 \times 5)$
$= 3.14 \times 25 = $ 78.5cm²

Example 2: The good old "Wagon Wheel" question:

This is a very common Exam question.
"How many turns must a wheel of diameter 1.2m make to go a distance of 12m?"

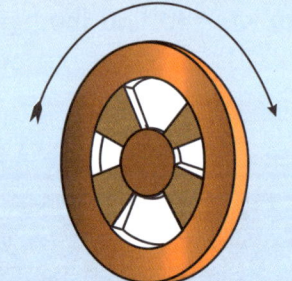

ANSWER:
Each full turn moves it one full circumference across the ground, so
1) find the circumference using "$C = \pi \times D$": $C = 3.14 \times 1.2 = $ 3.768m
2) then find how many times it fits into the distance travelled, by dividing:
    i.e.   12m ÷ 3.768m = 3.18   so the answer is 3.2 turns of the wheel

UNIT FOUR

Constructing Triangles

"Construct" means draw accurately using pencil, ruler and compasses.

If you are told to construct a triangle and you are told how long the three sides are, this is what to do.

> 1) Draw a rough sketch and label the lengths of the sides.
> 2) Draw the base line using a ruler.
> 3) Draw two arcs, one from each end of the base line, setting your compasses to the lengths of the sides.
> 4) Draw lines from the ends of the base line to where the two arcs cross.

Example:

Construct the triangle ABC where AB = 6cm, BC = 4cm, AC = 5cm.

ANSWER:

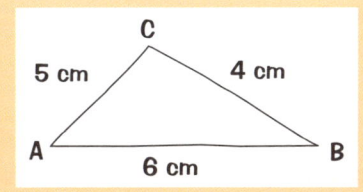

1) Sketch the triangle. Label the corners A, B and C. Label the lengths (AB means the side going from A to B).

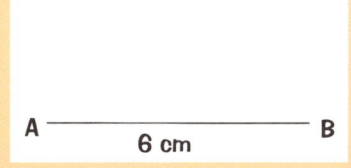

2) Pick a side for the base line — it doesn't matter which one. We'll pick AB. Draw a line 6cm long. Label the ends A and B.

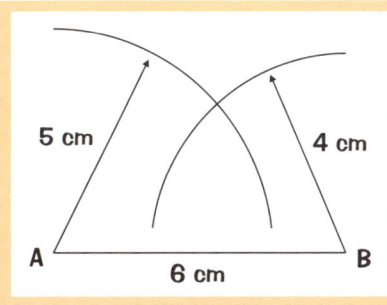

3) For AC, set the compasses to 5cm, put the point at A and draw an arc. For BC, set the compasses to 4cm, put the point at B and draw an arc.

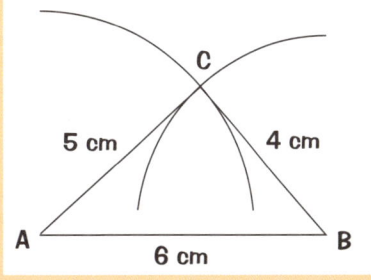

4) Where the arcs cross is the point C. Draw a line from A to C and another line from B to C to finish your triangle.

The Acid Test

1) Construct an equilateral triangle with sides 5cm.

2) Construct a triangle with sides 3cm, 4cm and 5cm. Check your drawing by measuring the sides.

UNIT FOUR

Loci and Constructions

A <u>LOCUS</u> (another ridiculous maths word) is simply:

> **A LINE that shows <u>all the points which fit in with a given rule</u>**

Make sure you <u>learn</u> how to do these <u>PROPERLY</u> using a <u>RULER AND COMPASSES</u> as shown.

1) The locus of points which are "A FIXED DISTANCE from a given POINT"

This locus is simply a <u>CIRCLE</u>.

- Pair of Compasses
- A given point
- The LOCUS of points a fixed distance from it

2) The locus of points which are "A FIXED DISTANCE from a given LINE"

This locus is an <u>OVAL SHAPE</u>

It has <u>straight sides</u> (drawn with a <u>ruler</u>) and <u>ends</u> which are <u>perfect semicircles</u> (drawn with <u>compasses</u>).

- Semicircle ends drawn with compasses
- A given line
- The LOCUS of points a fixed distance from it

3) The locus of points which are "EQUIDISTANT from TWO GIVEN LINES"

Equidistant just means "the same distance".

1) Keep the compass setting <u>THE SAME</u> while you make <u>all four marks</u>.
2) Make sure you <u>leave</u> your compass marks <u>showing</u>.
3) You get <u>two equal angles</u> — i.e. this <u>LOCUS</u> is actually an <u>ANGLE BISECTOR</u>.

- Step 1
- Step 2
- A given line
- The LOCUS
- Second Compass marks
- First Compass marks
- The other given line

4) The locus of points which are "EQUIDISTANT from TWO GIVEN POINTS"

(In the diagram below, A and B are the two given points)

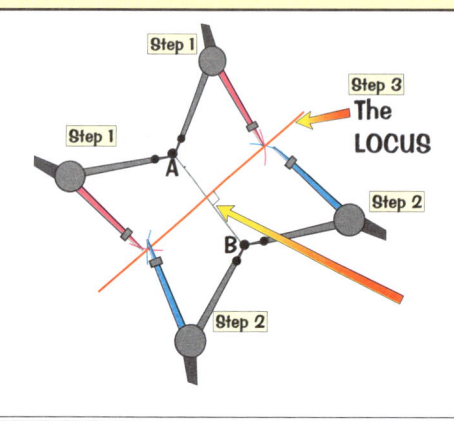

- Step 1
- Step 1
- Step 2
- Step 2
- Step 3 — The LOCUS

This <u>LOCUS</u> is all the points which are the <u>same distance</u> from A and B.

This time the locus is actually the **PERPENDICULAR BISECTOR** of the line joining the two points.

UNIT FOUR

Loci and Constructions

Constructing accurate 60° angles

1) They may well ask you to draw an accurate 60° angle.

2) One place they're needed is for drawing an equilateral triangle.

3) Make sure you follow the method shown in this diagram, and that you can do it entirely from memory.

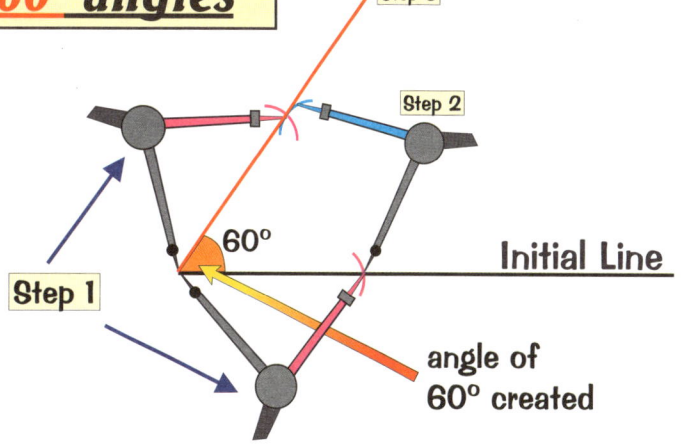

Constructing accurate 90° angles

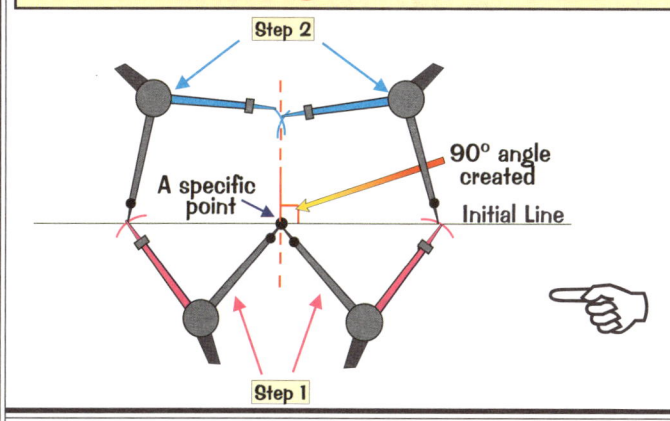

1) They might want you to draw an accurate 90° angle.

2) They won't accept it just done "by eye" or with a ruler — if you want to get the marks, you've got to do it the proper way with compasses like I've shown you here.

3) Make sure you can follow the method shown in this diagram.

Drawing the Perpendicular from a Point to a Line

1) This is similar to the one above but not quite the same — make sure you can do both.

2) Again, they won't accept it just done "by eye" or with a ruler — you've got to do it the proper way with compasses.

3) Learn the diagram.

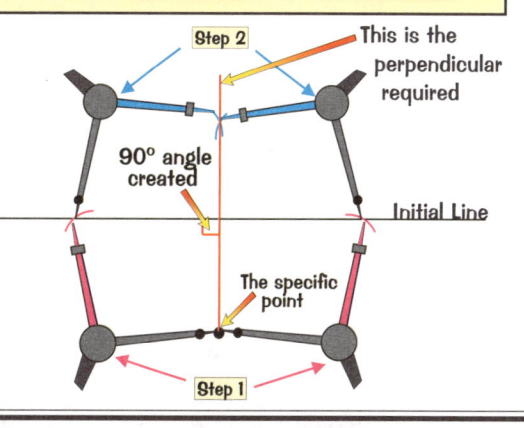

The Acid Test: LEARN EVERYTHING ON THESE TWO PAGES

Now cover up these two pages and draw an example of each of the four loci. Also draw an equilateral triangle and a square, both with fabulously accurate 60° and 90° angles. Also, draw a line and a point and construct the perpendicular from the point to the line.

UNIT FOUR

Symmetry

Symmetry is where a shape or picture can be put in different positions that look exactly the same. There are THREE types of symmetry:

1) Line Symmetry

This is where you can draw a MIRROR LINE (or more than one) across a picture and both sides will fold exactly together.

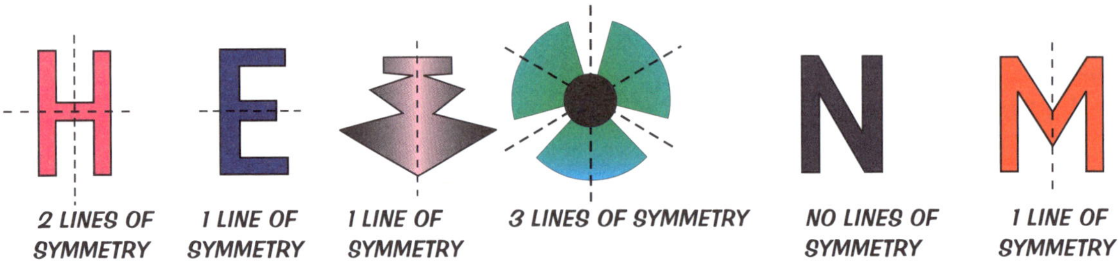

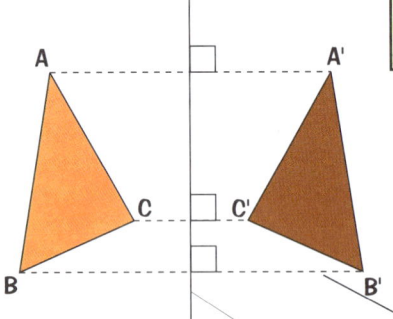

H	E	⬆	✿	N	M
2 LINES OF SYMMETRY	1 LINE OF SYMMETRY	1 LINE OF SYMMETRY	3 LINES OF SYMMETRY	NO LINES OF SYMMETRY	1 LINE OF SYMMETRY

How to draw a reflection:

1) Reflect each point one by one

2) Use a line which crosses the mirror line at 90° and goes EXACTLY the same distance on the other side of the mirror line, as shown.

A line which crosses at 90° is called a perpendicular

2) Plane Symmetry

Plane Symmetry is all to do with 3-D SOLIDS.

Just like flat shapes can have a mirror line, so solid 3-D objects can have a plane of symmetry.

A plane mirror surface can be drawn through, but the shape must be exactly the same on both sides of the plane (i.e. mirror images), like these are:

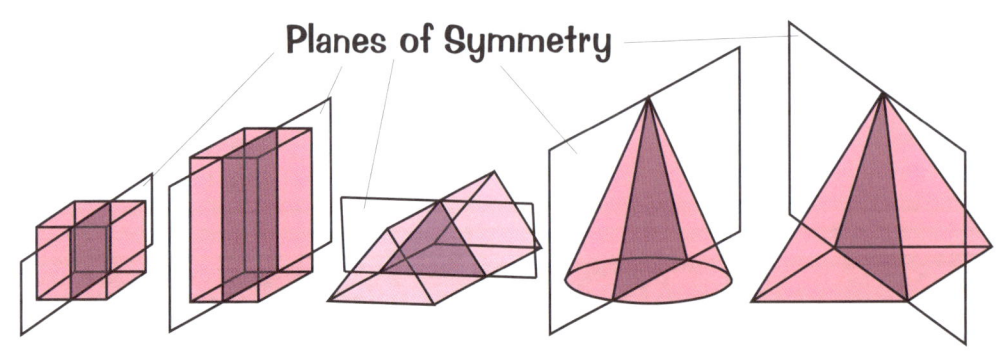

Planes of Symmetry

The shapes drawn here all have MANY MORE PLANES OF SYMMETRY but there's only one plane of symmetry drawn in for each shape, because otherwise it would all get really messy and you wouldn't be able to see anything.

UNIT FOUR

Symmetry

3) Rotational Symmetry

This is where you can ROTATE the shape or drawing into different positions that all look exactly the same.

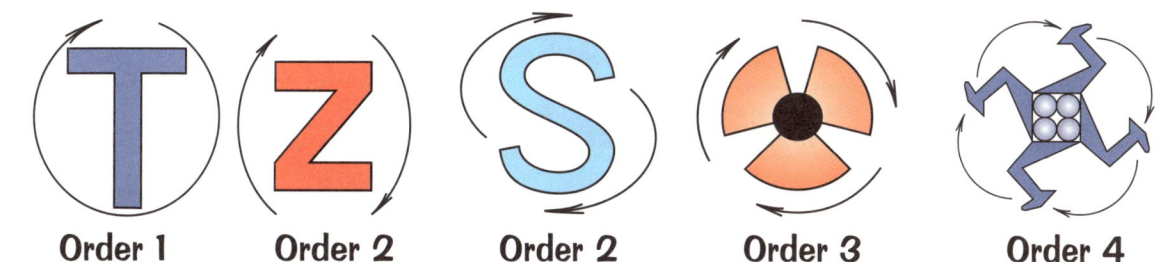

T	Z	S	(3-blade)	(4-blade)
Order 1	Order 2	Order 2	Order 3	Order 4

The ORDER OF ROTATIONAL SYMMETRY is the posh way of saying: "HOW MANY DIFFERENT POSITIONS LOOK THE SAME".
E.g. You should say the Z shape above has "Rotational symmetry order 2"
BUT...when a shape has ONLY 1 POSITION you can either say that it has "Rotational Symmetry order 1"   or that it has   "NO Rotational Symmetry"

Tracing Paper — this always makes symmetry a lot easier

1) For REFLECTIONS, trace one side of the drawing and the mirror line too. Then turn the paper over and line up the mirror line in its original position.

2) For ROTATIONS, just swizzle the paper round. It's really good for finding the centre of rotation (by trial and error) as well as the order of rotational symmetry.

3) You can use tracing paper in the EXAM — ask for it, or take your own in.

Tessellations — "Tiling patterns with no gaps"

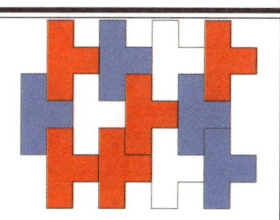

You must have done loads of these, but don't forget what the name "tessellation" means — "a tiling pattern with no gaps":

The Acid Test

Copy these letters and mark in all the lines of symmetry.
Also say what the rotational symmetry is for each one.

H   Z   T   N   E   X   S

UNIT FOUR

The Four Transformations

Translation — ONE Detail	1) Use the word **TERRY** to remember the 4 types.
Enlargement — TWO Details	
Rotation — THREE Details	2) You must always give
Reflection — ONE Detail	all the details for each type.
Y (The Y doesn't stand for anything)	

1) Translation

A translation is just a SLIDE. You must specify how far along and how far up the translation is.

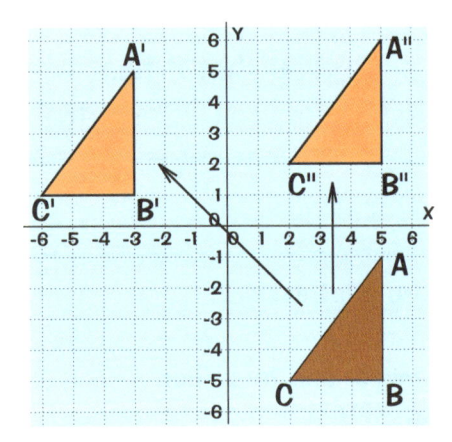

ABC to A'B'C' is a translation of 8 left and 6 up.

ABC to A"B"C" is a translation of 7 up.

You can describe translations with vectors which look like this. x is the number of spaces right, y is the number of spaces up. $\begin{pmatrix} x \rightarrow \\ y \uparrow \end{pmatrix}$

As vectors, the translations shown in the diagram are: $\begin{pmatrix} -8 \\ 6 \end{pmatrix}$ and $\begin{pmatrix} 0 \\ 7 \end{pmatrix}$

2) Enlargement

You must give these 2 details:
1) The SCALE FACTOR
2) The CENTRE of Enlargement

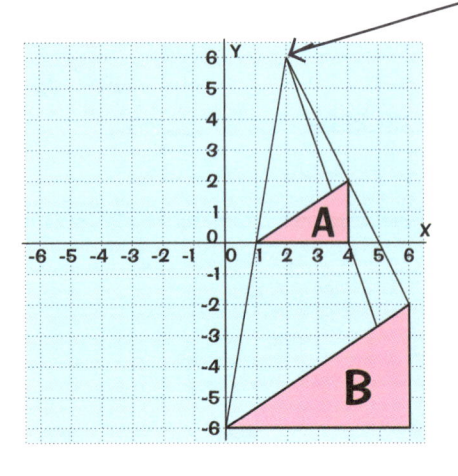

From A to B is an enlargement of scale factor 2, and centre (2,6)

N.B. Lengths doubled, distances from centre doubled too.

With enlargement, the ANGLES of the object remain unchanged. The RATIOS of the lengths of the sides, and the object's ORIENTATION remain unchanged. The size and position do change.

The Four Transformations

3) Rotation

You must give these 3 details:
1) **ANGLE** turned
2) **DIRECTION** (Clockwise or Anti-clockwise)
3) **CENTRE** of Rotation

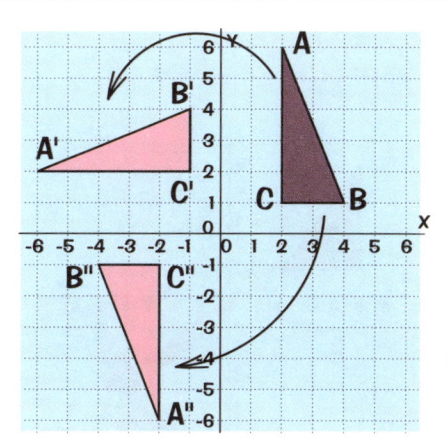

ABC to A'B'C' is a Rotation of 90°, anticlockwise, ABOUT the origin.

ABC to A"B"C" is a Rotation of half a turn (180°), clockwise, ABOUT the origin.

(For half-turns, it doesn't actually matter if you go clockwise or anticlockwise.)

The only things that *change* in a rotation are the *POSITION* and the *ORIENTATION* of the object. Everything else remains unchanged.

4) Reflection

You must give this **ONE detail**: 1) The **MIRROR LINE**

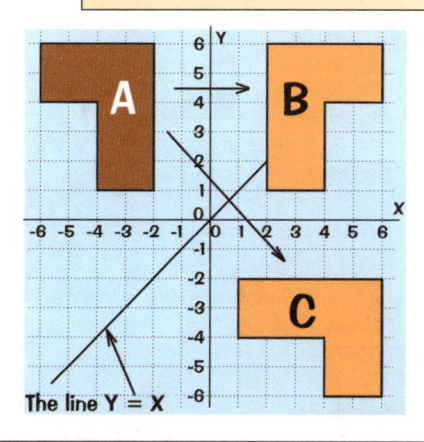

A to B is a reflection IN the Y-axis.

A to C is a reflection IN the line Y=X.

With reflection, the *POSITION* and *ORIENTATION* of the object are the only things that change.

The Acid Test

LEARN the names of the Four Transformations and the details that go with each. When you think you know it, turn over and write it all down.

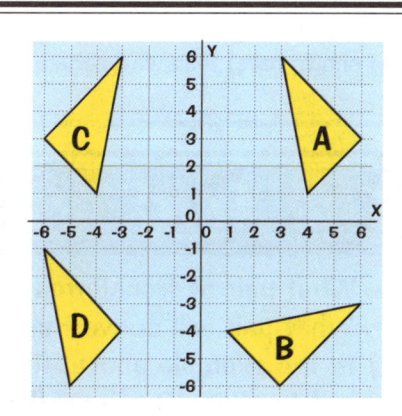

Describe **fully** these 4 transformations:

A → B,   B → C,   C → A,   A → D

UNIT FOUR

Combinations of Transformations

In the Exam questions they might do something horrid like stick two transformations together and say what single transformation gets you from shape A to shape B. Be ready.

The Better You Know Them All — The Easier it is

These kinds of question aren't so bad — but ONLY if you've LEARNT the four transformations on the last page really well — if you don't know them, then you certainly won't do too well at spotting a combination of one followed by another.
That's because the method is basically "Try it and see..."

Example

"What combination of two transformations takes you from triangle A to triangle B?"

(There's usually a few different ways of getting from one shape to the other — but remember you only need to find ONE of them.)

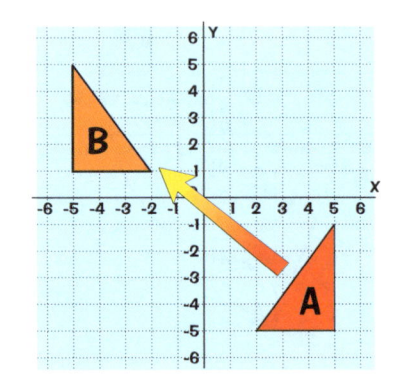

Method: Try an obvious transformation first, and See...

If you think about it, the answer can only be a combination of two of the four types shown on the last page, so you can immediately start to narrow it down:

1) Since the shapes are the same size we can rule out enlargements.
2) Next, try a reflection (in either the x-axis or the y-axis).
   Here we've tried a reflection in the y-axis, to give shape A':
3) You should now easily be able to see the final step

   from A' to B — it's a translation of $\begin{pmatrix} 0 \\ 6 \end{pmatrix}$.

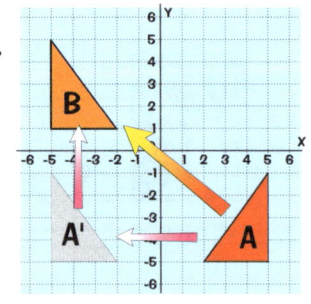

And that's it DONE — from A to B is simply a combination of:

A reflection in the y-axis followed by a translation of $\begin{pmatrix} 0 \\ 6 \end{pmatrix}$

At least that's one answer anyway. If instead we decided to reflect it in the x-axis first (as shown here) then we'd get another answer (see Acid Test below) — but both are right.

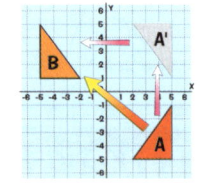

The Acid Test:
LEARN the main points on this page.
Then cover it up and write them all down.

1) What pair of transformations will convert shape C into shape D?:
   What pair will convert shape D to shape C?
2) In the example above, find the other transformation needed to get to shape B after reflecting shape A in the X-axis.

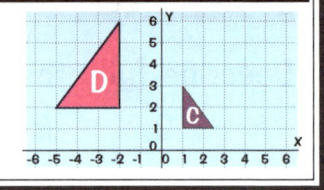

UNIT FOUR

Enlargement — Scale Factors

1) If the Scale Factor is <u>BIGGER THAN 1</u> then the shape gets <u>BIGGER</u>.

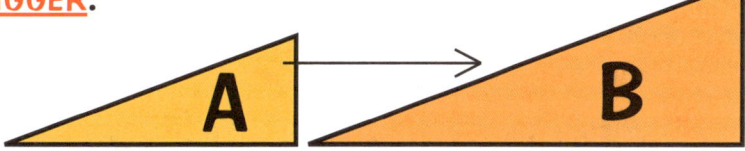

A to B is an Enlargement, Scale Factor 1½

2) If the Scale Factor is <u>SMALLER THAN 1</u> (i.e. a fraction like ½), then the shape gets <u>SMALLER</u>.

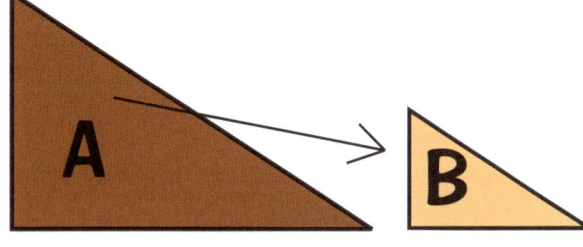

(Really this is a reduction, but you still call it an Enlargement, Scale Factor ½)

A to B is an Enlargement of Scale Factor ½

3) The <u>Scale Factor</u> also tells you the <u>RELATIVE DISTANCE</u> of old points and new points from the <u>Centre of Enlargement</u>.

This is very useful for drawing an enlargement, because you can use it to <u>trace out the positions of the new points</u> from the centre of enlargement, as shown in the diagram.

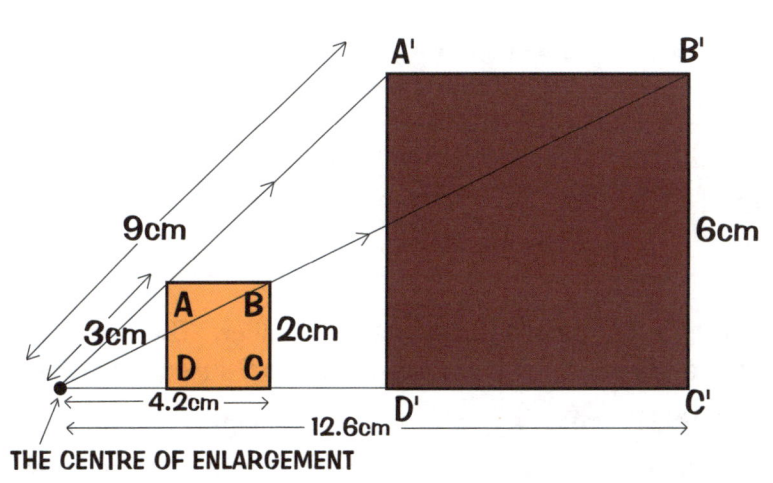

Enlargement Scale Factor 3

THE CENTRE OF ENLARGEMENT

The Acid Test: LEARN everything on the page.

Then, <u>when you think you know it</u>, cover the page and <u>write it all down again</u>, from <u>memory</u>, including the sketches and examples. Keep trying till you can.

UNIT FOUR

Enlargement — Scale Factors

Use the Formula Triangle for Calculations

The lengths of the big and small shapes are related to the Scale Factor by this very important Formula Triangle which you must learn:

EXAMPLE: Find the missing width, x, in the diagram.

[Formula Triangle: NEW LENGTH / SCALE FACTOR × OLD LENGTH]

For formula triangles, see p.44

To find the width of the enlarged photo we use the formula triangle TWICE, (firstly to find the Scale Factor, and then to find the missing side):

1) Scale Factor = New length ÷ Old length = 14.7 ÷ 8.4 = 1.75
2) New width = Scale Factor × Old width = 1.75 × 5.6 = 9.8 cm

BUT WITHOUT THE FORMULA TRIANGLE YOU'RE SCUPPERED!

Note — you can use the formula triangle to find perimeters in exactly the same way as lengths. E.g. a square with sides 1 cm is enlarged by a scale factor of 2.
New perimeter = scale factor × old perimeter = 2 × 4 = 8 cm.

Areas and Volumes of Enlargements

Ho ho! This little joker catches everybody out. The increase in area and volume is BIGGER than the scale factor.
For example, if the Scale Factor is 2, the lengths are twice as big, each area is 4 times as big, and the volume is 8 times as big. The rule is this:

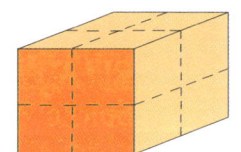

For a Scale Factor n:
The SIDES are   n times bigger
The AREAS are n^2 times bigger
The VOLUMES are n^3 times bigger   Simple... but VERY FORGETTABLE

EXAMPLE: Two bottles of water are similar. They have heights of 20 cm and 30 cm. If the volume of the smaller bottle is 2 litres, find the volume of the larger bottle.

ANSWER: 1) Scale Factor n = New height ÷ Old height = 30 ÷ 20 = 1.5
2) New volume = Old volume × (Scale Factor)^3 = 2 × 1.5^3 = 6.75 litres

The Acid Test:
LEARN the Enlargement Formula Triangle and the rules for Area and Volume enlargements. Then turn over and write everything down.

1) Two triangles which are similar have heights of 5 cm and 45 cm respectively. The smaller triangle has an area of 30 cm^2. Find the area of the larger triangle.
2) Two similar cones have base diameters of 20 cm and 50 cm. If the volume of the smaller one is 120 cm^3, find the volume of the other one.

UNIT FOUR

Length, Area And Volume

Identifying Formulas Just by Looking at Them

This isn't as bad as it sounds, since we're only talking about the formulas for 3 things:

LENGTH, AREA and VOLUME

The rules are as simple as this:

> AREA FORMULAS always have
> LENGTHS MULTIPLIED IN PAIRS
>
> VOLUME FORMULAS always have
> LENGTHS MULTIPLIED IN GROUPS OF THREE
>
> LENGTH FORMULAS (such as perimeter)
> always have LENGTHS OCCURRING SINGLY

In formulas of course, LENGTHS ARE REPRESENTED BY LETTERS,

so when you look at a formula you're looking for:

GROUPS OF LETTERS MULTIPLIED TOGETHER in ONES, TWOS or THREES.

BUT REMEMBER, π is NOT a length.

Examples:

$4\pi r^2 + 6d^2$ (area) $Lwh + 6r^2L$ (volume)   (r^2 means $r \times r$, don't forget)

$4\pi r + 15L$ (length) $6hp + \pi r^2 + 7h^2$ (area)

$5p^2L - 4k^3/7$ (volume) $2\pi d - 14r/3$ (length)

Watch out for these last two tricky ones: (Why are they tricky?)

$3p(2b + a)$ (area) $3\pi h(L^2 + 4P^2)$ (volume)

The Acid Test:

LEARN the Rules for Identifying Formulas.
Turn over and write it all down.

Identify each of these expressions as an area, volume, or perimeter:

πr^2 Lwh πd $\tfrac{1}{2}bh$

$2bh + 4lb$ $4r^2h + 3\pi d^3$ $2\pi r(3L + 5T)$

UNIT FOUR

3D Shapes & Converting Measures

SOLIDS

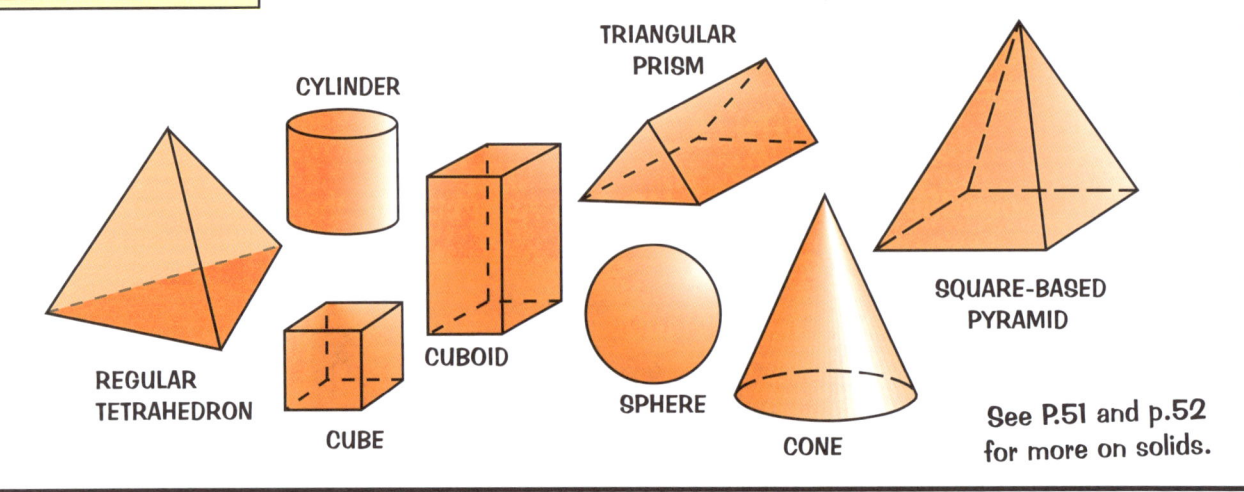

TRIANGULAR PRISM

CYLINDER

REGULAR TETRAHEDRON

CUBE

CUBOID

SPHERE

CONE

SQUARE-BASED PYRAMID

See P.51 and p.52 for more on solids.

Converting Area Measurements

Right then, this is dead easy stuff — you just have to remember...

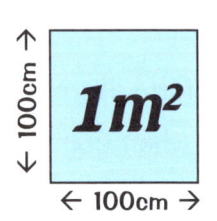

$$1m^2 = 100cm \times 100cm = 10,000cm^2$$

1m² (100cm × 100cm)

1) To change area measurements from m^2 to cm^2 multiply the area in m^2 by 10,000 (e.g. $3m^2 = 30,000cm^2$).

2) To change area measurements from cm^2 to m^2 divide the area in cm^2 by 10,000 (e.g. $45,000cm^2 = 4.5m^2$).

Converting Volume Measurements

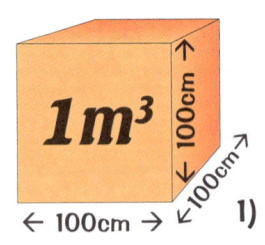

Same again really...

1m³ (100cm × 100cm × 100cm)

$$1m^3 = 100cm \times 100cm \times 100cm = 1,000,000cm^3$$

1) To change volume measurements from m^3 to cm^3 multiply the volume in m^3 by 1,000,000 (e.g. $3m^3 = 3,000,000cm^3$).

2) To change volume measurements from cm^3 to m^3 divide the volume in cm^3 by 1,000,000 (e.g. $4,500,000cm^3 = 4.5m^3$).

The Acid Test

1) Cover up the page, then name 8 types of solid object.
2) Convert these area measurements: a) 23 m² → cm²   b) 34,500 cm² → m²
3) Convert these volume measurements: a) 5.2m³ → cm³   b) 100,000 cm³ → m³

UNIT FOUR

Maps and Map Scales

1) The most usual map scale is "1 cm = so many km"

2) This just tells you how many km in real life it is for 1 cm measured on the actual map itself.

1) Converting "cm on the Map" into "Real km"

This map shows the original Roman M6 Motorway built by the Emperor Hadrian in the year AD120.

> The scale of the map is "1cm to 8km"
>
> "Work out the length of the section of M6 between Wigan and Preston."

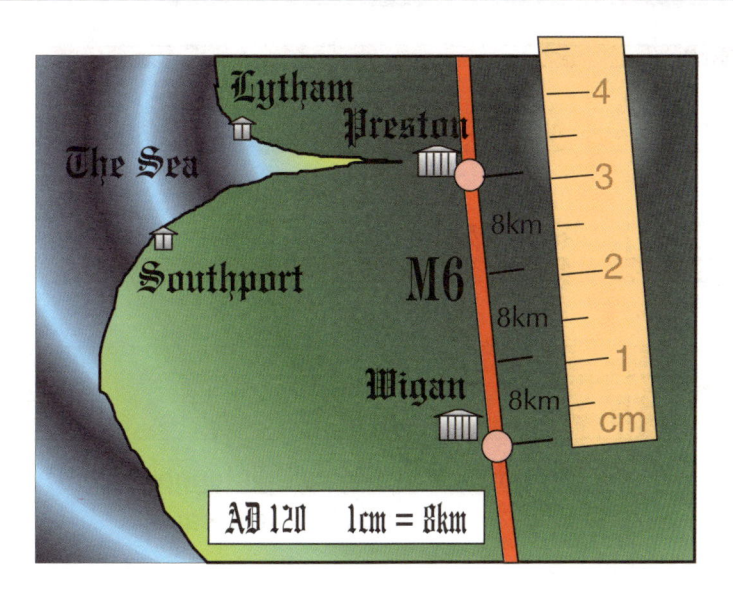

This is what you do (as shown on the diagram)

1) **PUT YOUR RULER AGAINST THE THING** you're finding the length of

2) **MARK OFF EACH WHOLE CM AND WRITE IN THE DISTANCE IN KM** next to each one

3) **ADD UP ALL THE KM DISTANCES TO FIND THE WHOLE LENGTH** of the road in km. (i.e. 8km + 8km + 8km = 24km)

Of course if they just tell you the thing is, say, 4 cm long you won't be able to put your ruler on it.

In that case you should draw an imaginary line 4cm long and then mark off the km on it using your ruler just the same, as shown in the example on the next page:

UNIT FOUR

Maps and Map Scales

2) Converting "Real km" into "cm on the Map"

Example:

"A map is drawn on a scale of 1cm to 2km. If a road is 12km long in real life, how long will it be in cm on the map?"

Answer:

1) Start by drawing the road as a straight line:

2) Mark off each cm and fill in how many km it is for each one

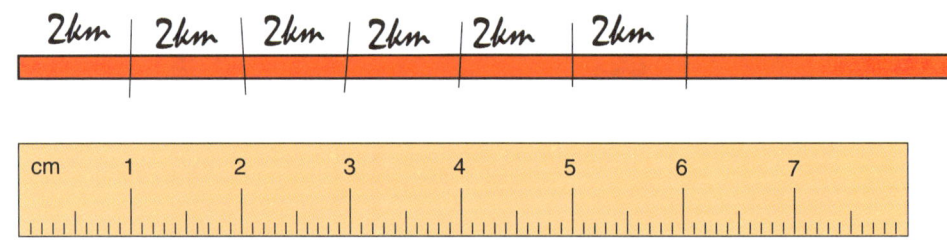

   2km | 2km | 2km | 2km | 2km | 2km

3) Keep going until the km add up to the full distance (12km in this case).

   Then just count how many cm long your line is (In this case 6cm).

The Acid Test

1) LEARN the 3 rules for working with map scales.

2) Work out the length in m of the runway shown here:

   SCALE: 1cm to 200m

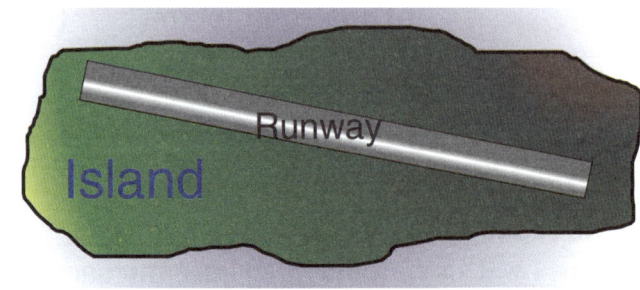

3) How many cm long would a 500m runway be?

UNIT FOUR

Revision Test for Unit Four

These are the final question pages — hurray. Remember, these questions will sort out quicker than anything else can, exactly what you know and what you don't. And that's exactly what revision is all about, don't forget: finding out what you DON'T know and then learning it until you do. Enjoy.

1) What is The Golden Rule for Ratio in the Home?

2) If 7 pints of milk cost £2.03, how much will 5 pints cost?

3) If 9 packs of Goldfish food weigh 2250g, how much will 4 packs weigh?

4) In a shop an item is reduced from £80 to £64. What percentage reduction is this?

5) Calculate a) 4/7 of 560   b) 2/5 of £150   c) 65% of 300

6) Work out without a calculator:

   a) $\frac{4}{6} \times 2\frac{12}{5}$ b) $\frac{25}{6} \div \frac{8}{3}$ c) $\frac{5}{8} + \frac{9}{4}$ d) $\frac{2}{3} - \frac{1}{7}$

7) "To find y you double x and add 4."   Write this as a formula.

8) Find x if $3^x = 81$ (Use trial and error)

9) Using the formula $F = \frac{9}{5}C + 32$, find the temperature in °F when it is 25 °C. Would that temperature be a hot day, a warm day or a cold day?

10) Solve these equations:
    a) $2x + 3 = 7$ b) $33 - 4x = 7x$ c) $5(x + 5) = -10$

11) For each of these, make y the subject:

    a) $6 - y = x$ b) $11 + 2y = x$ c) $y/3 = 7x + 3$

12) If $X^2 = 30$, find X accurate to one decimal place. (Trial and Improvement)

13) Solve these inequalities:
    a) $5x < 25$ b) $20 - 5x > 25$ c) $-6x < 30$ d) $10x > 170 - 7x$

14) Say if each of the following are straight line equations or quadratics.
    a) $x + 3 = y$ b) $y + x^2 = 2$ c) $y/2 = 1 - 2x$ d) $y^2 = x$

15) Find the gradient of the straight line that passes through the points (0, 1) and (3, 10). Use $y = mx + c$ to write down the equation of the line.

Unit Four

Revision Test for Unit Four

16) The travel graph shown on the right relates to a wandering goat ambling along a road. Describe what the goat is doing
    a) Between 4pm and 6pm
    b) Between 6pm and 7pm
    c) How far from home does the goat stray?
    d) What time does he get home?

17) Work out the exterior and interior angles for a regular octagon (8 sides).

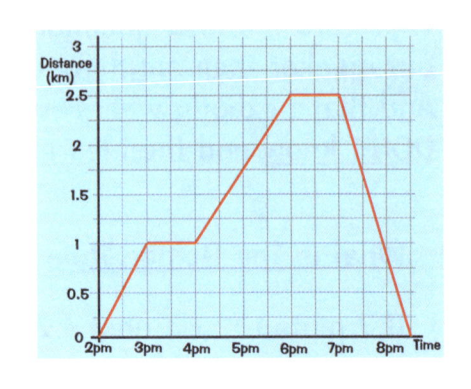

18) Draw the plan and side and front elevations for this cuboid: How many planes of symmetry does it have?

19) A car has a wheel of radius 0.5m. How many times will it need to rotate for the car to move forward 150m?

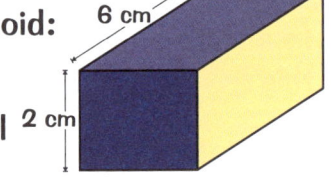

20) Use Pythagoras to calculate the missing lengths (to 1 d.p.) in these triangles:

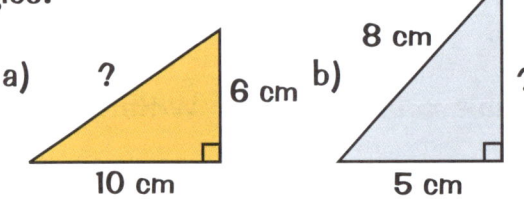

21) Are each of the following lengths, areas or volumes? (all letters are lengths)
    a) 5l + 6w   b) 5l² − 50lw   c) 25R² − 16r²   d) 25x³

22) Convert: a) 250 000 cm² to m²   b) 2.1 m³ to cm³

23) What transformation maps
    a) shape A onto shape B
    b) shape C onto shape D?

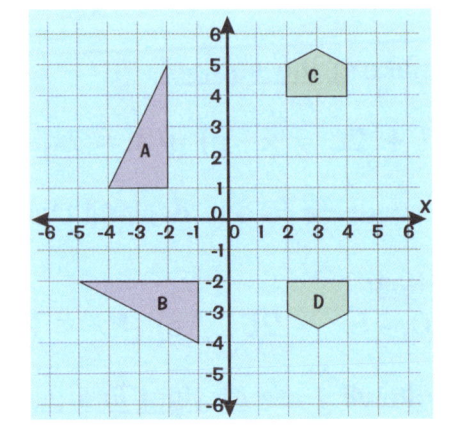

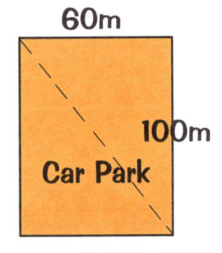

24) Do an accurate scale drawing of the car park shown to the left using a scale of 1 cm to 5 m.

UNIT FOUR

Answers

Unit Two — Acid Tests

P.3 Relative Frequency: **1) a)** 1/13 **b)** 6/13 **c)** 3/26
2) Landing on red: 0.43, landing on blue: 0.24, landing on green: 0.33

P.6 Tables, Charts and Graphs: **2)** They are NOT closely related. They have no correlation.

P.7 Pie charts: See pie chart to the right.

P.8 Mean, Median, Mode and Range:
1) First, do this: -14, -12, -5, -5, 0, 1, 3, 6, 7, 8, 10, 14, 18, 23, 25
   Mean = 5.27, Median = 6, Mode = -5, Range = 39

P.9 Grouped Frequency Tables: See table to the right.

P.10 1) a) Discrete, possible table:
Columns "Shoe Size" and "frequency",
Shoe size intervals: 3, 4, 5, 6, 7, 8, 9, 10, 11, 12.
b) Continuous, possible table:
Columns "Height (cm)" and "frequency", intervals:
$140 \leq h < 150$, $150 \leq h < 160$, $160 \leq h < 170$, etc.

P.11 (See table to the right.)
1) Mean = 17.4   **2)** Modal Group = $17.5 \leq L < 18.5$

Revision Test for Unit Two

1) 7/15 **2)** H-H, H-T, T-H, T-T   ¼   **3)** H-1, H-2, H-3, H-4, H-5, H-6, T-1, T-2, T-3, T-4, T-5, T-6   1/12   **4)** 0.8 **5)** Pictogram, 35 angry customers   **6)** Scattergraph, not good at all
7) Angles are: Blue 108°, Red 135°, Yellow 36°, White 81°. See pie chart.
8) First put in order: 2, 3, 4, 6, 7, 7, 12, 15 **a)** 7 **b)** 6.5 **c)** 7 **d)** 13   **9)** Values of w from 50 to 60 **including** 50, but **not including** 60. 60 would go in the next group up.
10) Modal group is $120 < t \leq 150$. Mean ≈ ((75×15) + (105×60) + (135×351) + (165×285) + (195×206) + (225×83)) ÷ 1000 = 160680 ÷ 1000 = <u>161 min</u>

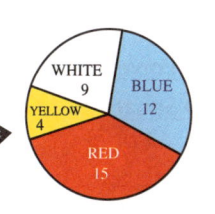

Unit Three — Acid Tests

P.13 Big Numbers:
1)a) One million, two hundred and thirty-four thousand, five hundred and thirty-one
b) Twenty-three thousand, four hundred and fifty-six   **c)** Two thousand, four hundred and fifteen
d) Three thousand, four hundred and two   **e)** Two hundred and three thousand, four hundred and twelve
2) 56,421   **3)** 9, 23, 87, 345, 493, 1029, 3004 **4)** 0.008, 0.09, 0.1, 0.2, 0.307, 0.37

P.14 Multiplying by 10, 100, 1000: **1a)** 1230 **b)** 3450 **c)** 9650   **2a)** 48 **b)** 450 **c)** 180,000

P.15 Dividing by 10, 100, 1000: **1a)** 0.245 **b)** 6.542 **c)** 0.00308 **2a)** 1.6 **b)** 12 **c)** 5

P.16-17 Multiplying and Dividing without a calculator: **1)** 336 **2)** 616 **3)** 832 **4)** 12 **5)** 121 **6)** 12 **7)** 179.2
8) 6.12 **9)** 56.1 **10)** 56 **11)** 46 **12)** 12

P.18) Rounding off: **2) a)** 3.2 **b)** 1.8 **c)** 2.3 **d)** 0.5 **e)** 9.8 **3) a)** 3 **b)** 5 **c)** 2 **d)** 7 **e)** 3

P.19) Rounding off: **1) a)** 450 **b)** 680 **c)** 50 **d)** 100 **e)** 10 **2) a)** 350 **b)** 500 **c)** 12.4 **d)** 0.036
3) a) 2900 **b)** 500 **c)** 100

P21 Accuracy and Estimating: **1) a)** 35g **b)** 134 mph **c)** 850g **d)** 76cm or 76.2cm
2) a) Approx 600 miles × 150 miles = 90,000 sq. miles **b)** Approx 7cm × 7cm × 10cm high = 490cm³
3) a) Actual answer = 5.831. Accept anything from 5.5 to 5.9 **b)** 2.236. Accept 2.1 to 2.5
c) 7.810. Accept 7.5 to 7.9 **d)** 4.690. Accept 4.5 to 4.9

Answers

P22 Special Number Sequences:
1) a) EVENS: 2,4,6,8,10,12,14,16,18,20,22,24,26,28,30
b) ODDS: 1,3,5,7,9,11,13,15,17,19,21,23,25,27,29
c) SQUARES: 1,4,9,16,25,36,49,64,81,100,121,144,169,196,225
d) CUBES:1,8,27,64,125,216,343,512,729,1000,1331,1728,2197,2744,3375
e) POWERS OF 2: 2, 4, 8, 16, 32, 64, 128, 256, 512, 1024, 2048, 4096, 8192, 16384, 32768;
POWERS OF 10: 10, 100, 1000, 10 000, 100 000, 1 000 000, 10 000 000, 100 000 000, 1 000 000 000, 10 000 000 000, 100 000 000 000, 1 000 000 000 000, 10 000 000 000 000, 100 000 000 000 000, 1 000 000 000 000 000 hmm...
f) TRIANGLE Nos: 1,3,6,10,15,21,28,36,45,55,66,78,91,105,120   **2) a)** 56, 134, 156, 36, 64
b) 23, 45, 81, 25, 97, 125, 1   **c)** 81, 25, 36, 1, 64   **d)** 125, 1, 64   **e)** 64   **f)** 45, 36, 1

P23 Prime numbers: **1)** 2,3,5,7,11,13,17,19,23,29,31,37,41,43,47
2) 97, 101, 103, 107, 109

P24 Multiples, Factors, Prime Factors: **1)** 7,14,21,28,35,42,49,56,63,70 and 9,18,27,36,45,54,63,72,81,90
2) 1,2,3,4,6,9,12,18,36 and 1,2,3,4,6,7,12,14,21,28,42,84
3) a) 990 = 2×3×3×5×11   **b)** 160 = 2×2×2×2×2×5

P25 LCM and HCF: 1) 8,16,24,32,40,48,56,64,72,80   and   9,18,27,36,45,54,63,72,81,90   LCM = 72
2) 1,2,4,7,8,14,28,56 and 1,2,4,8,13,26,52,104   HCF = 8
3) 63   **4)** 12

P.26 Fractions: 1) a) 5/6, **b)** 2/3   **c)** 15/22   **2)** 3/5, 2/3, 11/15

P27 Fractions, Decimals, Percentages: **a)** 6/10 = 3/5   **b)** 2/100 = 1/50   **c)** 77/100   **d)** 555/1000 = 111/200
e) 56/10 = 28/5 or 5 3/5

P28 Powers: 1) a) 3^8 **b)** 4   **c)** 8^{12} **d)** 1   **e)** 7^6 **2) a)** 5^{12} **b)** 36 or 6^2 **c)** 2^5

P29 Square and Cube Roots: 1) a) 14.14   **b)** 20, other value for a) is -14.14   **2) a)** g = 6 or -6   **b)** b = 4
c) r = 3 or -3

P31 Standard Index Form: **1)** 1. The front number must always be between 1 and 10. 2. The power of 10, n, is purely: how far the d.p. moves. 3. n is +ive for big numbers, n is –ive for small numbers (This is much better than rules based on which way the d.p. moves.)   **2)** 9.58×10^5 **3)** 1.8×10^{-4}
4) 4560   **5)** 2×10^{21} , 2,000,00.....(21 zeros!)

P33 Calculator Buttons: **1) a)** 11/4   **b)** 33/2   **c)** 33/4   **2) a)** 1.70   **b)** 39.96

P34 Negative Numbers and Letters: 1) a) +12 (Rule 1)   **b)** -6 (Rule1/Rule 2)
c) X (Rule 2, then Rule 1)   **d)** -3 (Rule 1)
2) a) +18   **b)** -216   **c)** 2   **d)** -27   **e)** -336

P35 Basic Algebra: **1) a)** 4x + y – 4   **b)** 9x + 5xy – 5   **c)** 5x + 3x² + 5y²   **d)** 6y – 4xy   **2) a)** 2x – 4   **b)** 5x + x²
c) y² + xy   **d)** 6xy – 18y

P36 Basic Algebra: **1) a)** x² + 3x + 2   **b)** y² + y – 12   **c)** x² + 10y + 25   **d)** 3x² – 13x + 4   **e)** 2x² + 5x + 2
f) 4x² – 4x + 1   **2) a)** 5x(y + 3)   **b)** a(5 – 7b)   **c)** 6y(2x + 1 – 6y)

P.38 Number patterns and Sequences: 1) a) 20, 27 "Add one extra each time"   **b)** 2,000   20,000 "Multiply the previous term by 10"   **c)** 4, 2 "Divide the previous term by 2"   **2)** 2n + 5

P.39 Metric and Imperial units: 1) a) 200   **b)** 65   **2) a)** 2.5   **b)** 1.5   **3)** 3 feet 10 inches   **4) a)** 200 or 220 yards   **b)** 187.5cm

P.42 Conversion Factors: 1) 160kg   **2)** 20 pints

P.43 Clock time questions: 1) 5:15pm **2)** 4:05pm **3)** 1,440 ; 86,400 **4)** 3hrs 30 min; 5hrs 45 min

P.45 Density and Speed: 1) Density = Mass ÷ Volume   **2)** 16.5 g/cm³   **3)** 603g   **4)** Speed = Distance ÷ Time
5) Time = 7½ hrs   Dist = 11.2km

P.47 Perimeters: 2) 42cm

P.49 Areas: 1) 12cm²   **2)** 12m²   **3)** 21m²   **4)** 78cm²

P.51 Solids and Nets: 1) 128.8cm²   **2)** 294cm²   **3)** 174cm²   **4)** 96cm²

P.52 Volume or Capacity: **a)** Trapezoidal Prism, V = 148.5 cm³   **b)** Cylinder, V = 0.700 m³

Answers

P.53 Lines and Angles: **1)** Actual angles given — accept answers within 10°:
a) 36° **b)** 79° **c)** 162° **d)** 287°

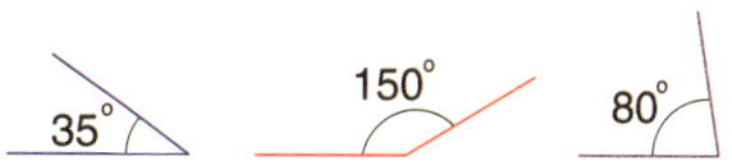

P.54 Measuring Angles with Protractors: 2) See P.54 **3)** See angles to the right.

P.55 Compass Directions and Bearings: 3) See diagram to the right.

P.57 Parallel Lines: See diagram to the right.

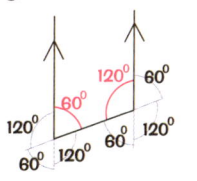

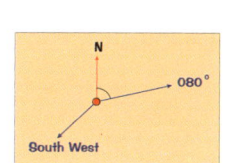

P.58 X, Y and Z Coordinates:
A(4,5) B(6,0) C(5,-5) D(0,-3) E(-5,-2) F(-4,0) G(-3,3) H(0,5)

P.59 Midpoint of a Line Segment: 1) (3,5) **2)** (5,1)

P.61 Drawing Graphs from Equations: 2)

x	-4	-2	-1	0	1	2	4
y	-6	-4	-3	-2	-1	0	2

3)

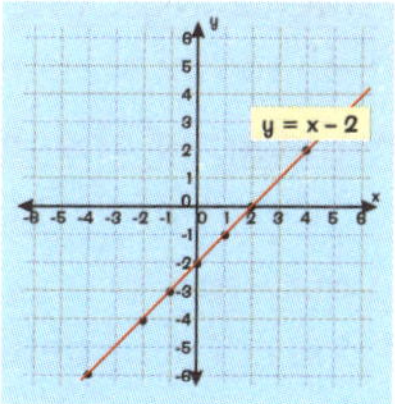

Revision Test for Unit Three

1) Twenty-one million, three hundred and six thousand, five hundred and fifteen.
2) a) 2, 23, 45, 123, 132, 789, 2200, 6534 **b)** -7, -6, -2, 0, 4, 5, 8, 10
3) a) +6 **b)** −32 **c)** −3 **d)** +5 **4)** 14 **5)** 40 **6)** 41, 43, 47, 53, 59
7) a) 210 = 2 × 3 × 5 × 7 **b)** 1050 = 2 × 3 × 5 × 5 × 7 **8) a)** 5.3 **b)** 3.5 **c)** 6.2
9) a) 250 **b)** 900 **10) a)** 2 **b)** 2 **c)** 1 **d)** 3 **e)** 2 **11)** 10 **12)** 4/5
13) 645/1000 = 129/200 **14)** 5x **15) a)** 12g + 20h − 4 **b)** $x^2 - 4x - 12$
16) 2x(1 + 3y) **17)** See graph on right **18) a)** 68° **b)** 26° **c)** 270° **d)** 224°
19) See P.46 **20)** See P.22 **21) a)** +16, −16 **b)** 6
22) a) 1296 **b)** 16807 **c)** 16 **d)** 248832 **e)** 2048000 **f)** 512 **23)** 3.56×10^{10}
24) nth number = 4n − 3 **25)** BDE = 40°, AED = 140°, BDC = 140°
26) See P.47; Perimeter = 32cm, Area = 32cm² **27)** 27cm³, 32cm³
28) See right **29)** 2 feet 6 inches

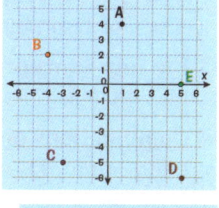

x	-5	-3	-1	0	1	2	4	6
y	-2	0	2	3	4	5	7	9

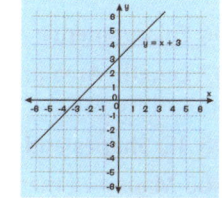

Unit Four — Acid Tests

P.64 Ratio in the Home: 1) 56p **2)** £1000 : £1400

P.65 Rat 'n' Toad Pie: Recipe for 9: 9 rats, 4.5 toads, 11.25 Oz of "Froggatt's Lumpy Sprout Ketchup", 18 'taties, a very big wodge of pastry (2.25 times as big in fact)

P.66 The Best Buy: Large size is best value at 1.90g per penny.

P.67 More Fractions: 1) a) 5/32 **b)** 32/35 **c)** 23/20 **d)** 1/40 **e)** 167/27   **2) a)** 220 **b)** £1.75

P.70 Percentages: 1) £120   **2)** 30%

P.71 Making Formulas from Words: 1) y = 5x − 3 **2)** C = 95n

P.72 Substituting values into formulas: 2) 25

P.73 Solving equations: 1) x = 8 **2)** x = 7

P.74 Solving equations: 1) a) x = 4   **b)** q = 32   **c)** y = −2   **2)** b = ½a + 3

P.75 Trial and improvement: x = 1.6

P.76 Inequalities: 1) x ⩾ -2 **2)** x ⩾ -4, x < 2, x = -4, -3, -2, -1, 0, 1

P.77 Straight Line Graphs — Gradients: Gradient = -1.5

P.78 Straight Line Graphs — "y = mx + c":

1) 2)

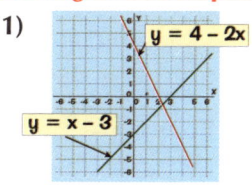

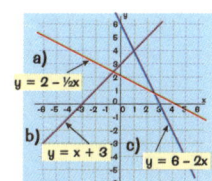

Answers

P.79 Simultaneous equations with graphs: 2) a) x=2, y=4 **b)** x=1½, y=3

P.80 Quadratic graphs:
See graph to the right. Using graph, solutions are x = -2 and x = 3.

P.83 Regular Polygons:
1) A regular polygon is a many-sided shape where all the sides and angles are the same **2)** Equilateral triangle, square, regular pentagon, regular hexagon, regular heptagon, regular octagon **3)** See P.83 **4)** Ext. angle = 72°, Int. angle = 108°
5) Ext. angle = 30°, Int. angle = 150°

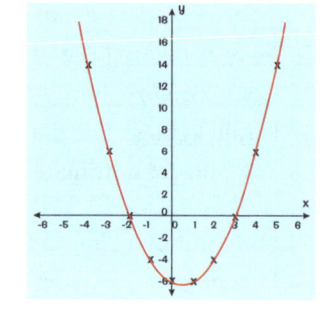

P.84 Projections, Congruence and Similarity: 1) See P.85 and check it looks right.
2) a) i, ii and iv are similar. **b)** i and ii are congruent.

P.85 Pythagoras' Theorem: 1) BC = 8m,
2) 5m, 12m, 13m is a right angled triangle because $a^2 + b^2 = h^2$ works.

P.91 Symmetry:
H : 2 lines of symmetry, Rot^n symmetry Order 2,   Z : 0 lines of symmetry, Rot^n symmetry Order 2,
T : 1 line of symmetry, No Rotational symmetry,   N : 0 lines of symmetry, Rot^n symmetry Order 2,
E : 1 line of symmetry, No Rotational symmetry,   X : 4 lines of symmetry, Rot^n symmetry Order 4,
S : 0 lines of symmetry, Rot^n symmetry Order 2

P.93 The four transformations: 1) A → B Rotation ¼ turn clockwise about the origin. **2)** B → C reflection in the line Y=X. **3)** C → A reflection in the y-axis. **4)** A → D translation of 9 left and 7 down

P.94 Combinations of Transformations: 1) C→D, Reflection in the y-axis, and an enlargement SF 2, centre the origin, D→C, Reflection in the y-axis, and an enlargement SF ½, centre the origin.
2) A'→B, Rotation of 180° clockwise or anticlockwise about the point (0,3).

P.96 Enlargements: 1) 2430 cm^2 **2)** 1875 cm^3

P.97 Length, Area and Volume: πr^2 = Area, Lwh = Volume, πd = Perimeter, ½bh = Area,
2bh + 4lb = Area, $4r^2h + 3\pi d^3$ = Volume, $2\pi r(3L + 5T)$ = Area

P.98 3D Shapes and converting measures: 2) a) 230,000cm^2 **b)** 3.45m^2 **3) a)** 5,200,000cm^3 **b)** 0.1m^3

P.100 Maps and map scales: 2) 1400m **3)** 2½cm

Revision Test for Unit Four

1) See P.64 **2)** £1.45 **3)** 1000g **4)** 20% **5) a)** 320 **b)** 60 **c)** 195 **6) a)** 88/30 = 44/15 **b)** 75/48 = 25/16
c) 23/8 **d)** 11/21 **7)** y = 2x + 4 **8)** x = 4 **9)** 77°F Warm/hot day **10) a)** x = 2 **b)** x = 3 **c)** x = -7
11) a) y = 6 – x **b)** y = (x – 11) / 2 **c)** y = 3(7x + 3) or y = 21x + 9 **12)** x = 5.5 to 1 d.p.
13) a) x < 5 **b)** x < -1 **c)** x > -5 **d)** x > 10 **14) a)** straight line **b)** quadratic **c)** straight line **d)** quadratic
15) Gradient m = 3, eqn is y = 3x + 1 **16) a)** Wandering away from home. **b)** Stood still chomping grass.
c) 2½ km **d)** 8:30pm **17)** 45° and 135° **18)** Elevations — the follow <u>rectangles</u> should be sketched: 6 cm × 3 cm (plan), 6 cm × 2 cm (side), 3 cm × 2 cm (front). 3 planes of symmetry. **19)** 47.8 turns
20) a) 11.7 cm **b)** 6.2 cm **21) a)** length **b)** area **c)** area **d)** volume **22) a)** 25 m^2 **b)** 2100000 cm^3
23) a) rotation 90° anticlockwise about (0, 0) **b)** reflection in the line y = 1 **24)** Scale drawing should have the dimensions 12 cm × 20 cm

Index

Symbols

3D shapes 98

A

a.m. 43
accuracy and estimating 20, 21
acute angles 54
algebra 35, 36, 72, 76
alternate angles 57
angles 53, 54, 56, 57
appropriate degree of accuracy 20
arc 50
area 50, 97
area formulas 48, 49
area of enlargement 96
area of circle 50, 86

B

bar charts 5
bar-line graphs 5
bearings 55
best buy 66
big numbers 13
bodmas 33, 72
brackets buttons 33

C

calculator buttons 32, 33
cancelling down 26
capacity 52
centre of enlargement 92, 95
chocco-burgers 71
chord 50
circle formulas 86
circles 50, 88
circumference 50, 86
clock time questions 43
compass directions 55
compasses 88
congruent 84
constructing accurate 60° angles 89
constructing accurate 90° angles 89
constructing triangles 87
constructions 88, 89
continuous data 10
conversion factors 41, 42
conversion graphs 82
converting area measurements 98
converting decimals to fractions 27
converting volume measurements 98
coordinates 58, 59
correlation 6

corresponding angles 57
cross-section 52
cube numbers 22
cube root 29
cuboid 52

D

decimal numbers 18
decimal places 18
decimals 27
density 45
density = mass ÷ volume 45
diameter 50
discount 69
discrete data 9
distance 45, 82
divide 15
dividing whole numbers 17
dividing with decimals 17
dividing without a calculator 17
double brackets 36
drawing quadratic curves 80
drawing a straight line 78
drawing graphs from equations 61

E

edge 51
elevation (front, side, plan) 84
enlargement 92, 94, 95, 96
equal probabilities 1
equation of a straight line graph 78
equilateral triangle 83
equivalent fractions 26
estimating angles 53
estimating areas 21
estimating calculations 20
estimating square roots 21
estimating volumes 21
even numbers 22
exterior angle 83

F

face 51
factor tree 24
factorising 36
factors 24
fair or biased 3
finding gradients 77
finding the nth number 38
formula triangles 44, 96
fraction button 32
fraction calculations 67
fractions 26, 27
frequency polygons 4
frequency tables 4

Froggatt's Homespun Rat 'n' Toad Pie 65
Froggatt's Lumpy Sprout Ketchup 42
front elevation 84

G

geometry rules 56
giant sea-slug called Kevin 41
gradient of a graph 81
gradients 77
grouped frequency tables 9, 10, 11

H

highest common factor (HCF) 25
horizontal line 60

I

imperial units 39
inequalities 76
inequality symbols 76
interior angle 83
isometric projection 84

L

length 97
line graphs 4
line of best fit 6
line segment 59
line symmetry 90
locus 88, 89
lowest common multiple (LCM) 25

M

main diagonal 60
making formulas from words 71
map scales 99, 100
mass 45
mean 8, 11
meaning of the gradient 81
measuring angles 54
median 8
memory buttons 32
metric units 39
metric-imperial conversions 39
mid-interval values 10, 11
midpoint of a line segment 59
mirror line 93
modal group 11
mode 8
move the decimal point 14, 15
multiples 24
multiply 14
multiplying decimals 16

Index

multiplying whole numbers 16
multiplying without a calculator 16

N

negative numbers and letters 34
net 51
northline 55
number patterns 37, 38
number sequences 37, 38

O

obtuse angles 54
odd numbers 22
ordering fractions 26
orientation 93
original value 70

P

p.m. 43
parallel lines 57
percentages 27, 68, 69, 70
perimeters 47
perpendicular 89
pi 50, 85
pictograms 5
pie charts 7
plan 84
plane symmetry 90
plot each point 61
postage rates 40
powers 22, 28
powers button 33
prime factors 24
prime numbers 23, 24
prism 52
probability 1, 2, 3
profit 70
projection 84
proportion 27
protractor 54
Pythagoras' theorem 85

Q

quadratic equations 80
quadratic graphs 80
quadrilaterals 46

R

radius 50
range 8
ratio in the home 64
rearranging formulas 74
recipe 65
recurring decimals 27
reduced price 69

reduction 70
reflection 90, 93, 94
reflex angles 54
regular heptagon 83
regular hexagon 83
regular octagon 83
regular pentagon 83
regular polygons 83
relating angles to fractions 7
relative frequency 3
right angles 54
right-angled triangles 85
rotation 93
rotational symmetry 91
rounding off 18, 19, 40
rounding off measurements 40
rounding whole numbers 19

S

scale factor 92, 95, 96
scatter graphs 6
sector 50
segment 50
shapes 46
side elevation 84
significant figures 19, 20
similar 84
simplifying algebra 35
simultaneous equations 79
sloping line 60
solids 98
solving equations 73, 74, 96
solving simultaneous equations 79
speed 45
speed = distance ÷ time 45
square 83
square numbers 22
square roots 29
squared brackets 36
standard form 30, 31
stem and leaf diagrams 5
straight line graphs 60, 77, 78
straight line equations 60
substituting values into formulas 72
supplementary angles 57
surface area 51
symmetry 90, 91

T

table of values 61, 80
tally 9
tangent 50
tessellation 91
three letter angle notation 53
throwing a dice 1
time 45, 82

tossing a coin 1
tracing paper 91
transformations 92, 93, 94
translation 92, 94
travel graphs 82
trial and error method 73
trial and improvement 75
triangle numbers 22
triangles 46
two-way tables 4
typical graph questions 81

U

unequal probabilities 2

V

VAT 69
vectors 92
vertex 51
vertical line 60
volume 45, 52, 97
volumes of enlargement 96

X

X- coordinates 58

Y

$y = mx + c$ 78
Y- coordinates 58

Z

Z- coordinates 58

CW01197365

Yule need a Drink

Yule Need a Drink

Copyright © 2025 by Cider Mill Press Book Publishers LLC.

This is an officially licensed book by Cider Mill Press Book Publishers LLC.

All rights reserved under the Pan-American and International Copyright Conventions.

No part of this book may be reproduced in whole or in part, scanned, photocopied, recorded, distributed in any printed or electronic form, or reproduced in any manner whatsoever, or by any information storage and retrieval system now known or hereafter invented, without express written permission of the publisher, except in the case of brief quotations embodied in critical articles and reviews.

The scanning, uploading, and distribution of this book via the internet or via any other means without permission of the publisher is illegal and punishable by law. Please support authors' rights, and do not participate in or encourage piracy of copyrighted materials.

13-Digit ISBN: 978-1-40035-271-5
10-Digit ISBN: 1-40035-271-1

Books published by Cider Mill Press Book Publishers are available at special discounts for bulk purchases in the United States by corporations, institutions, and other organizations. For more information, please contact the publisher.

Without limiting the exclusive rights of any author, contributor or the publisher of this publication, any unauthorized use of this publication to train generative artificial intelligence (AI) technologies is expressly prohibited. HarperCollins also exercise their rights under Article 4(3) of the Digital Single Market Directive 2019/790 and expressly reserve this publication from the text and data mining exception.

HarperCollins Publishers, Macken House, 39/40 Mayor Street Upper, Dublin 1, D01 C9W8, Ireland (https://www.harpercollins.com)

Cider Mill Press Book Publishers
"Where good books are ready for press"
501 Nelson Place
Nashville, Tennessee 37214, USA

cidermillpress.com

Typography: Bembo Std, Brilon, Panel

Printed in Malaysia

25 26 27 28 29 SEA 5 4 3 2 1

First Edition

Yule Need a Drink

100+ cocktails to keep your season bright

CIDER MILL PRESS
BOOK PUBLISHERS

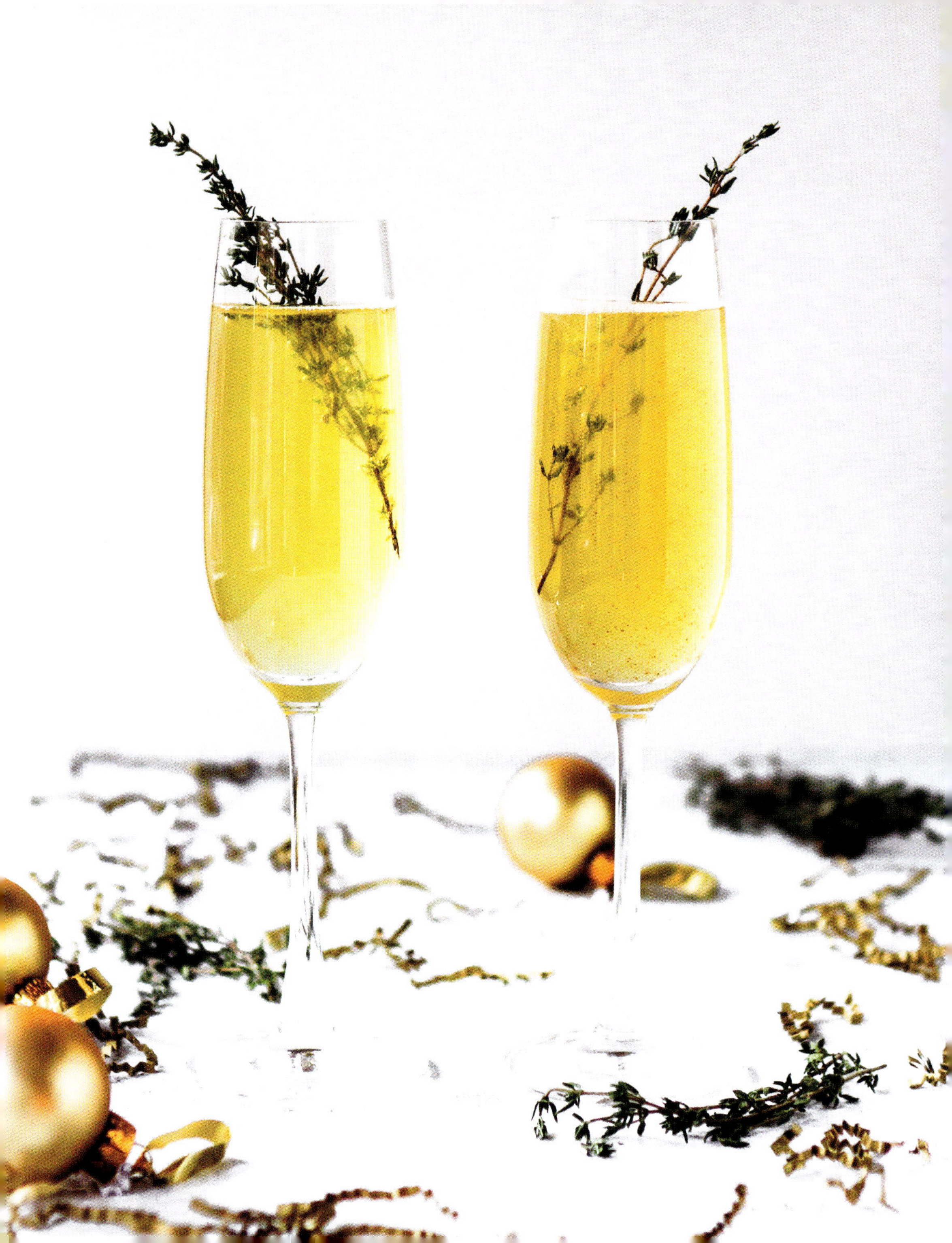

Contents

Welcome to the Naughty List ✳ 6

How to Survive Holiday Gatherings 101 ✳ 10

Sweater Weather, but Make It Boozy ✳ 78

Old-Fashioned Holiday Cheer ✳ 112

All I Want for Christmas Is a Sparkly Drink ✳ 170

'Tis the Season to Keep Spirits Bright ✳ 204

Index ✳ 235

WELCOME TO THE NAUGHTY LIST!

This isn't your grandmother's dusty cocktail book. It's a totally unapologetic ode to the best part of the season. Spoiler alert—it's not the parking lot panic at the mall or listening to that one uncle rant about inflation. It's cocktails. This is your ultimate guide to surviving the season in style—and by style, we clearly mean with a cocktail firmly in hand. Whether you're braving the holiday chaos or escaping it altogether, these drinks are here to make sure your glass (and your patience) stay full.

These beverages are designed to pair perfectly with every merry—and not-so-merry—moment the holidays throw your way. We're talking drinks for when you're flying solo with *Love Actually* on repeat in your coziest PJs and cocktails that'll outshine the overpriced champagne at your friend's posh holiday party. Need something to make opening socks from your office Secret Santa slightly less soul-crushing? There's a drink for that. Hosting Christmas dinner and want to stun your in-laws? We've got you covered. This book is here to help you sip your way through the season, from the first holiday playlist in November (we see you, Mariah) to that blurry New Year's Eve countdown.

Forget the endless gift-wrapping sessions, the passive-aggressive family group chats, and the atrocity that is fruitcake. Inside these pages, you'll find chapters to help you survive every up and down of the season. When you need to defrost after hauling in that overpriced Christmas tree, head straight to our chapter on hot drinks. These spiked delights will restore feeling to your hands and hopefully to your icy heart. When you need a companion to sit with through yet another round of holiday karaoke Shame, keep your spirits bright (pun intended) with our collection of festive sippers. When you need something to distract that one cousin who insists on talking politics over dinner, dazzle them with timeless, show-stopping classics. When you're searching for the willpower to help you survive Grandma's annual "Why aren't you married yet?" interrogation, arm yourself with a strategically timed glass of bubbly. There's even a chapter for the perfect party provisions in our batch cocktail chapter—because if your tree still isn't lit, your guests definitely should be. With drinks that are equal parts delicious and festive, you'll be so busy mixing, shaking, and toasting that you might even enjoy the holidays this year. Or at least make it through without texting your ex. Probably.

Now grab your shaker, raise your glass, lower your stress, and get ready to sleigh the holidays. Cheers to a season of strong spirits, zero regrets, and fewer awkward family conversations!

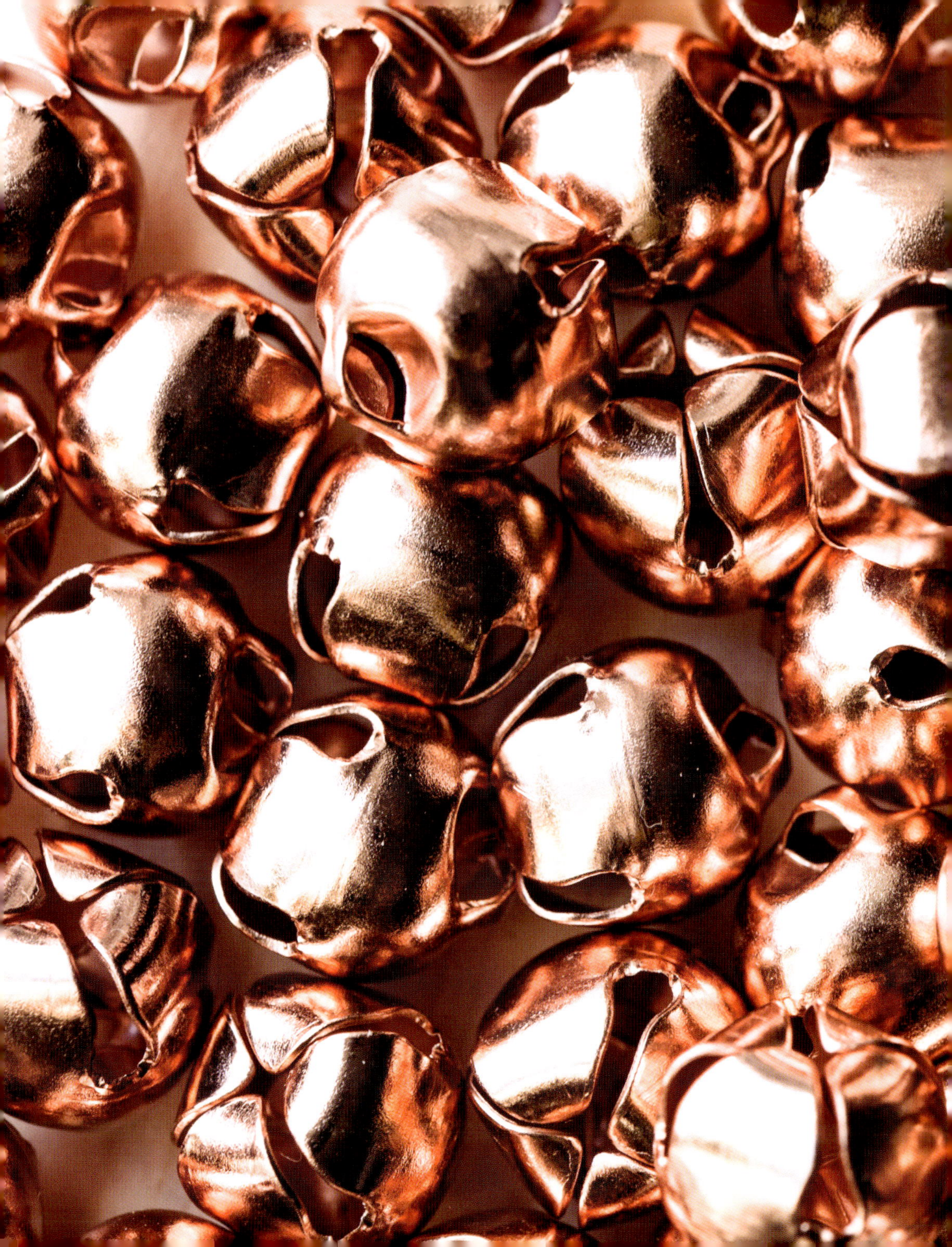

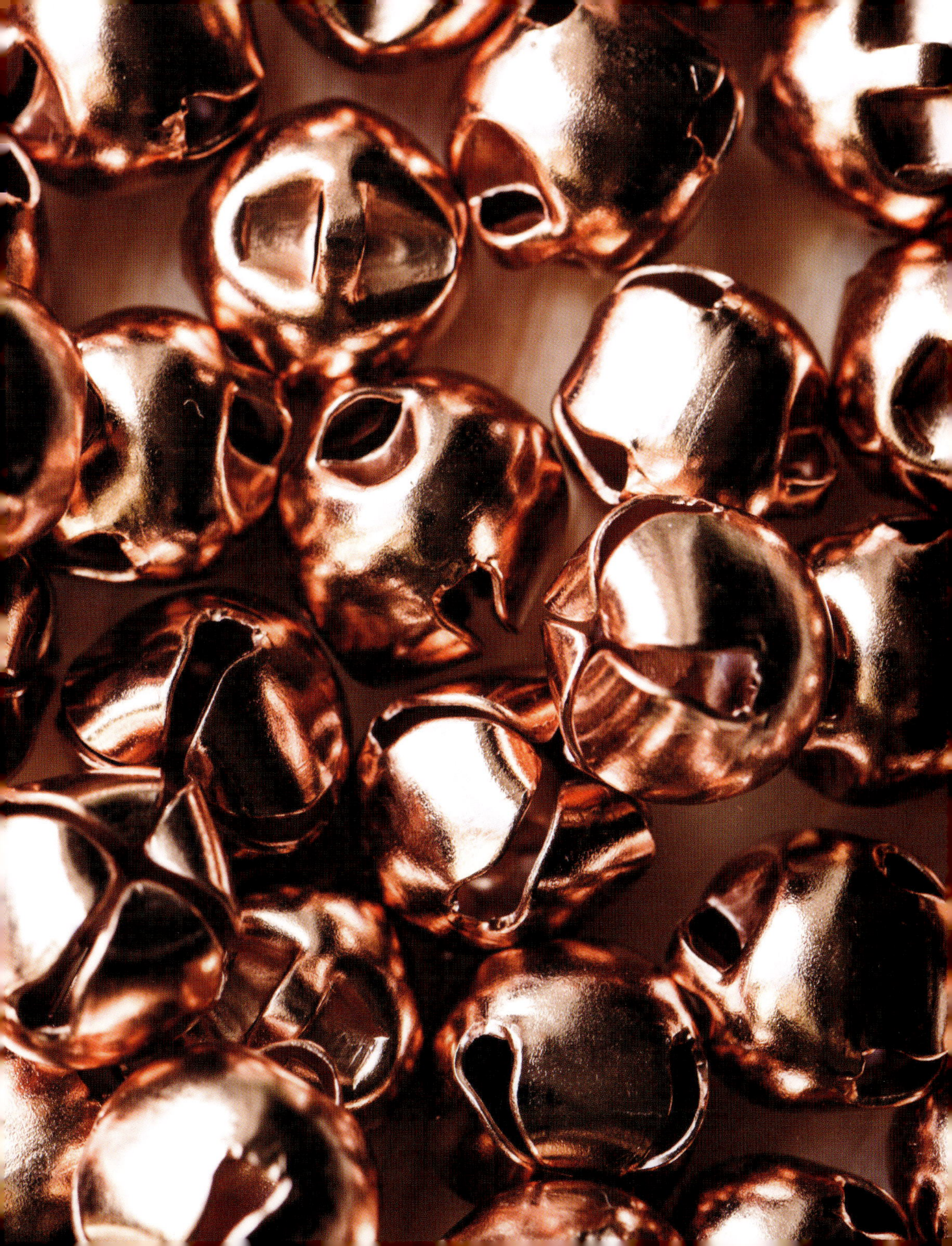

HOW TO SURVIVE HOLIDAY GATHERINGS 101

Ah, the holiday gathering—a delightful tradition where everyone pretends to enjoy each other's company while silently panicking about overcooked turkey, cringeworthy small talk, and whether Aunt Carol is about to say something weird again. Fear not, for this chapter is your lifeline! With the right cocktail in hand, you can face anything—judgy in-laws? Boom, you're bulletproof. Random holiday party invite from "that one coworker"? You're suddenly the life of the cubicle convoy. Surprise visit from your neighbor bringing *fruitcake*? Ew. Smile, sip, and keep them standing on the porch. These batch drinks are less about spreading cheer and more about faking it until the last sleigh bell rings. Strap in, mix up, and get ready to conquer every awkward moment with a little liquid courage.

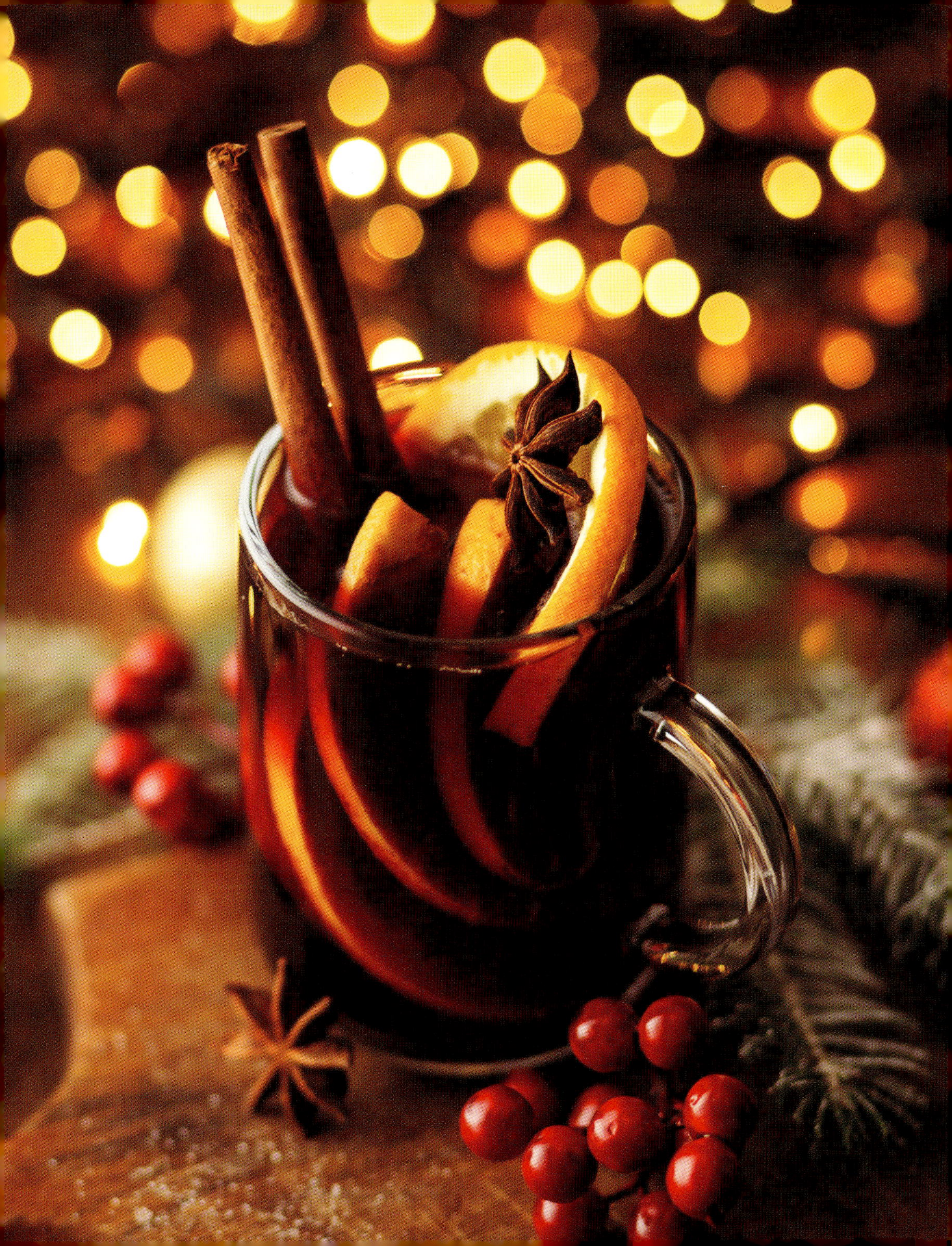

MERRY MIMOSA-THON

Sugar, for the rims (optional)

1½ cups Grand Marnier

3 (750 ml) bottles of Champagne

3 cups fresh orange juice

If using the sugar, pour ¼ cup of the Grand Marnier into a bowl. Dip the rims of the champagne flutes into the liqueur and then coat them with the sugar.

Place the remaining orange liqueur, Champagne, and orange juice in a large punch bowl, stir gently, and pour into the rimmed glasses.

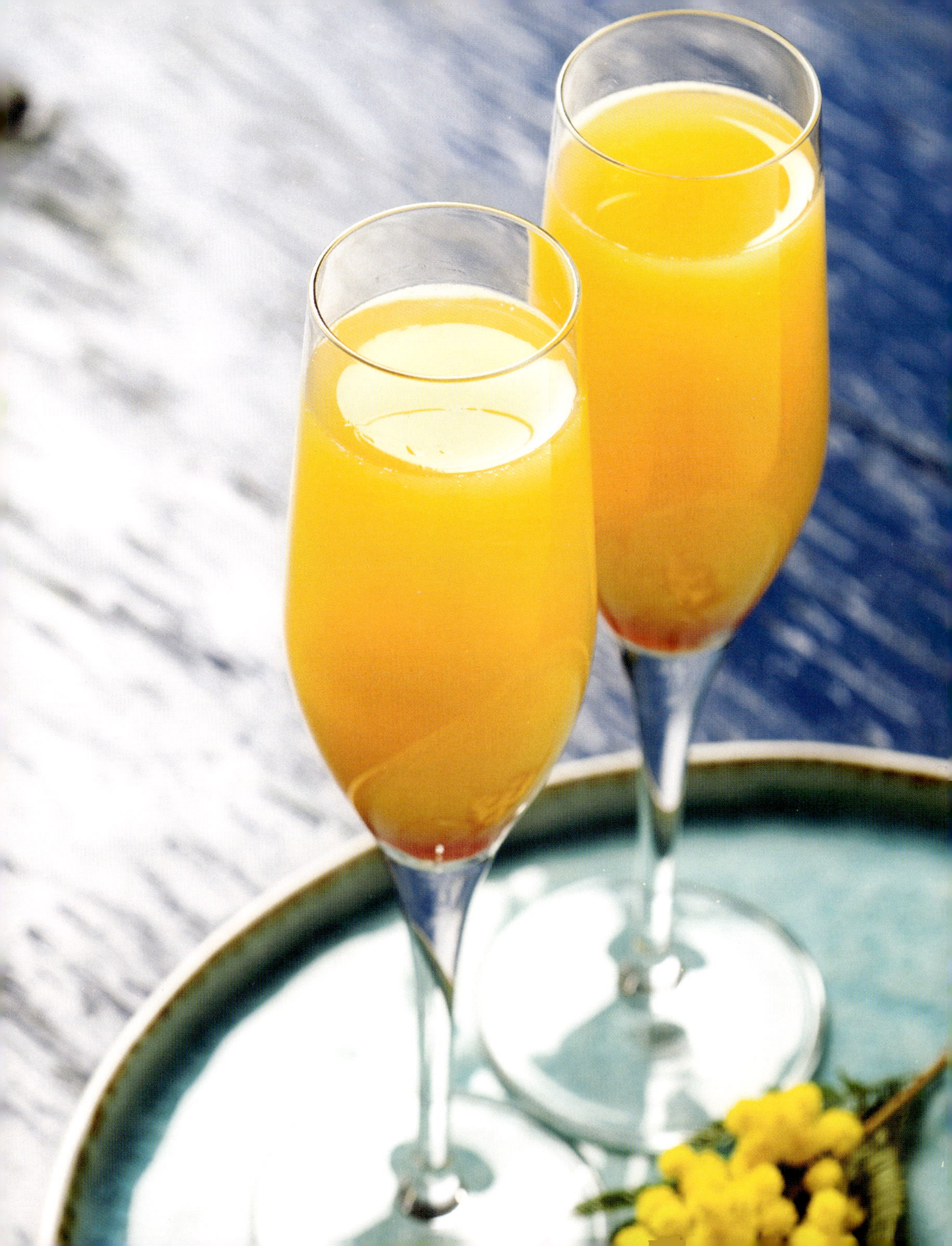

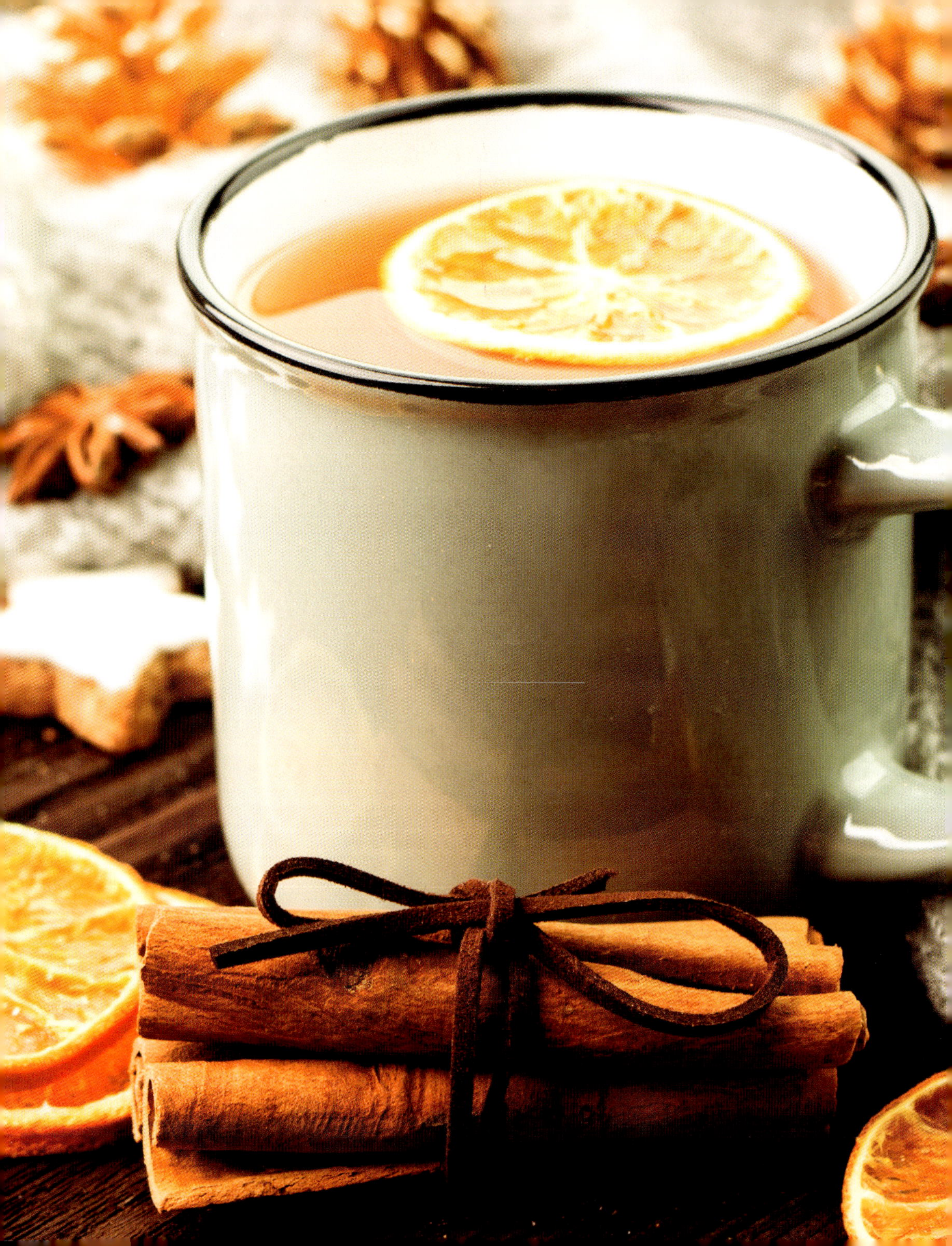

APPLE-LUJAH, IT'S BOOZY

6 cups apple cider

3 cups bourbon

5 cinnamon sticks

3 orange peels, for garnish

30 to 40 whole cloves, for garnish

Place the apple cider, bourbon, and cinnamon sticks in a slow cooker and cook on low for 2 hours, making sure the mixture does not come to a boil.

Cut the orange peels into rectangles and press the cloves into them. Garnish each glass with a clove-studded orange peel.

MOCHA ME FORGET MY FAMILY DRAMA

8 cups whole milk

1 cup heavy cream

½ cup sugar, plus more to taste

½ cup freshly brewed espresso

8 oz. bittersweet chocolate, chopped

1 cup aged rum

1 tablespoon orange zest

½ teaspoon fine sea salt

Place the milk, cream, sugar, and espresso in a saucepan and warm it over medium heat.

Place the chocolate in a bowl. When the milk mixture is hot, ladle 1 cup of it over the chocolate and whisk until the chocolate is completely melted, adding more of the warm milk mixture if the melted chocolate mixture is too thick.

Pour the melted chocolate mixture into the pot of warm milk and whisk to combine. Add the rum, orange zest, and salt and stir to combine. Pour into mugs and enjoy.

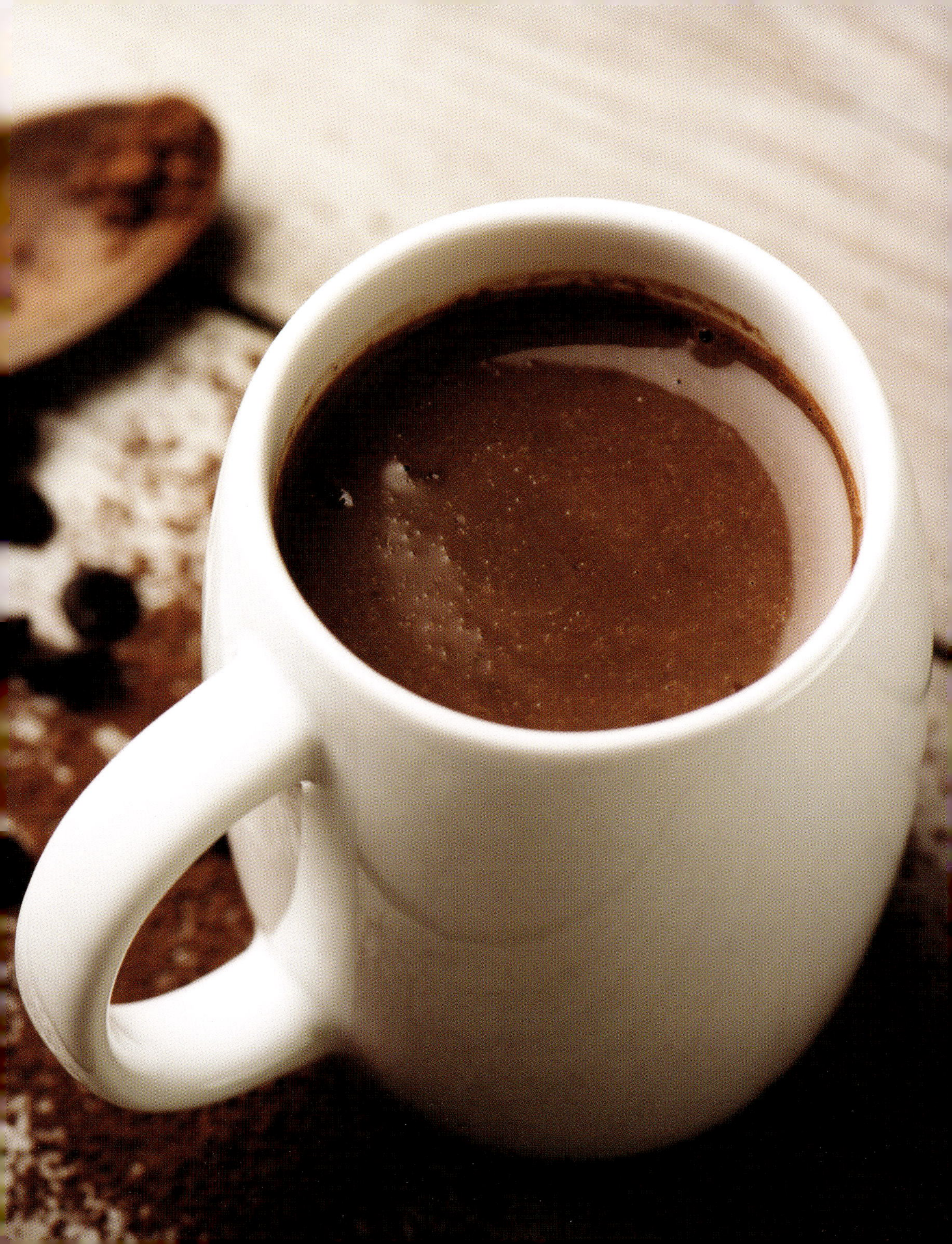

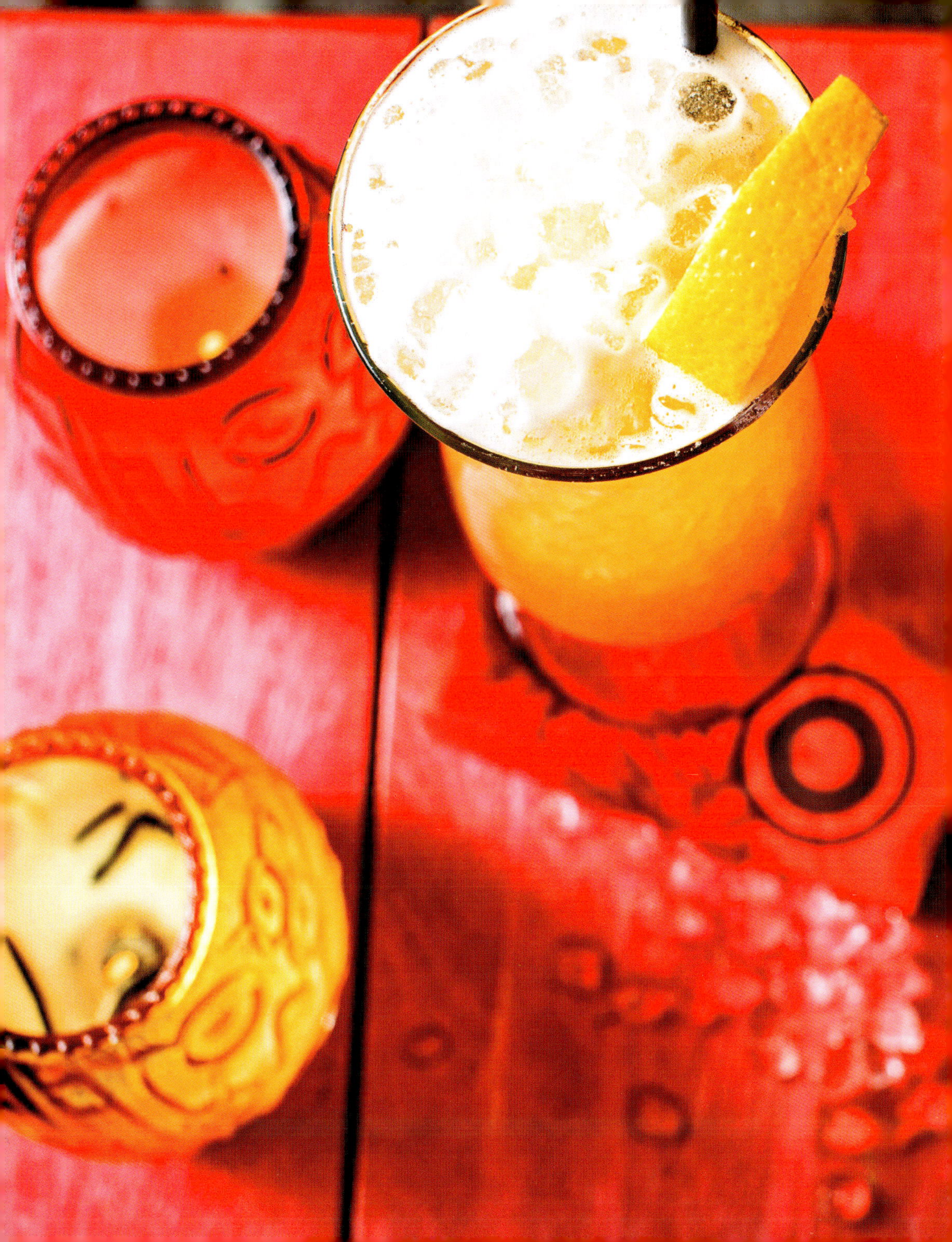

LOVE ACTUALLY SUCKS PUNCH

3 cups light rum

1½ cups dark rum

1 oz. Angostura Bitters

3 cups orange juice

½ cup pineapple juice

1 cup triple sec

2 oz. grenadine

Orange slices, for garnish

Place all of the ingredients, except for the orange slices, in a large punch bowl, add blocks of ice, and stir to combine.

Serve over ice in Collins glasses and garnish with orange slices.

I'D RATHER BE HOME WITH MY DOG

3 cups bourbon

1 cup whole milk

1 oz. Simple Syrup (see sidebar)

1 teaspoon pure vanilla extract

Freshly grated nutmeg, for garnish

Place all of the ingredients, except for the nutmeg, in a large punch bowl, add large blocks of ice, and stir to combine.

Garnish with the nutmeg and serve in coupes or rocks glasses.

SIMPLE SYRUP

Named due to its humble components—equal parts sugar and water—and the ease of making it—just place the sugar (or honey) and water in a saucepan, stir as it comes to a boil in order to help the sugar dissolve, and then let it cool—there is nothing basic about the role simple syrup plays in cocktail making. Whether it is there to offset the lemon or lime juice, allow a tucked-away flavor to surface, or add body and viscosity to a drink, simple syrup definitively transcends its modest construction.

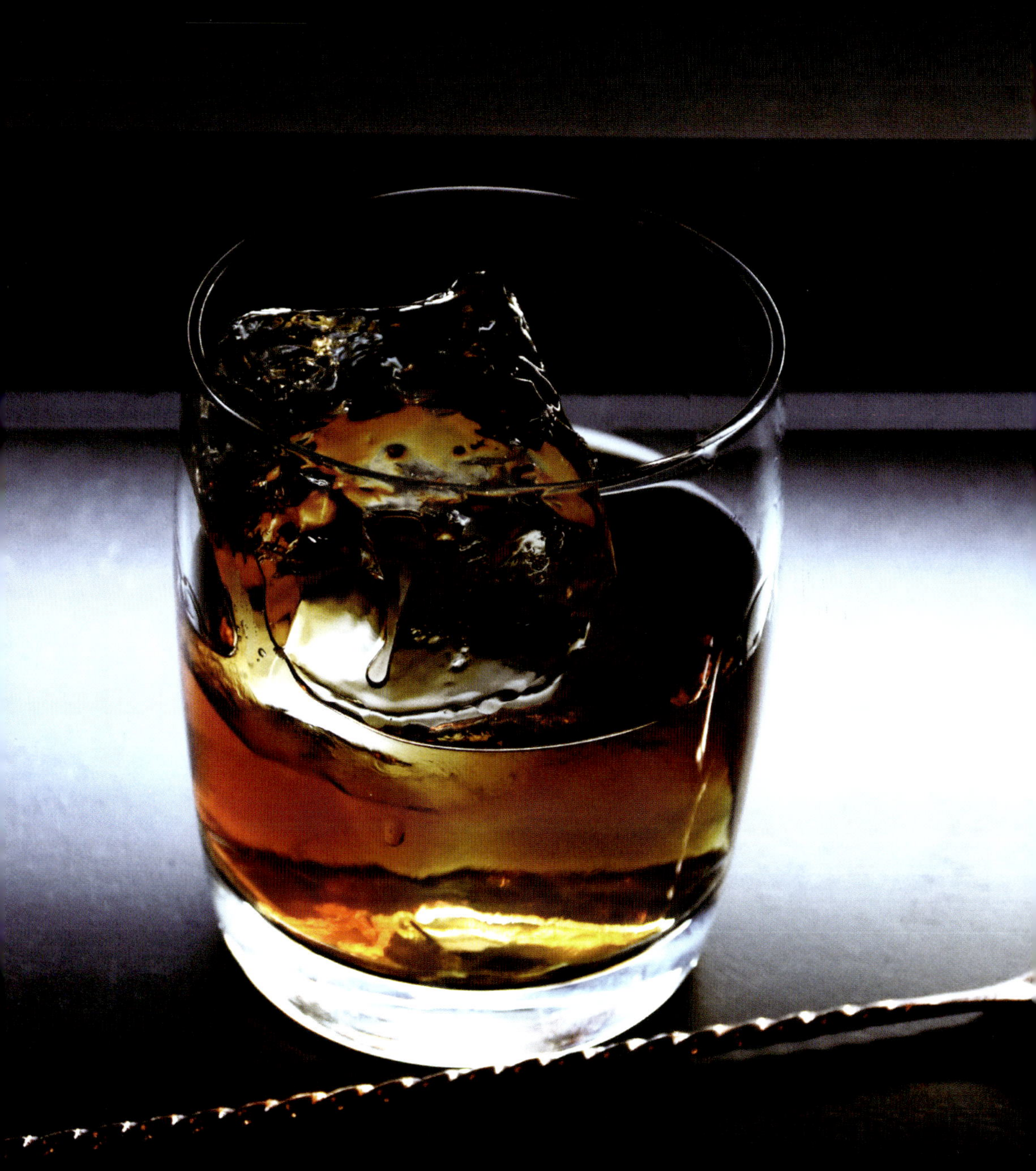

WHEN IN-LAWS COME A-KNOCKING

2 cups rum

2 cups Crown Royal whiskey

2 cups brandy

½ oz. grenadine

Maraschino cherries, for garnish

Place all of the ingredients, except for the maraschino cherries, in a large punch bowl, add blocks of ice, and stir to combine.

Serve over ice in rocks glasses and garnish with the maraschino cherries.

FAMILY FIASCO FIXER

2 cups aged rum

1 cup bourbon

1 cup Simple Syrup (see page 20)

2 cups heavy cream

Freshly grated nutmeg, for garnish

Place all of the ingredients, except for the nutmeg, in a large punch bowl, add large blocks of ice, and stir to combine.

Garnish with the nutmeg and serve in coupes or over ice in rocks glasses.

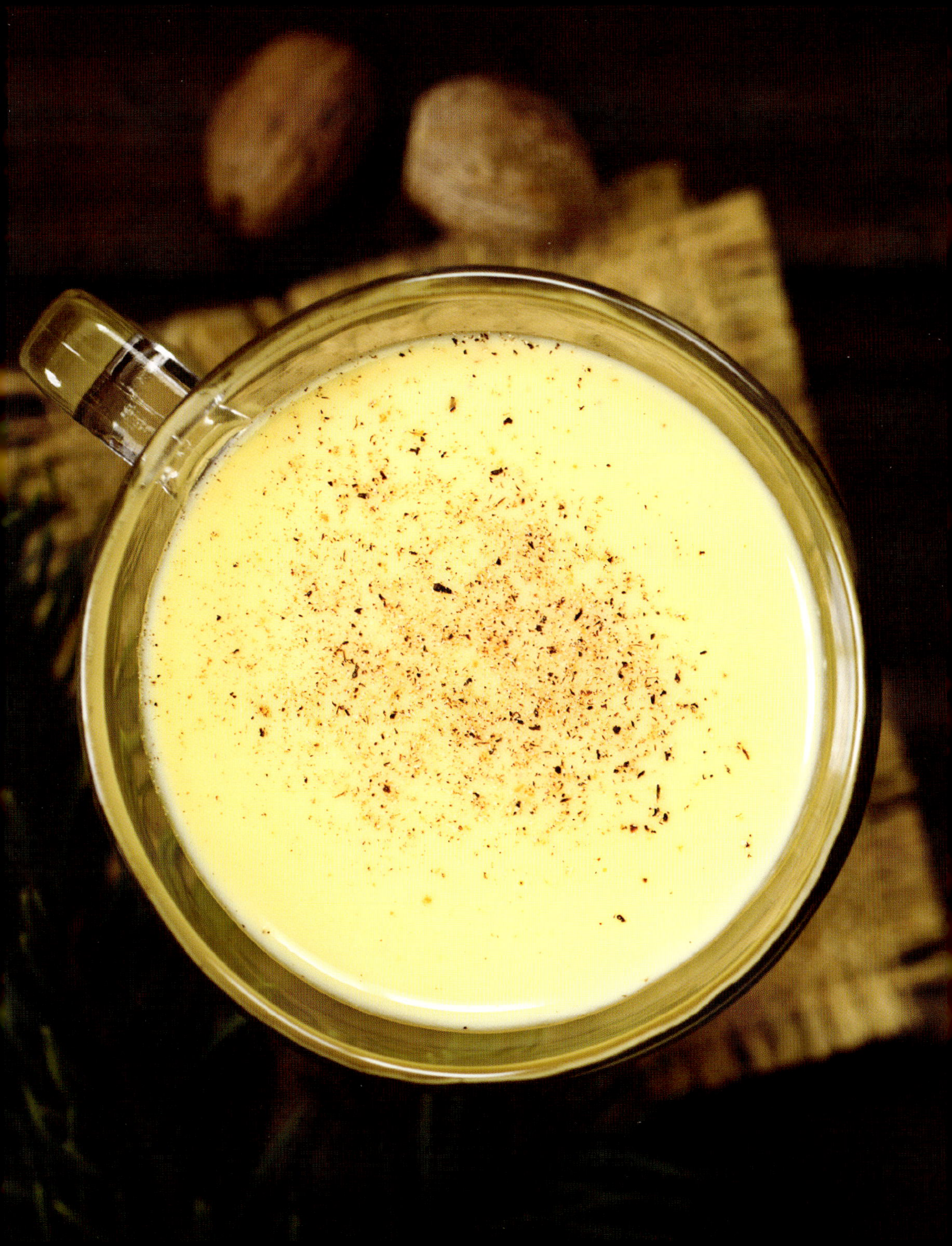

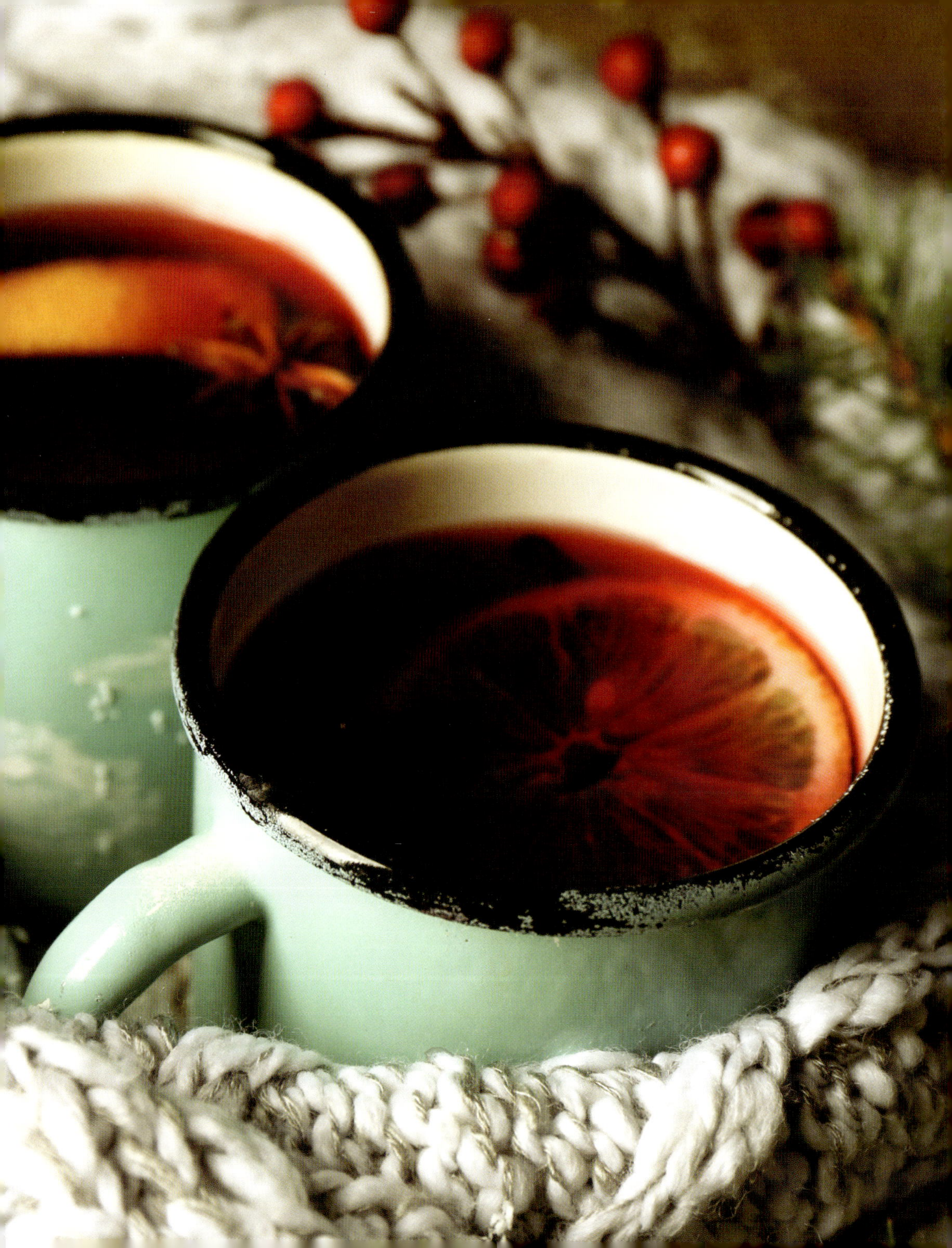

'TWAS THE NIGHTCAP BEFORE CHRISTMAS

1 (750 ml) bottle of bourbon

6 cups orange juice

2 cups fresh lemon juice

¼ oz. blood orange bitters

½ cup Simple Syrup (see page 20)

Maraschino cherries or orange wheels, for garnish

Place all of the ingredients, except for the maraschino cherries, in a large punch bowl, add large blocks of ice, and stir until chilled.

Serve over ice in mugs or Collins glasses and garnish with maraschino cherries or orange wheels.

DEAD AFTER THE GIFT RUSH

6 lemons

1 cup sugar

8 bags of chai tea

4 cups boiling water

1 cup bourbon

1 (12 oz.) bottle of ginger beer

Lemon wheels, for garnish

Cinnamon sticks, for garnish

Whole cloves, for garnish

Star anise pods, for garnish

Allspice berries, for garnish

Peel the lemons and set the fruit aside. Place the lemon peels and the sugar in a bowl, muddle, and let stand for 1 hour. Juice the lemons and strain to remove all pulp.

Place the tea bags in the boiling water and steep for 5 minutes. Remove the tea bags and discard. Add the sugar-and-lemon peel mixture to the tea and stir until the sugar has dissolved. Strain and discard the solids.

Add the bourbon and the lemon juice, stir to combine, and chill the punch in the refrigerator for 1 hour.

Add ginger beer and large blocks of ice just before serving. Gently stir to combine, serve over ice in rocks glasses, and garnish with lemon wheels, cinnamon sticks, cloves, star anise pods, and allspice berries.

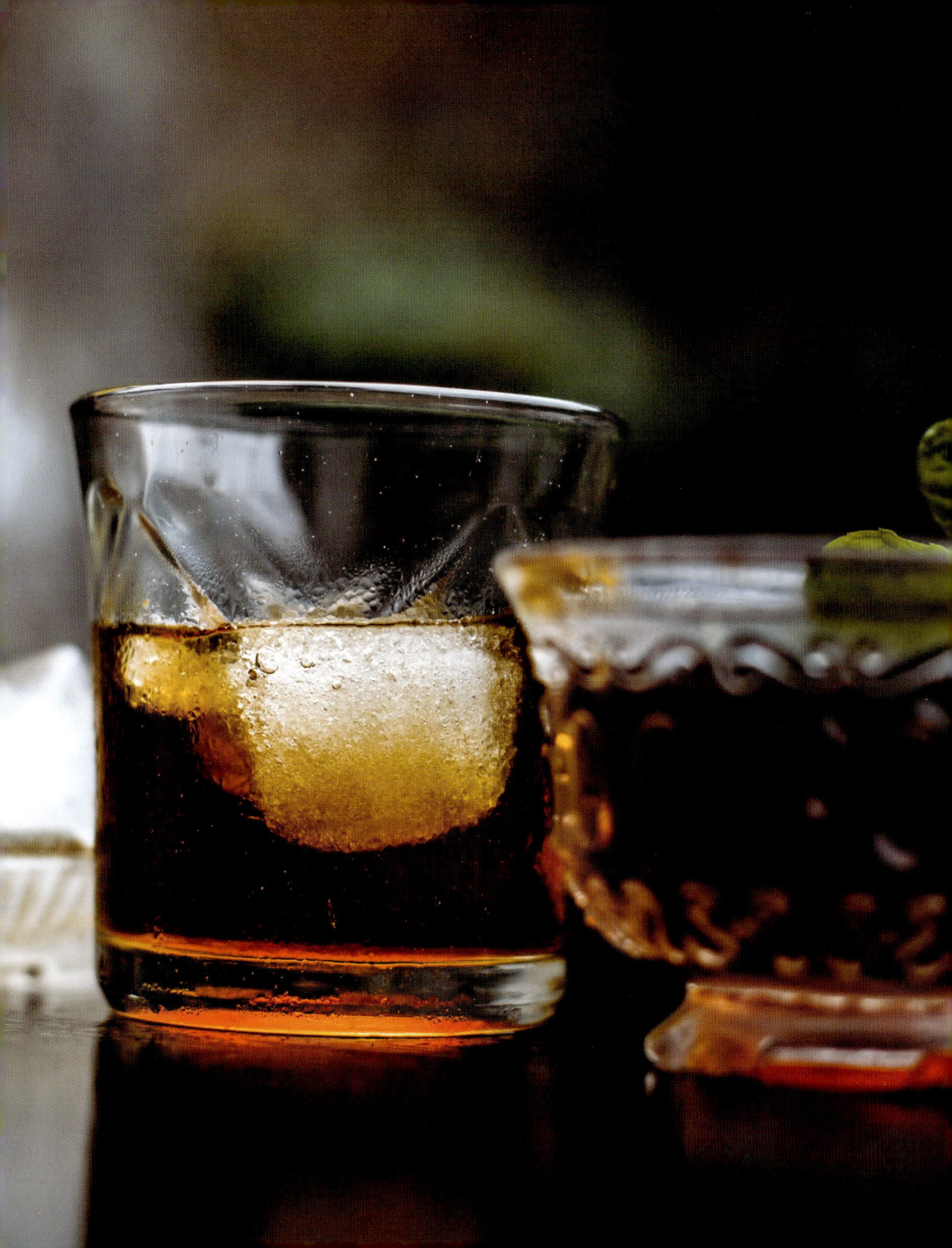

ROSEMARY SYRUP

Place 1 cup sugar and 1 cup water in a small saucepan and bring to a boil over medium heat, stirring to dissolve the sugar. Add 3 sprigs of fresh rosemary, remove the pan from heat, and let the syrup cool completely. Strain before using.

HAVE A PEAR-Y LITTLE CHRISTMAS

4 pears

2 cups fresh lemon juice

½ oz. Rosemary Syrup (see sidebar)

4 cups Scotch whisky

1½ cups Grand Marnier

Sprigs of fresh rosemary, torched, for garnish

Place the pears, lemon juice, and syrup in a mixing bowl and muddle.

Transfer the mixture to a large punch bowl, add large blocks of ice, the Scotch whisky, and Grand Marnier and stir to combine.

Serve over ice in wine glasses or rocks glasses and garnish with sprigs of torched rosemary.

IS IT TOO SOON TO FAKE AN EMERGENCY?

2 cups Domaine de Canton ginger liqueur

1½ cups bourbon

1½ cups Amontillado sherry

2 cups brewed black tea, cooled to room temperature

2 cups ginger beer

2 cups fresh lemon juice

1¼ cups Oleo Saccharum (see sidebar)

Place all of the ingredients in a large punch bowl, add blocks of ice, and stir until chilled.

Serve over ice in Collins glasses.

OLEO SACCHARUM

Place the peels of 8 lemons and 2 oranges and 2½ cups sugar in a large bowl and toss to combine. Using some serious elbow grease, use a muddler or the back of a heavy wooden spoon to mash the peels until they express all of their oil. Let the mixture macerate for 30 minutes to 1 hour. Strain the liquid and discard the peels.

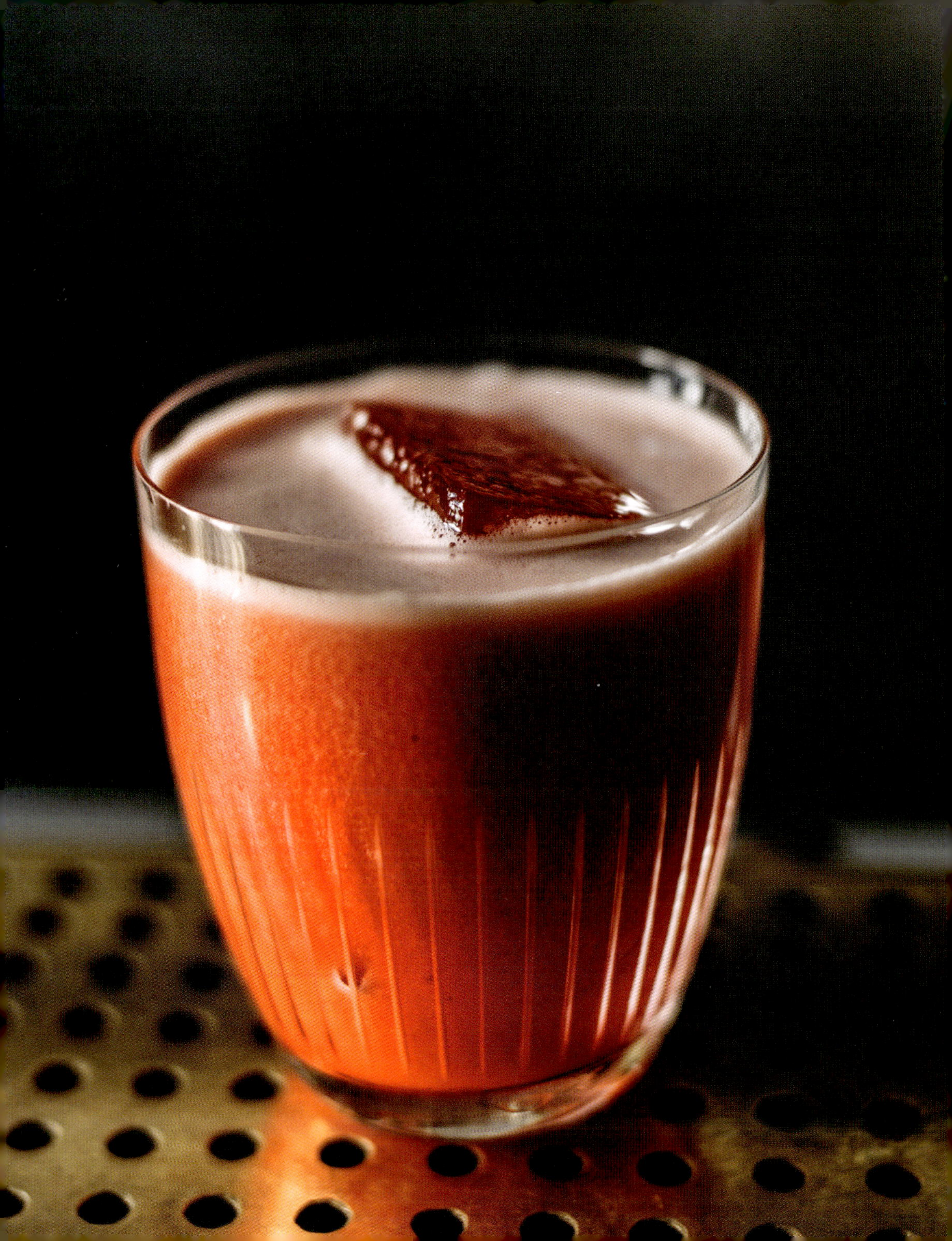

BLITZ THE HALLS

3 cups gin

1½ cups Lillet Rosé

1 cup orange liqueur

2 cups fresh grapefruit juice

½ cup fresh lime juice

Grapefruit twists, for garnish

Place all of the ingredients, except for the grapefruit twists, in a large punch bowl, add large blocks of ice, and stir until chilled.

Serve in coupes or over ice in rocks glasses and garnish with the grapefruit twists.

BABY, IT'S WAY TOO COLD OUTSIDE

2 cups absinthe

1 cup Herbsaint

1 cup white crème de menthe

2 cups heavy cream

¼ oz. Simple Syrup (see page 20)

Dash of orange blossom water

1 egg white

Fresh mint, for garnish

Place all of the ingredients, except for the mint, in a blender and puree until combined.

Place the mixture in a large punch bowl, add large blocks of ice, and stir until chilled.

Serve in coupes or over ice in rocks glasses and garnish with fresh mint.

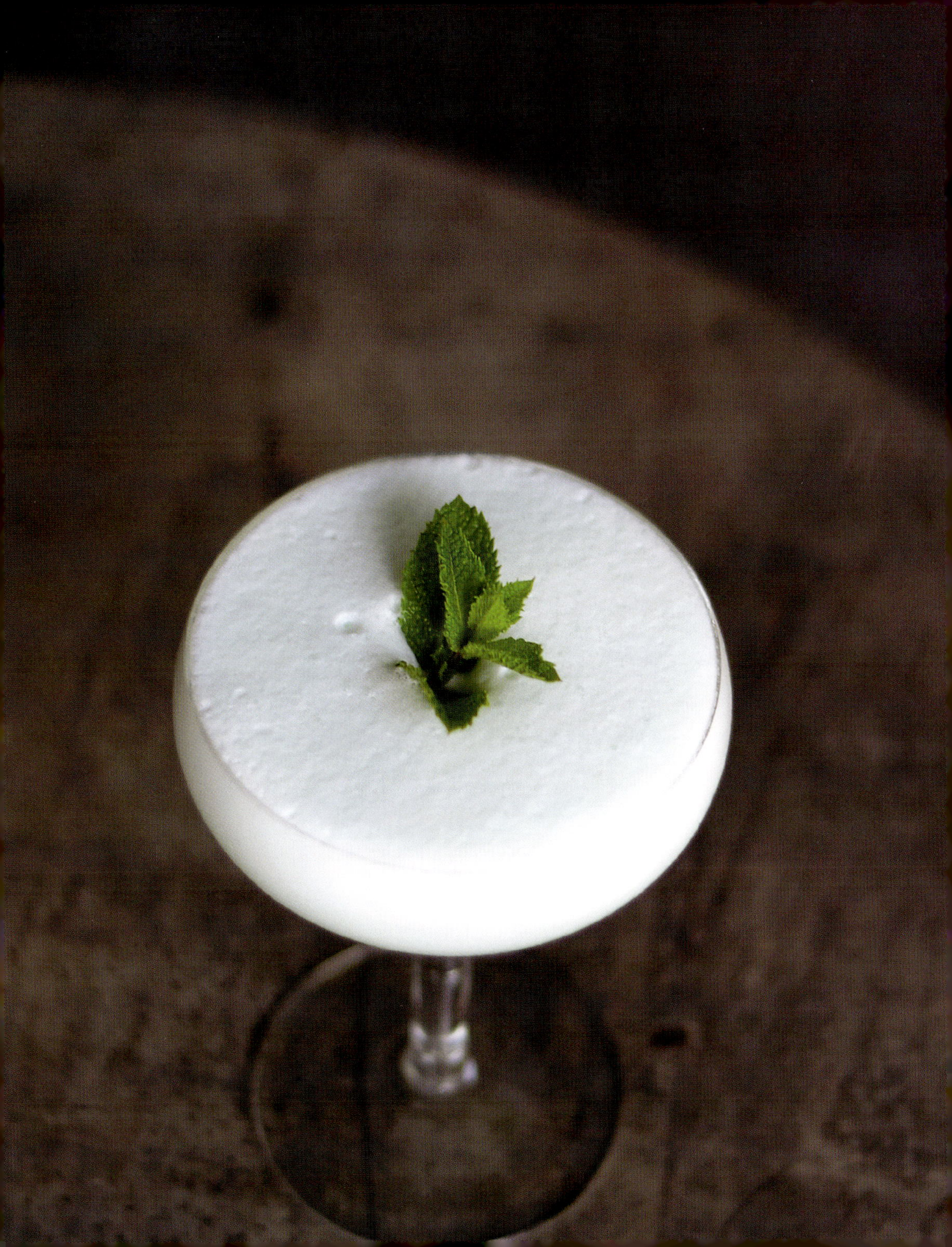

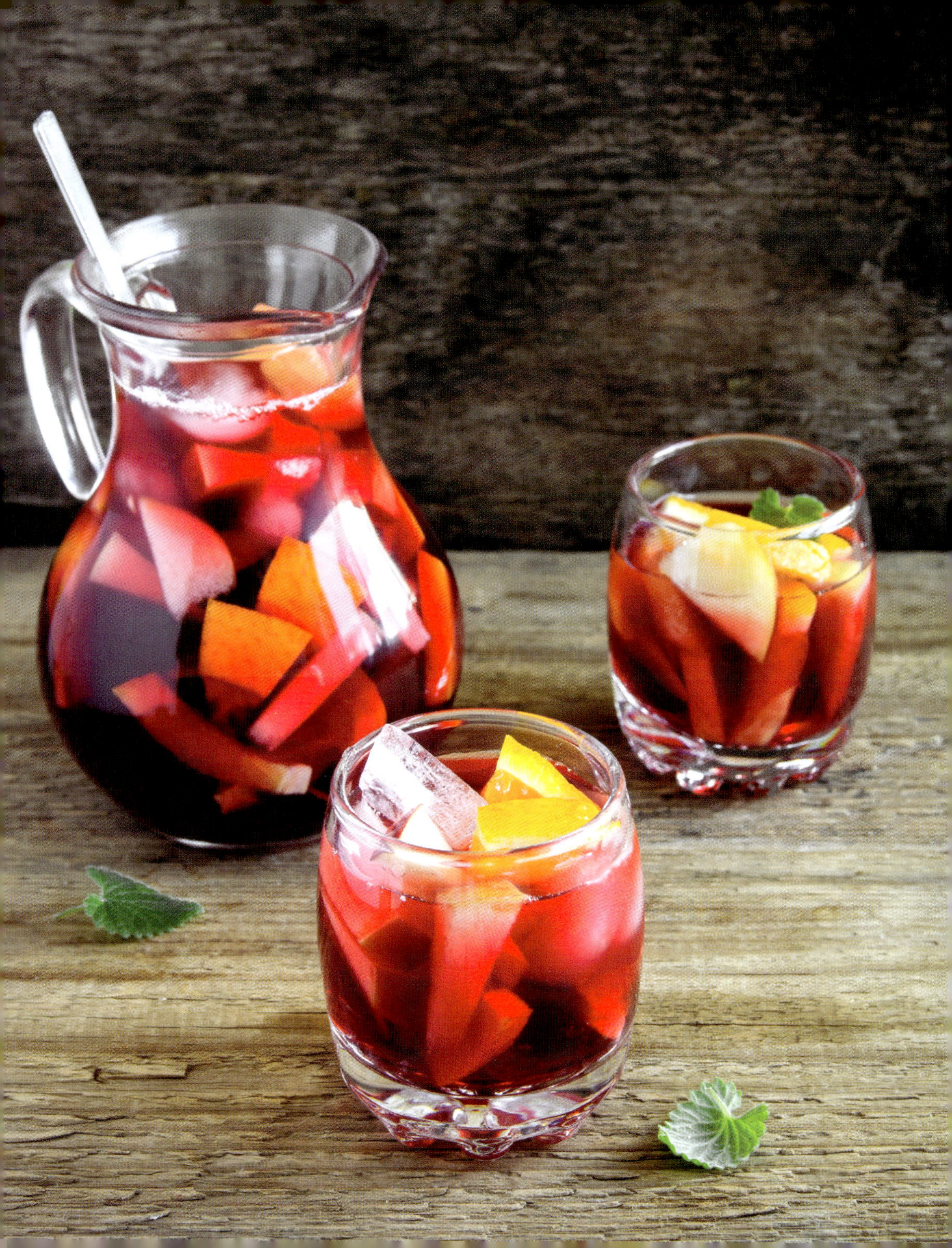

JINGLE JUICE SANGRIA

2 (750 ml) bottles of red wine

1½ cups brandy

½ cup Simple Syrup (see page 20)

1 cup orange juice

2 apples, cored, seeded, and diced

2 oranges, peeled and sliced thin

5 lemon wheels

5 lime wheels

Place all of the ingredients into a large, airtight container and seal.

Refrigerate for 24 hours to allow the flavors to combine and pour the sangria into a punch bowl when ready to serve.

WHY'D YOU GIVE ME A PATRIDGE IN A PEAR TREE?

2 (750 ml) bottles of dry red wine

4 pears, cored, seeded, and diced

3 cups seedless grapes, frozen

3 cups orange juice

1 (12 oz.) can of cream soda

Place all of the ingredients, except for the soda, in a large pitcher or punch bowl. Cover and refrigerate for 4 or more hours.

When ready to serve, add large blocks of ice and the soda and gently stir. Serve in wine glasses or champagne flutes.

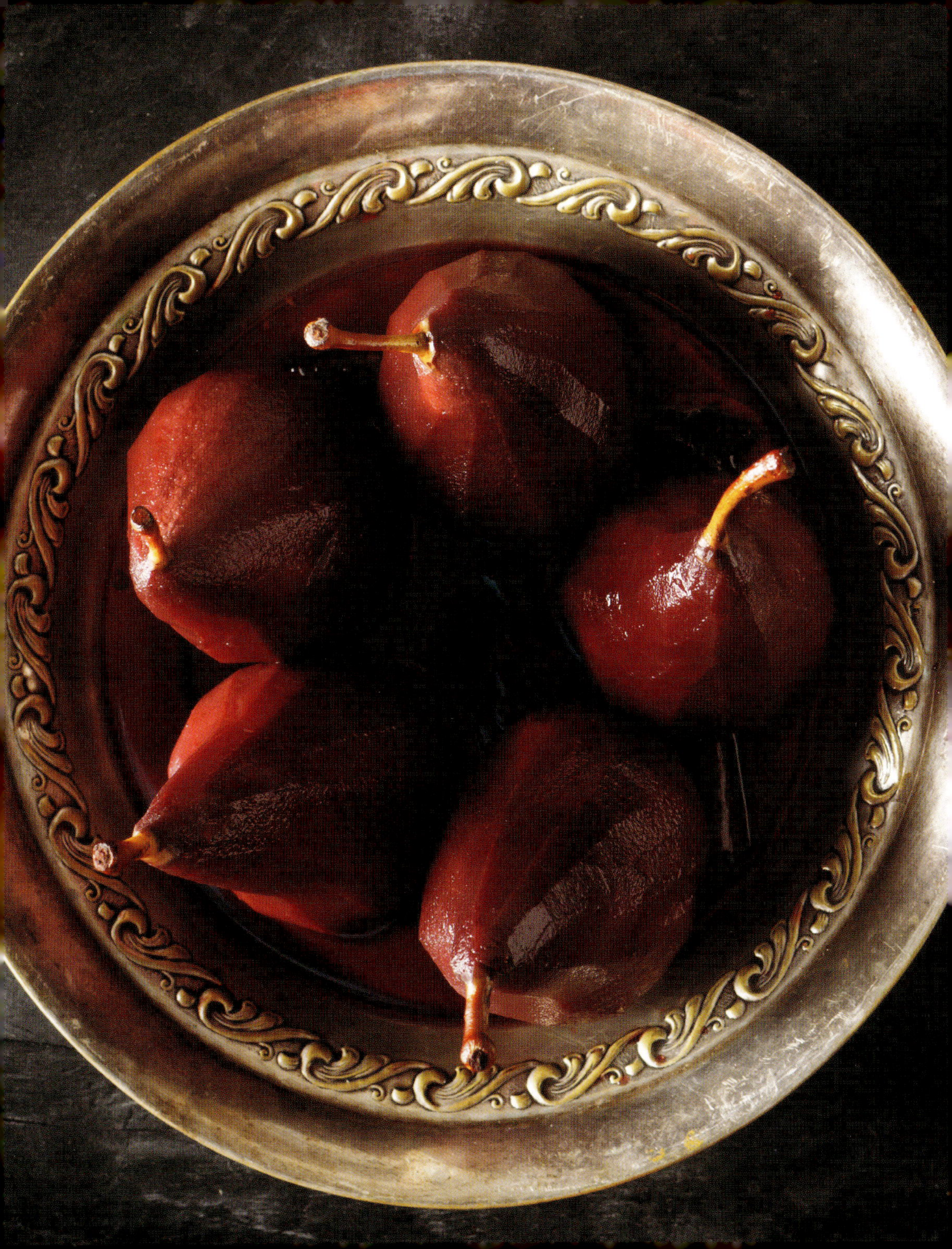

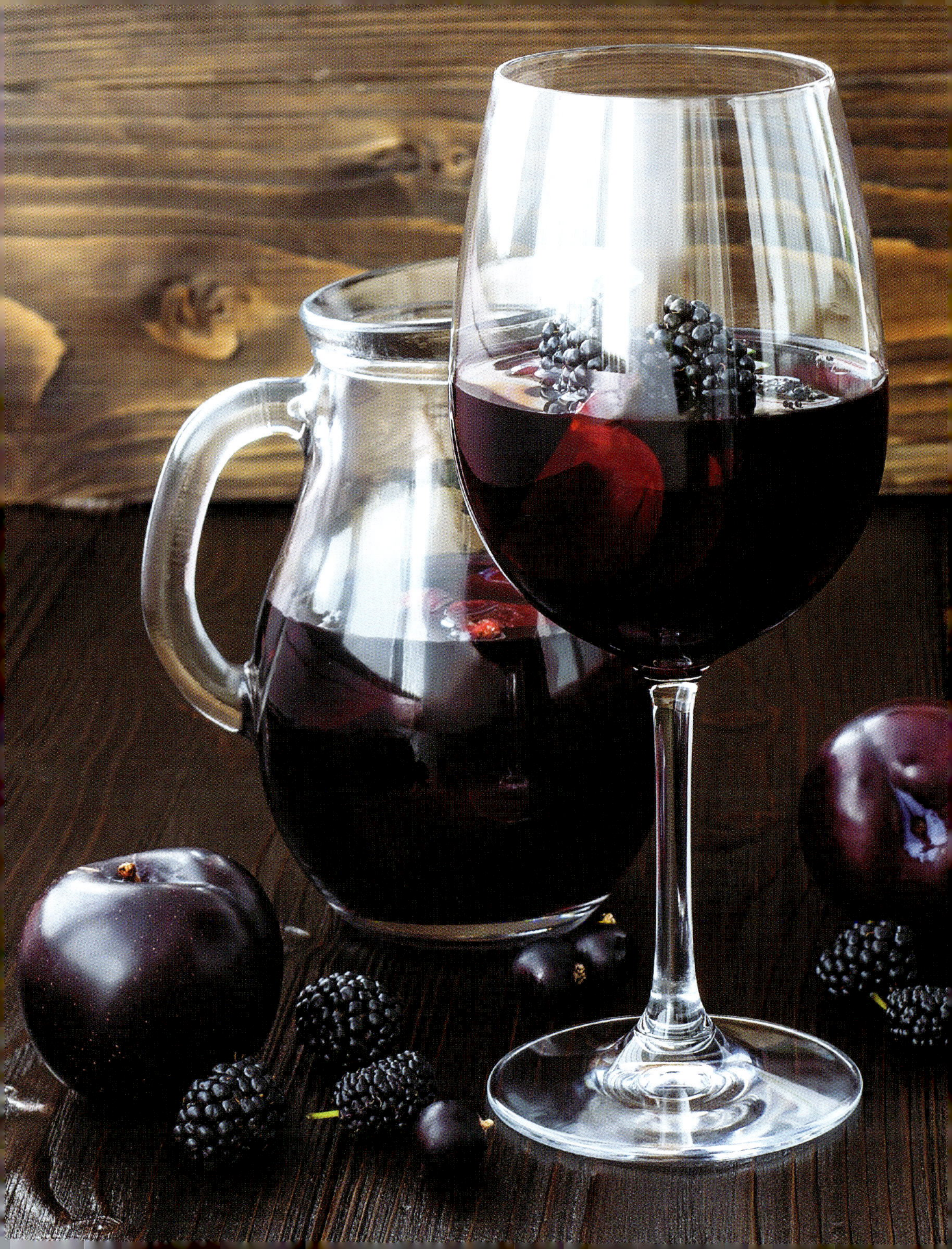

MORE CHEER? PASS THE WINE

2 (750 ml) bottles of dry red wine

2 plums, pitted, sliced thin, and frozen

1 cup cherries, pitted and halved

1 cup blackberries

½ cup Grand Marnier

4 cups seltzer water

Place all of the ingredients, except for the seltzer water, in a large pitcher or punch bowl. Cover and refrigerate for 4 or more hours.

When ready to serve, add large blocks of ice and the seltzer and gently stir to combine. Serve in wine glasses or champagne flutes.

YULE BE FINE (EVENTUALLY)

2 (750 ml) bottles of dry red wine

4 apples, cored, seeded, and diced

2 oranges, sliced thin

½ cup quality apple vodka

2 cups apple cider

Dash of cinnamon

Pomegranate seeds, for garnish

Place all of the ingredients, except for the pomegranate seeds, in a large pitcher or punch bowl. Cover and refrigerate for 4 or more hours.

Serve over ice in wine glasses and garnish with the pomegranate seeds.

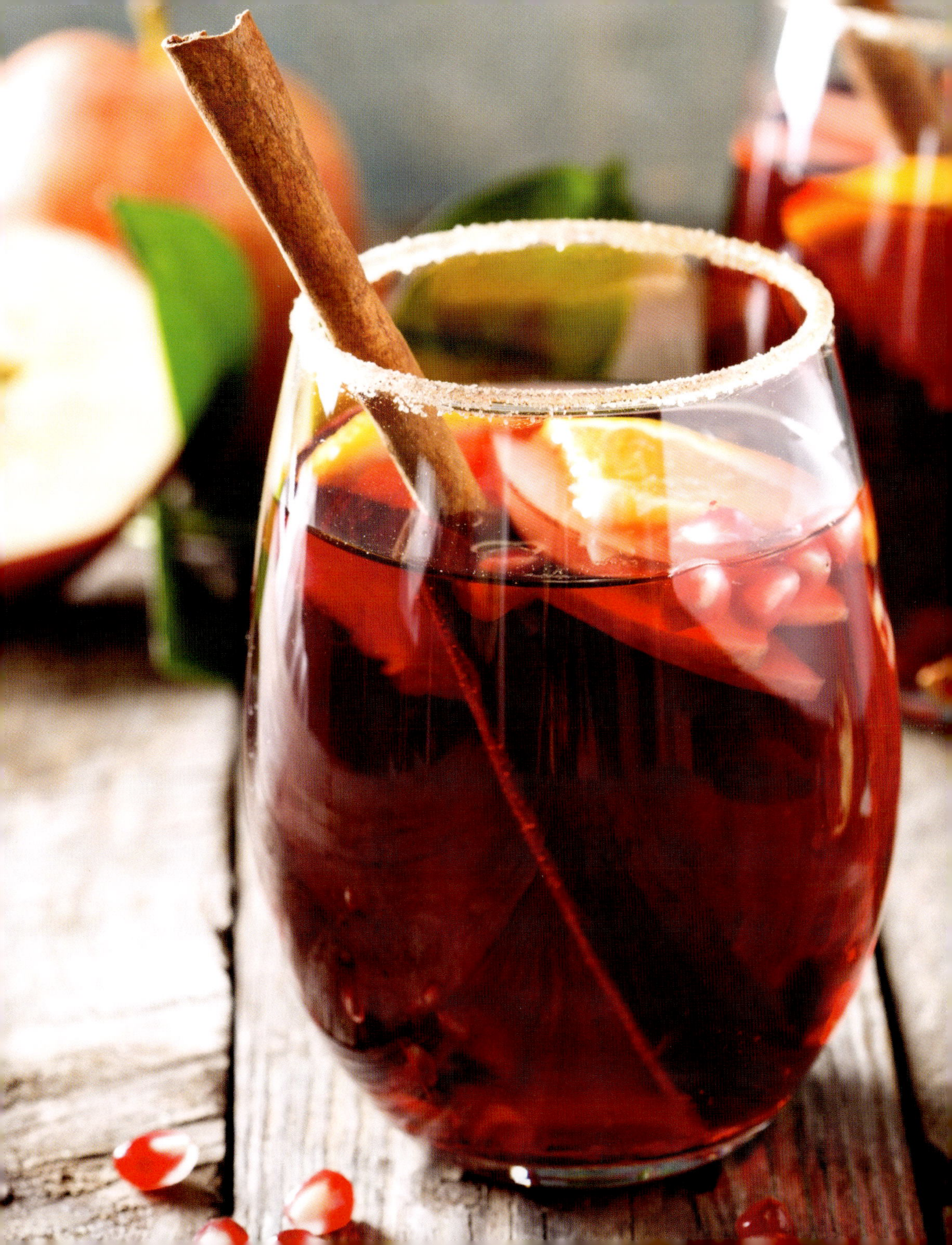

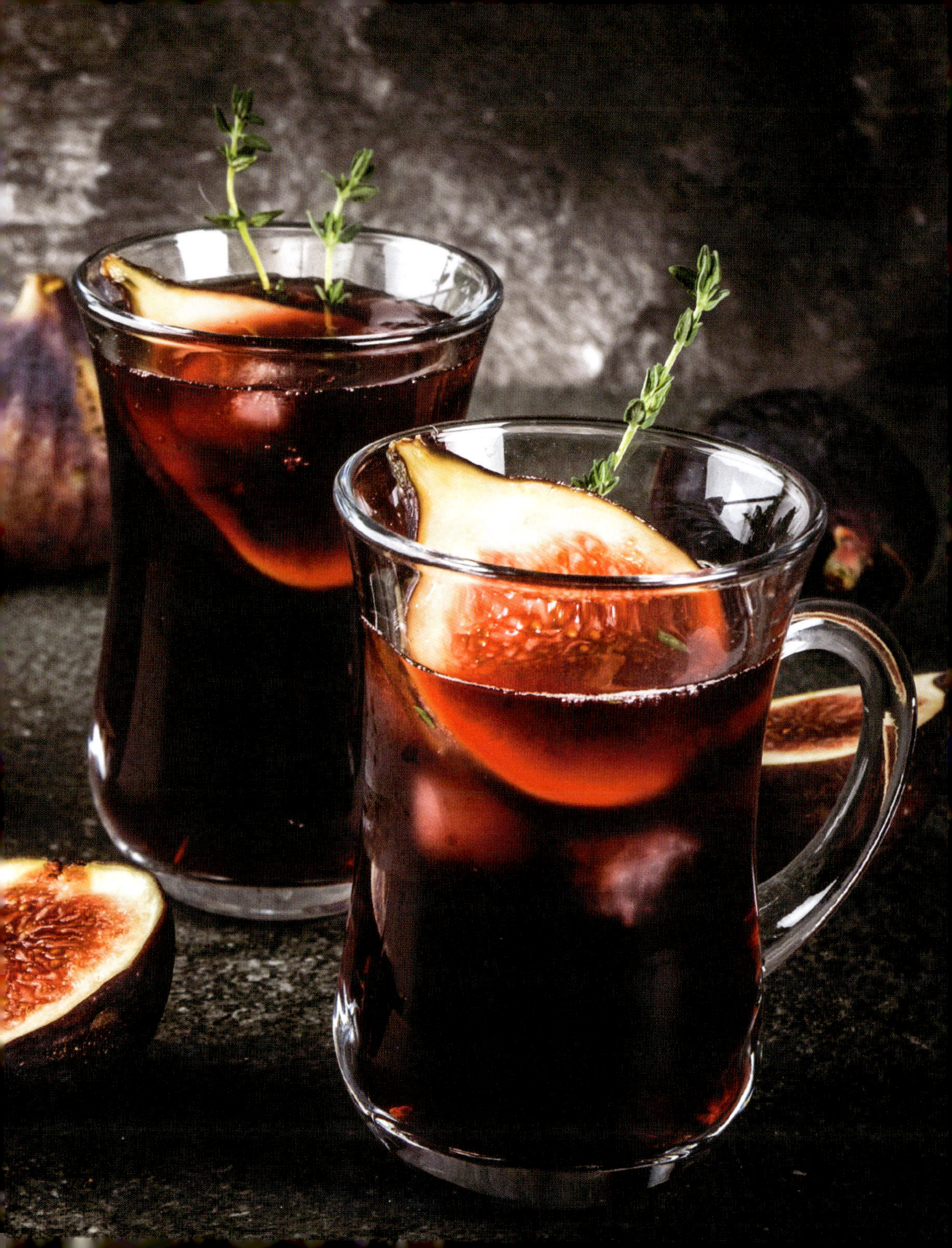

DON'T MAKE ME EAT FIGGY PUDDING

2 (750 ml) bottles of dry red wine

2 cups fresh raspberries

6 figs, diced and frozen

2 cups fig juice

1 cup pomegranate juice

2 cups seltzer water

Sprigs of fresh thyme, for garnish

Place all of the ingredients, except for the seltzer and thyme, in a large pitcher or punch bowl. Cover and refrigerate for 4 or more hours.

When ready to serve, add the seltzer water and gently stir. Serve over ice and garnish each with a sprig of thyme.

SLEIGH MY SANITY

2 (750 ml) bottles of dry white wine

2 cups seedless red grapes, halved and frozen

4 plums, pitted, diced, and frozen

¾ cup Ginger Syrup (see sidebar)

2 cups seltzer water

Place all of the ingredients, except for the seltzer water, in a large pitcher or punch bowl. Cover and refrigerate for 4 or more hours.

When ready to serve, add the seltzer and gently stir. Serve over ice in wine glasses.

GINGER SYRUP

Place 1 cup sugar and 1 cup water in a saucepan and bring to a boil, stirring to dissolve the sugar. Remove the pan from heat, stir in ¼ cup of peeled and thinly sliced fresh ginger, and let the mixture steep for 2 hours. Strain before using.

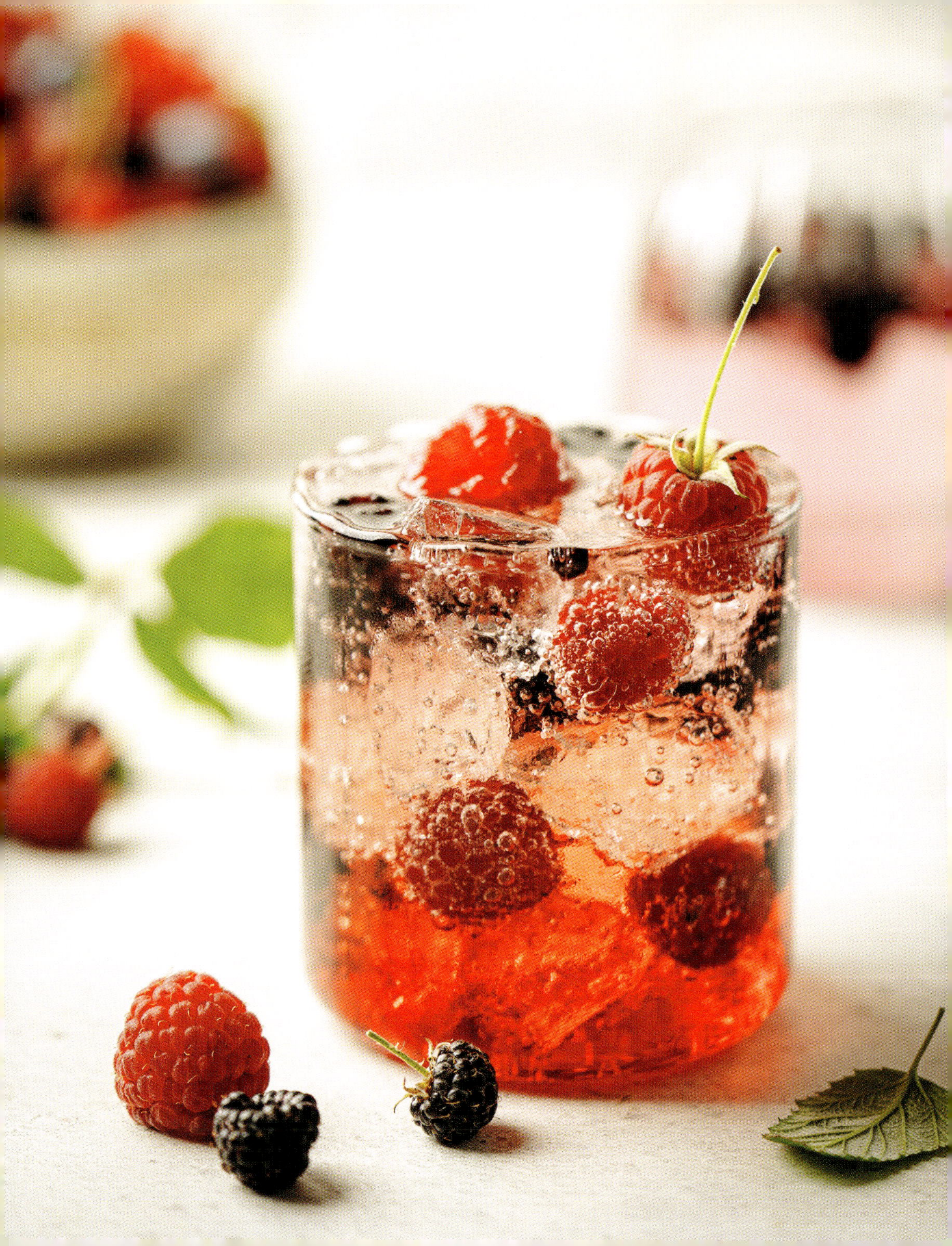

SCROOGE-APPROVED SPARKLE

1 cup fresh lemon juice

½ cup gin

24 blackberries

12 raspberries

2 (750 ml) bottles of sparkling wine, very cold

Place the lemon juice and gin in a pitcher and stir to combine.

Divide this mixture and the berries between rocks glasses or champagne flutes and top with the sparkling wine.

APRÈS THIS, I'M DONE

4 cups frozen raspberries

2 cups frozen blueberries

1 cup Lavender Syrup (see sidebar)

2 (750 ml) bottles of white wine, very cold

Fresh mint, for garnish

Place the raspberries, blueberries, and syrup in a large pitcher or punch bowl, stir to combine, cover, and refrigerate for 1 hour.

Divide the mixture between wine glasses or champagne flutes and top with the wine. Garnish with fresh mint.

LAVENDER SYRUP

Place 1 cup water and 1 cup sugar in a saucepan and bring to a boil, stirring to dissolve the sugar. Stir in 2 tablespoons of dried lavender, remove the pan from heat, and let the syrup cool. Strain before using.

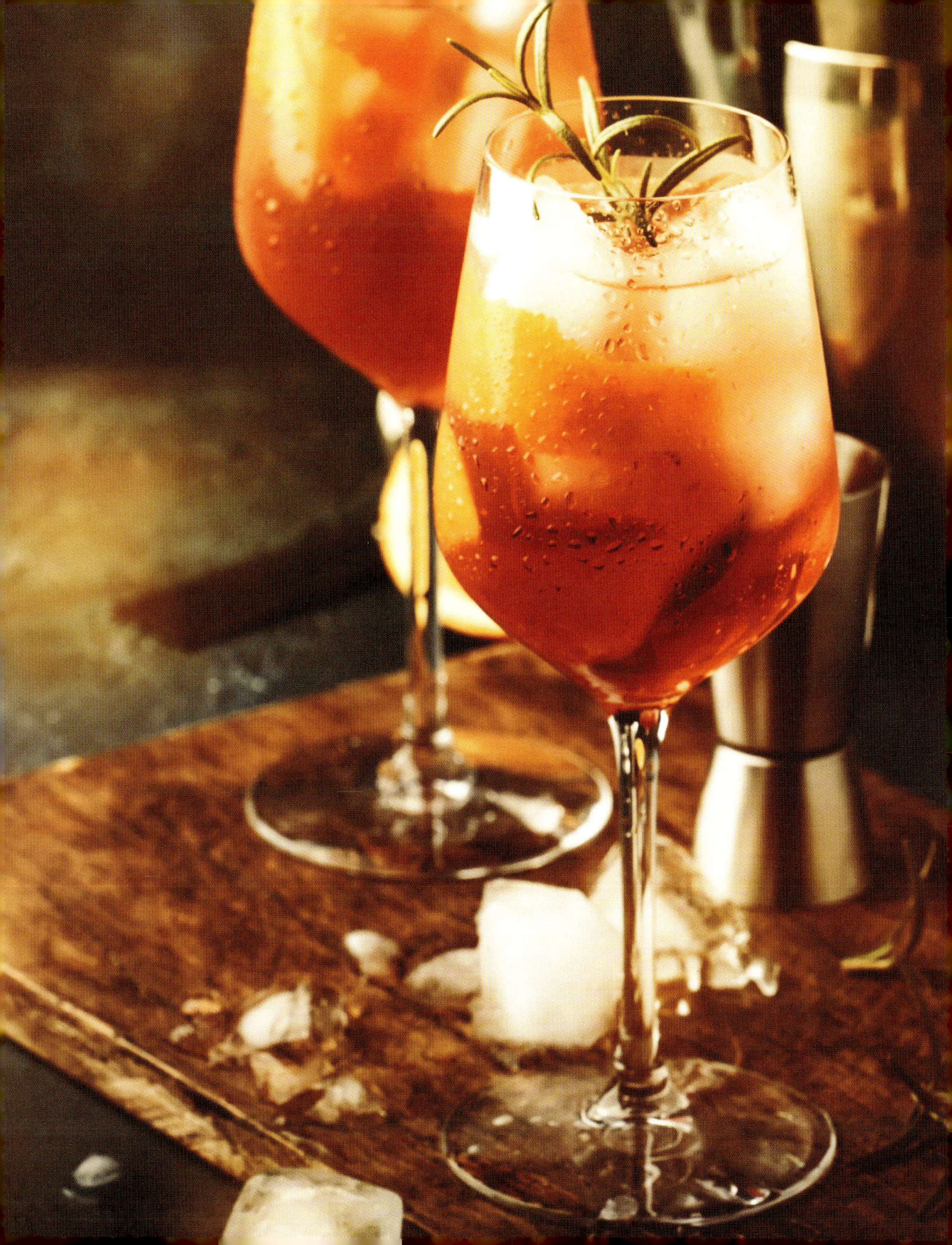

BAH HUMBUG

2 navel oranges, sliced thin

¼ cup fresh lemon juice

½ cup Grand Marnier

12 raspberries

2 (750 ml) bottles of sparkling wine, very cold

Reserve six slices of orange and place the rest in a bowl.

Add the lemon juice and Grand Marnier, stir to combine, cover, and refrigerate for 1 hour.

Divide this mixture, the reserved orange slices, and the raspberries between wine glasses or champagne flutes and top with the sparkling wine.

PEAKED LAST CHRISTMAS

4½ cups whole milk

1½ cups half-and-half

3 cups brandy

1½ cups Simple Syrup (see page 20)

2 tablespoons pure vanilla extract

Freshly grated nutmeg, for garnish

Place all of the ingredients, except for the nutmeg, in a punch bowl, add large blocks of ice, and stir until chilled.

Garnish with the nutmeg and serve over ice in Nick & Nora glasses or coupes.

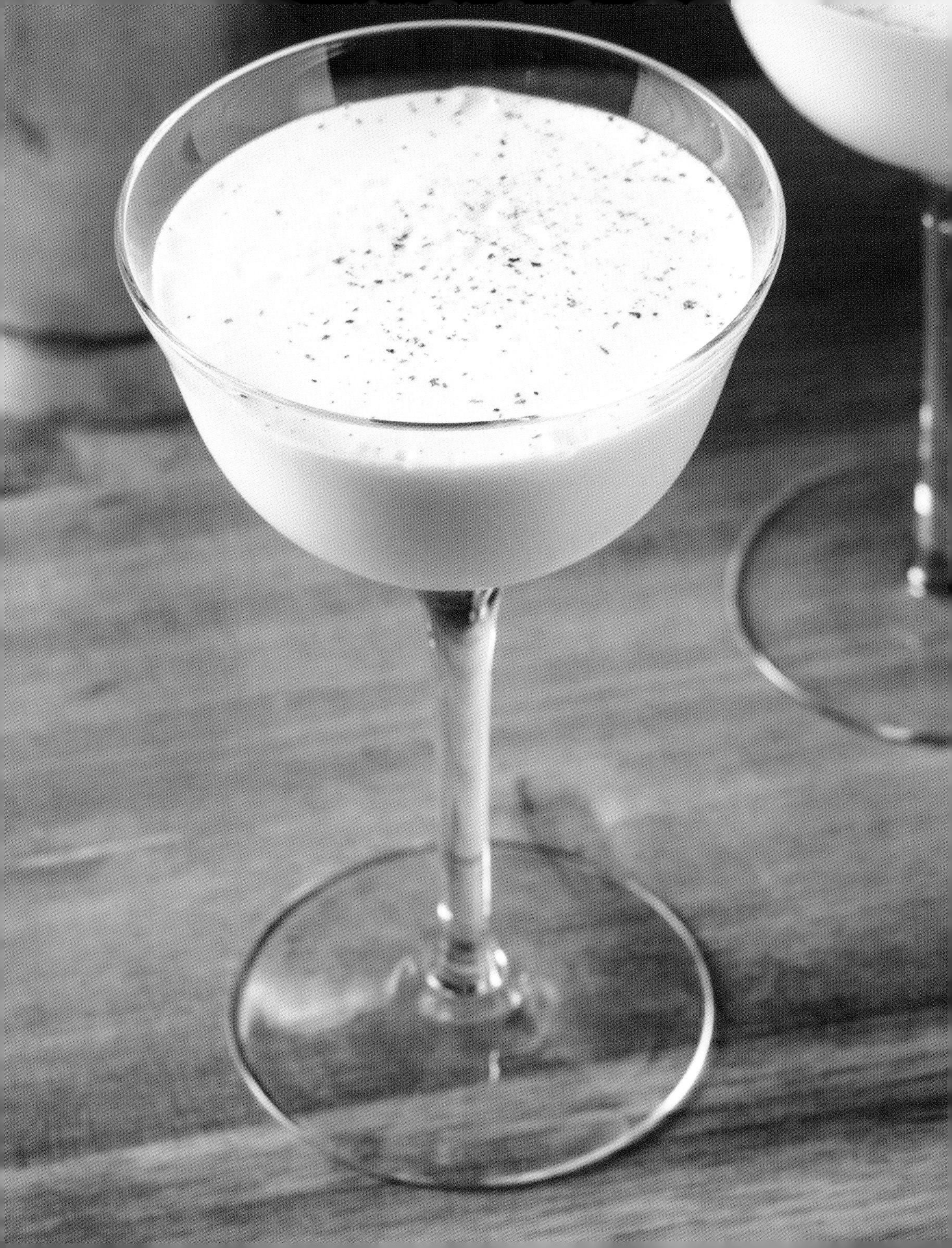

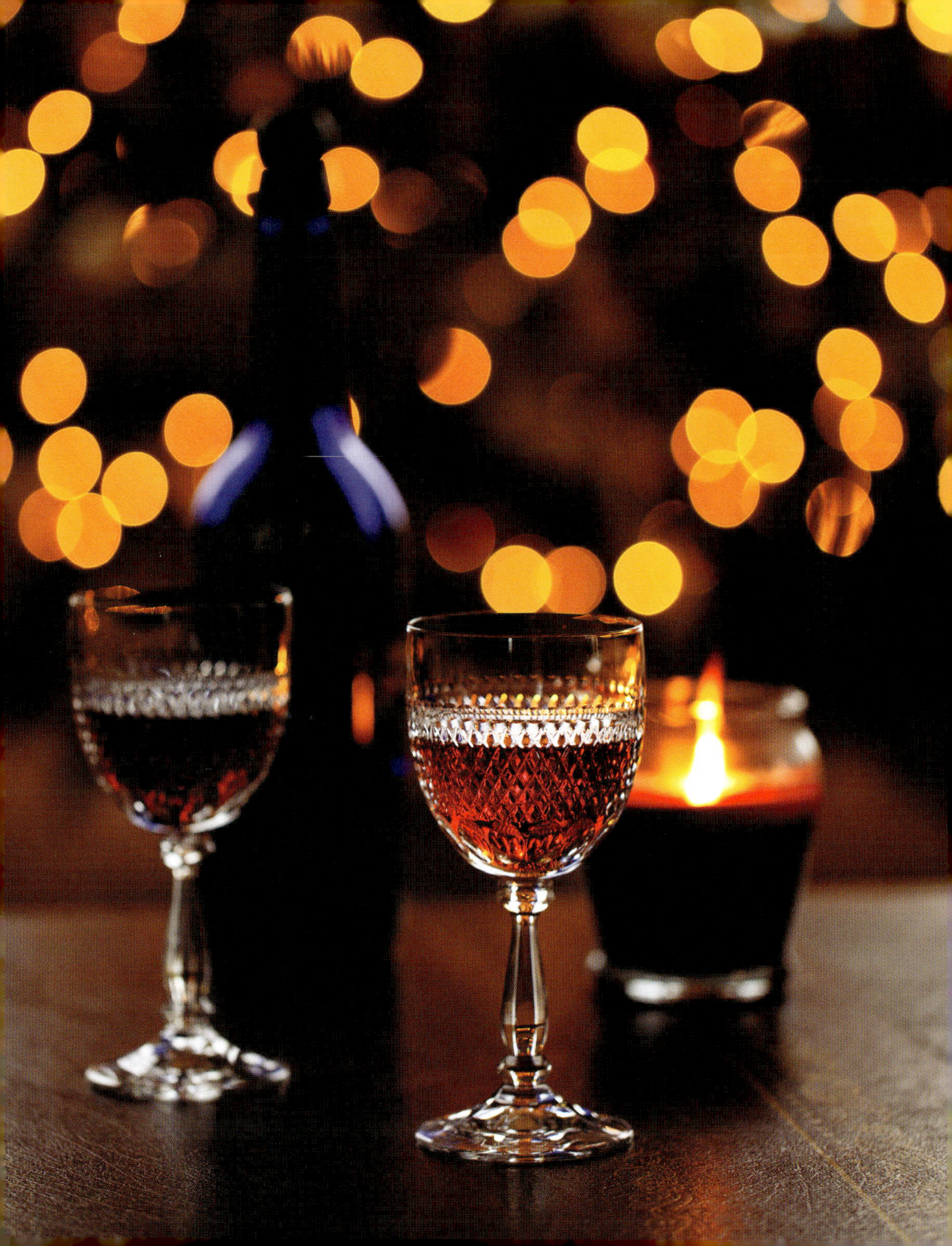

NIPPING AT YOUR NOSE

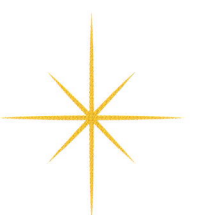

3 cups fresh lemon juice

2 cups Cognac

1 cup Simple Syrup (see page 20)

¼ cup orange liqueur

3 cups Port wine

Lemon wedges, for garnish

Place the lemon juice, Cognac, simple syrup, orange liqueur, and Port in a punch bowl, add large blocks of ice, and stir until chilled.

Serve in coupes or over ice in Collins glasses and garnish with lemon wedges.

How to Survive Holiday Gatherings 101

BLITZEN'S BACKUP PLAN

3 cups applejack

1½ cups Bénédictine

2 oz. Dolin Blanc

2 cups apple juice

1 cup club soda

Place the applejack, Bénédictine, Dolin Blanc, apple juice, and club soda in a large punch bowl, add large blocks of ice, and stir until chilled.

Add the club soda, gently stir, and serve over ice in Collins glasses or mugs.

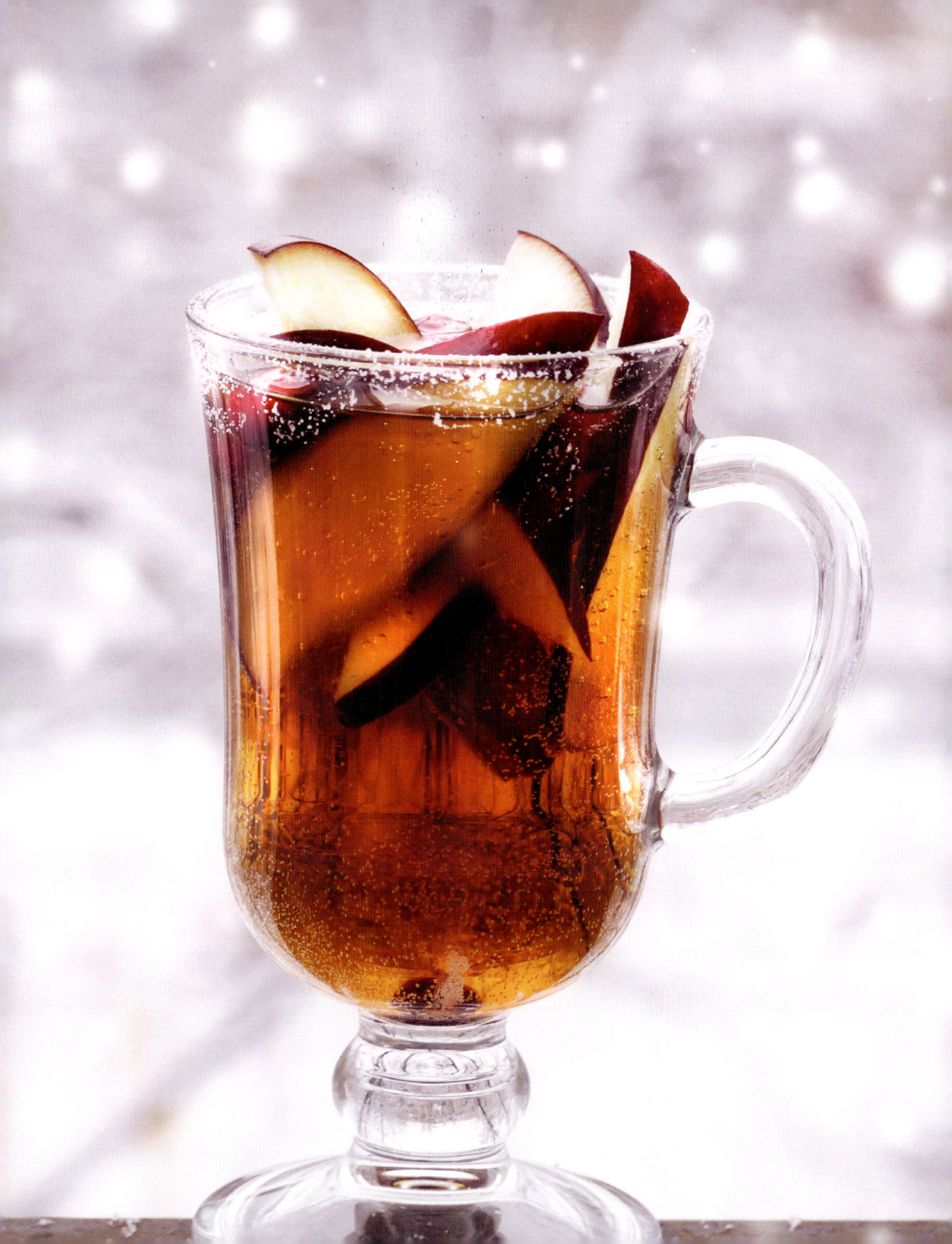

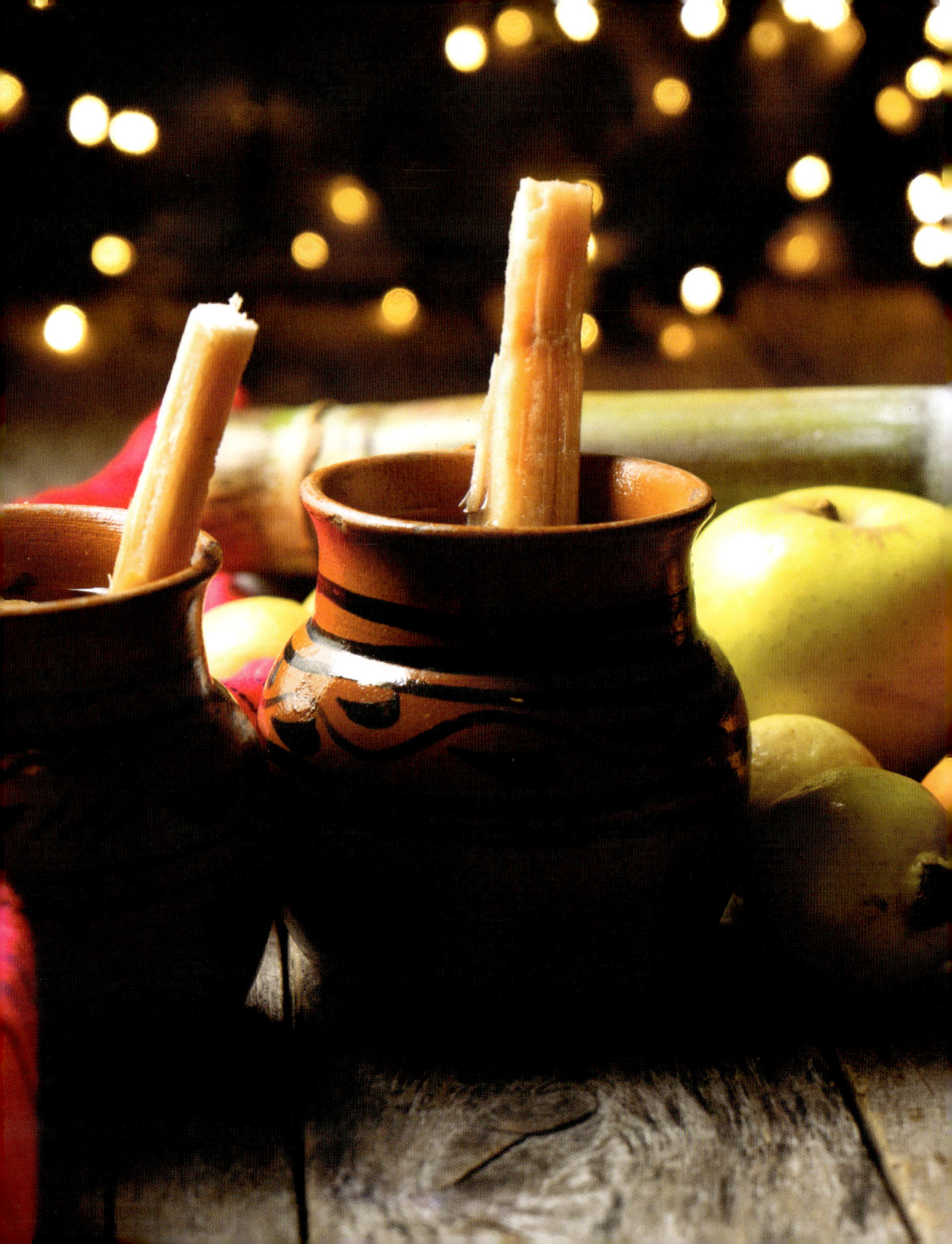

SPICE SPICE BABY

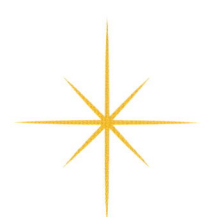

3 cups spiced rum

½ cup apple schnapps

1½ cups cinnamon schnapps

1 cup lemon-lime seltzer

Fresh mint, for garnish

Place the rum and schnapps in a large punch bowl, add large blocks of ice, and stir until chilled.

Add the seltzer and stir gently to combine.

Serve over ice in rocks glasses and garnish with fresh mint.

ALL FROST, NO CHILL

3 cups Absolut Citron

1½ cups triple sec

1½ cups white cranberry juice

½ cup fresh lime juice

1½ cups lemon-lime seltzer

Fresh mint or rosemary, for garnish

Lime wedge, for garnish

Place the vodka, triple sec, and white cranberry juice in a large punch bowl, add large blocks of ice, and stir until chilled.

Add the seltzer and stir gently to combine.

Serve over ice in rocks glasses and garnish with fresh mint, rosemary, or lime.

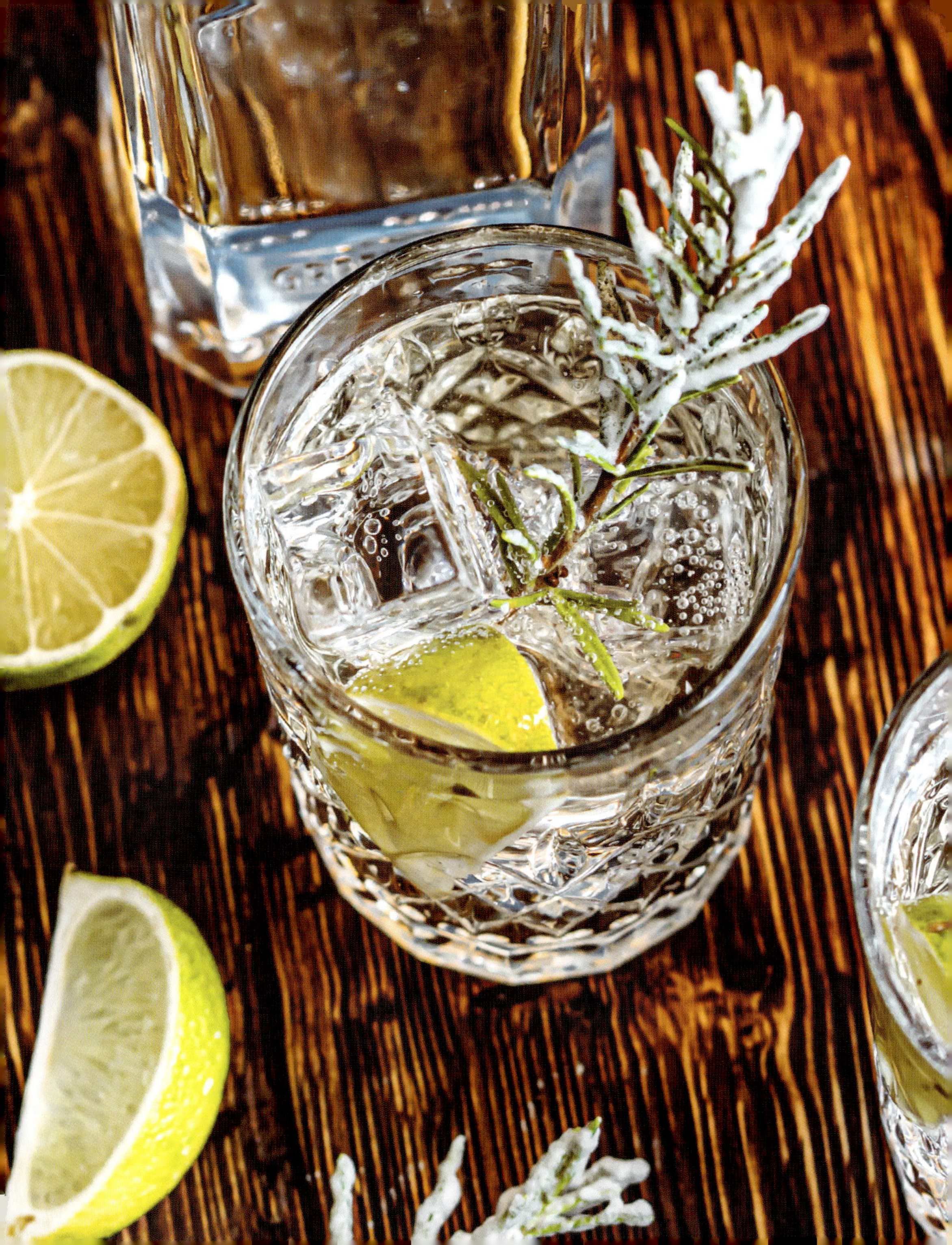

SPICED SYRUP

In a small saucepan, combine 1 cup water, 1 cup pomegranate juice, 3 cinnamon sticks, 5 whole cloves, 5 allspice berries, and 3 cardamom pods. Cook over low heat, stirring frequently, until the sugar has dissolved. Remove from heat, let the syrup cool, and strain before using.

HONK IF YOU'RE LIT

6 cups pear cider

1 (375 ml) bottle of brandy

¾ cup aged rum

2 (12 oz.) bottles of spicy ginger beer

⅓ cup Spiced Syrup (see sidebar)

2 dashes of Peychaud's Bitters

Pear slices, for garnish

Lemon wheels, for garnish

Place all of the ingredients, except for the garnishes, in a large punch bowl, add large blocks of ice, and stir until chilled.

Serve over ice in rocks glasses and garnish with the pear slices and lemon wheels.

ESPRESSO YOURSELF (OR DON'T, I DON'T CARE)

2½ oz. Simple Syrup (see page 20)

2 cups Scotch whisky

1 cup Kahlúa

4 cups milk

2 cups half-and-half

3 tablespoons instant coffee

6 eggs

2 cups ice

Cinnamon, for garnish

Place all of the ingredients, except for the cinnamon, in a large mixing bowl and stir to combine.

Working in batches, add the mixture to a blender and puree until smooth.

Serve over ice in rocks glasses and garnish each drink with cinnamon.

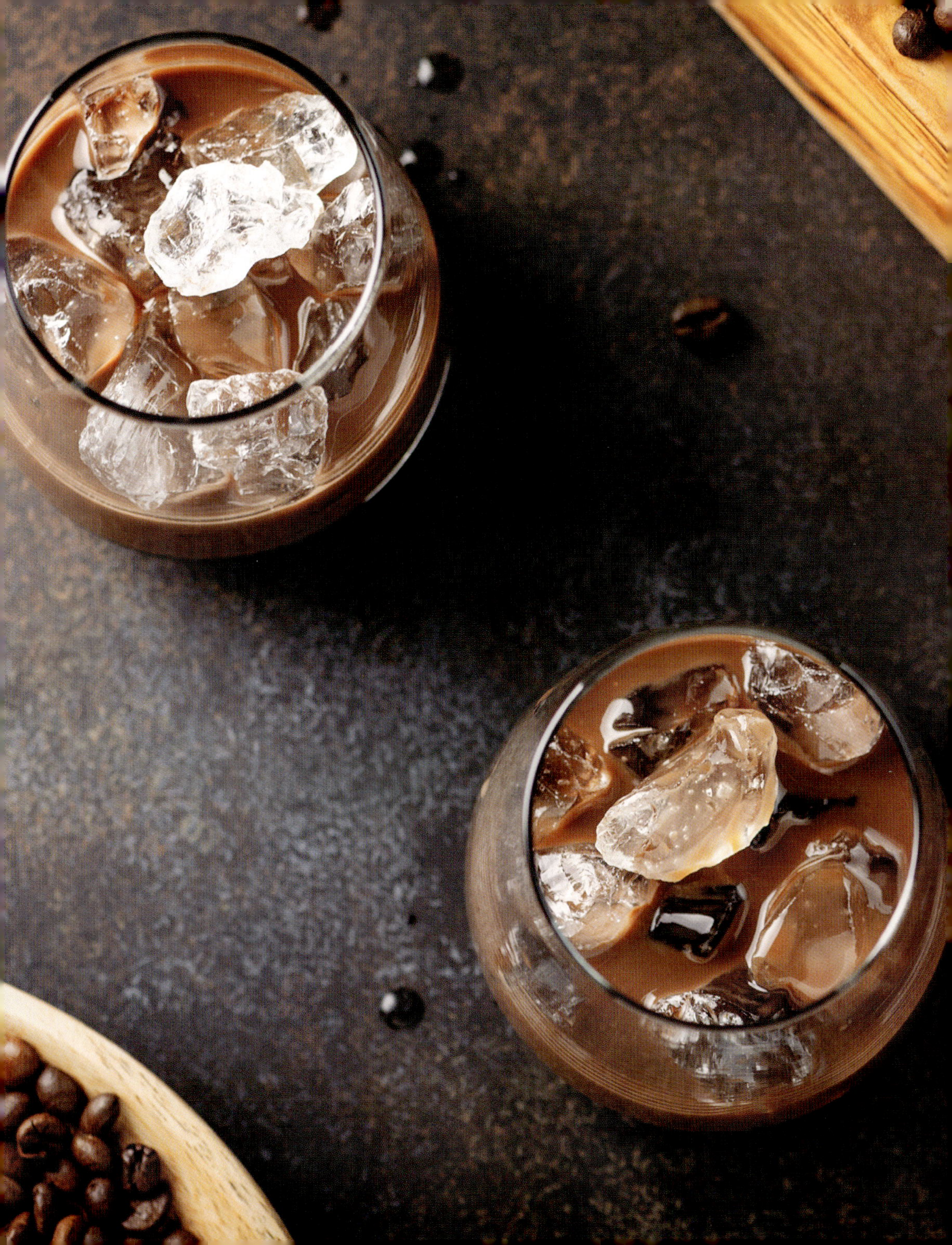

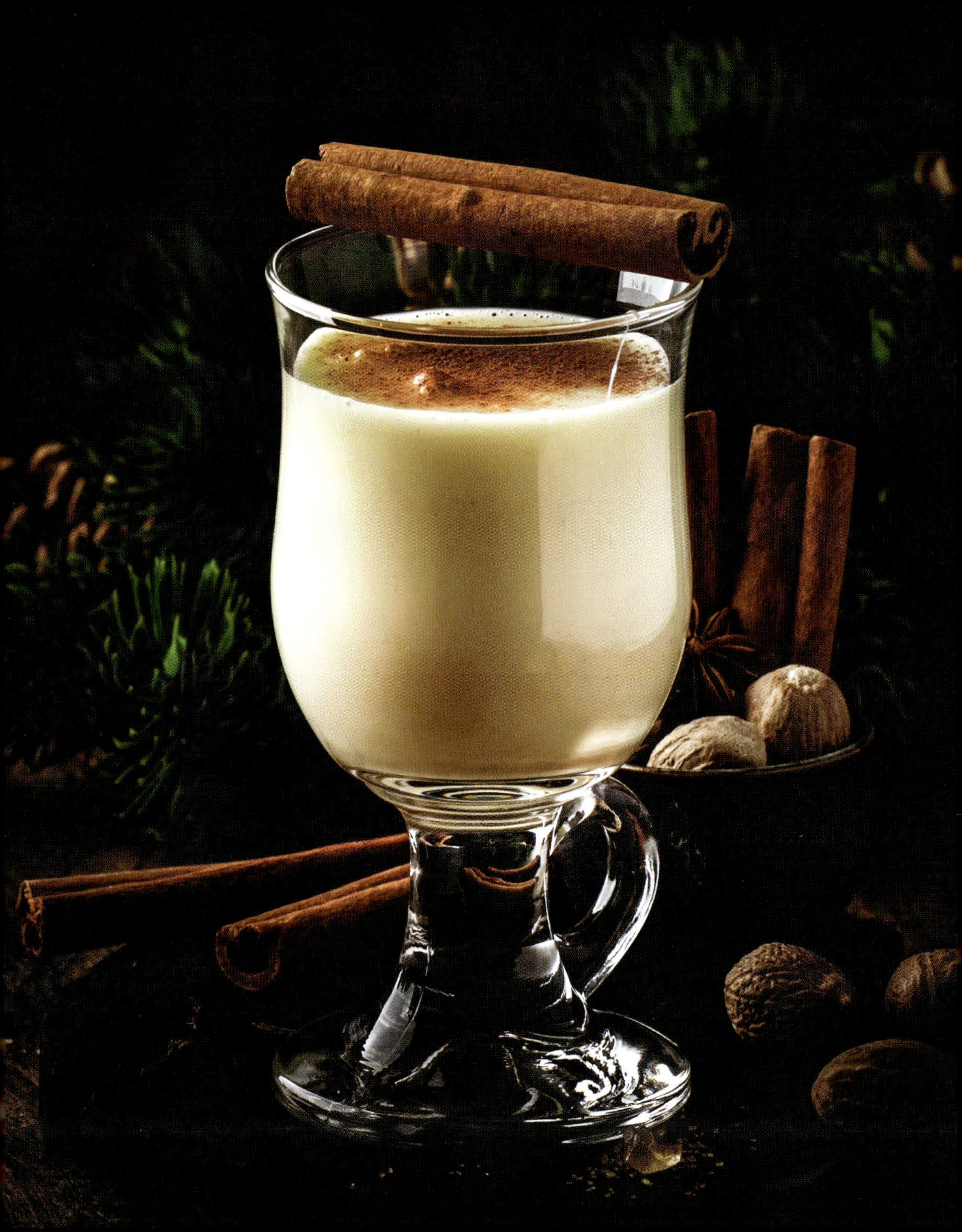

NOG YOURSELF OUT

12 eggs, yolks and whites separated

2 cups caster sugar

2 cups Cognac

1 cup dark rum

1 cup Madeira

6 cups milk

2 cups heavy cream

Freshly grated nutmeg, for garnish

Place the egg yolks and sugar in a bowl and beat until the mixture is pale and thick.

Stir in the Cognac, rum, Madeira, milk, and cream. Refrigerate until thoroughly chilled.

When ready to serve, beat the egg whites until they hold stiff peaks. Transfer the chilled base to a large, chilled punch bowl and then fold in the beaten egg whites. Do not stir.

Serve in cocktail glasses or rocks glasses and garnish with nutmeg.

POUR SOME MULLING ON ME

2 (750 ml) bottles of red wine

2 star anise pods

2-inch piece of fresh ginger

5 whole cloves

3 cardamom pods

2 tablespoons orange zest

2 tablespoons lemon zest

¾ cup honey

¾ cup Cognac

Cinnamon sticks, for garnish

Orange slices, for garnish

Place all of the ingredients, except for the Cognac and garnishes, in a saucepan and bring to a simmer over medium heat.

Remove from heat and stir in the Cognac.

Pour into warmed mugs and garnish with cinnamon sticks and orange slices.

If you'd prefer something other than Cognac, Calvados is a solid alternative.

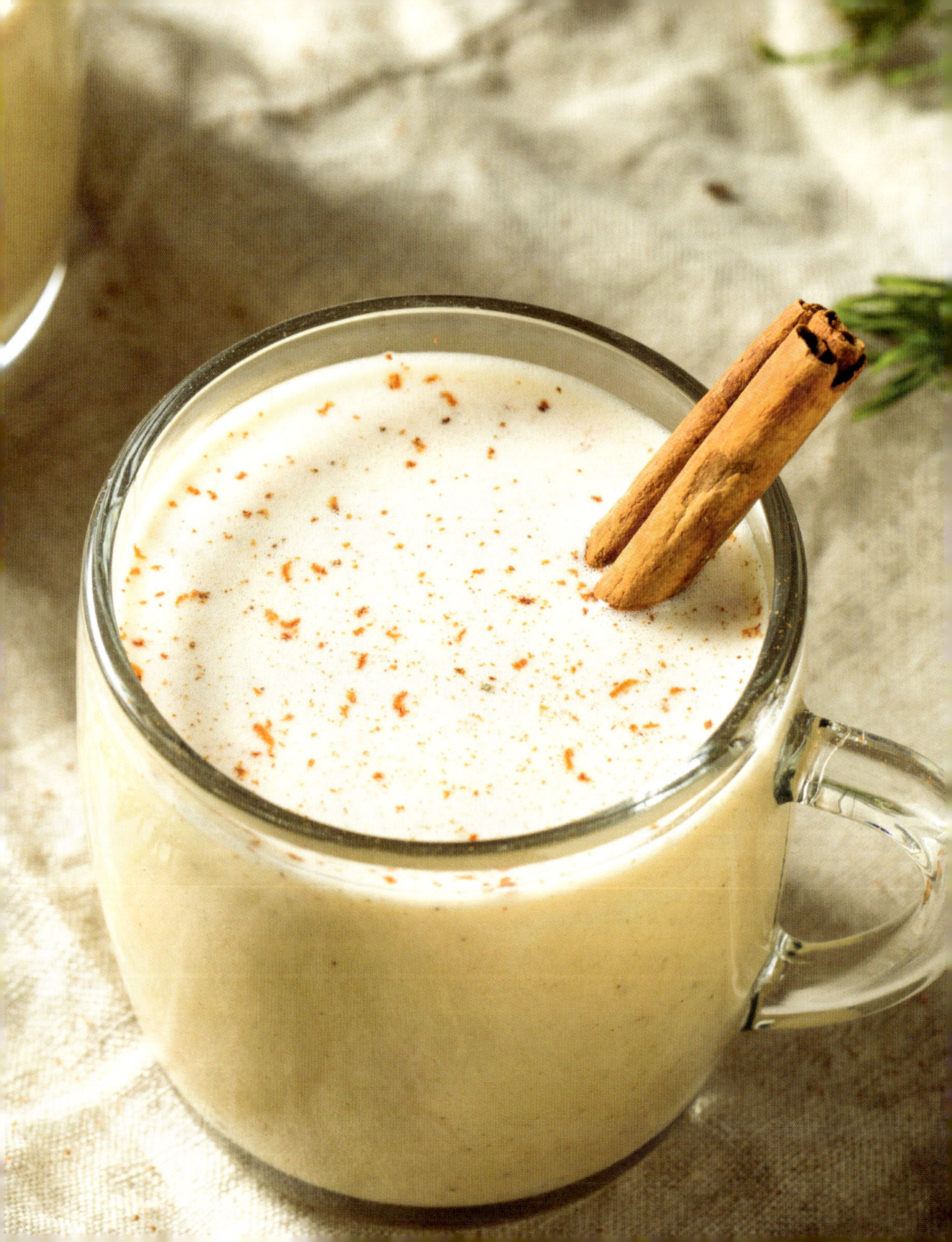

EGGNOG'S OVERRATED

6 eggs, beaten until frothy

½ teaspoon pure vanilla extract

¼ teaspoon freshly grated nutmeg, plus more for garnish

1 cup sugar, plus 1 tablespoon

¾ cup brandy

⅓ cup dark rum

2 cups heavy cream

2 cups milk

Cinnamon sticks, for garnish

Place all of the ingredients, except for the cinnamon sticks, in a large punch bowl and whisk to combine.

Chill in the refrigerator until ready to serve, garnishing each glass with additional nutmeg and cinnamon sticks.

FA-LA-LA-LA LIT

1 (375 ml) bottle of aged rum or Cognac

¾ cup orange liqueur

¼ cup Spiced Hibiscus Syrup (see sidebar)

3 dashes of Peychaud's Bitters

2 (750 ml) bottles of sparkling wine

Cranberries, for garnish

Place all of the ingredients, except for the sparkling wine and cranberries, in a large punch bowl, add large blocks of ice, and stir until chilled.

Add the sparkling wine and gently stir to combine.

Serve in wine glasses or champagne flutes and garnish with cranberries.

SPICED HIBISCUS SYRUP

Place 1 cup water, ½ cup dried hibiscus blossoms (or 6 bags of hibiscus tea), 1 cinnamon stick, 5 whole cloves, 5 allspice berries, and 1 split vanilla bean pod in a small saucepan and bring to boil over medium heat. Remove from heat and let the mixture steep for 15 to 20 minutes. Strain, discard the solids, and return the liquid to the pan. Bring to a boil over medium heat and add ¾ cup Demerara sugar. Stir until the sugar has dissolved, remove from heat, and let cool before using.

SWEATER WEATHER, BUT MAKE IT BOOZY

When the temps outside are colder than your ex's heart, there's only one cure—a steaming mug of something spiked and spectacular. This chapter is dedicated to drinks that hug you from the inside out, because sometimes a sweater just isn't enough. From rich, buttery concoctions that taste like Christmas in a cup to coffee that's gone gloriously rogue with a splash of whiskey, these toasty treats are here to warm your soul (and defrost your attitude). Perfect for fireside chats, snowy-night sipping, or braving yet another round of *that one cousin's* off-key caroling, these drinks are the seasonal serotonin boost you didn't know you needed.

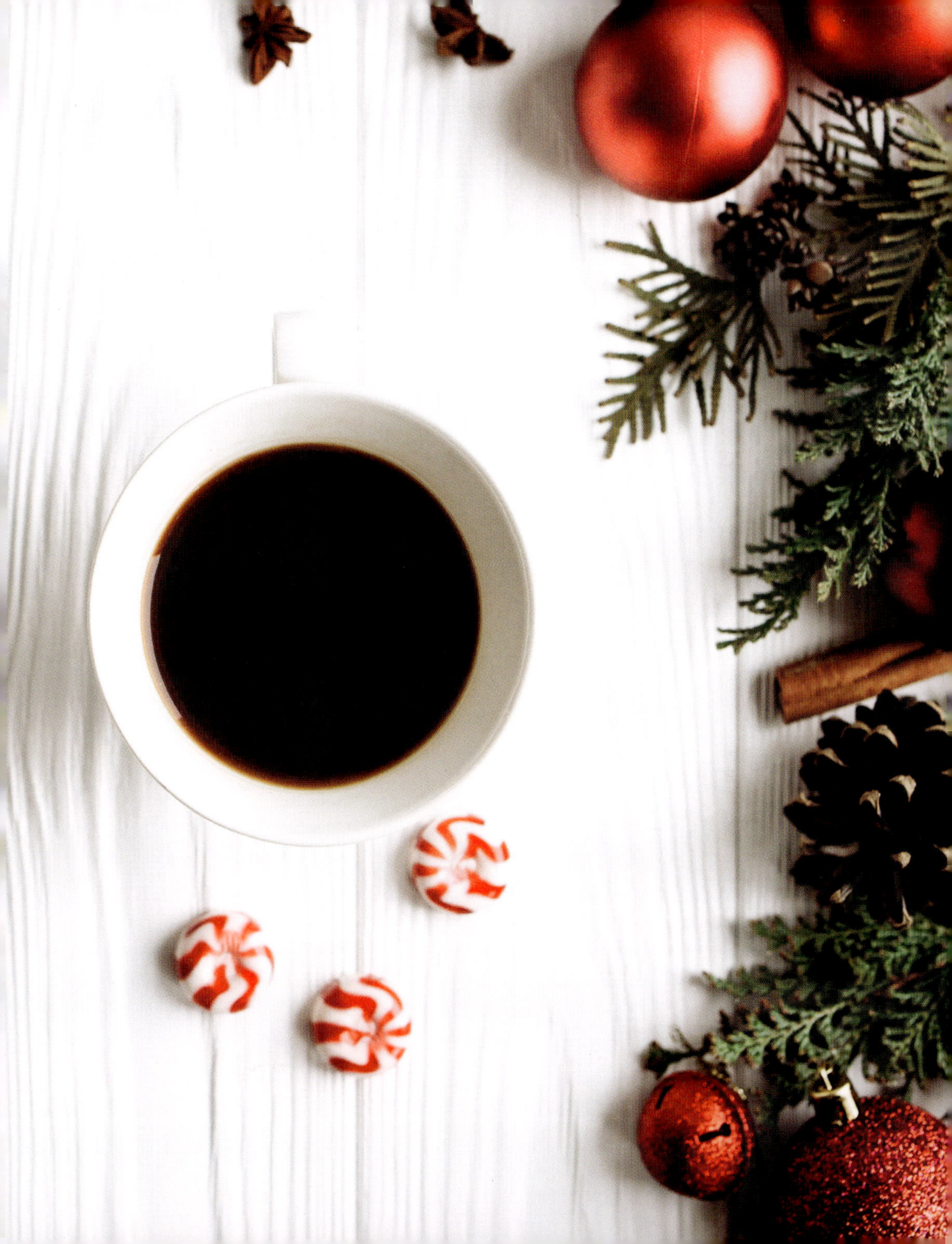

TODDY CLAUS IS COMIN' TO TOWN

2 oz. blended Scotch whisky

½ oz. fresh lemon juice

¼ oz. Simple Syrup (see page 20)

Boiling water, to top

1 lemon wedge, for garnish

1 cinnamon stick, for garnish

Place the Scotch, lemon juice, syrup, and water in a mug or Irish Coffee glass and stir to combine.

Garnish with the lemon wedge and cinnamon stick.

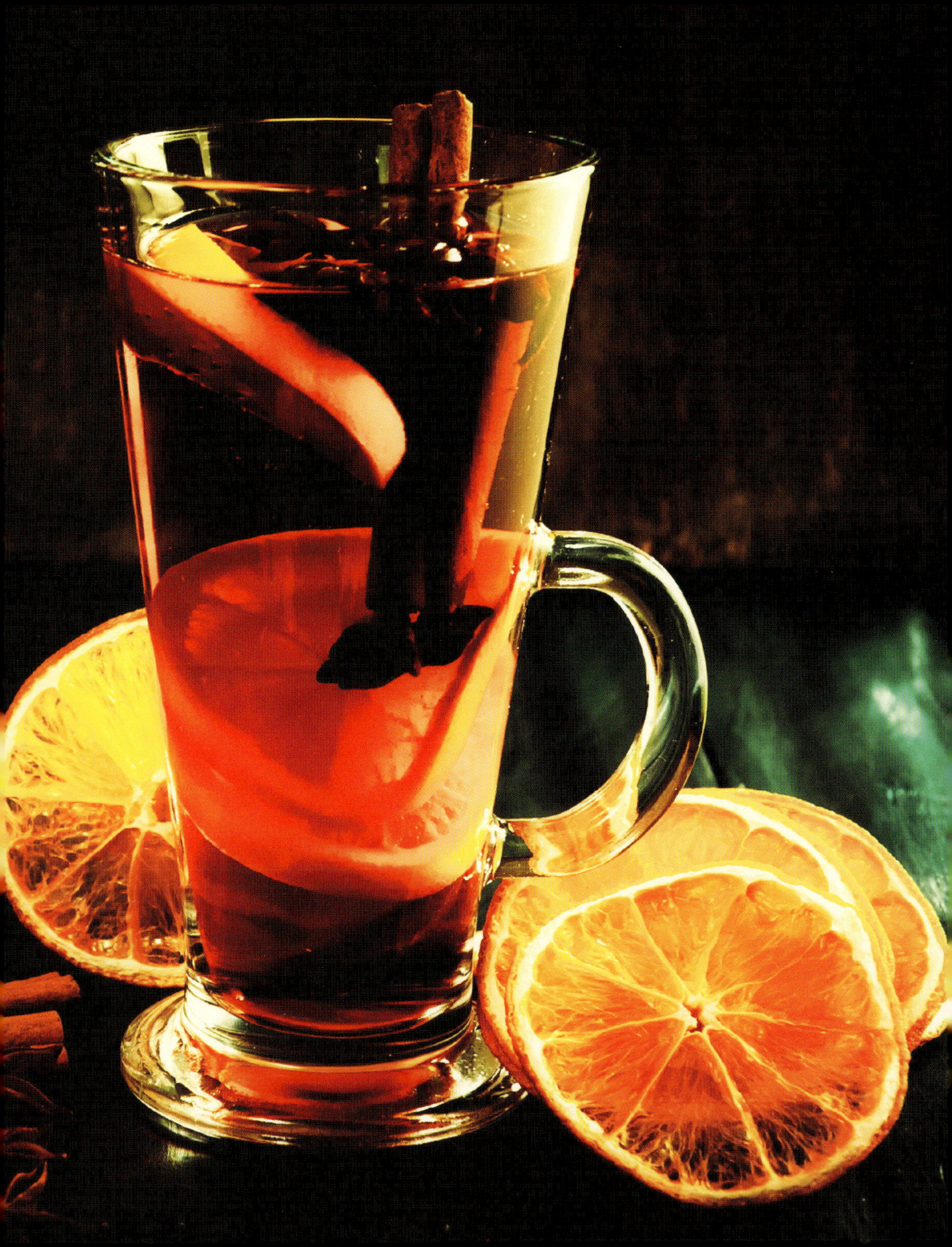

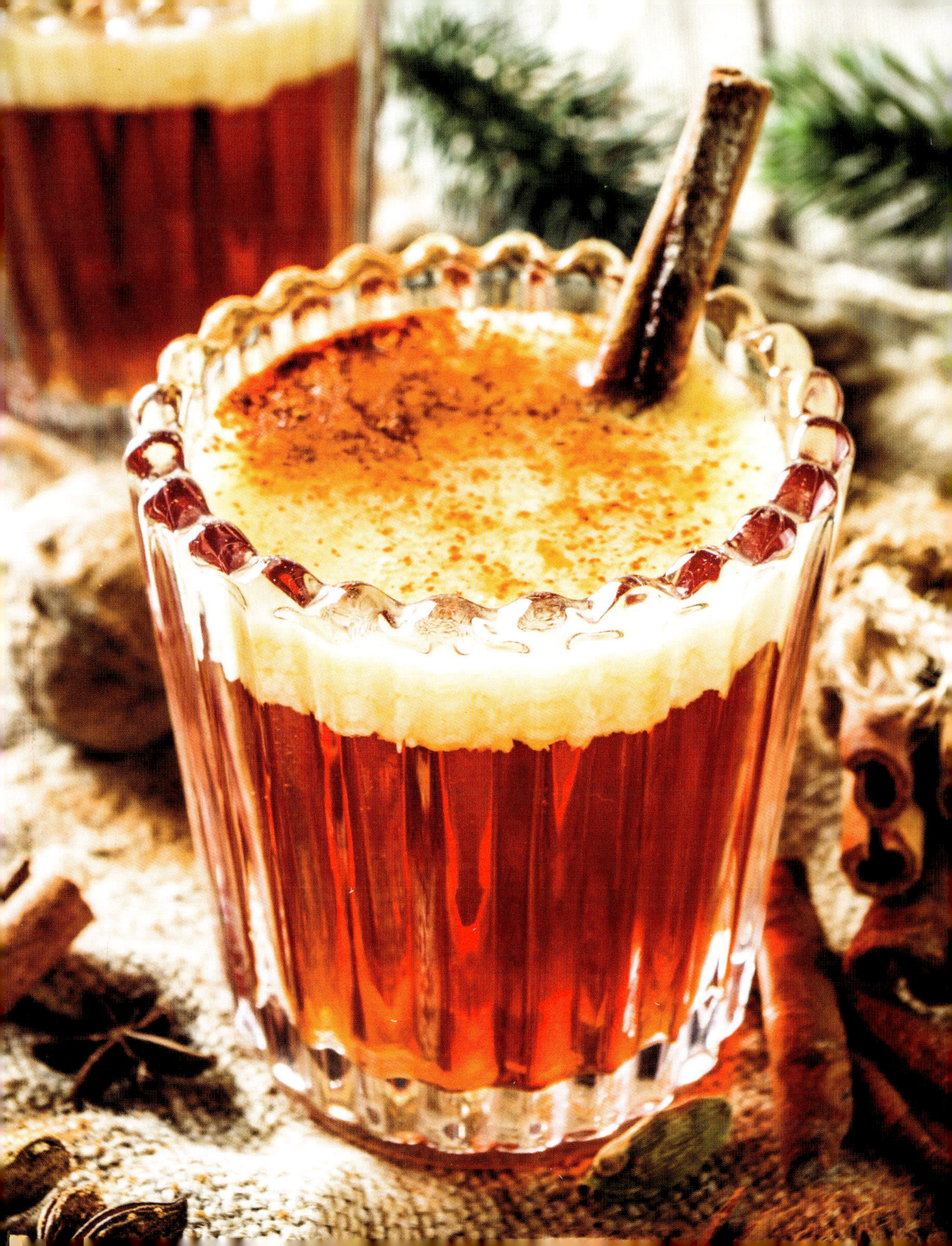

SANTA'S NIGHTCAP

1 small pat of butter

1 teaspoon brown sugar

Dash of cinnamon, plus more to taste

Dash of freshly grated nutmeg, plus more to taste

Dash of orange zest, plus more to taste

Splash of pure vanilla extract

6 oz. boiling water

2 oz. aged rum

1 cinnamon stick, for garnish

Place the butter, brown sugar, cinnamon, nutmeg, and orange zest in the bottom of a mug and stir to combine.

Add the vanilla extract, water, and rum and stir to combine.

Adjust to taste and garnish with the cinnamon stick.

Sweater Weather, but Make It Boozy

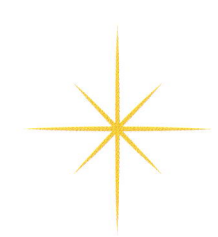

CLOVE ACTUALLY

2 oz. applejack

1 teaspoon maple syrup

6 oz. freshly brewed cinnamon apple tea

1 lemon twist, for garnish

4 whole cloves, for garnish

Place the applejack, maple syrup, and tea in a mug and stir to combine.

Garnish with the lemon twist and whole cloves.

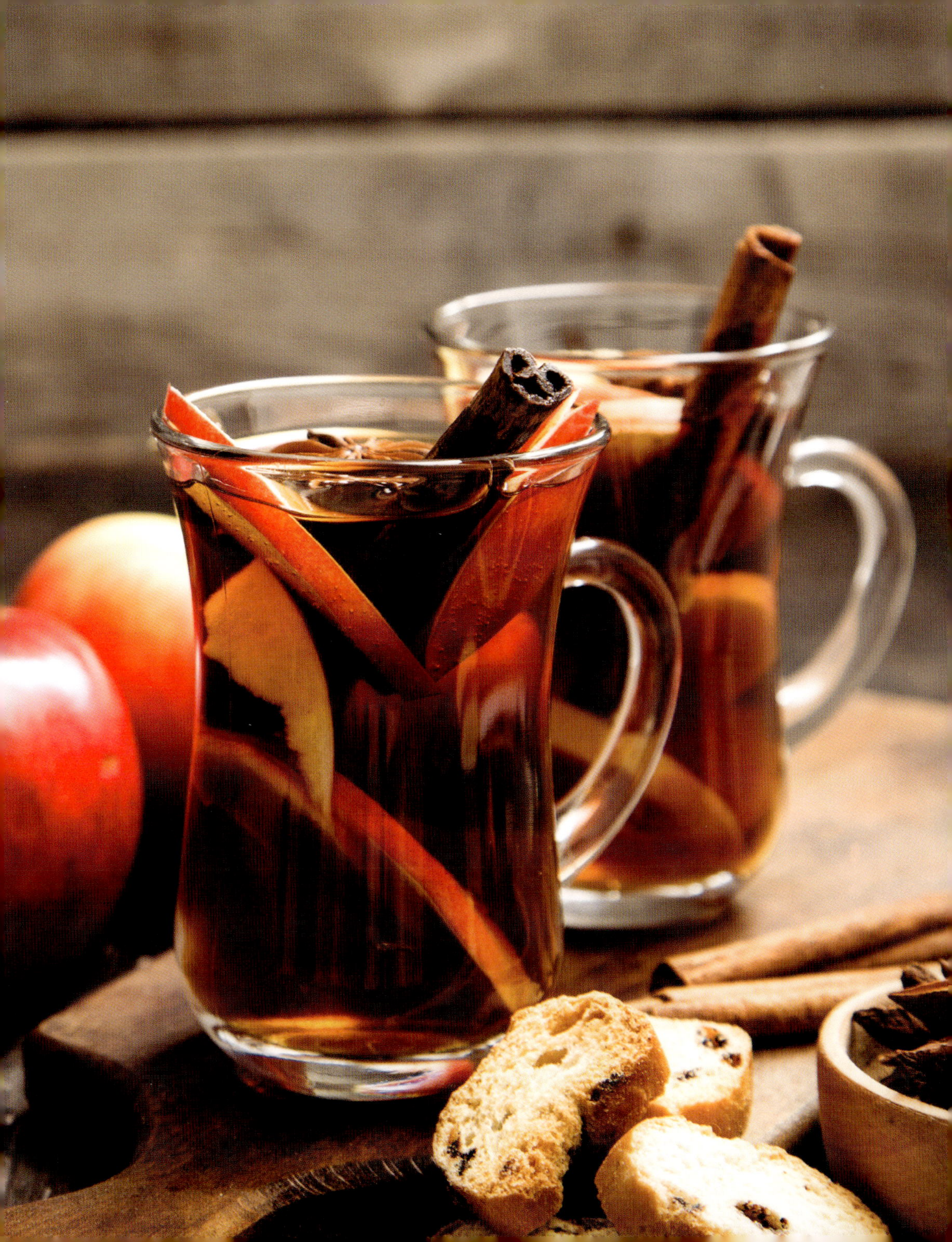

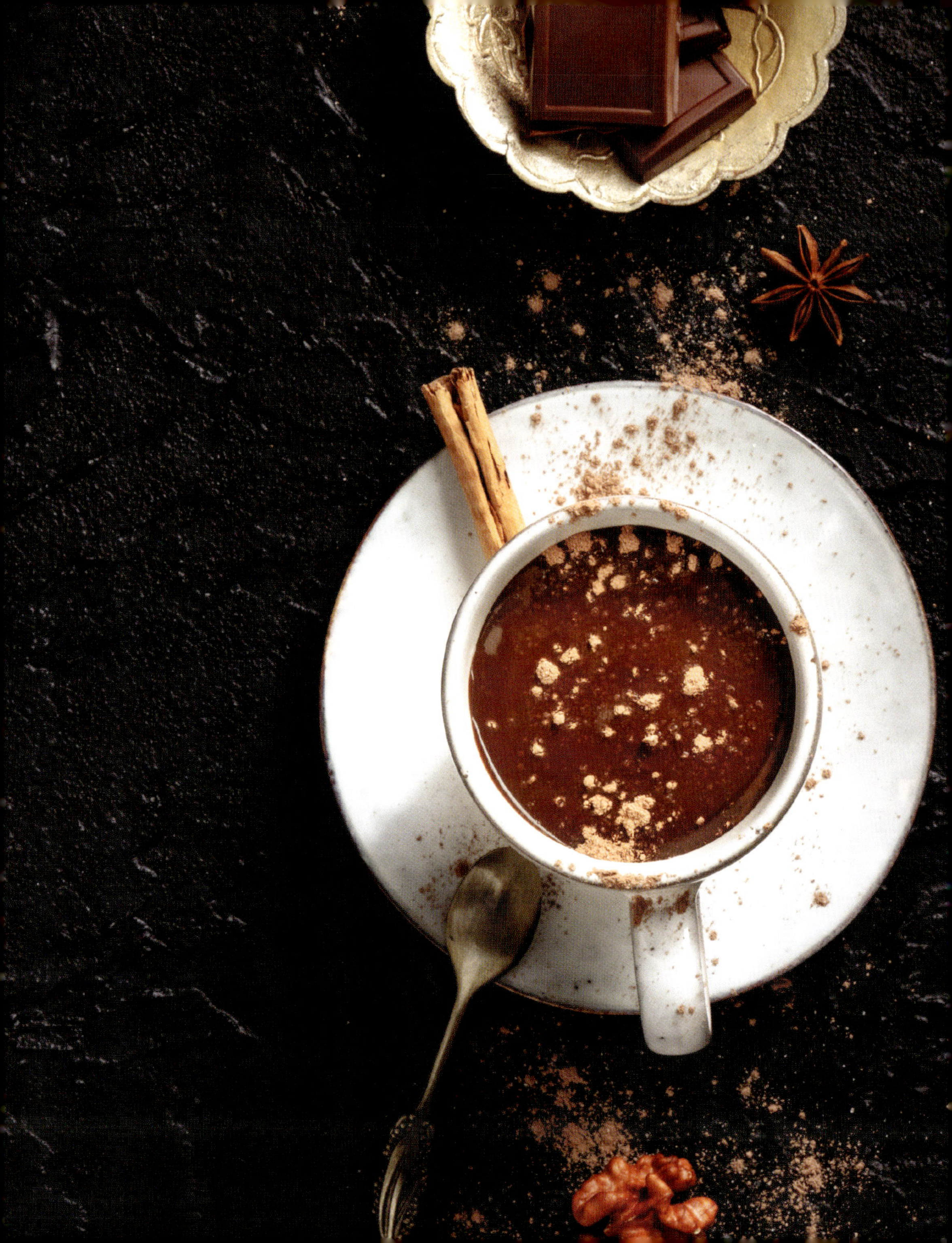

FLAKE IT TIL YOU MAKE IT

8 oz. milk

1 oz. quality chocolate

1 oz. aged rum

Handful of miniature marshmallows

Place the milk in a small saucepan and warm it over medium-low heat, stirring constantly, until it just starts to simmer.

Place the chocolate in a mug, pour the warmed milk on top, and stir until smooth.

Stir in the rum, top with the marshmallows, and enjoy.

LIQUID COURAGE

1 oz. Simple Syrup (see page 20)

1 oz. dark rum

1 oz. brandy

2 oz. eggnog, warmed

1 cinnamon stick, for garnish

Place the syrup, rum, brandy, and eggnog in a mug or Irish coffee glass and stir to combine.

Garnish with the cinnamon stick.

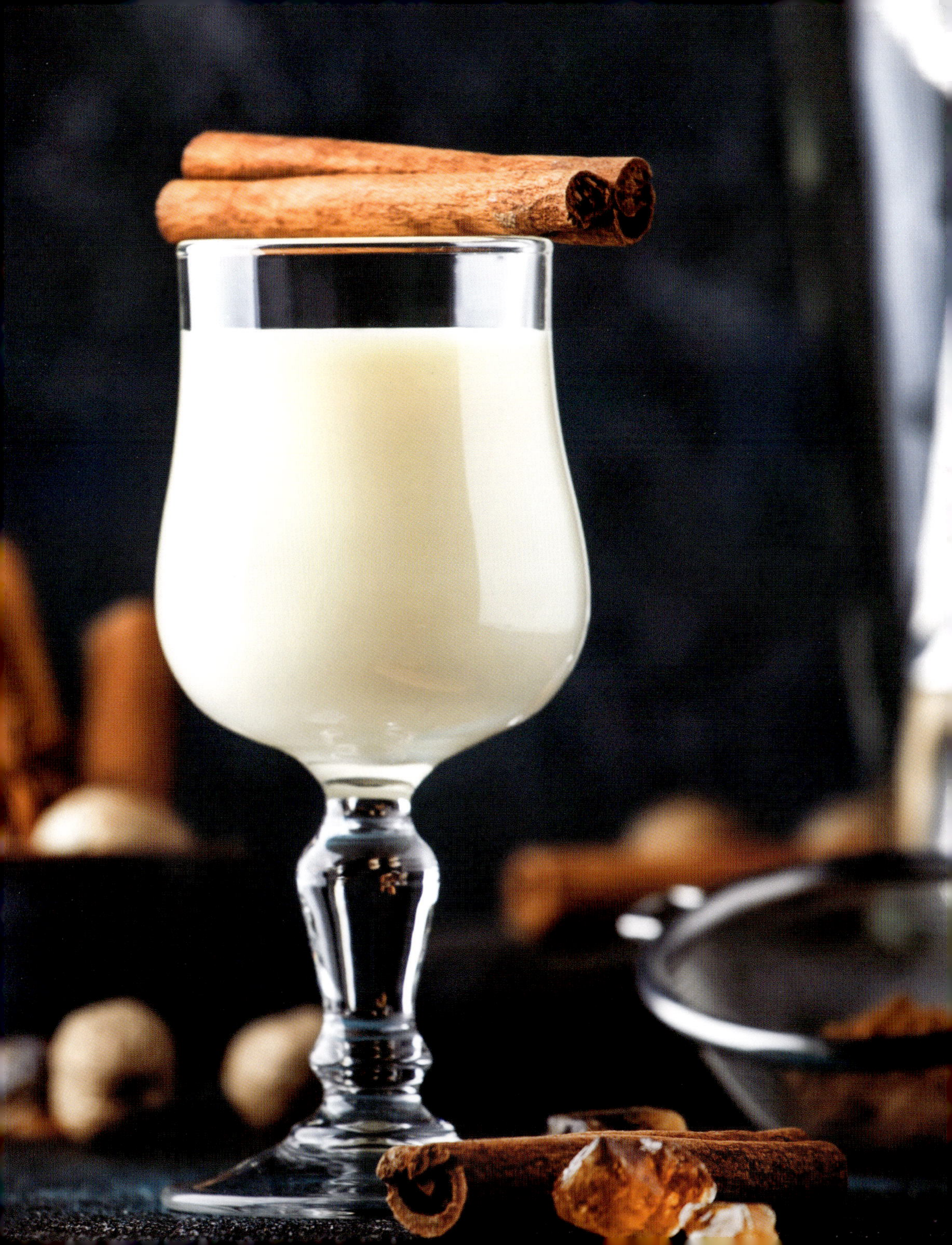

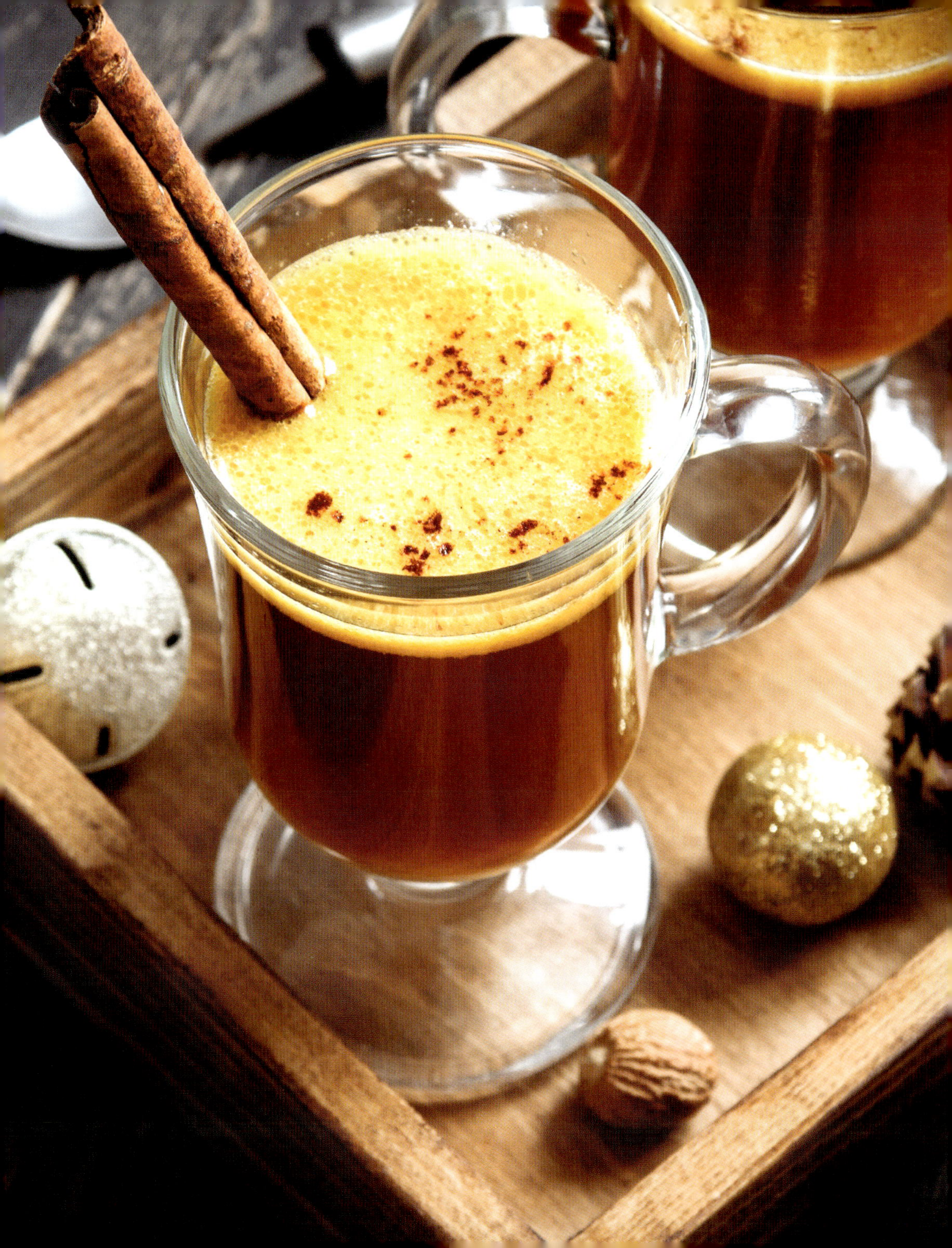

BUTTER LATE THAN SOBER

1 small pat of butter

1 teaspoon brown sugar

Dash of cinnamon

Dash of freshly grated nutmeg

Pinch of kosher salt

1½ oz. bourbon

Dash of Angostura Bitters

6 oz. boiling water

1 cinnamon stick, for garnish

Place the butter, brown sugar, cinnamon, nutmeg, salt, bourbon, and bitters in a mug and stir to combine.

Pour the boiling water on top, stir to combine, and garnish with the cinnamon stick.

Sweater Weather, but Make It Boozy

I'M ALLERGIC TO THIS MUCH JOY

2 oz. gin

1 oz. Simple Syrup (see page 20)

Juice of ½ lemon

6 oz. freshly brewed hibiscus tea

Cranberries, to taste

Fresh mint, for garnish

Place the gin, syrup, and lemon juice in a mug and stir to combine.

Add the tea and cranberries, stir to combine, and garnish with the fresh mint.

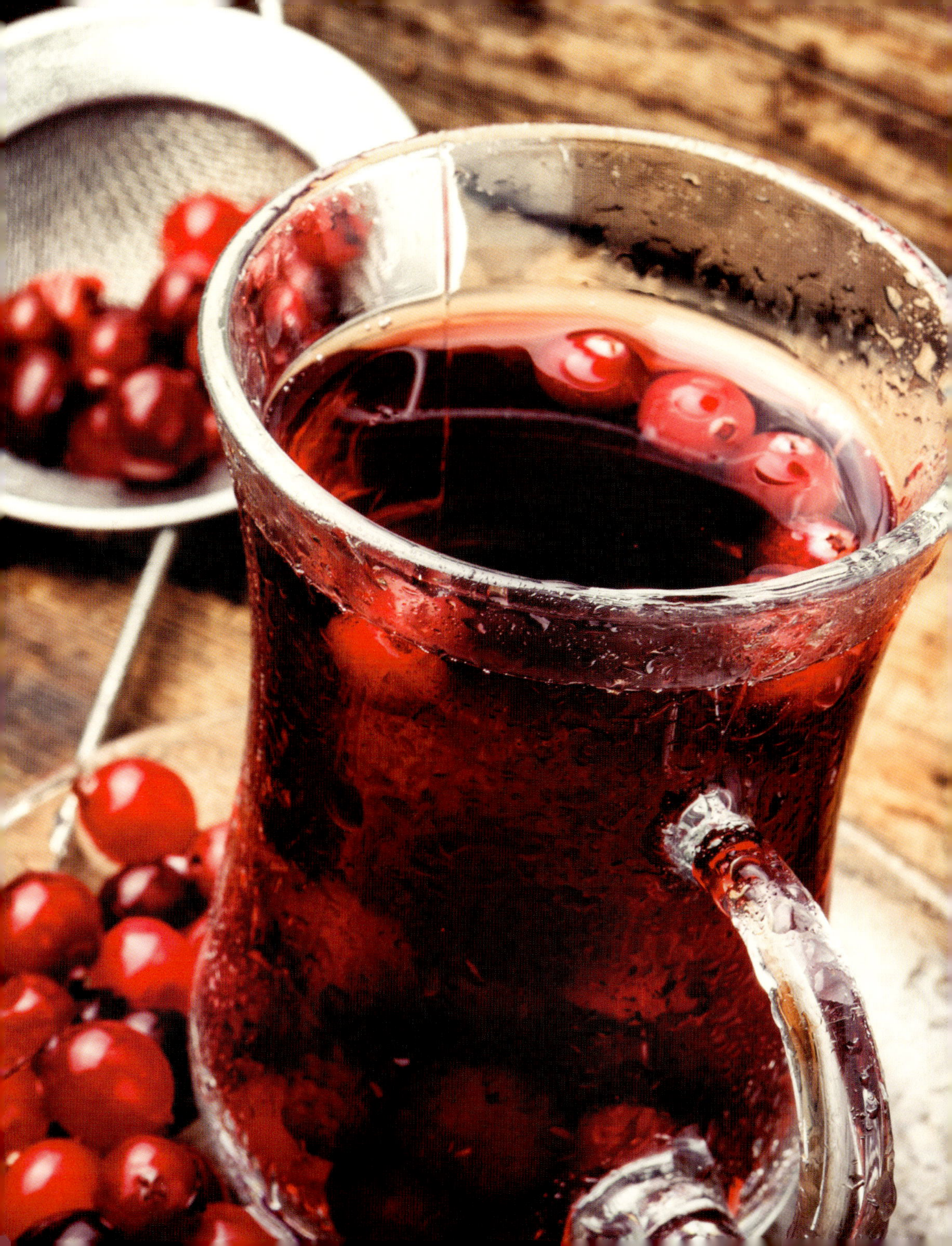

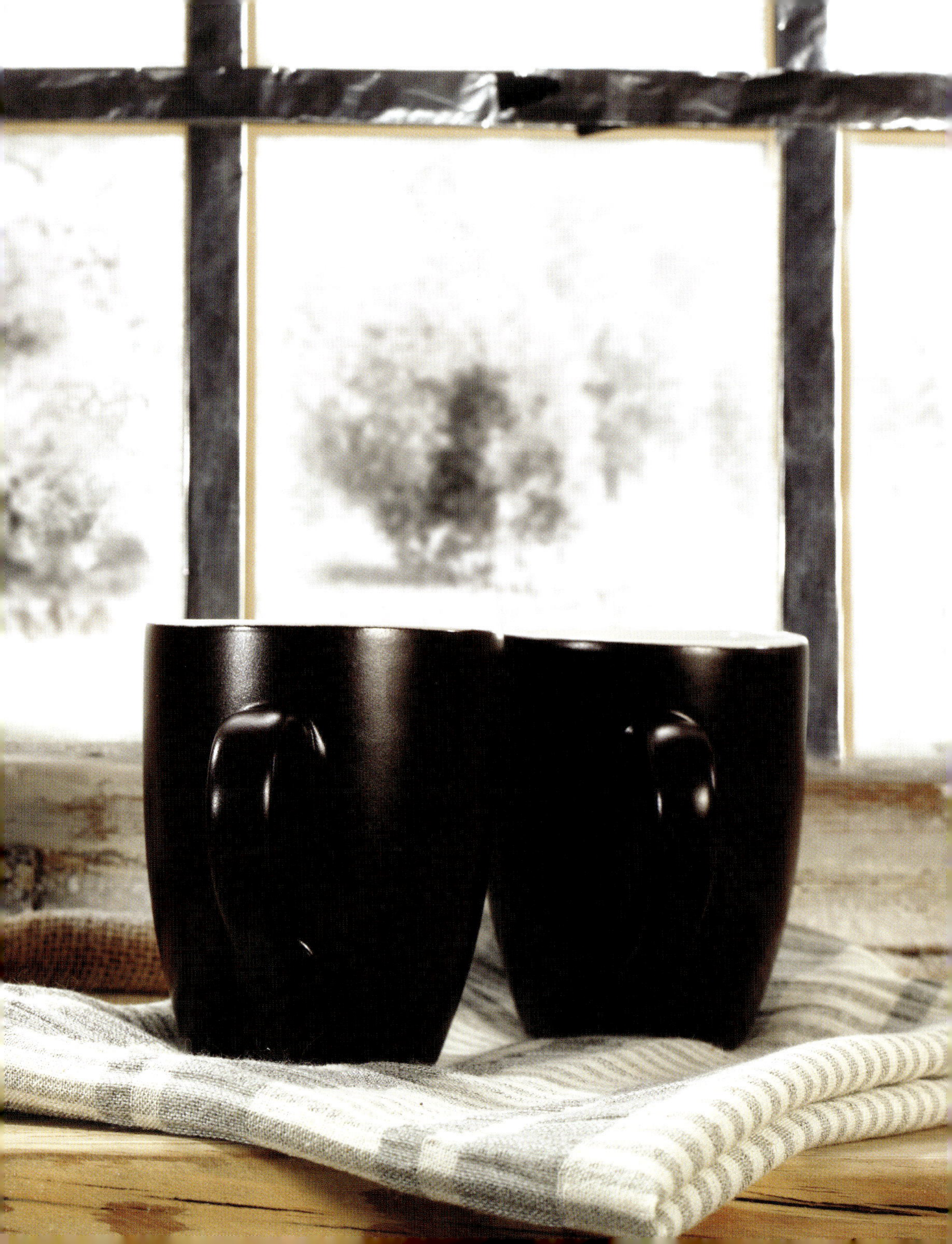

SNOW WAY OUT

1 bag of English Breakfast tea

1 bag of Earl Grey tea

6 oz. very hot water (170°F)

¼ oz. Simple Syrup (see page 20)

1¼ oz. Hendrick's Gin

Dollop of whipped cream

Place the tea bags and the hot water in a mug and steep for 3 minutes.

Stir in the simple syrup and gin, top with the whipped cream, and enjoy.

FROTHY THE SNOWMAN

1 oz. Scotch whisky

2 oz. Kahlúa

2 oz. crème de cacao

1 oz. freshly brewed espresso or strong coffee

4 oz. crème fraîche

Place all of the ingredients, except for the crème fraîche, in a mug and stir to combine.

Layer the crème fraîche on top and enjoy.

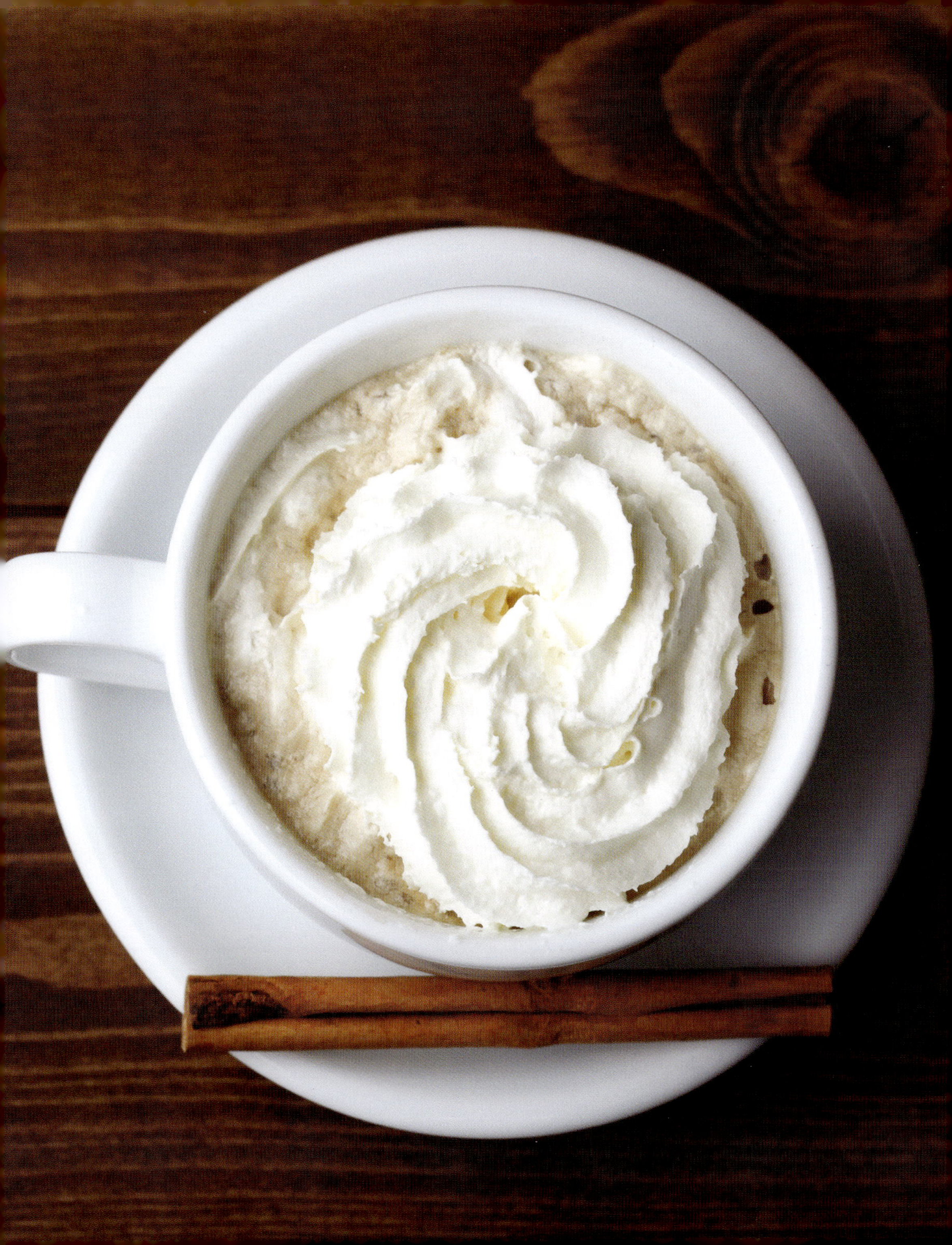

SAFFRON SYRUP

Place 1 cup water and 1 cup sugar in a small saucepan and bring to a boil. Stir in ⅛ teaspoon saffron threads, remove the pan from heat, and let cool completely. Strain before using.

HARK! THE VERBENA SINGS

8 oz. water

2 oz. sugar

6 large lemon verbena leaves, plus more for garnish

1¼ oz. gin

½ oz. fresh key lime juice

¼ oz. Saffron Syrup (see sidebar)

Place the water and sugar in a small saucepan and bring to a boil. Add the lemon verbena leaves, remove the pan from heat, and let steep for 5 minutes.

Strain into a mug, add the gin, key lime juice, and syrup, and stir to combine.

Garnish with the additional lemon verbena leaf and enjoy.

CHAI'LL BE TIPSY FOR THE HOLIDAYS

2 oz. single-malt Scotch whisky

5 oz. freshly brewed chai tea

½ oz. milk

½ tablespoon honey

1 cinnamon stick, for garnish

1 star anise pod, for garnish

Place the whisky, tea, milk, and honey in a mug and stir to combine.

Garnish with the cinnamon stick and star anise and enjoy.

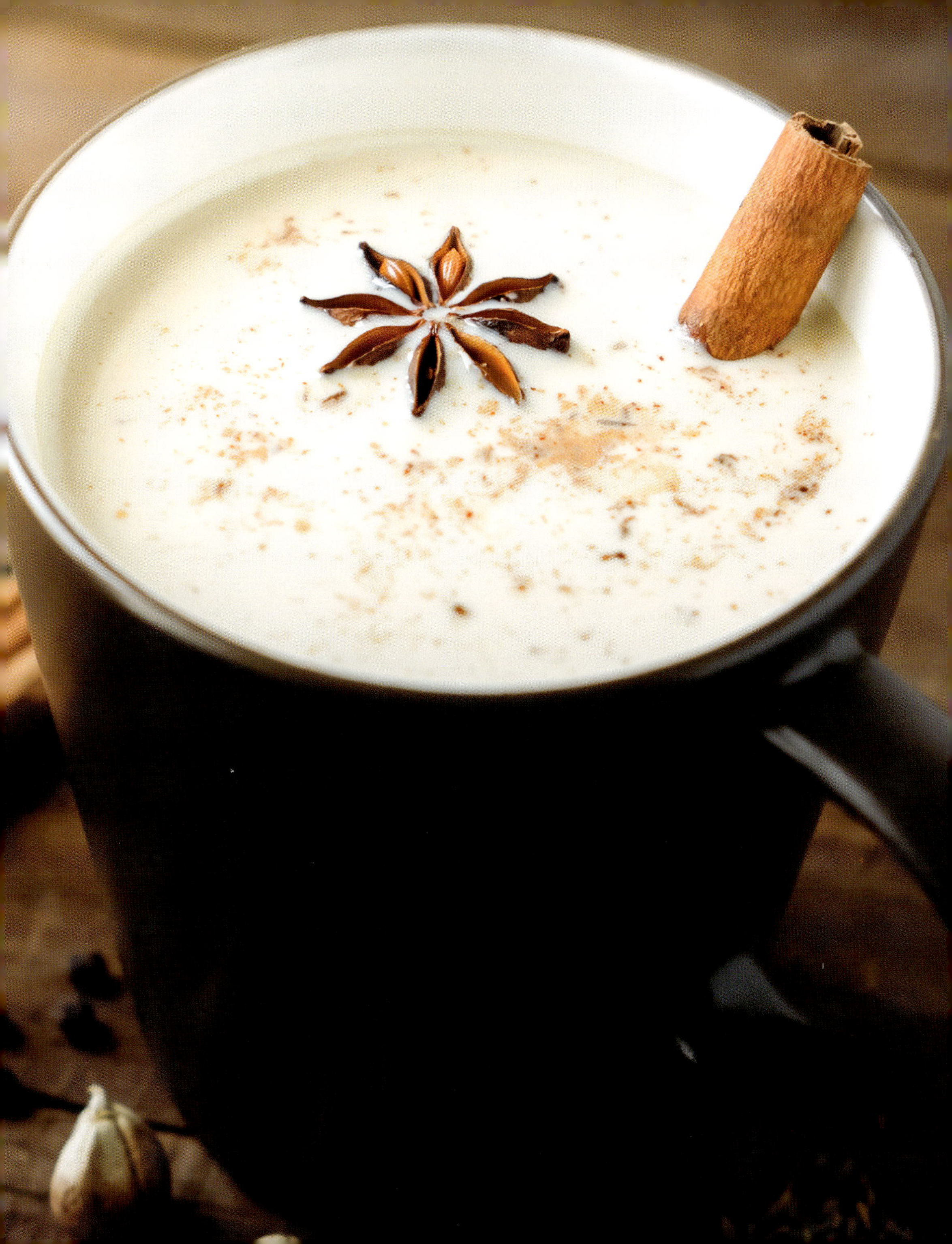

EARL GREY SYRUP

Place 1 cup water and 1 cup sugar in a small saucepan and bring to a boil, stirring to dissolve the sugar. Add 3 teabags of Earl Grey tea, remove the pan from heat, and let the syrup cool completely. Remove the tea bags before using.

WARM MY ICY HEART

1½ oz. Irish whiskey

3 oz. hot apple cider

½ oz. Earl Grey Syrup (see sidebar)

½ oz. fresh lemon juice

Splash of hot water

2 oz. sparkling wine

1 lemon twist, for garnish

Place the whiskey, cider, syrup, and lemon juice in a mug and stir to combine.

Add the splash of hot water, stir, and top with the sparkling wine.

Garnish with the lemon twist and enjoy.

IRISH YOU A MERRY HANGOVER

½ cup freshly brewed coffee

Dash of sugar

1 oz. Irish whiskey

1 oz. Baileys Original Irish Cream

Pour the coffee into a mug or Irish Coffee glass and add the sugar. Stir until the sugar has dissolved.

Add the whiskey and stir again. Top with Baileys. If you can, pour the Baileys over the back of a spoon to layer it on top rather than stirring it in.

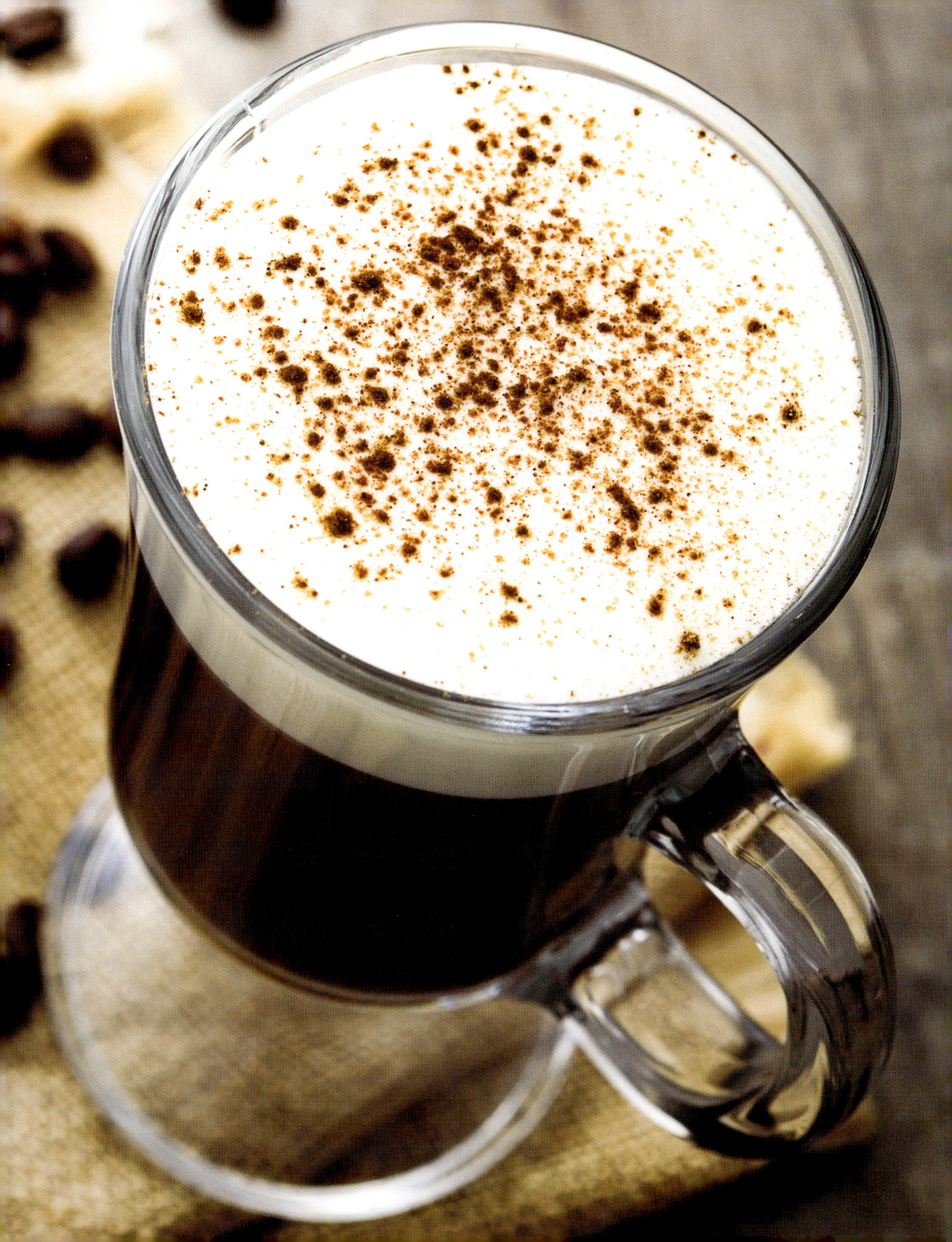

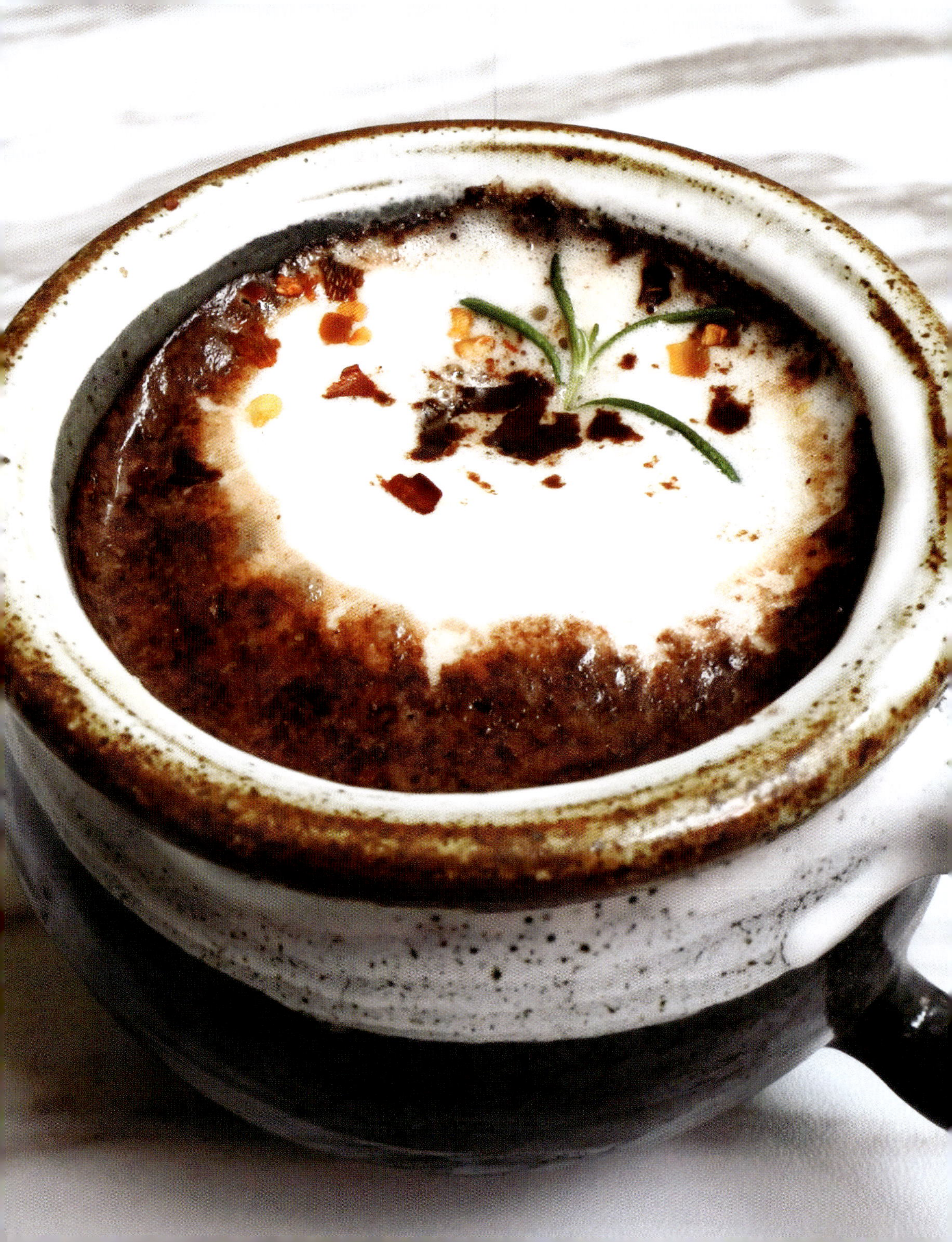

FELIZ NAVI-DONE

6 oz. whole milk

2 oz. half-and-half

3 cinnamon sticks

1 red chili pepper, stemmed and seeded

1 oz. sweetened condensed milk

½ teaspoon pure vanilla extract

1 teaspoon freshly grated nutmeg

½ teaspoon fine sea salt

1 oz. tequila

1 oz. Abuelita Mexican Hot Chocolate

Whipped cream, for garnish

Place the milk, half-and-half, cinnamon sticks, and chili pepper in a saucepan and warm the mixture over medium-low heat for 5 to 6 minutes, making sure it does not come to a boil. When the mixture starts to steam, remove the cinnamon sticks and chili pepper.

Add the sweetened condensed milk and whisk until combined. Stir in the vanilla, nutmeg, and salt.

Place the tequila and chocolate in a mug. Pour the warmed milk over them and stir until the chocolate has melted. Top with whipped cream and enjoy.

Sweater Weather, but Make It Boozy

HOW DO I "IRISH GOODBYE" THIS SHINDIG?

¾ oz. Bushmills Black Bush Irish Whiskey

½ oz. Simple Syrup (see page 20)

½ teaspoon Pedro Ximénez Sherry

2 oz. freshly brewed medium-roast espresso

Hot water, to top

Heavy cream, lightly whipped, for garnish

Fill an Irish Coffee glass with boiling water. When the glass is warm, discard the water.

Add the whiskey, syrup, and sherry to the glass and stir to combine.

Add the espresso and the hot water—reserving room for the cream—and stir to incorporate.

Float the cream on top by pouring it over the back of a spoon.

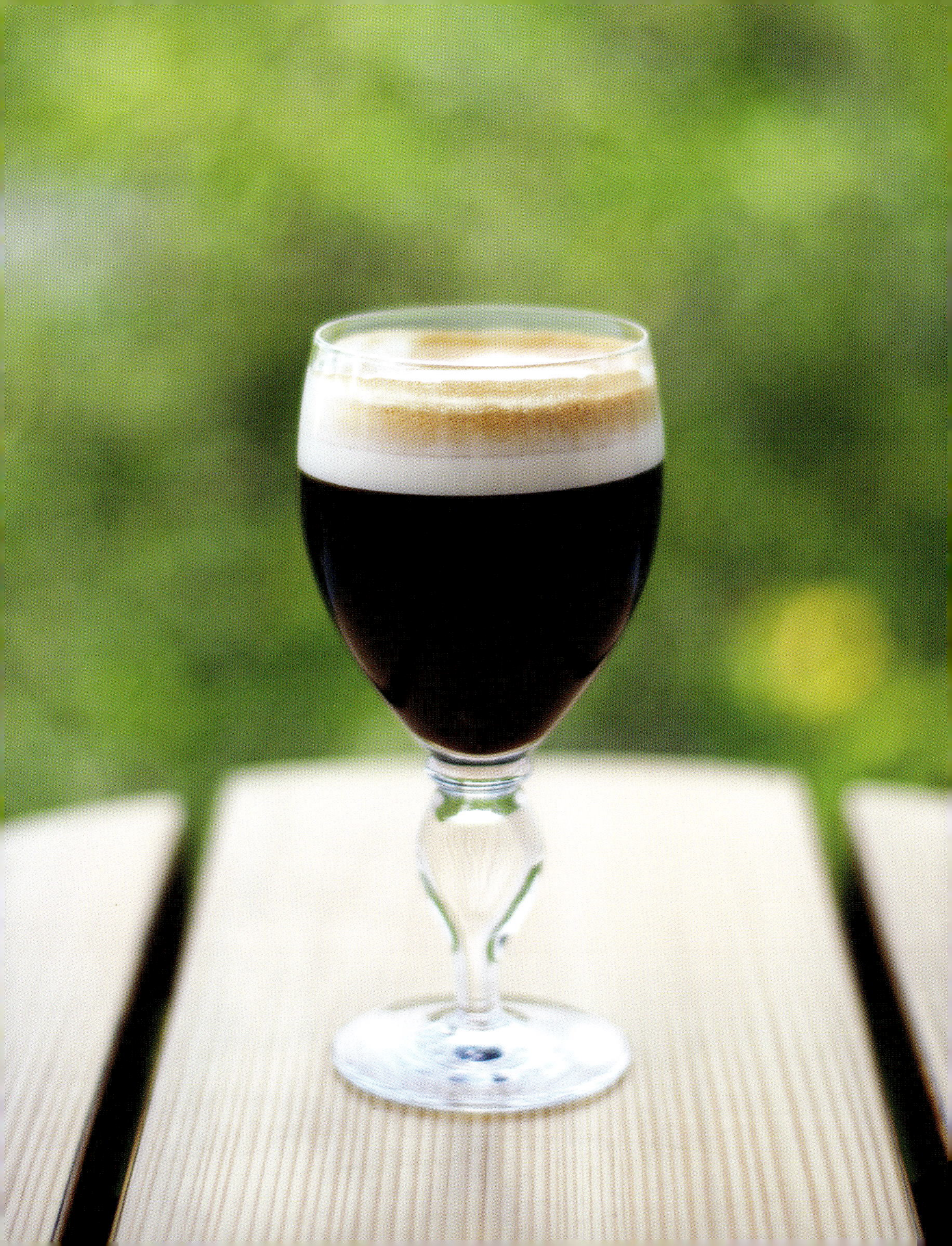

CINNAMON SYRUP

Place 1 cup sugar and 1 cup water in a small saucepan and bring to a boil, stirring to dissolve the sugar. When the sugar has dissolved, add 3 cinnamon sticks, cook for another minute, and remove the pan from heat. Let it cool completely and strain before using.

SHHH, IT'S SPIKED

6 oz. freshly brewed coffee

2 oz. mezcal

½ oz. Cinnamon Syrup (see sidebar)

1 strip of orange peel, for garnish

Place the coffee, mezcal, and syrup in a mug and stir to combine.

Garnish with the strip of orange peel and enjoy.

OLD-FASHIONED HOLIDAY CHEER

They say holiday traditions never go out of style, just like Grandma's tinsel-covered tree or her unsolicited opinions about your love life. This chapter is an ode to the classics—the cocktails that have been gracing holiday gatherings since long before your weird cousin Greg decided to bring his own "artisan kombucha." These aren't fussy or overcomplicated drinks; these are the timeless crowd-pleasers that get the job done with grace (and maybe just a hint of bourbon-soaked chaos). Perfect for anyone who loves their holiday spirit with a splash of nostalgia and zero irony, these staples will have you raising your glass to simpler times—all while subtly side-eyeing Greg's mason jar of fermented nightmare juice. Cheers!

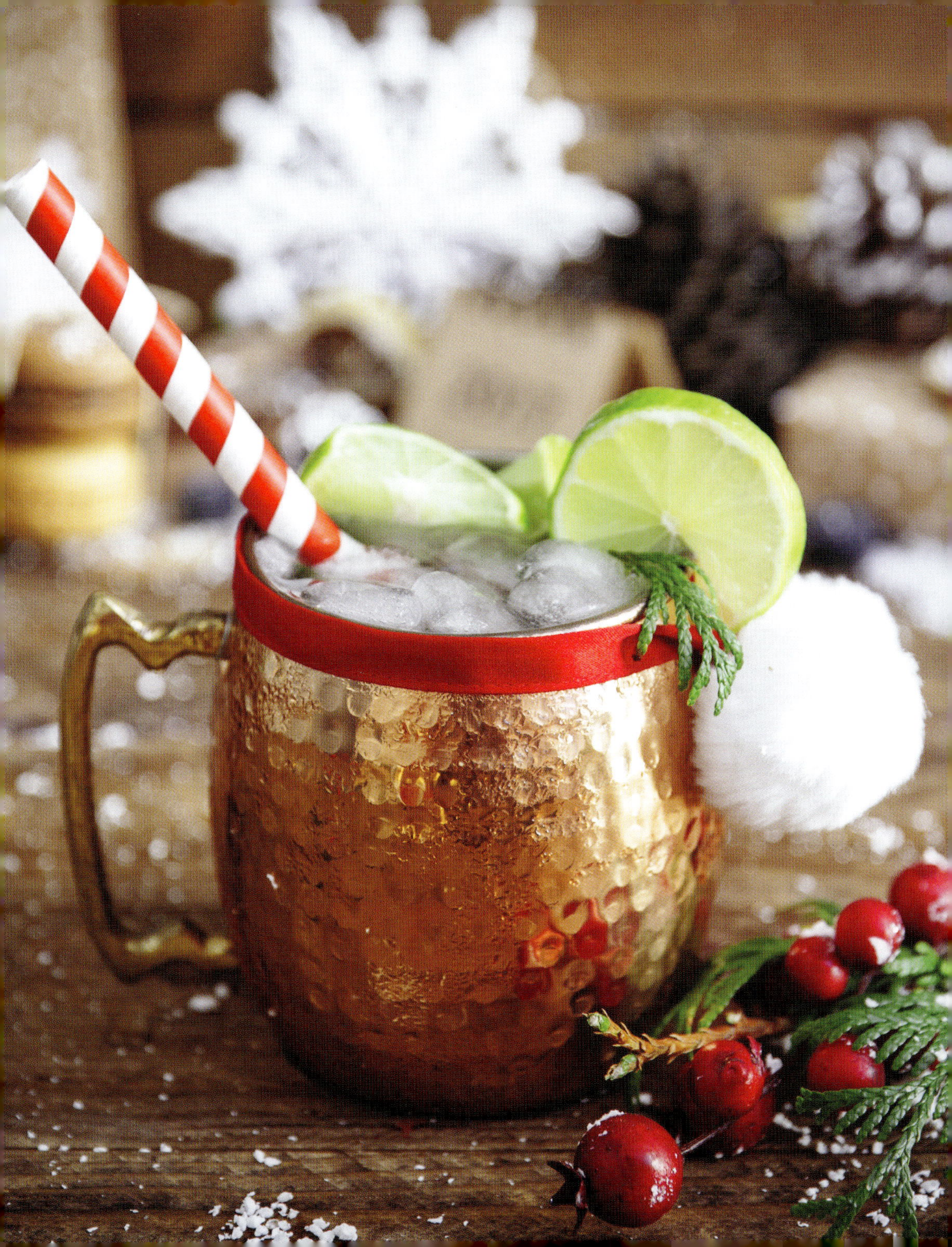

MERRY-RITA

Salt, for the rim

2 oz. tequila

1 oz. orange liqueur

1 oz. fresh lime juice

1 lime slice, for garnish

Rim a coupe with the salt and, if desired, add ice to the glass.

Place the tequila, liqueur, and lime juice in a cocktail shaker, fill it two-thirds of the way with ice, and then shake vigorously until chilled.

Strain the cocktail into the glass and garnish with the lime slice.

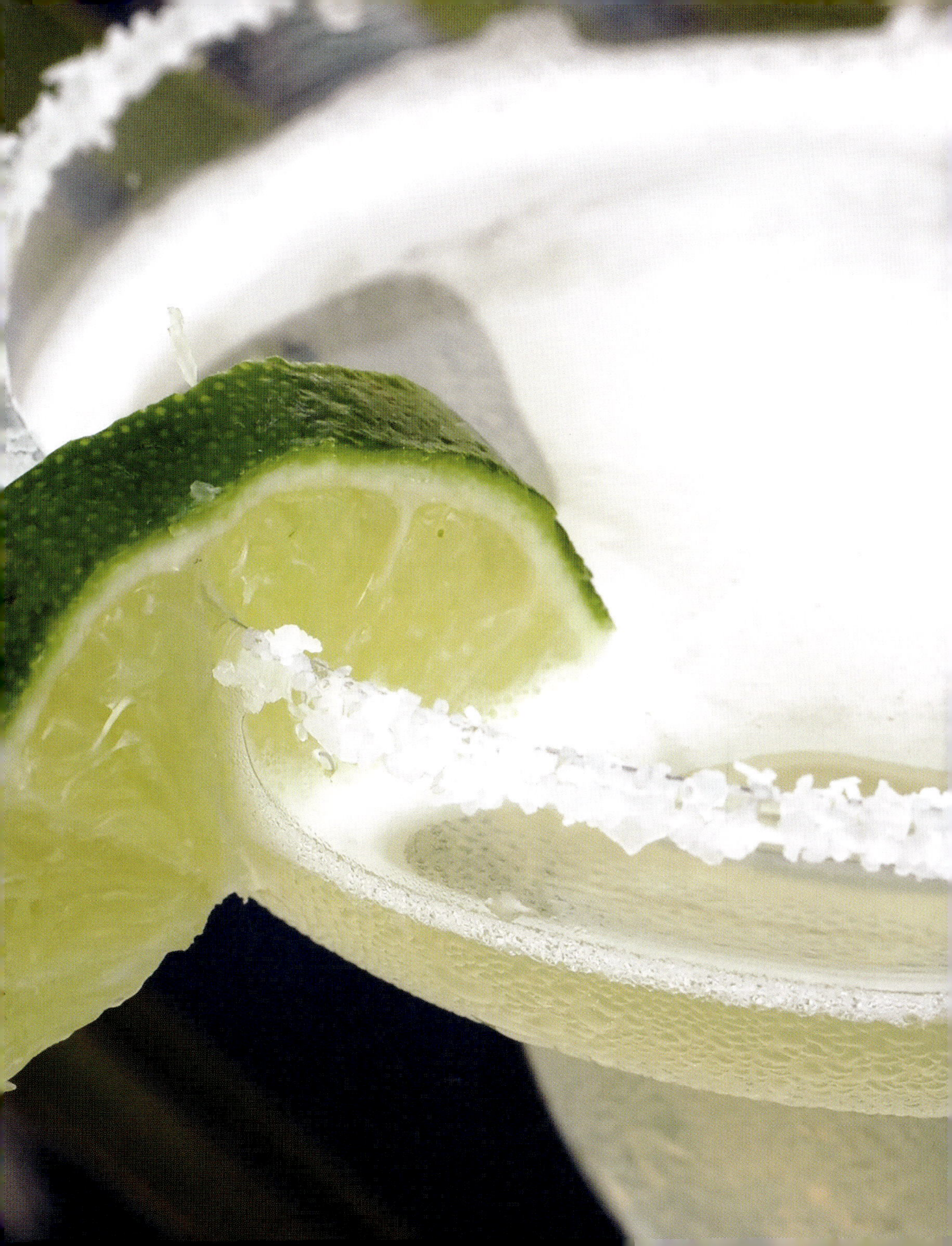

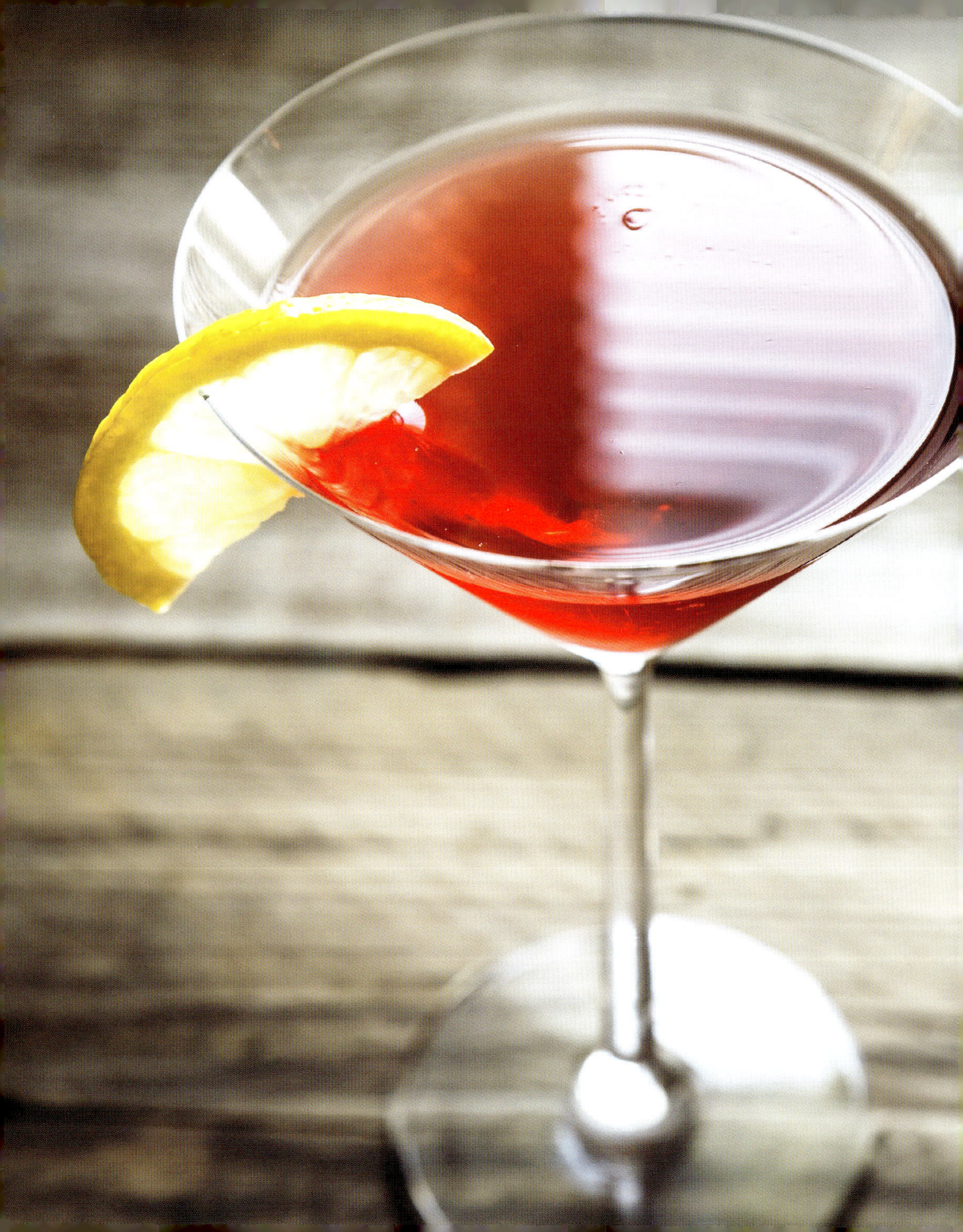

COSMO CLAUS

1 oz. vodka

1 oz. triple sec

1½ oz. cranberry juice

½ oz. fresh lime juice

1 lemon slice, for garnish

Chill a cocktail glass in the freezer.

Place the vodka, triple sec, cranberry juice, and lime juice in a cocktail shaker, fill it two-thirds of the way with ice, and shake until chilled.

Strain into the chilled cocktail glass and garnish with the lemon slice.

OLD-FASHIONED CHRISTMAS CHEER

1 teaspoon caster sugar (see sidebar)

2 to 3 dashes of Angostura Bitters

Dash of water

2 oz. bourbon or rye whiskey

1 strip of lemon peel, for garnish

1 maraschino cherry, for garnish

Place the sugar, bitters, and water in a double rocks glass and stir until the sugar has dissolved.

Add the whiskey and ice to the glass and stir until chilled. Express the strip of lemon peel over the cocktail, drop it into the glass, and garnish the cocktail with the maraschino cherry.

CASTER SUGAR

Caster sugar is a superfine sugar with a consistency that sits somewhere between granulated and confectioners' sugar. Since it can dissolve without heat, unlike granulated sugar, it is tailor-made for cocktails. This ideal fit comes with a hefty price tag at the store, but you can easily make caster sugar at home with nothing more than a food processor or a blender and some granulated sugar. Place the granulated sugar in the food processor or blender and pulse until the consistency is superfine but short of powdery. Let the sugar settle in the food processor, transfer it to a container, and label to avoid future confusion.

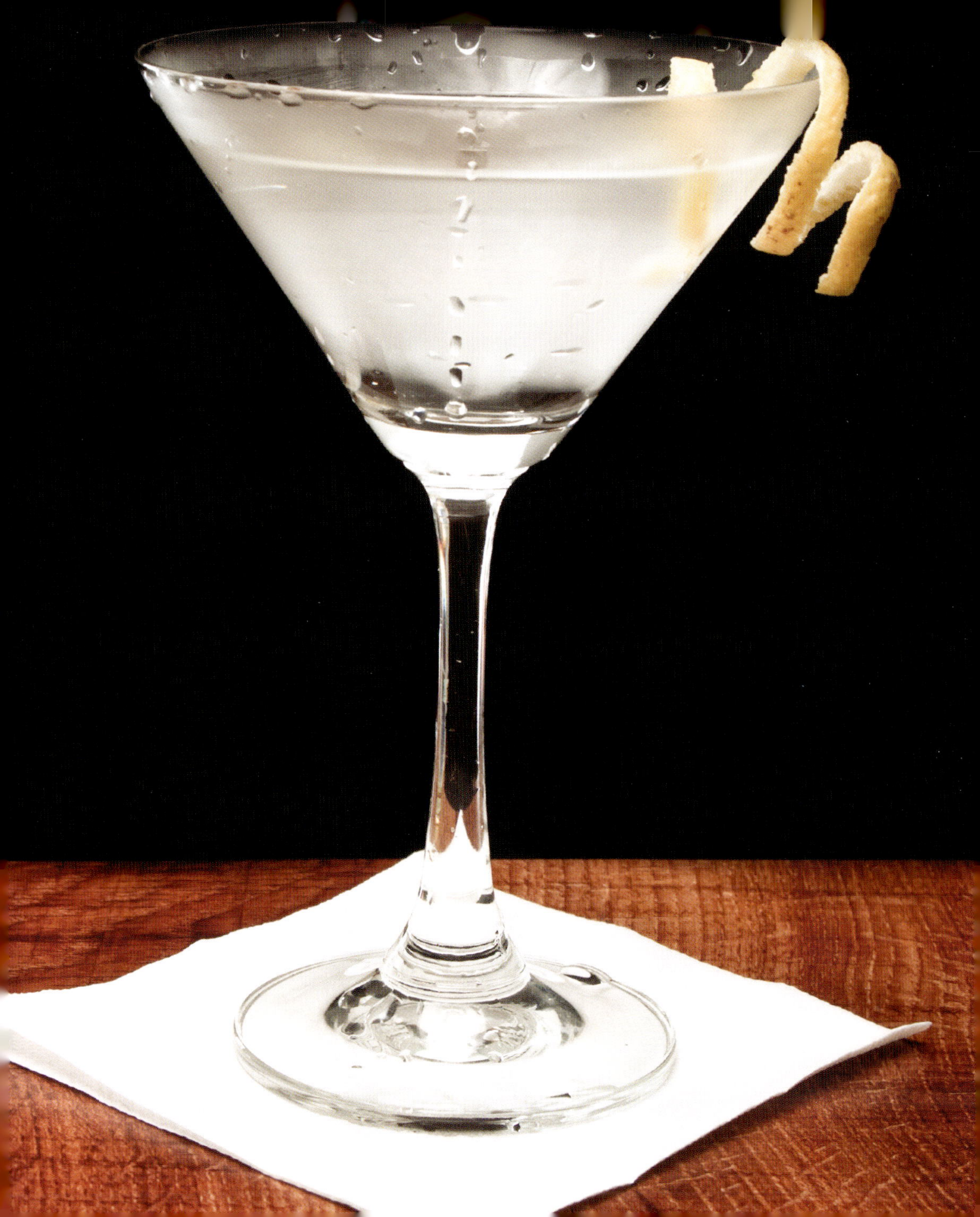

MARTINI, NAUGHTY AND STIRRED

3 oz. London Dry gin

½ oz. dry vermouth

1 lemon twist, for garnish

Chill a cocktail glass in the freezer.

Place the gin and vermouth in a mixing glass, fill it two-thirds of the way with ice, and stir until chilled.

Strain into the chilled glass and garnish with a lemon twist.

GIN-GLE ALL THE WAY

2½ oz. gin

2½ oz. tonic water

Splash of fresh lime juice

1 lime wedge, for garnish

Fill a rocks glass with ice, add the gin and tonic water, and stir until chilled.

Top with the lime juice and garnish with the lime wedge.

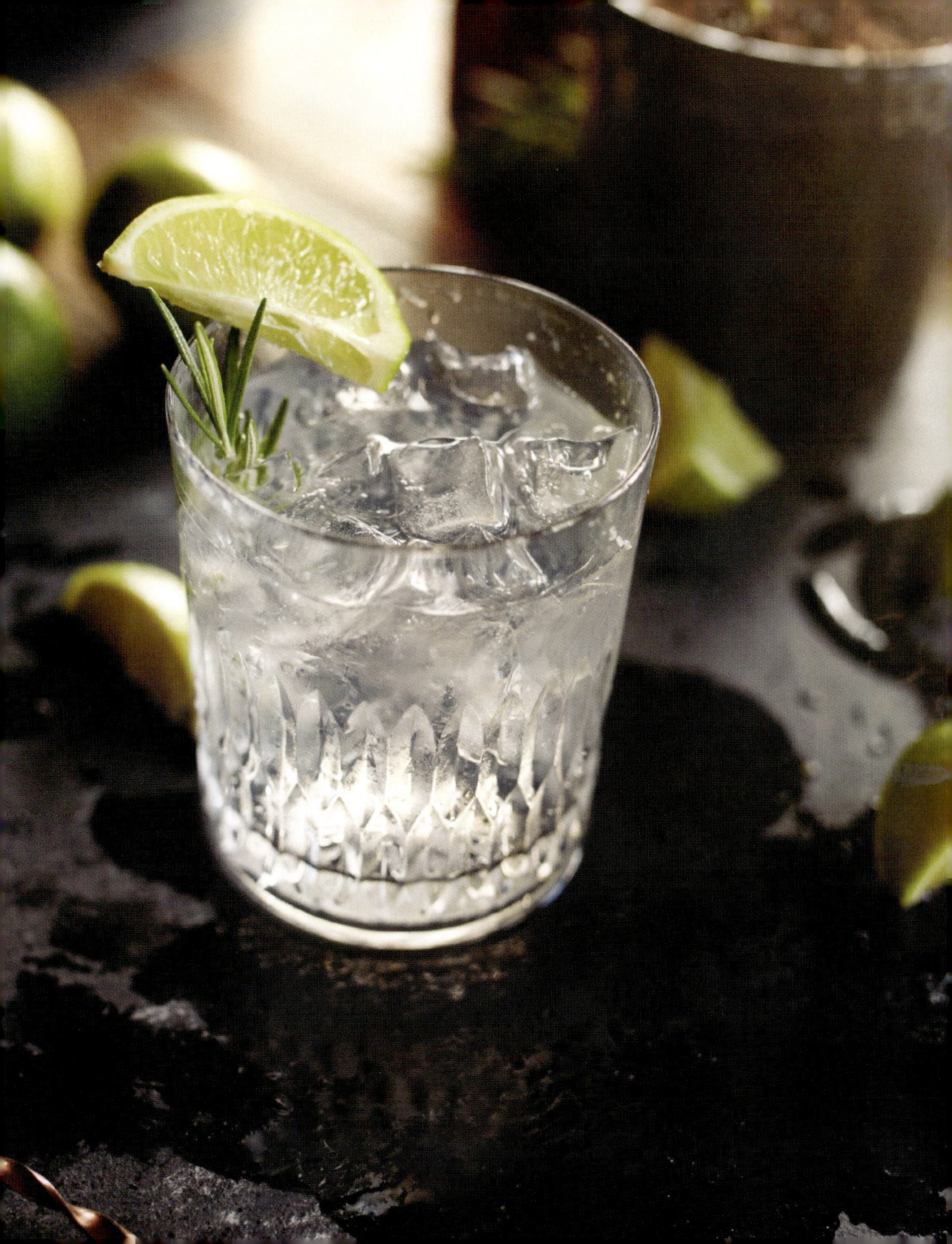

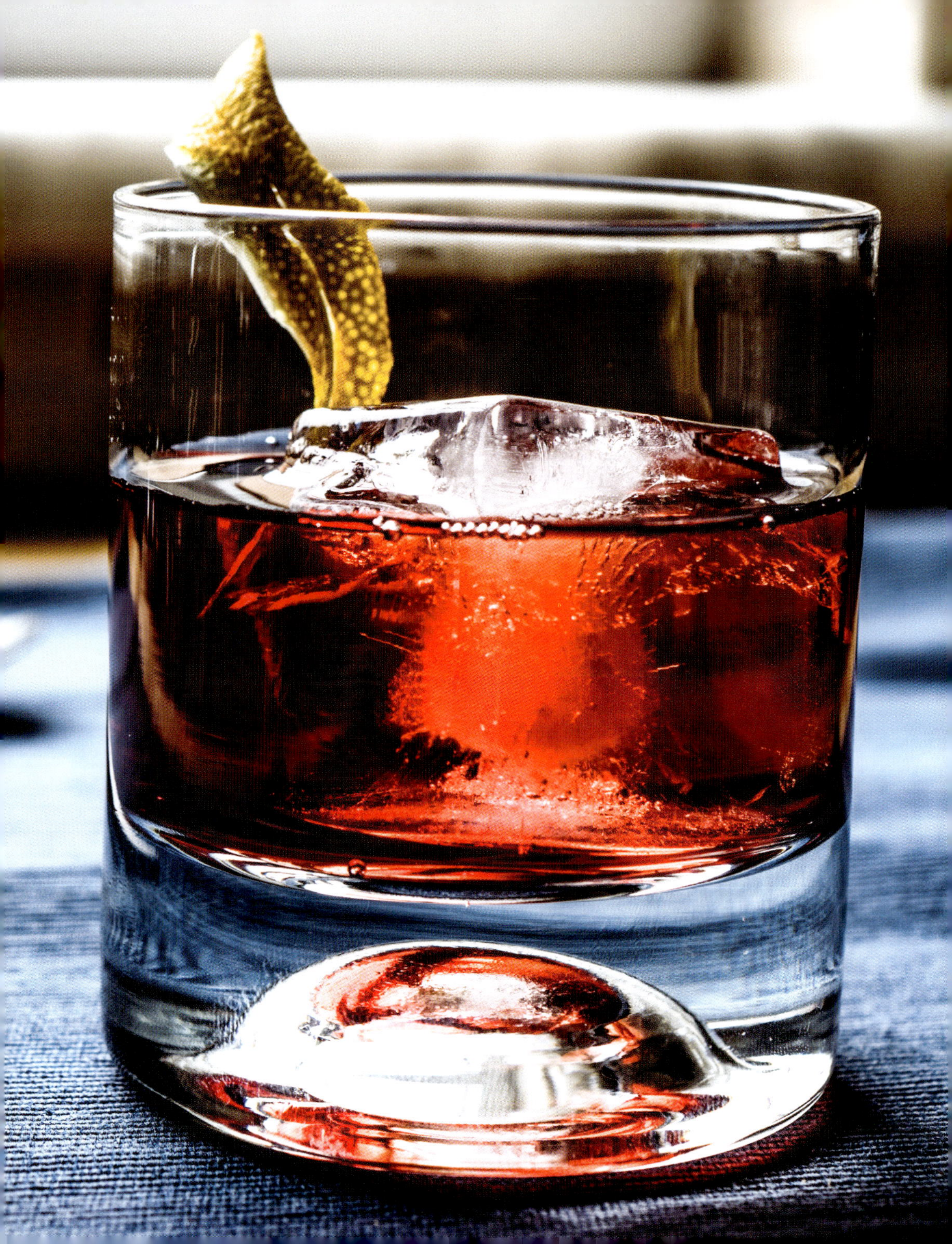

ALL I WANT FOR CHRISTMAS IS A NEGRONI

⅔ oz. Campari

⅔ oz. sweet vermouth

2 oz. gin

1 orange twist, for garnish

Place the Campari, sweet vermouth, and gin in a mixing glass, fill the glass two-thirds of the way with ice, and stir until chilled.

Strain the cocktail over ice into a rocks glass and garnish with the orange twist.

BLOODY MERRY

1 tablespoon fresh lemon juice

1 tablespoon fresh lime juice

4 oz. tomato juice

2 dashes of Worcestershire sauce

Pinch of sea salt

Pinch of celery salt

Pinch of coarsely ground black pepper

¼ teaspoon peeled and grated horseradish

2 oz. vodka

Place all of the ingredients in a cocktail shaker, fill it two-thirds of the way with ice, and shake vigorously until chilled.

Strain into a pint glass filled with ice and garnish as desired.

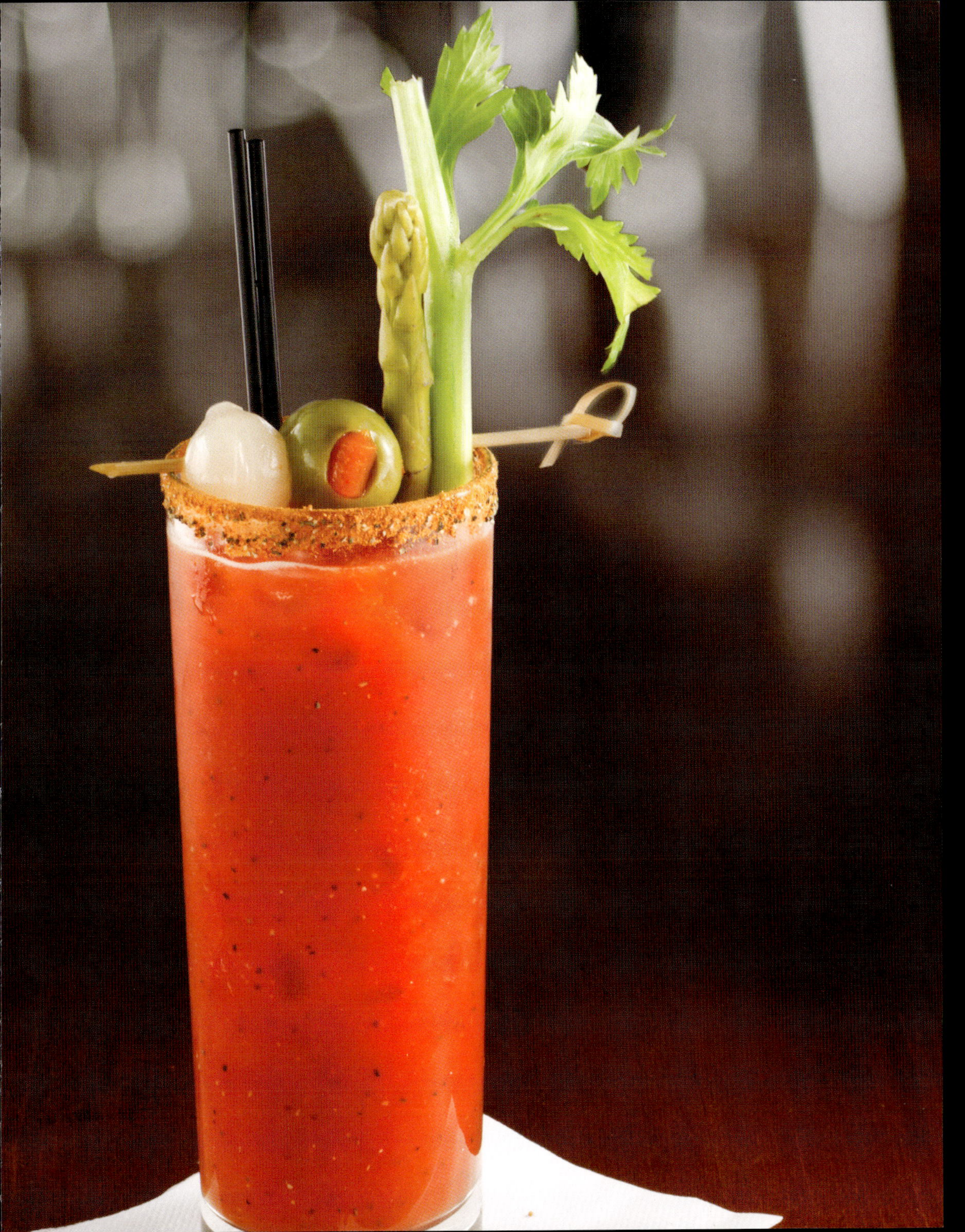

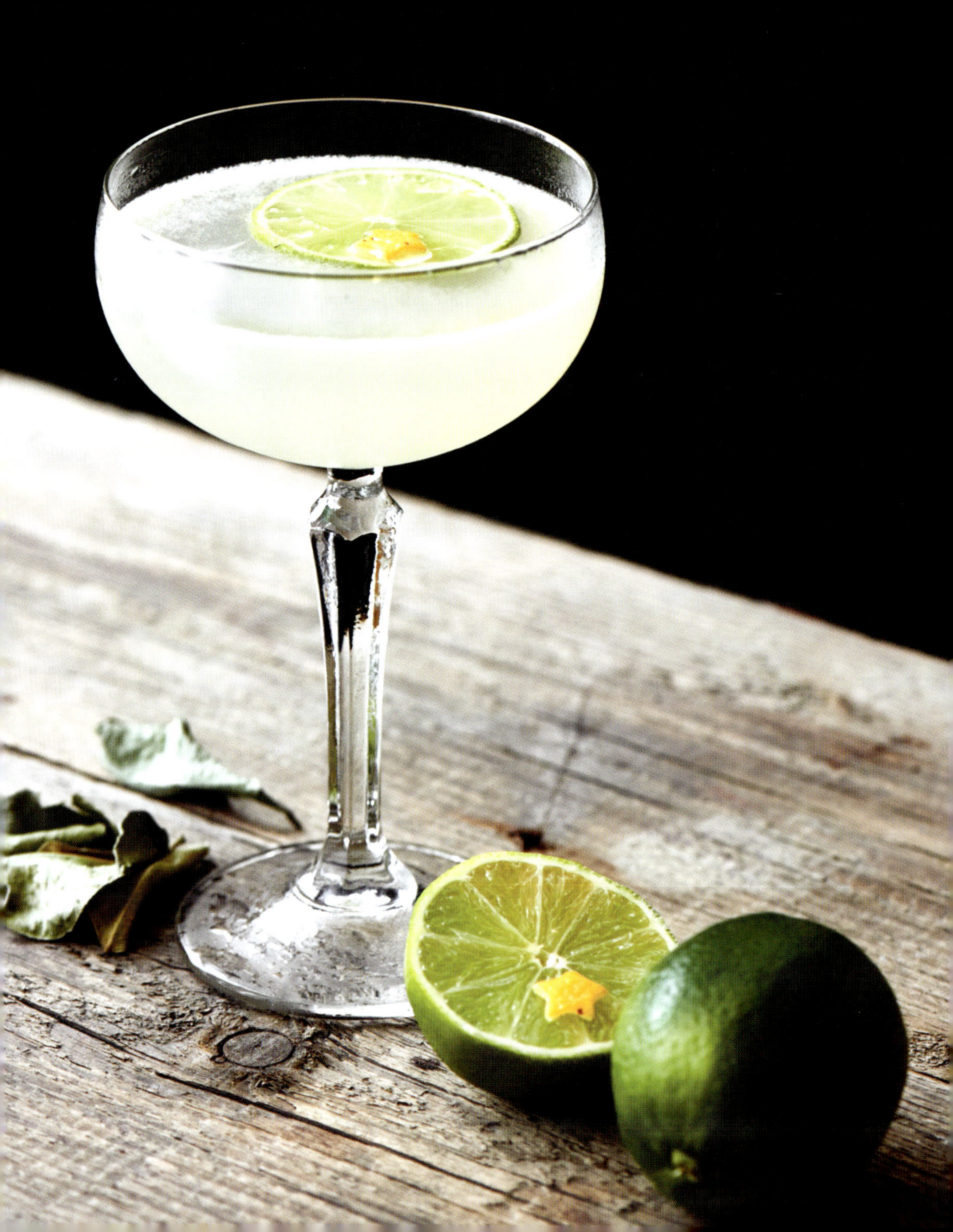

SILENT NIGHT, DAIQUIRI BRIGHT

2 oz. white rum

½ oz. fresh lime juice

½ teaspoon caster sugar

1 lime wheel, for garnish

Chill a coupe in the freezer.

Add the rum, lime juice, and caster sugar to a cocktail shaker, fill it two-thirds of the way with ice, and shake until chilled.

Strain into the chilled coupe and garnish with the lime wheel.

RYE AND SHINE, IT'S CHRISTMAS- TIME

2 oz. rye whiskey

⅔ oz. sweet vermouth

2 drops of aromatic bitters

1 maraschino cherry, for garnish

Chill a cocktail glass in the freezer.

Place the whiskey, vermouth, and bitters in a mixing glass, fill it two-thirds of the way with ice, and stir until chilled.

Strain into the cocktail glass and garnish with the maraschino cherry.

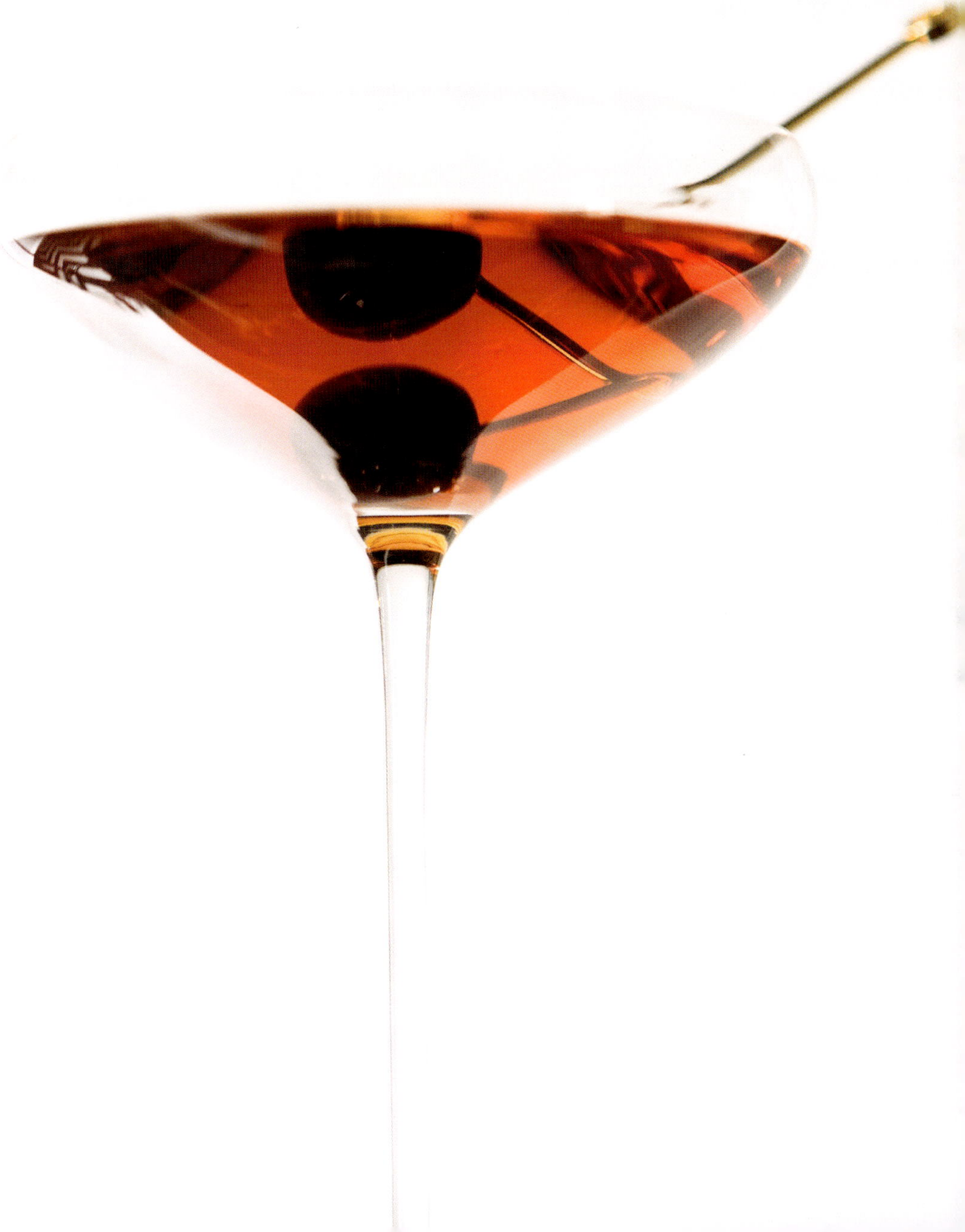

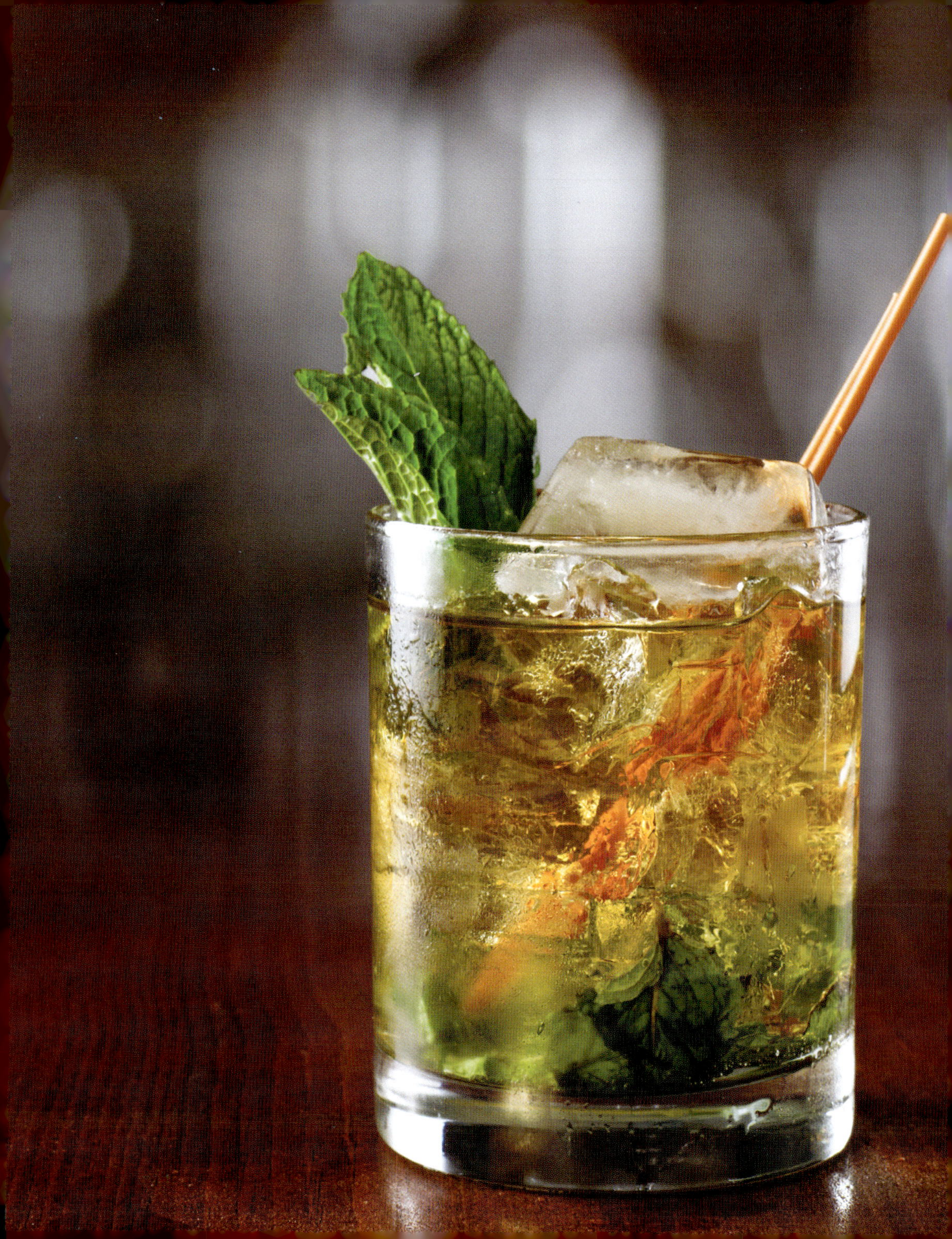

MINT JULEP FOR THE JADED

4 fresh mint leaves

1 teaspoon caster sugar

Splash of water

2 oz. bourbon

1 sprig of fresh mint, for garnish

Place the mint leaves, sugar, and water in a rocks glass and muddle.

Fill the glass with crushed ice, add the bourbon, and stir until chilled.

Garnish with the sprig of mint.

NEW YEAR, NEW NERVES

¾ oz. rye whiskey

¾ oz. Cognac

¾ oz. sweet vermouth

1 barspoon of Bénédictine

Dash of Peychaud's Bitters

Dash of Angostura Bitters

1 lemon twist, for garnish

Place the rye, Cognac, vermouth, Bénédictine, and bitters in a mixing glass, fill it two-thirds of the way with ice, and stir until chilled.

Strain over one large ice cube into a rocks glass and garnish with the lemon twist.

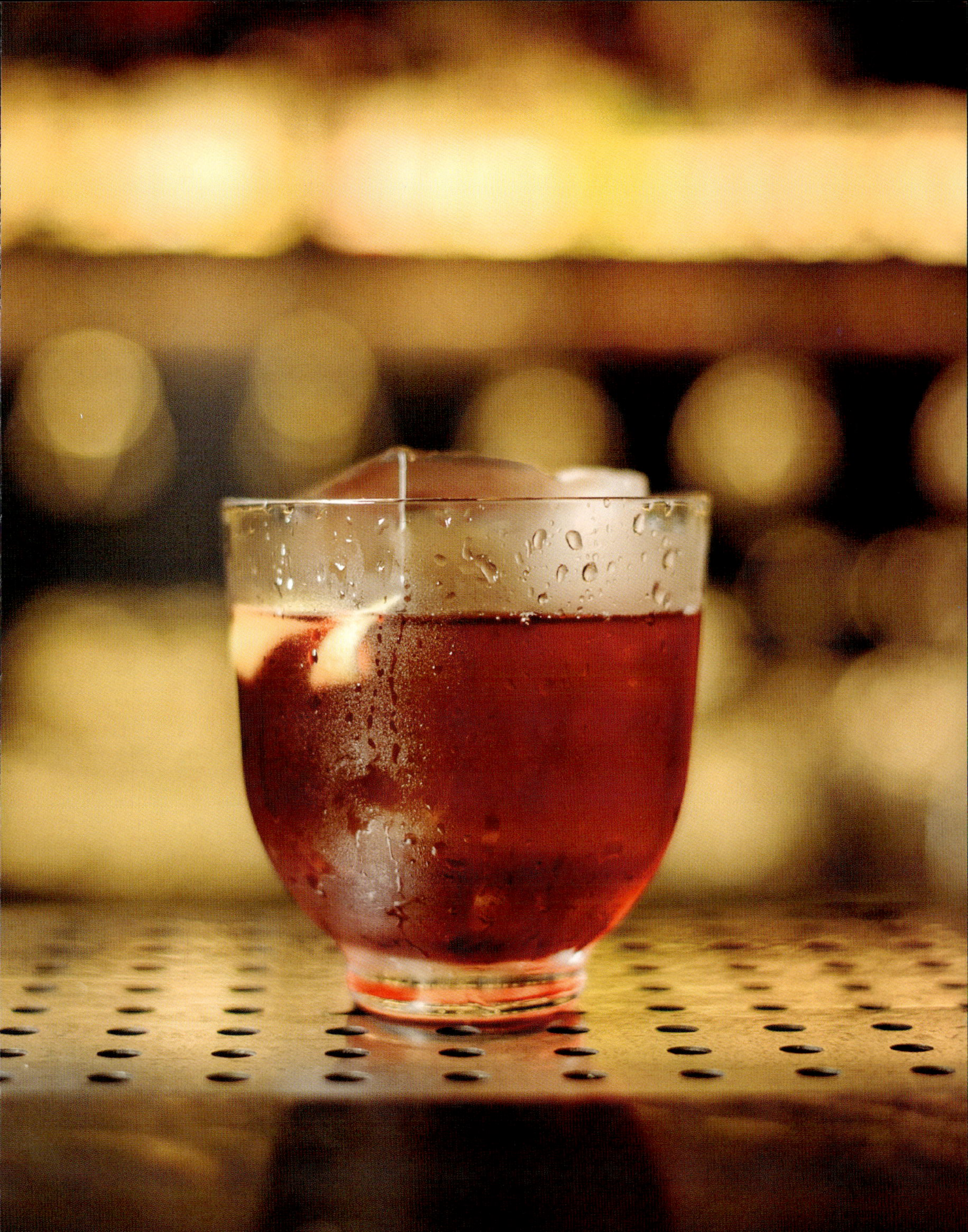

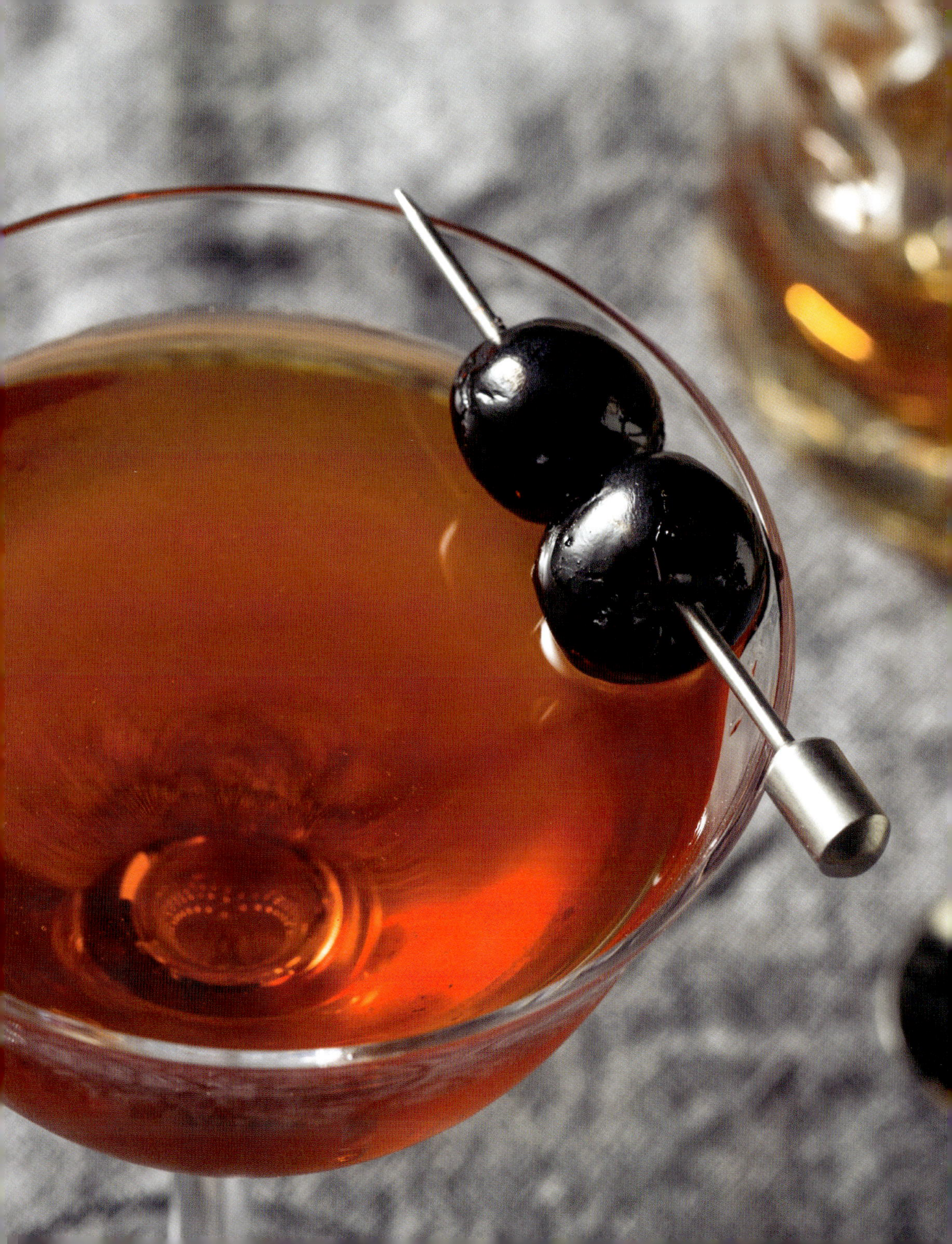

ROYALLY OVER THE HOLIDAYS

2 oz. Scotch whisky

1 oz. sweet vermouth

2 drops of Angostura Bitters

2 Luxardo maraschino cherries, for garnish

Add the Scotch, vermouth, and bitters to a mixing glass, fill it two-thirds of the way with ice, and stir until chilled.

Strain into a cocktail glass and garnish with the Luxardo maraschino cherries.

FIZZ THE SEASON

2 oz. Old Tom gin

1 oz. Simple Syrup (see page 20)

¾ oz. fresh lemon juice

Club soda, to top

1 lemon slice, for garnish

1 maraschino cherry, for garnish

Fill a Collins glass with ice and place it in the freezer.

Place the gin, syrup, and lemon juice in a cocktail shaker, fill it two-thirds of the way with ice, and shake until chilled.

Strain into the chilled Collins glass and top with the club soda.

Garnish with the lemon slice and cherry.

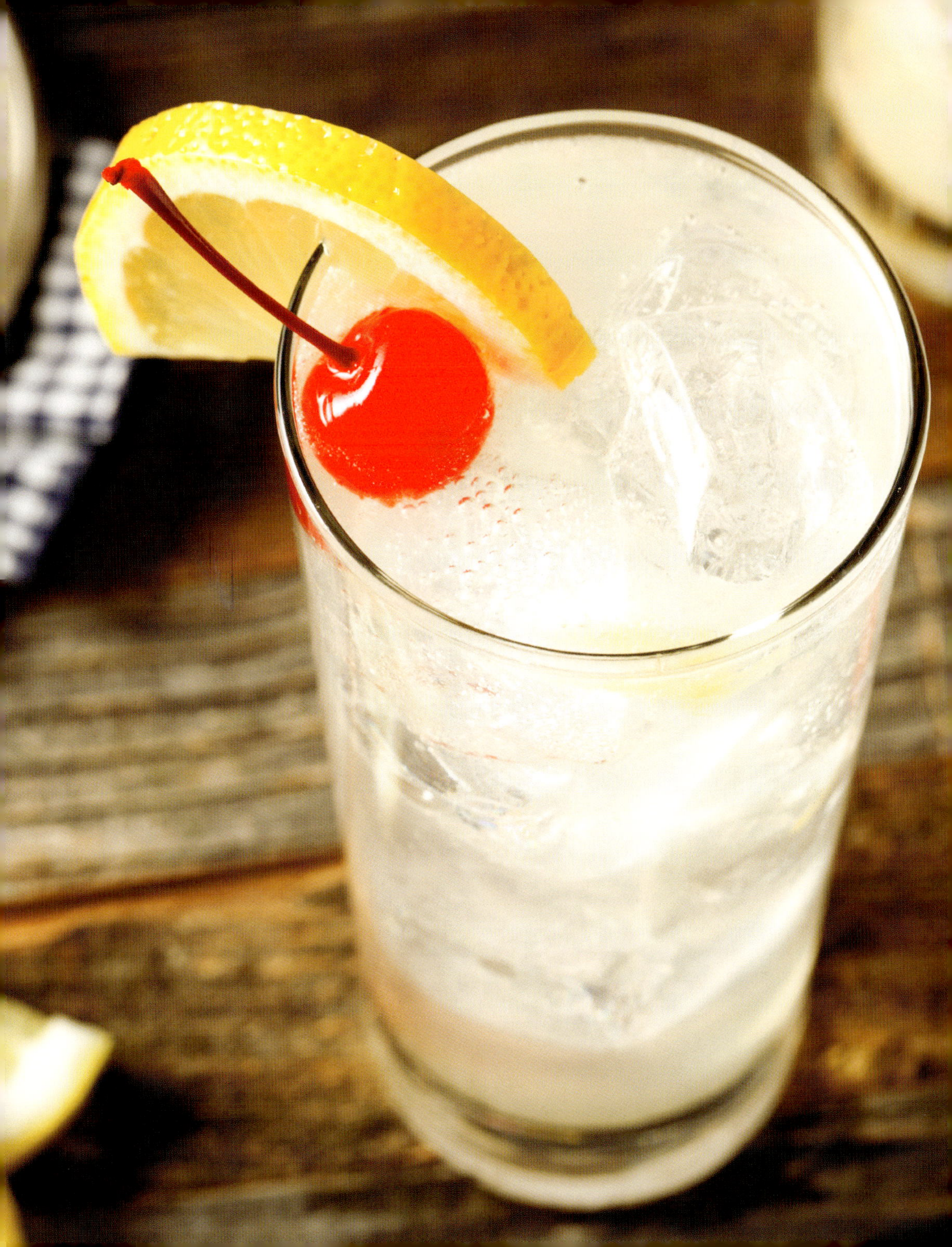

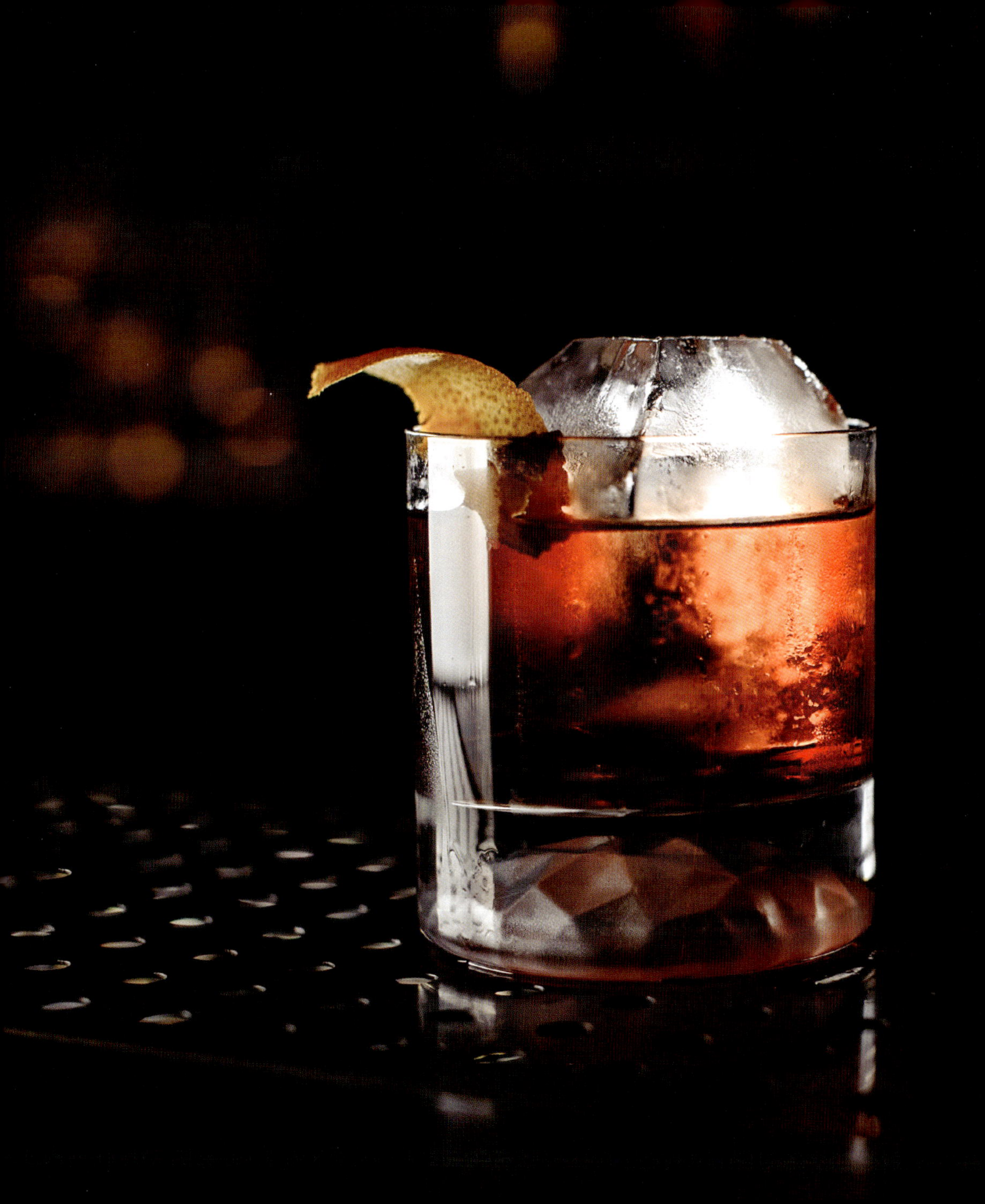

COAL FOR THE SOUL

1 oz. bourbon

1 oz. Campari

1 oz. sweet vermouth

1 orange twist, for garnish

Place the bourbon, Campari, and vermouth in a mixing glass, fill it two-thirds of the way with ice, and stir until chilled.

Strain over ice into a rocks glass and garnish with the orange twist.

SANTA'S LITTLE HELPER

2 oz. London Dry gin

½ oz. Luxardo maraschino liqueur

¼ oz. crème de violette

½ oz. fresh lemon juice

1 maraschino cherry, for garnish

Chill a cocktail glass in the freezer.

Place the gin, Luxardo, crème de violette, and lemon juice in a cocktail shaker, fill it two-thirds of the way with ice, and shake until chilled.

Strain into the chilled glass and garnish with the cherry.

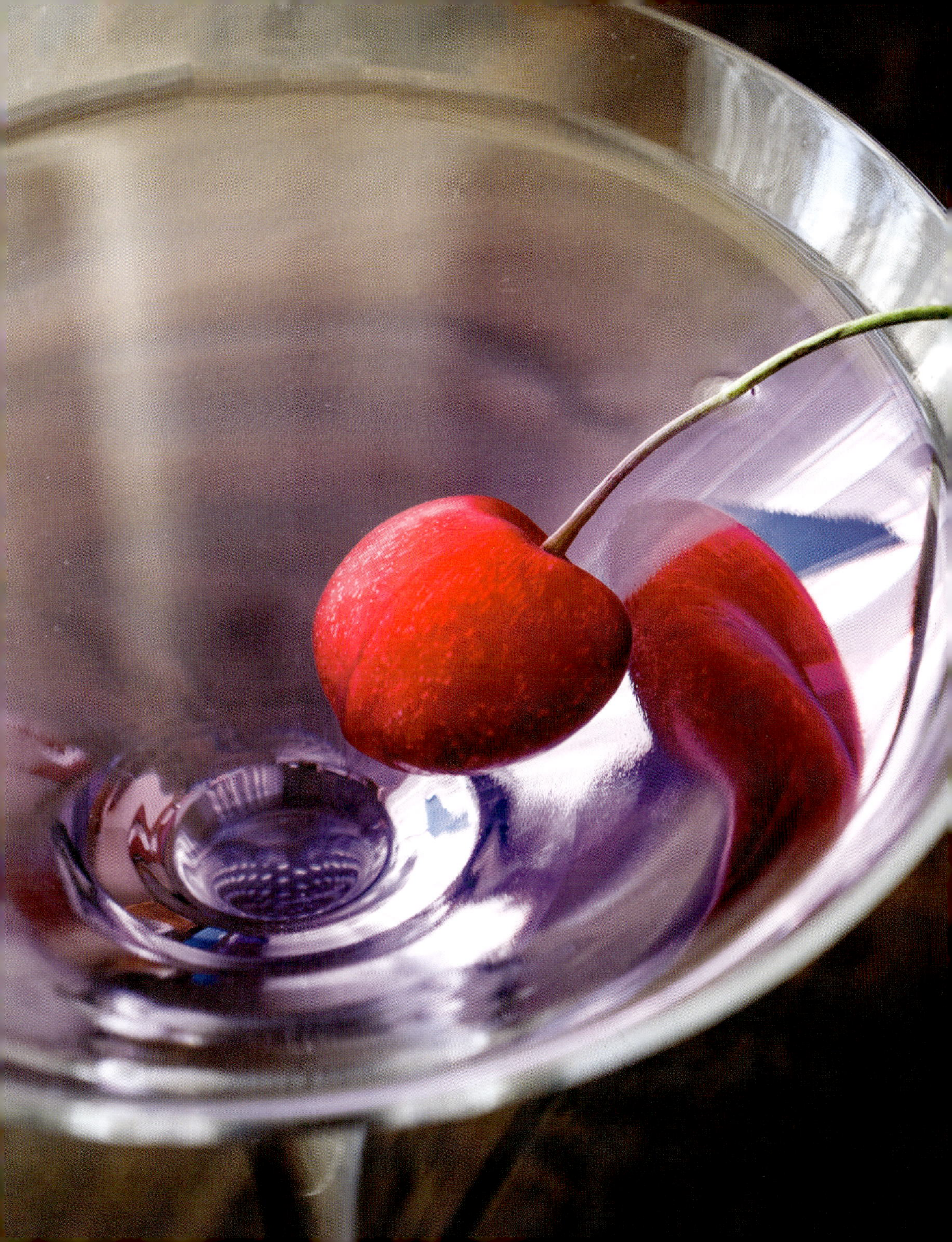

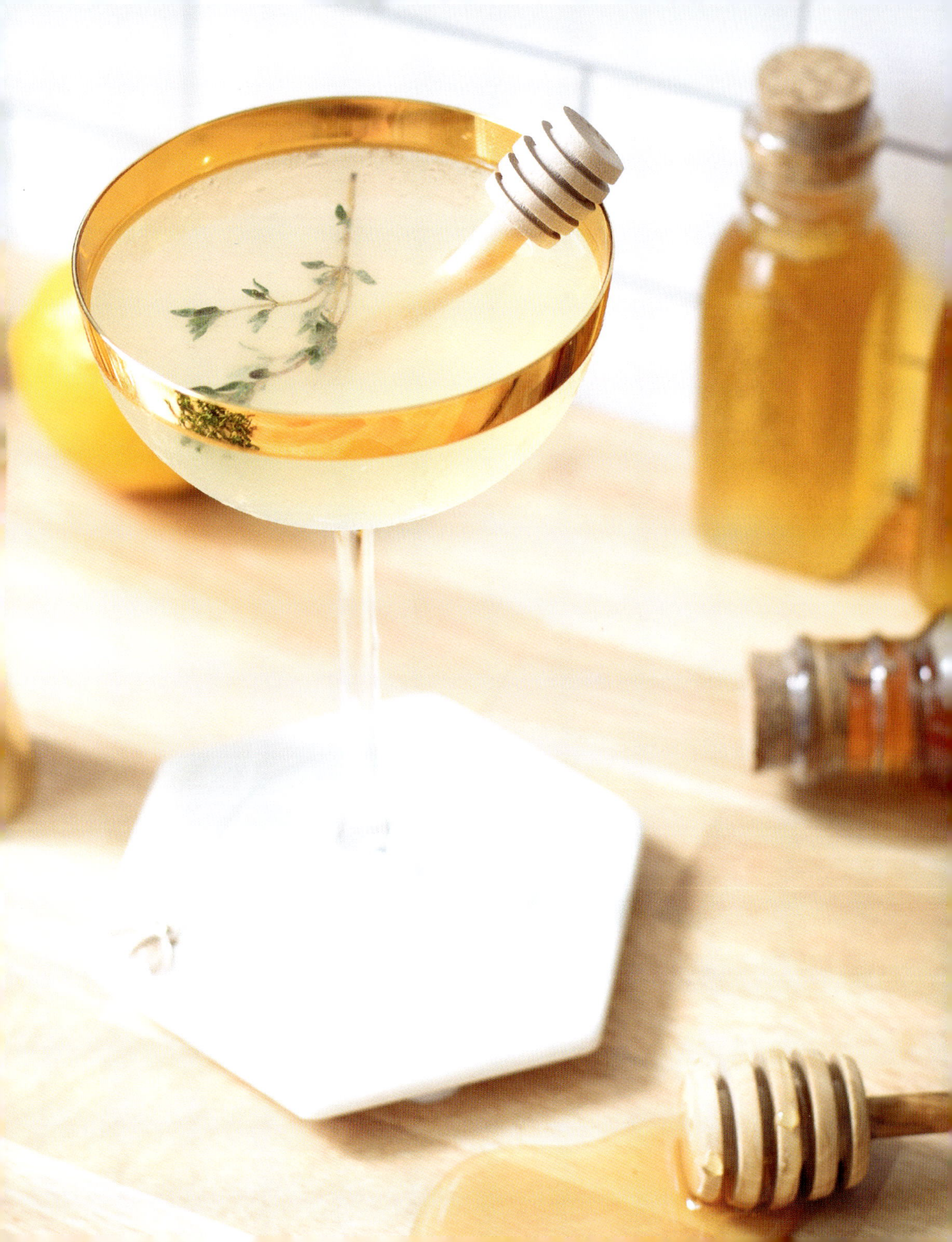

BUZZ OFF, HOLIDAY DRAMA

2 oz. dry gin

¾ oz. fresh lemon juice

¾ oz. honey syrup

Sprig of fresh thyme, for garnish

Chill a coupe in the freezer.

Place the gin, lemon juice, and honey syrup in a cocktail shaker, fill it two-thirds of the way with ice, and shake until chilled.

Strain into the chilled coupe and garnish with the sprig of thyme.

LIME, GIN, AND ZERO PATIENCE

1½ oz. gin

½ oz. fresh lime juice

1 lime twist, for garnish

Place the gin and lime juice in a cocktail shaker, fill it two-thirds of the way with ice, and shake until chilled.

Strain into a cocktail glass and garnish with the lime twist.

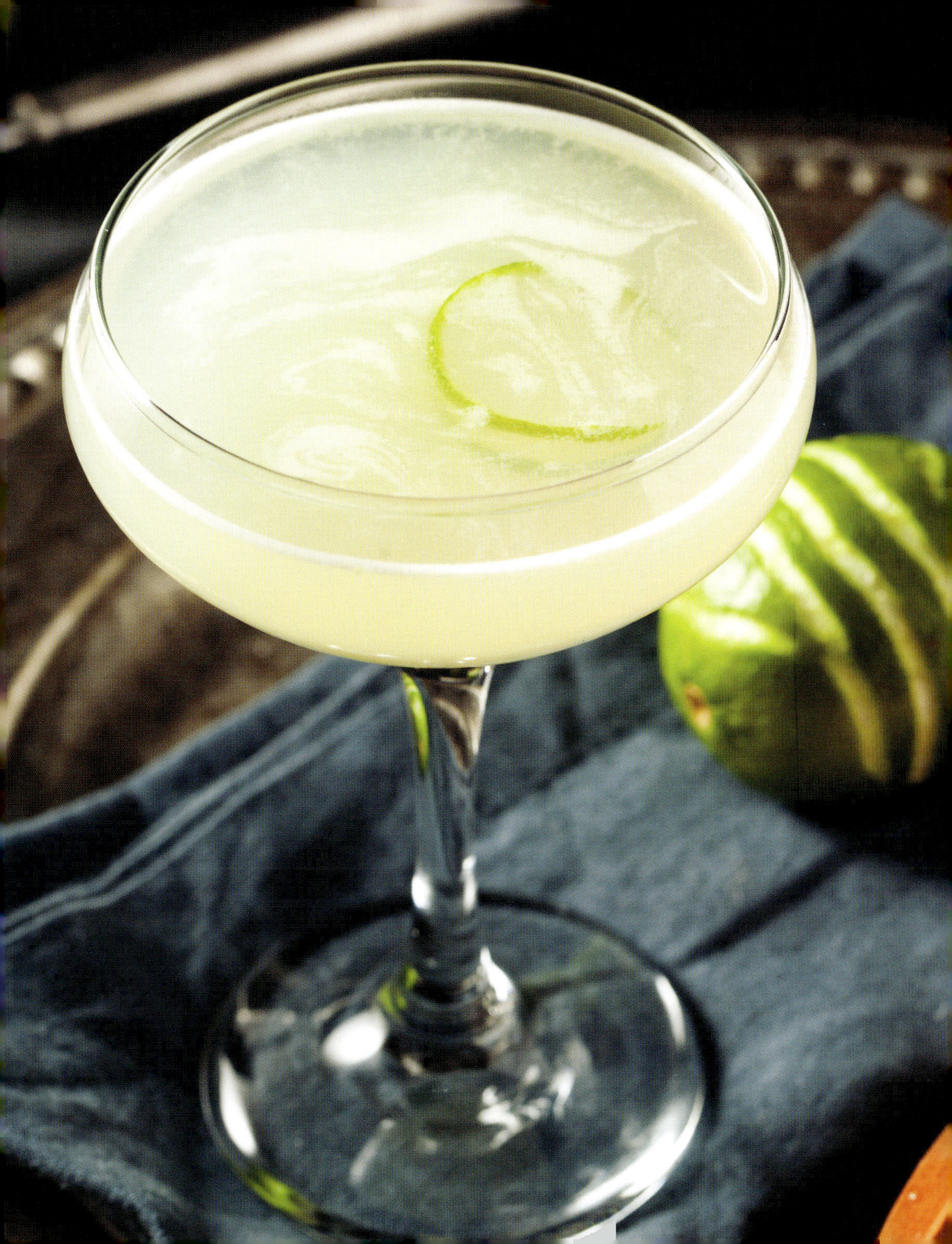

Swapping blue cheese–stuffed olives in for the garnish is a much-loved variation among Martini devotees.

MERRY CHRISTMAS, YA FILTHY ANIMAL

3 oz. gin

¾ oz. dry vermouth

Splash of olive brine

3 pimento-stuffed olives, for garnish

Place the gin, vermouth, and olive brine in a mixing glass, fill it two-thirds of the way with ice, and stir until chilled.

Strain into a cocktail glass and garnish with the olives skewered on a toothpick.

NOT ANOTHER HOLIDAY MELTDOWN

2 oz. London Dry gin

1 oz. dry vermouth

½ oz. triple sec

3 dashes of absinthe

1 lemon twist, for garnish

Place the gin, vermouth, triple sec, and absinthe in a mixing glass, fill it two-thirds of the way with ice, and stir until chilled.

Strain into a coupe and garnish with the lemon twist.

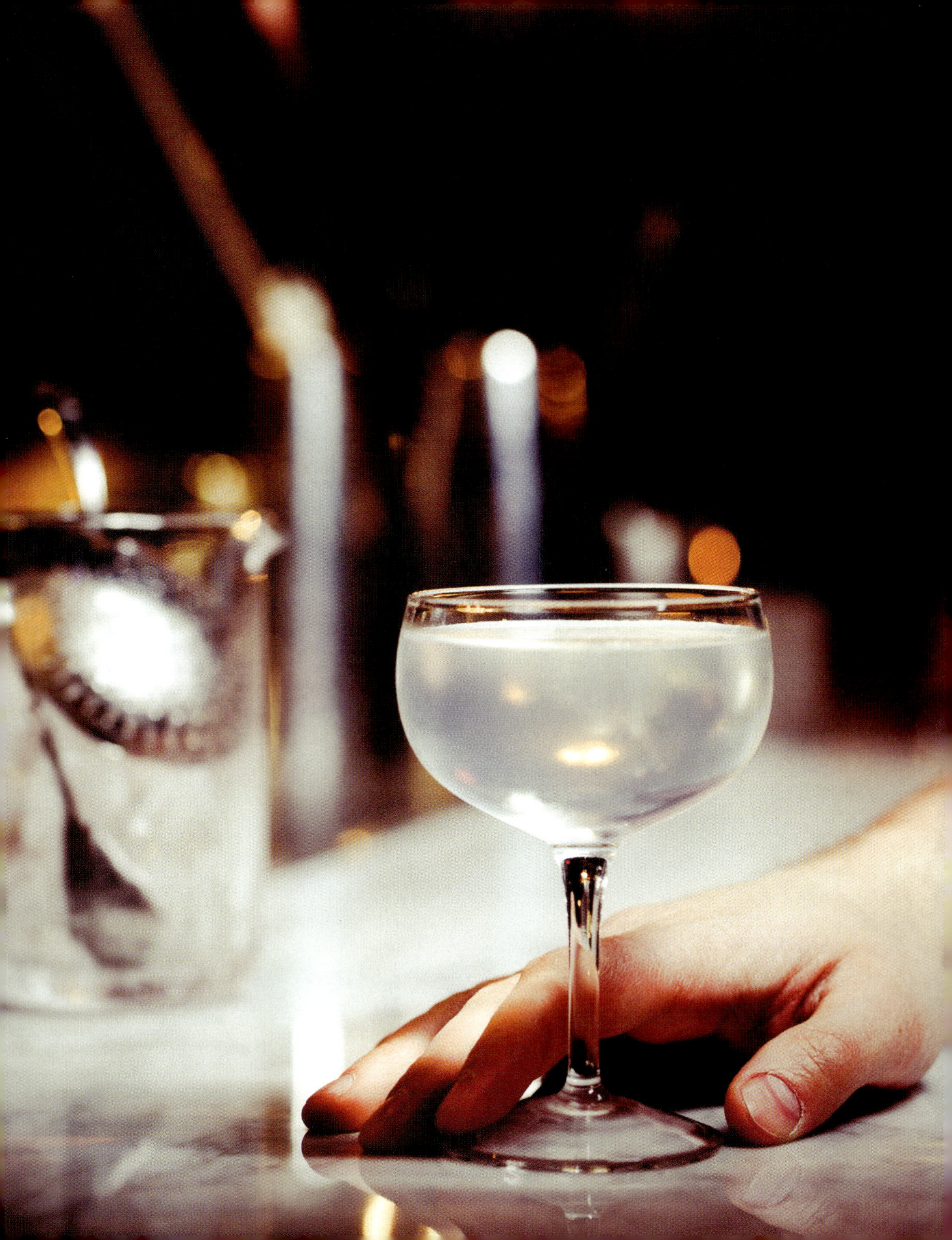

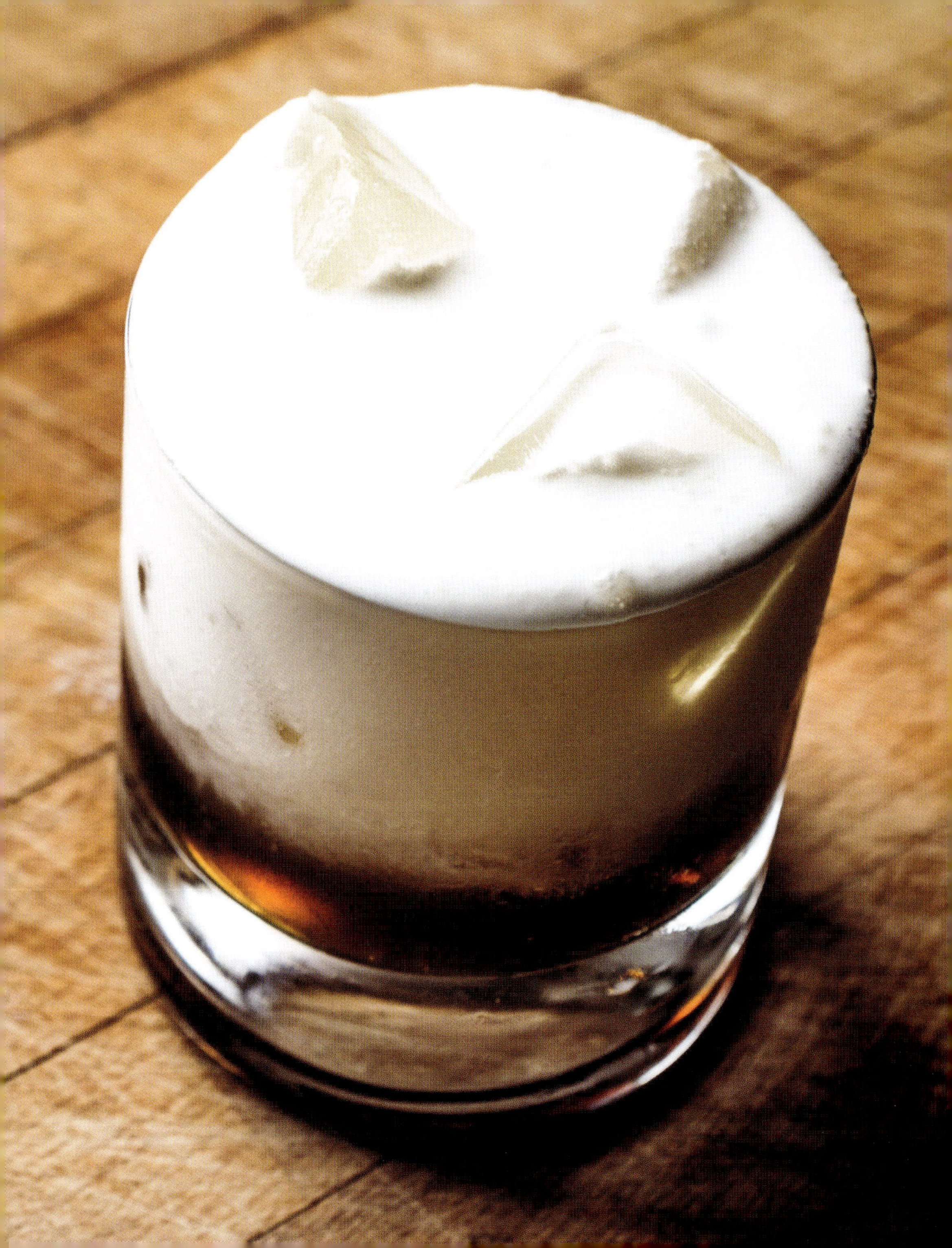

WHITE ELEPHANT

2 oz. vodka

1 oz. Kahlúa

Heavy cream, to taste

Place a few ice cubes in a rocks glass.

Add the vodka and Kahlúa and stir until chilled. Top with a generous splash of heavy cream and slowly stir until combined.

IF I GET RUN OVER BY A REINDEER, CAN I BAIL?

4 fresh mint leaves

Juice of ½ lime

2 oz. vodka

6 oz. ginger beer

1 lime wedge, for garnish

Place the mint leaves at the bottom of a copper mug, add the lime juice, and muddle.

Add crushed ice to the mug, add the vodka and ginger beer, and garnish with the lime wedge.

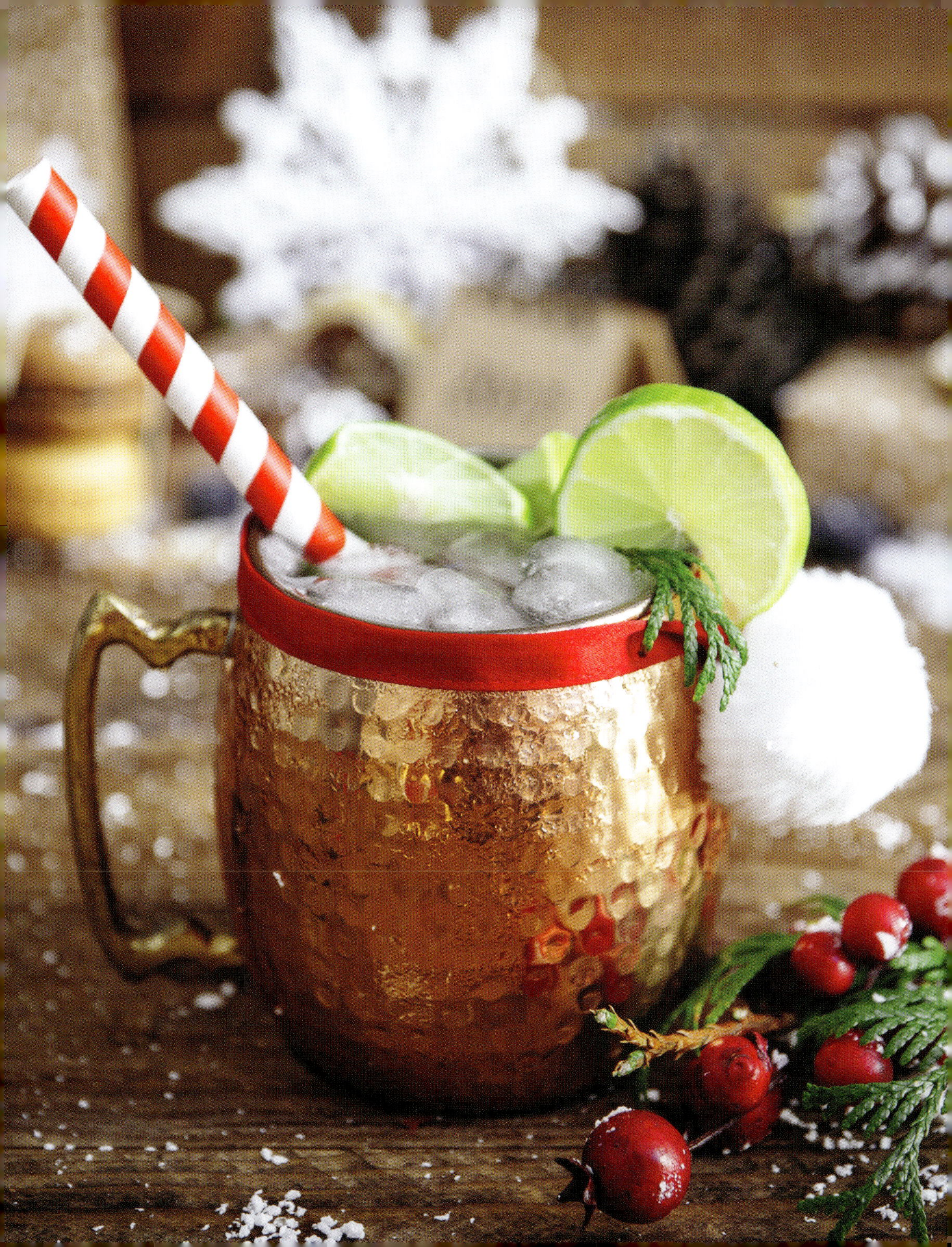

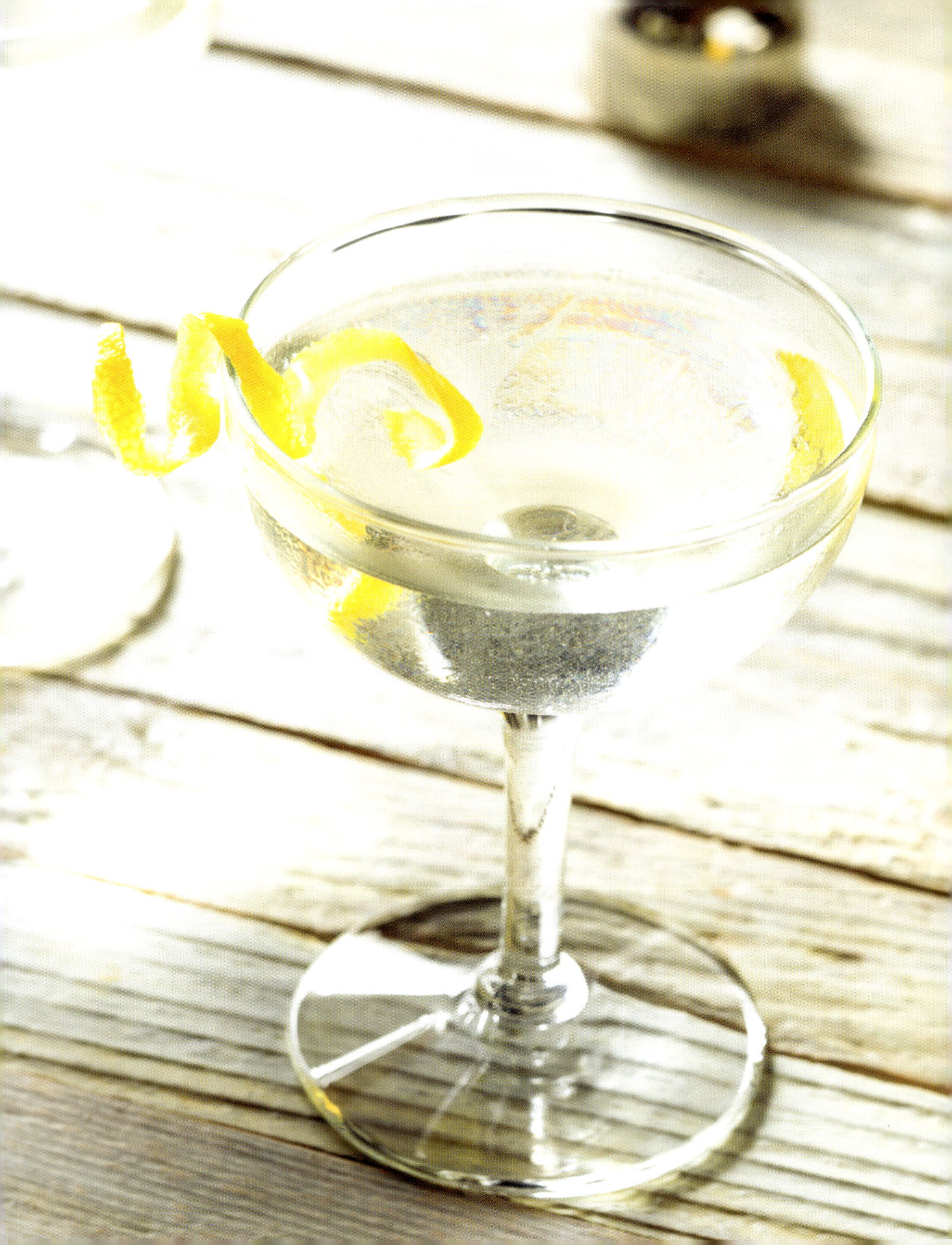

LICENSE TO CHILL

3 oz. gin

1 oz. vodka

½ oz. Lillet Blanc or Cocchi Americano

1 lemon twist, for garnish

Chill a coupe in the freezer.

Add the gin, vodka, and Lillet or Cocchi Americano to a cocktail shaker, fill it two-thirds of the way with ice, and shake until chilled.

Strain into the chilled coupe and garnish with the lemon twist.

I JUST WANT TO GO TO BED

2 oz. vodka

1 oz. freshly brewed espresso

½ oz. Kahlúa

3 espresso beans, for garnish

Chill a cocktail glass in the freezer.

Place the vodka, espresso, and Kahlúa in a cocktail shaker, fill it two-thirds of the way with ice, and shake until chilled.

Double-strain into the chilled glass and garnish with the espresso beans.

Even though it will cool in the shaker, be sure to use a steaming hot shot of espresso so that the cocktail retains the crema.

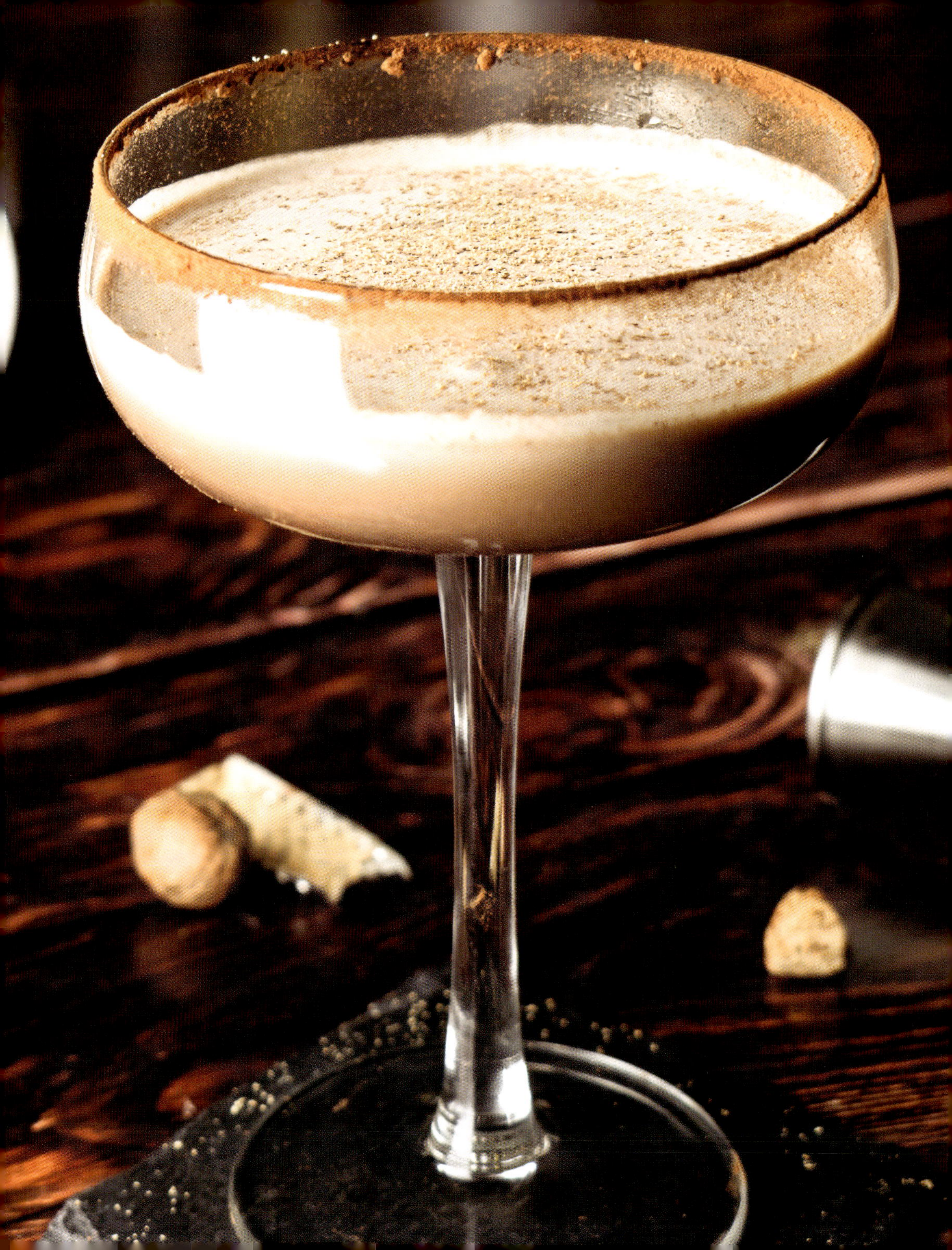

CALORIES DON'T COUNT AT CHRISTMASTIME

1½ oz. brandy or Cognac

1 oz. crème de cacao

¾ oz. heavy cream

Freshly grated nutmeg, for garnish

Chill a cocktail glass in the freezer.

Place the ingredients, except for the nutmeg, in a cocktail shaker, fill it two-thirds of the way with ice, and shake until chilled.

Strain into the chilled cocktail glass and garnish with the nutmeg.

"TOO MUCH FAMILY TIME" MOJITO

8 fresh mint leaves

1 oz. Simple Syrup (see page 20)

1 oz. fresh lime juice

2 oz. white rum

1 sprig of fresh mint, for garnish

Place the mint leaves in the palm of one hand and slap them to activate their aroma. Place them in the bottom of a Collins glass and add the syrup and lime juice.

Fill the glass halfway with crushed ice. Gently stir until lightly chilled, about 10 seconds. Add the rum and more crushed ice and briefly stir to combine.

Fill the remainder of the glass with crushed ice and garnish with the sprig of mint.

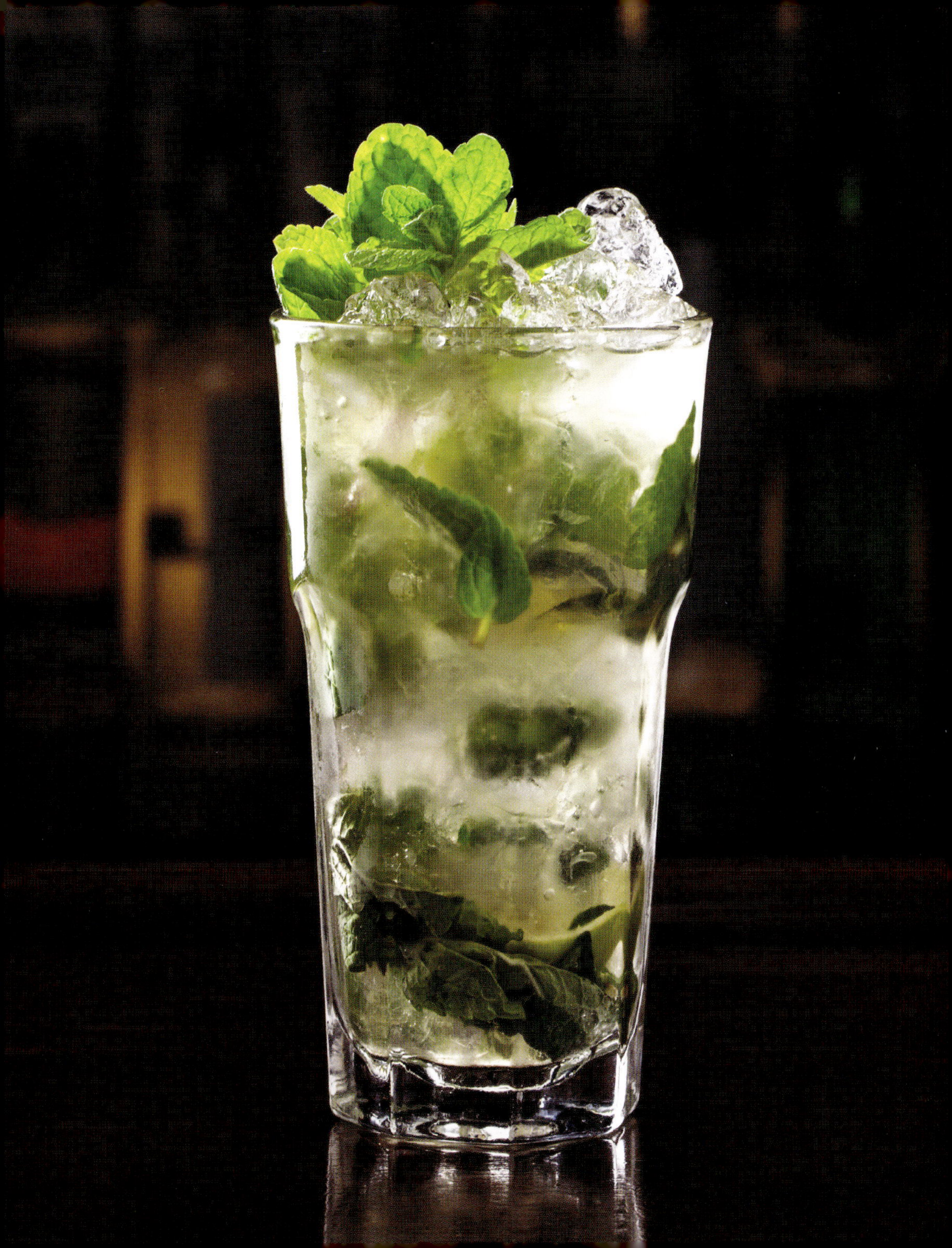

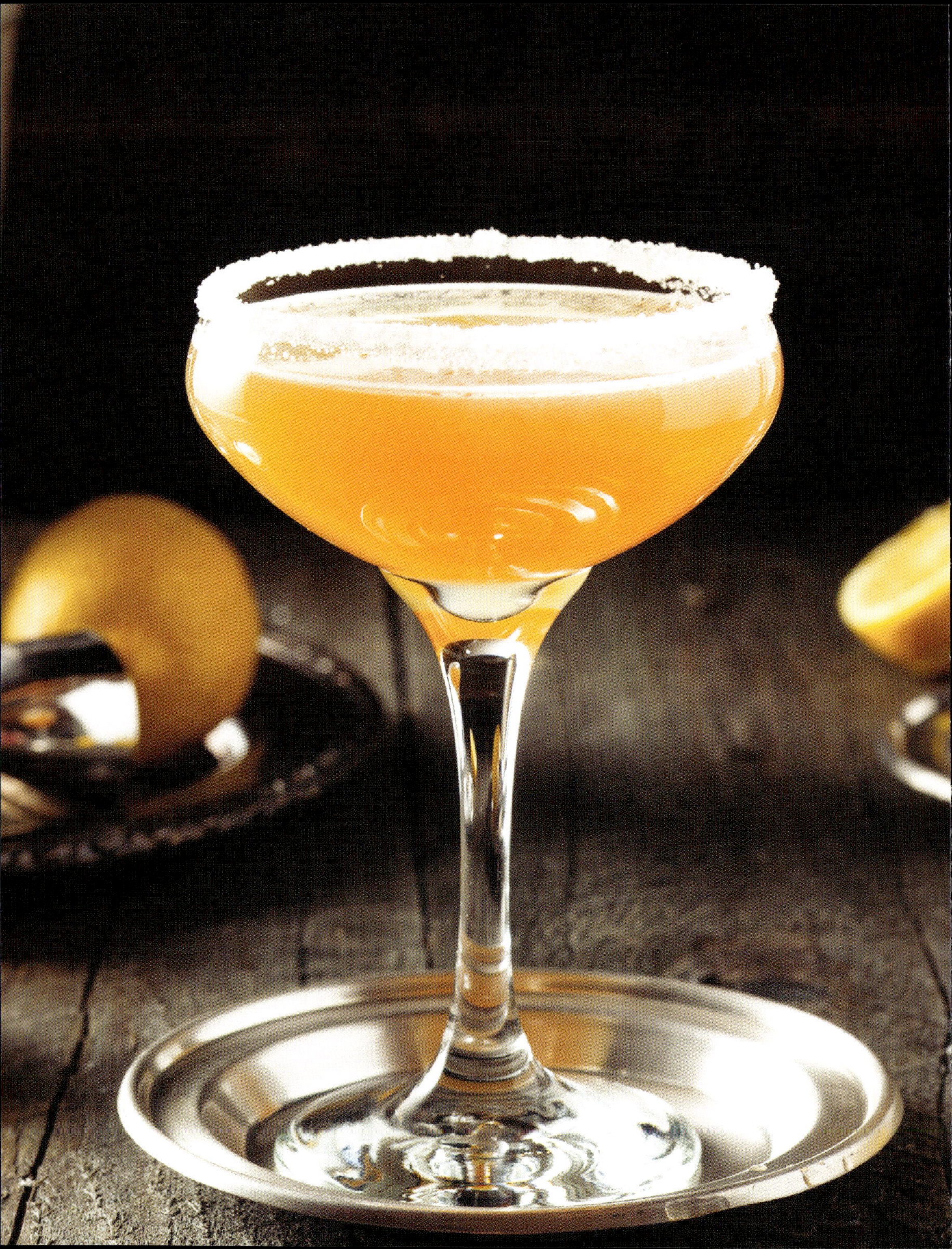

I'M JUST HERE FOR THE BOOZE

Sugar, for the rim (optional)

1½ oz. Cognac

¾ oz. Cointreau

¾ oz. fresh lemon juice

1 lemon twist, for garnish

If desired, rim a coupe with sugar.

Place the Cognac, Cointreau, and lemon juice in a cocktail shaker, fill it two-thirds of the way with ice, and shake until chilled.

Strain into the coupe and garnish with the lemon twist.

MY FACE HURTS FROM FAKE SMILING

1 oz. green crème de menthe

1 oz. white crème de cacao

1 oz. heavy cream

Chill a cocktail glass or champagne flute in the freezer.

Place the ingredients in a cocktail shaker, fill it two-thirds of the way with ice, and shake until chilled.

Strain into the chilled glass.

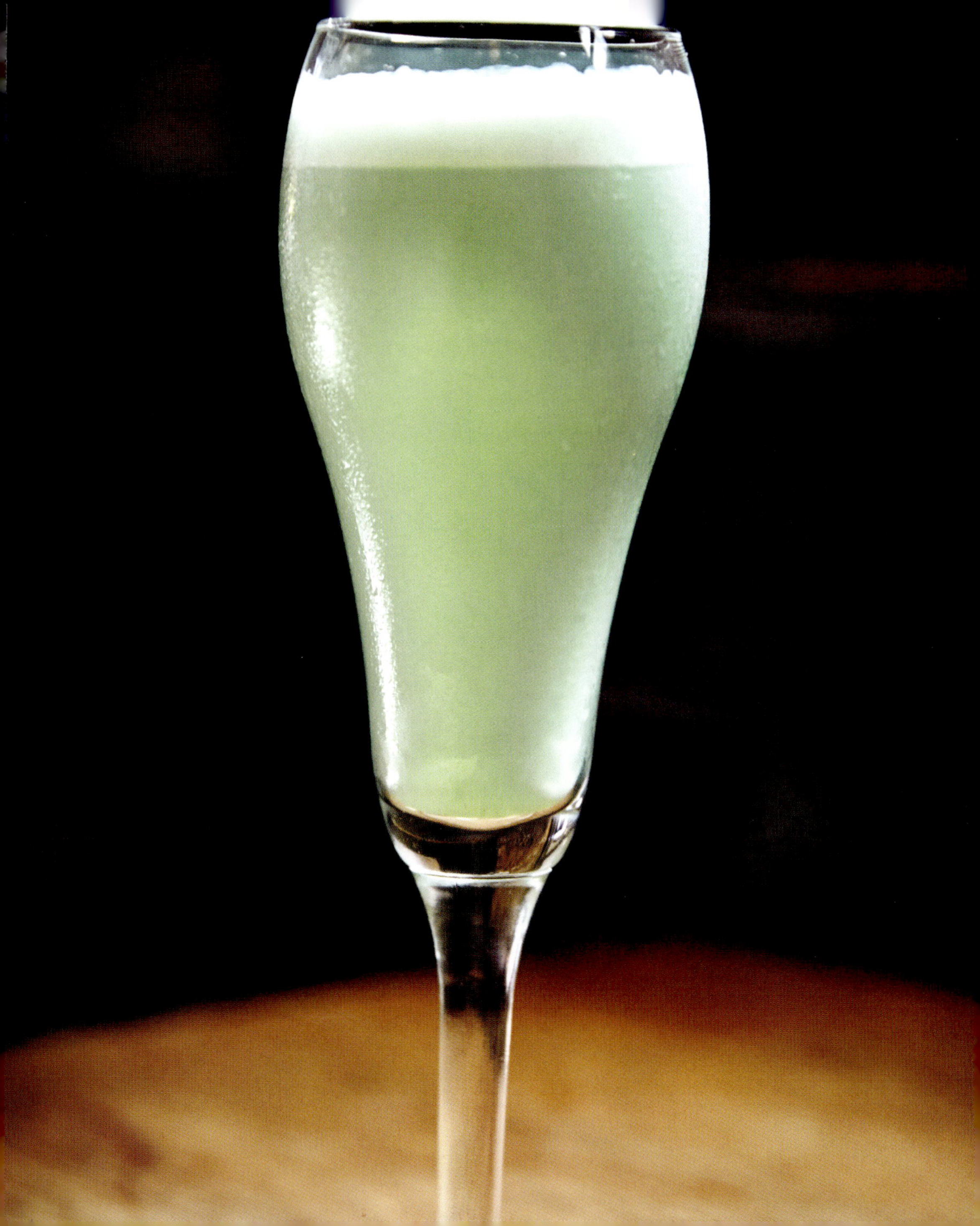

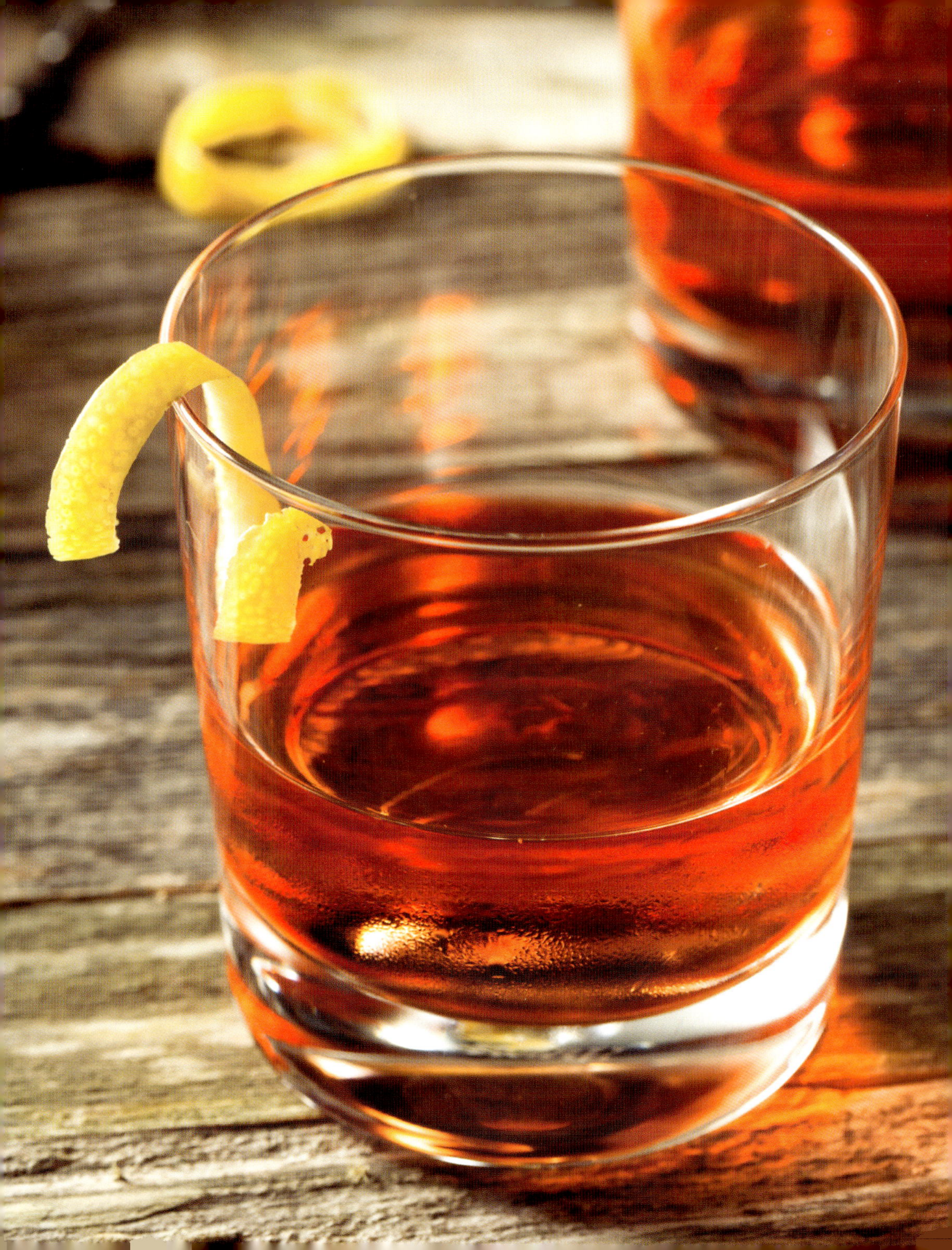

HO-HO-HOLY CRAP THAT'S STRONG

⅛ oz. Herbsaint

1 sugar cube

3 dashes of Peychaud's Bitters

1½ oz. Sazerac Rye whiskey

1 lemon twist, for garnish

Chill a rocks glass in the freezer.

Remove the glass from the freezer, add the Herbsaint, and rinse the glass with it. Discard any excess and set the glass aside.

Drop the sugar cube in a mixing glass, add the bitters, and muddle. Add the rye along with ice, stir until chilled, and strain the cocktail into the glass.

Garnish with the lemon twist.

ALL I WANT FOR CHRISTMAS IS A SPARKLY DRINK

It's not the holidays without a little sparkle, and by sparkle, we mean booze with bubbles. This chapter is your one-stop shop for all things fizzy and fabulous—because nothing says "festive" like a drink that's as over-the-top as your neighbor's synchronized holiday light show. Whether you're raising a glass to New Year's Eve, toasting at yet another holiday brunch, or just trying to distract everyone from the fact that you forgot to buy a gift, these cocktails have you covered. Because if Mariah Carey taught us anything, it's that all we really want for Christmas is *this*.

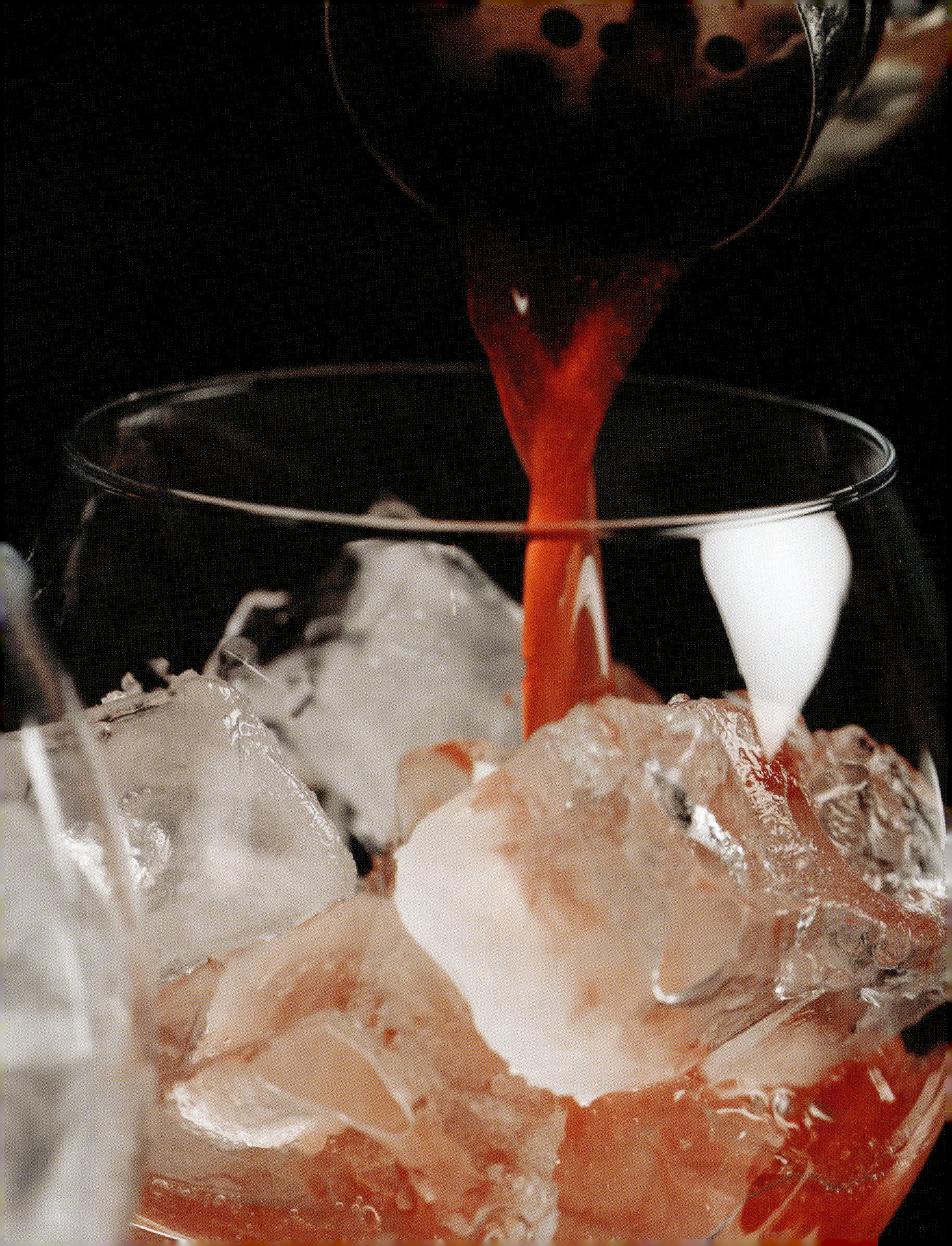

IT'S 10 A.M. SOMEWHERE

3 oz. orange juice

3 oz. Champagne

1 orange wheel, for garnish

Place the orange juice in a champagne flute and top with the champagne Garnish with the orange wheel.

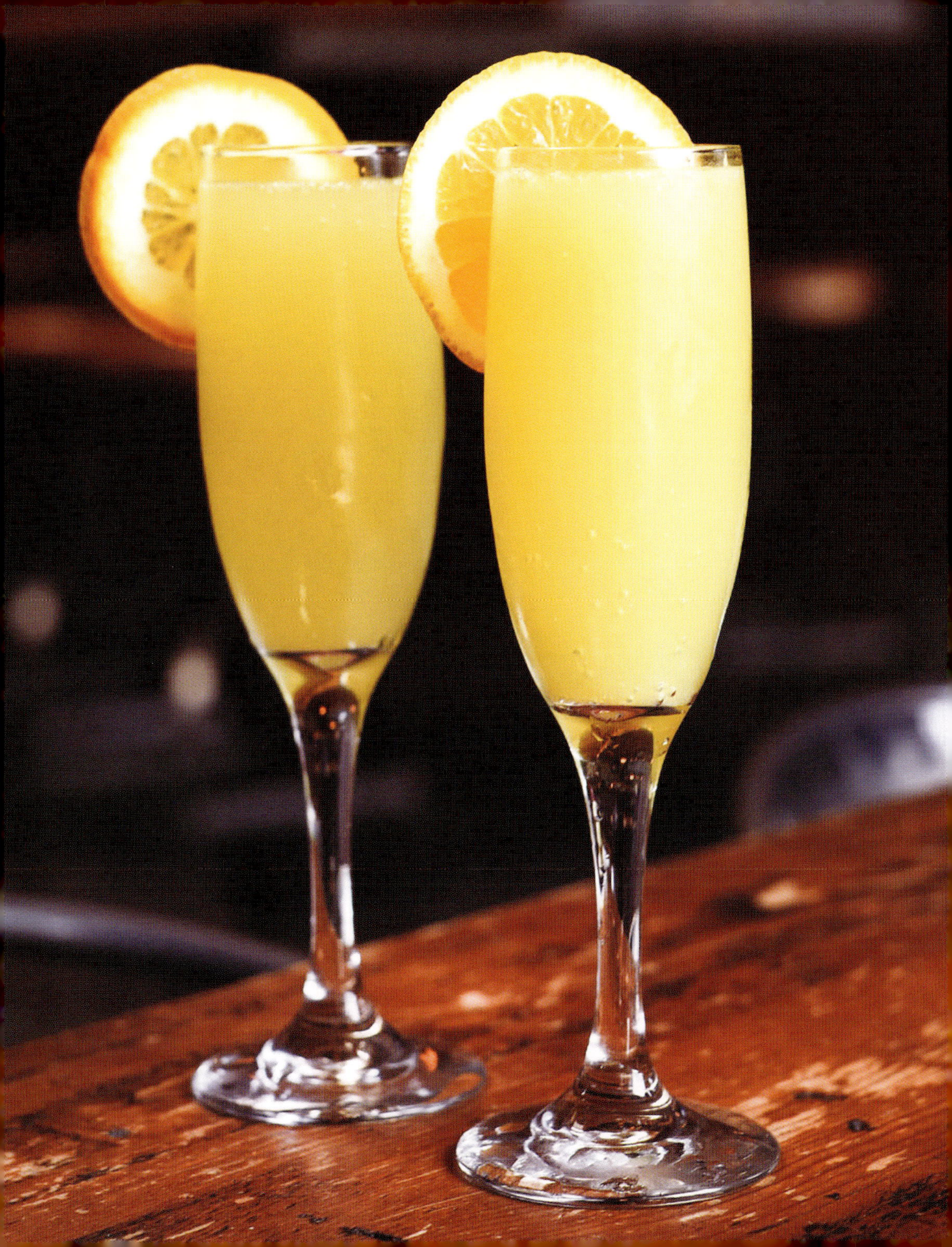

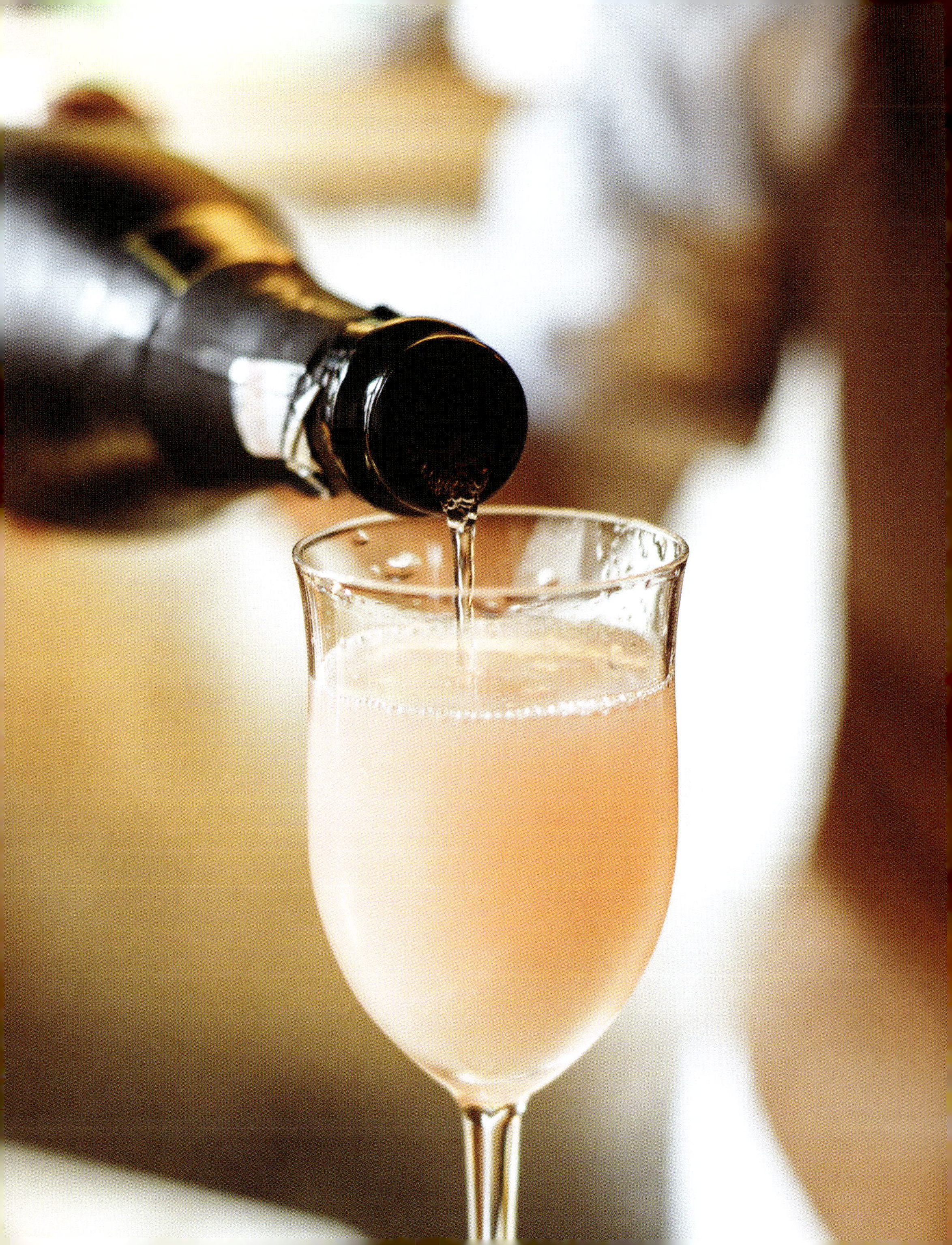

MARIAH CAREY IS MY VILLAIN ORIGIN STORY

2 oz. single-malt whisky

1 oz. Averna Amaro

2 oz. dry sparkling wine

Chill a champagne flute in the freezer.

Place the whisky and amaro in a mixing glass, fill it two-thirds of the way with ice, and stir until chilled.

Strain into the chilled champagne flute and top with the sparkling wine.

THIS IS MY EMOTIONAL SUPPORT DRINK

1 sugar cube

Juice of 1 lemon wedge

1 oz. gin

2 oz. Champagne

1 lemon twist, for garnish

1 Luxardo maraschino cherry, for garnish

Place the sugar cube in a champagne flute and add the lemon juice.

Add the gin and top with the Champagne.

Garnish the cocktail with the lemon twist. Skewer the cherry with a toothpick, place it over the mouth of the champagne flute, and enjoy.

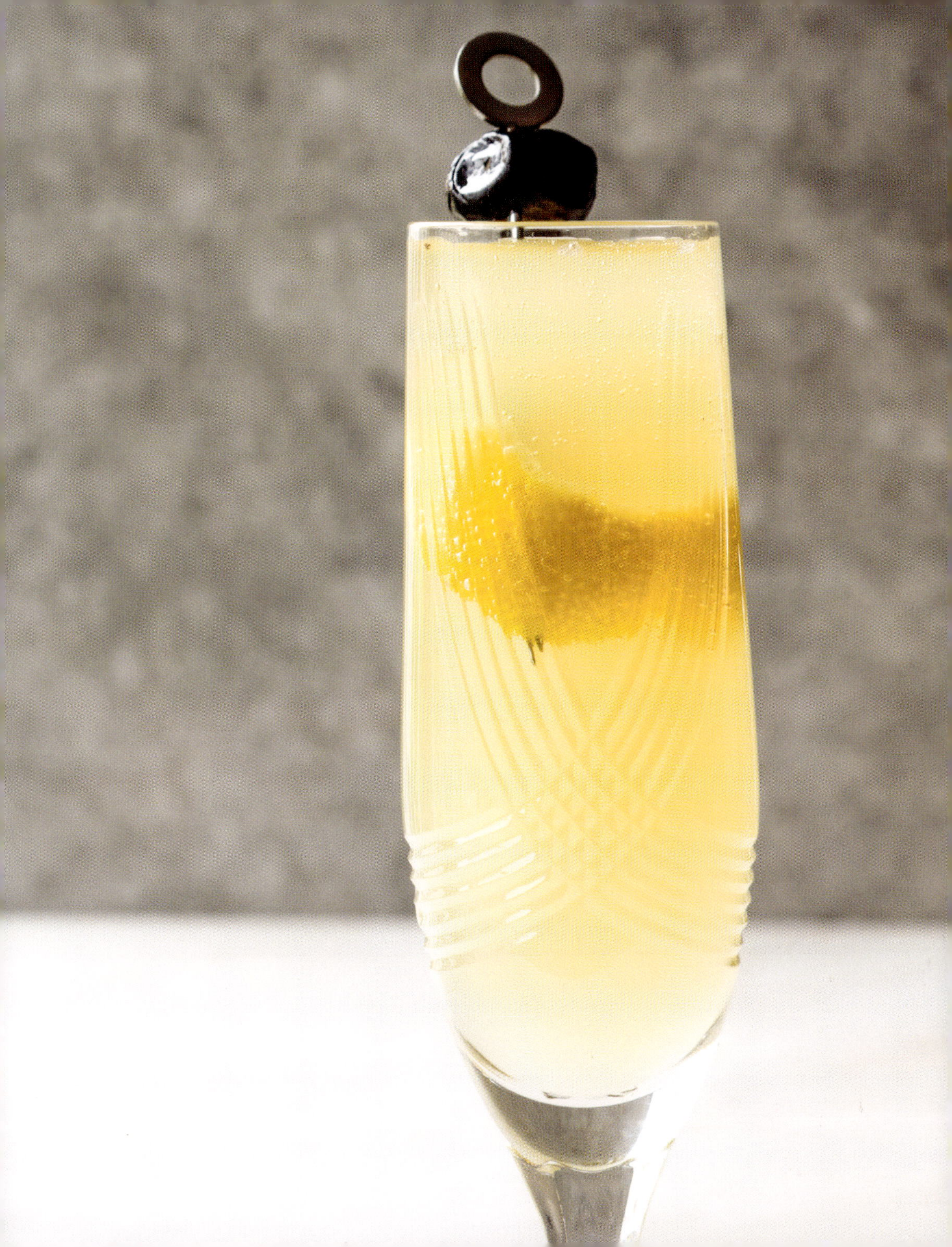

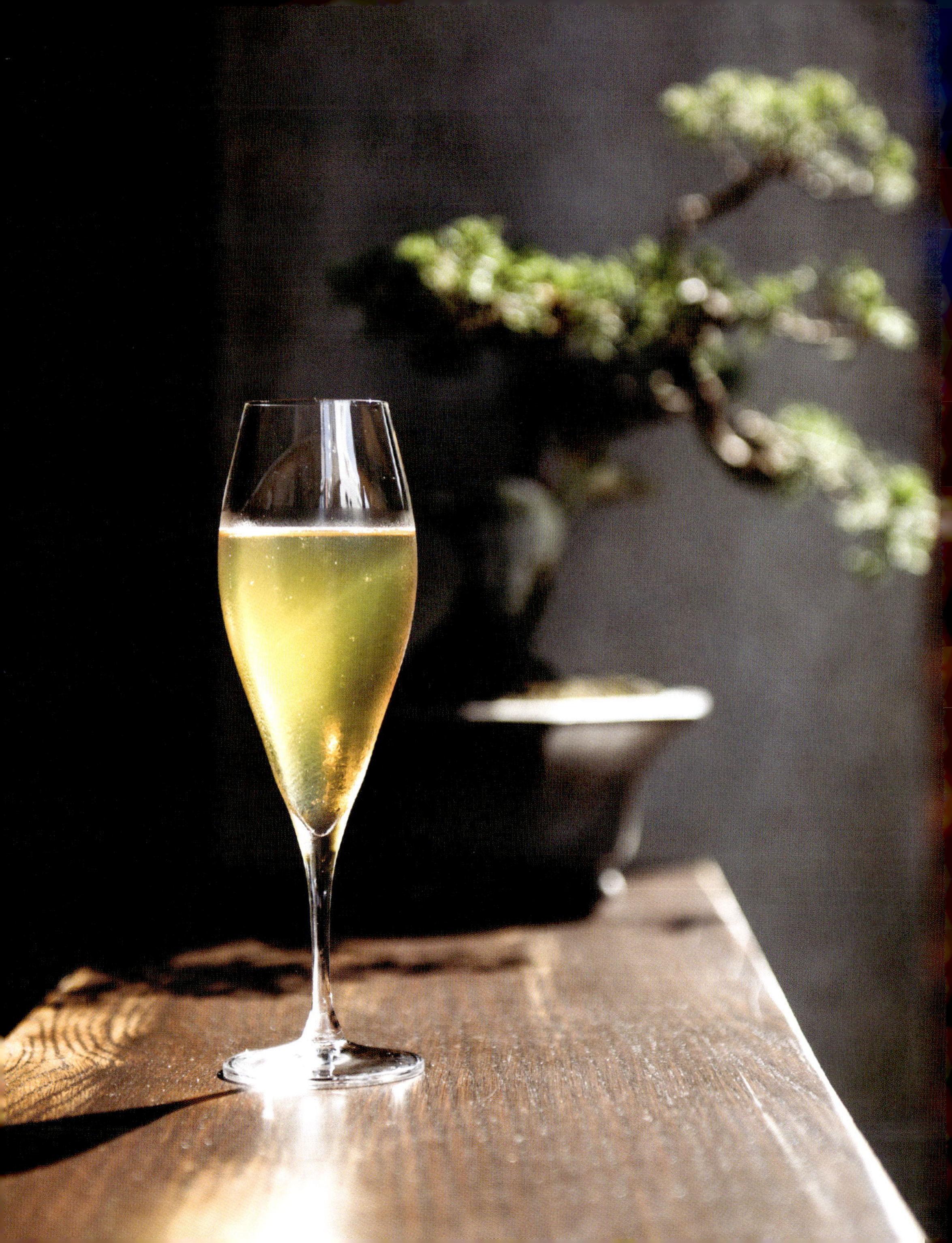

I'LL CAROL AFTER THIS ONE

1 oz. Old Tom gin

½ oz. fresh lemon juice

½ oz. Simple Syrup (see page 20)

Champagne, to top

1 lemon twist, for garnish

Place the gin, lemon juice, and syrup in a cocktail shaker, fill it two-thirds of the way with ice, and shake until chilled.

Strain into a champagne flute, top with the Champagne, and garnish with the lemon twist.

I'D RATHER BE STUCK IN TRAFFIC

1 oz. tequila

1 oz. grapefruit soda

2 oz. Champagne

Place the tequila and soda in a champagne flute and gently swirl to combine.

Top with the Champagne and enjoy.

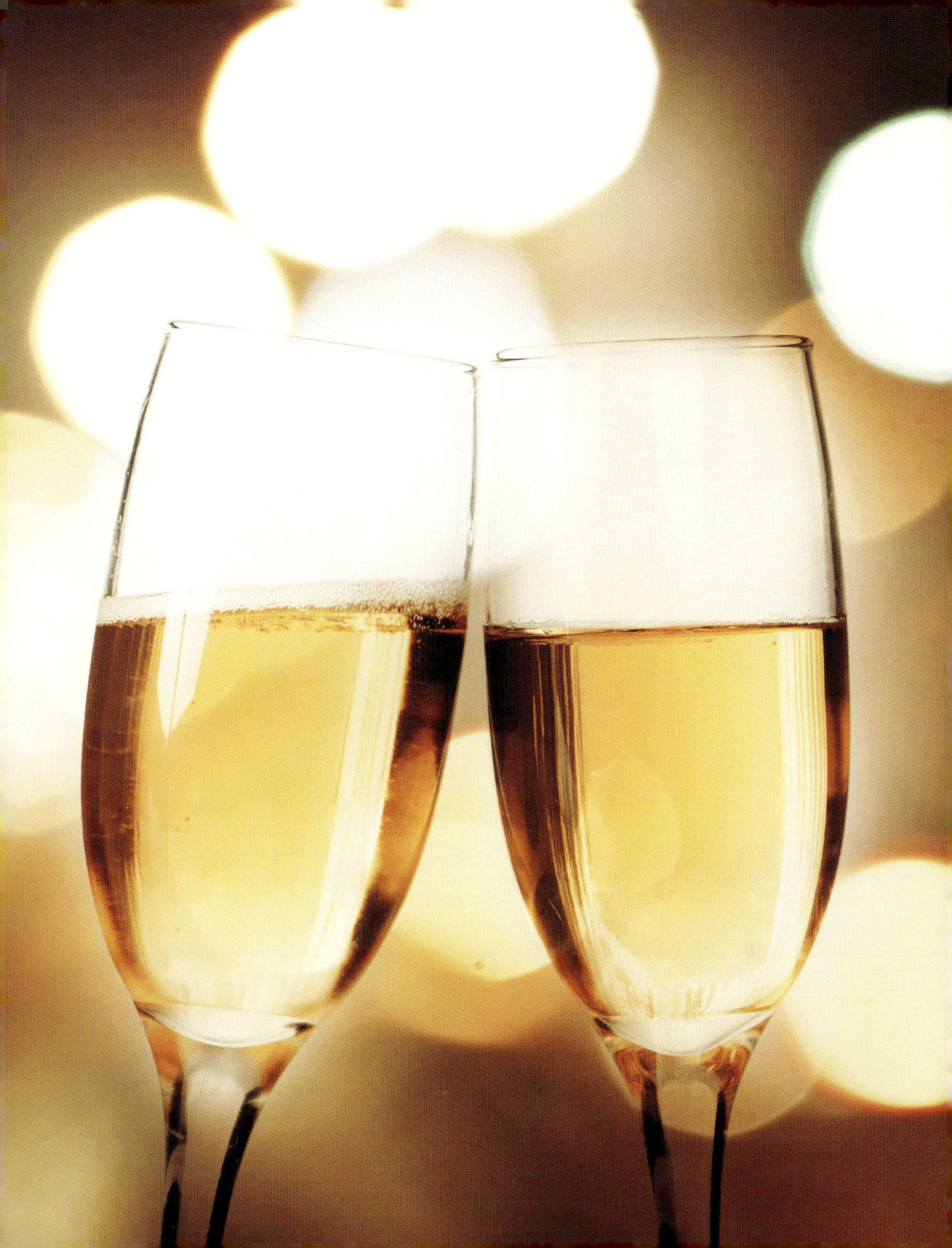

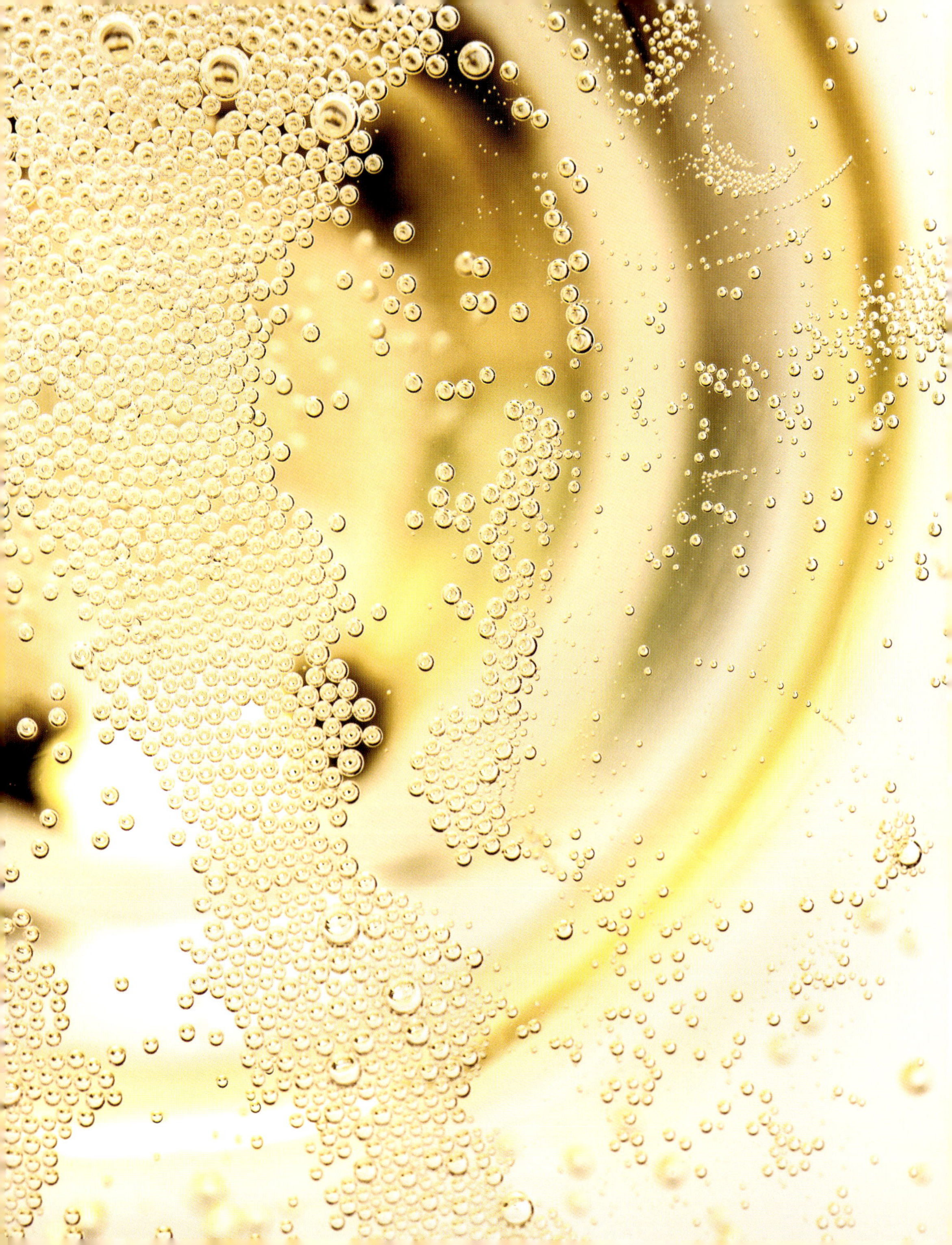

ASK ME ABOUT MY JOB AGAIN, I DARE YOU

Fleur de sel, for the rim

2 oz. premium tequila

1 oz. Grand Marnier

1 oz. fresh lime juice

4 oz. Champagne

1 lime twist, for garnish

Rim a rocks glass with the fleur de sel and add ice to the glass.

Place the tequila, Grand Marnier, and lime juice in a cocktail shaker, fill it two-thirds of the way with ice, and shake until chilled.

Strain into the rocks glass, top with the Champagne, and garnish with the lime twist.

THE "I CAN'T EVEN"

1 oz. Peach Vodka (see sidebar)

1 oz. cranberry juice

Sparkling wine, to top

1 lemon twist, for garnish

Place the vodka and cranberry juice in a mixing glass, add ice, and stir until chilled.

Strain into a champagne flute, top with sparkling wine, and garnish with the lemon twist.

PEACH VODKA

Place three halved peaches and a 750 ml bottle of vodka in a mason jar, cover, and store in a cool dark place for 48 minutes. Strain before using or storing.

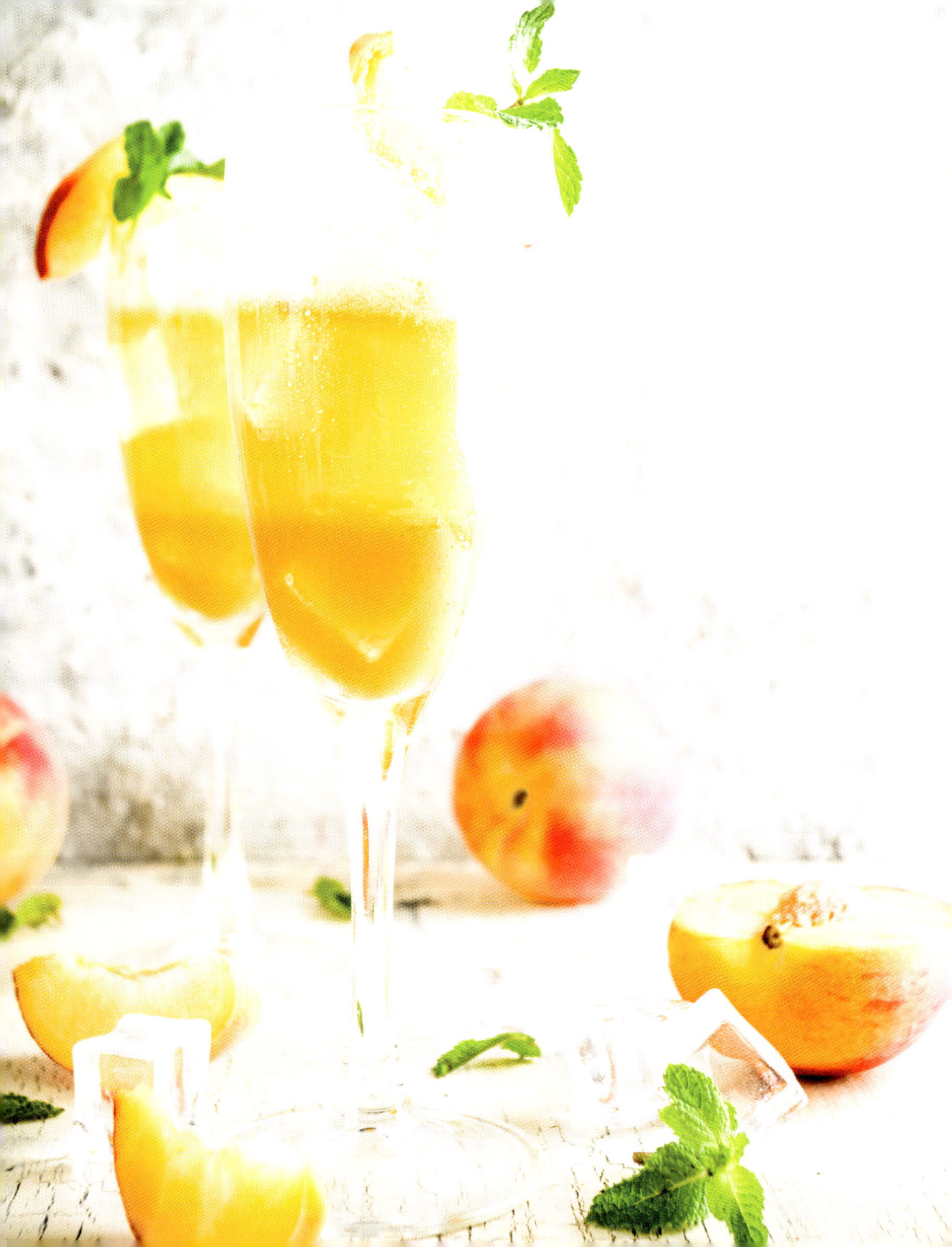

I'M CLASSY, I SWEAR

2 oz. peach nectar

¼ oz. fresh lemon juice

Champagne, to top

Place the peach nectar and lemon juice in a cocktail shaker, fill it two-thirds of the way with ice, and shake until chilled.

Strain into a champagne flute and top with Champagne.

I'M STEALING SANTA'S ROSY GLOW

¾ oz. Aperol

¾ oz. amaretto

¾ oz. fresh lemon juice

3 oz. Prosecco

1 lemon twist, for garnish

Place the Aperol, amaretto, and lemon juice in a cocktail shaker, fill it two-thirds of the way with ice, and shake until chilled.

Strain into a champagne flute, top with the Prosecco, and garnish with the lemon twist.

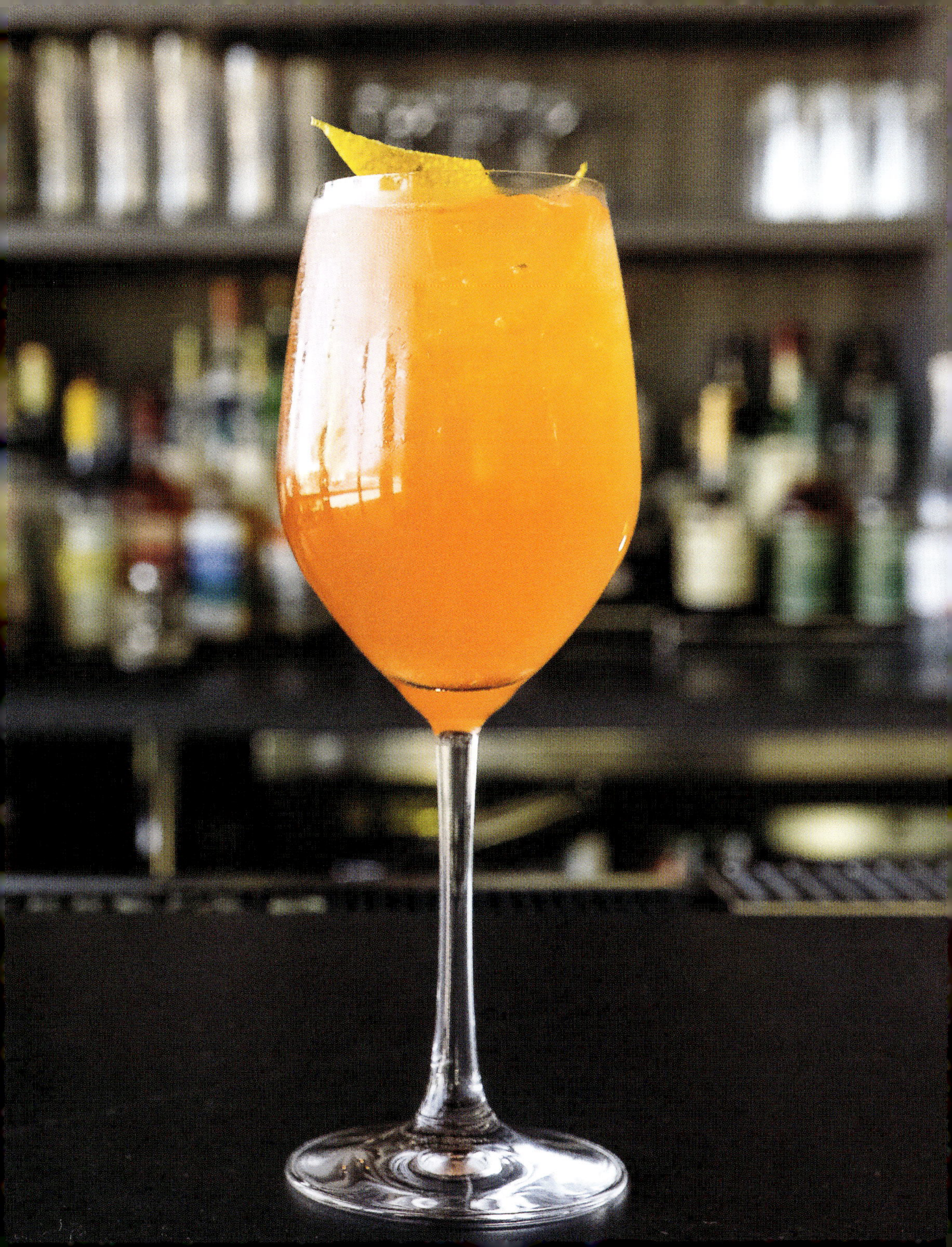

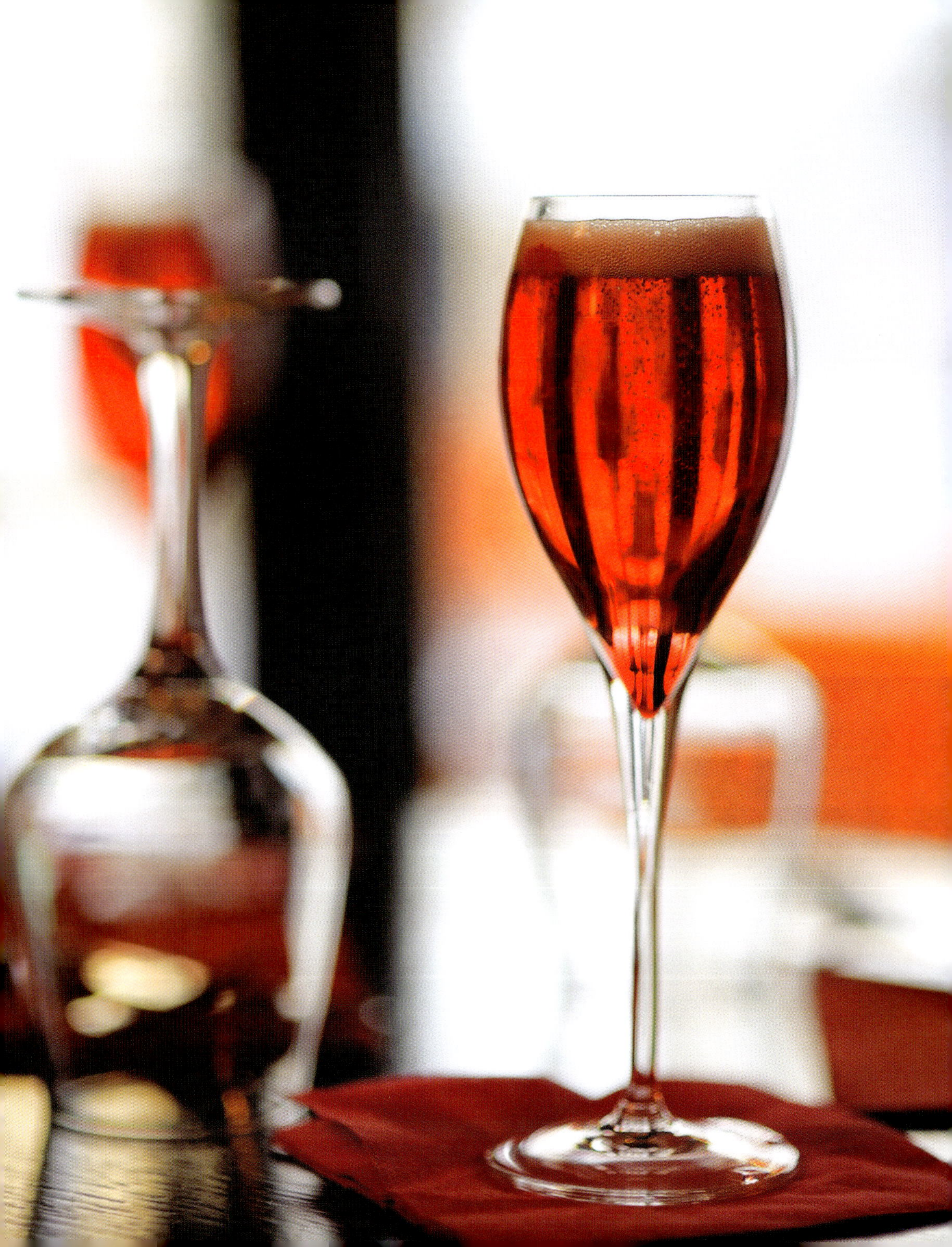

MITTENS OFF, SPIRITS UP

½ oz. St-Germain

1 oz. Giffard Crème de Pamplemousse Rose

Champagne, to top

1 grapefruit twist, for garnish

Pour the liqueurs into a champagne flute, top with Champagne, and garnish with the grapefruit twist.

PLEASE, NO NIGHTMARES BEFORE CHRISTMAS

1 oz. whiskey

2 oz. apple cider

2 oz. hard sparkling cider

Place the whiskey and apple cider in a rocks glass, add ice as desired, and gently stir until chilled.

Top with the sparkling cider and enjoy.

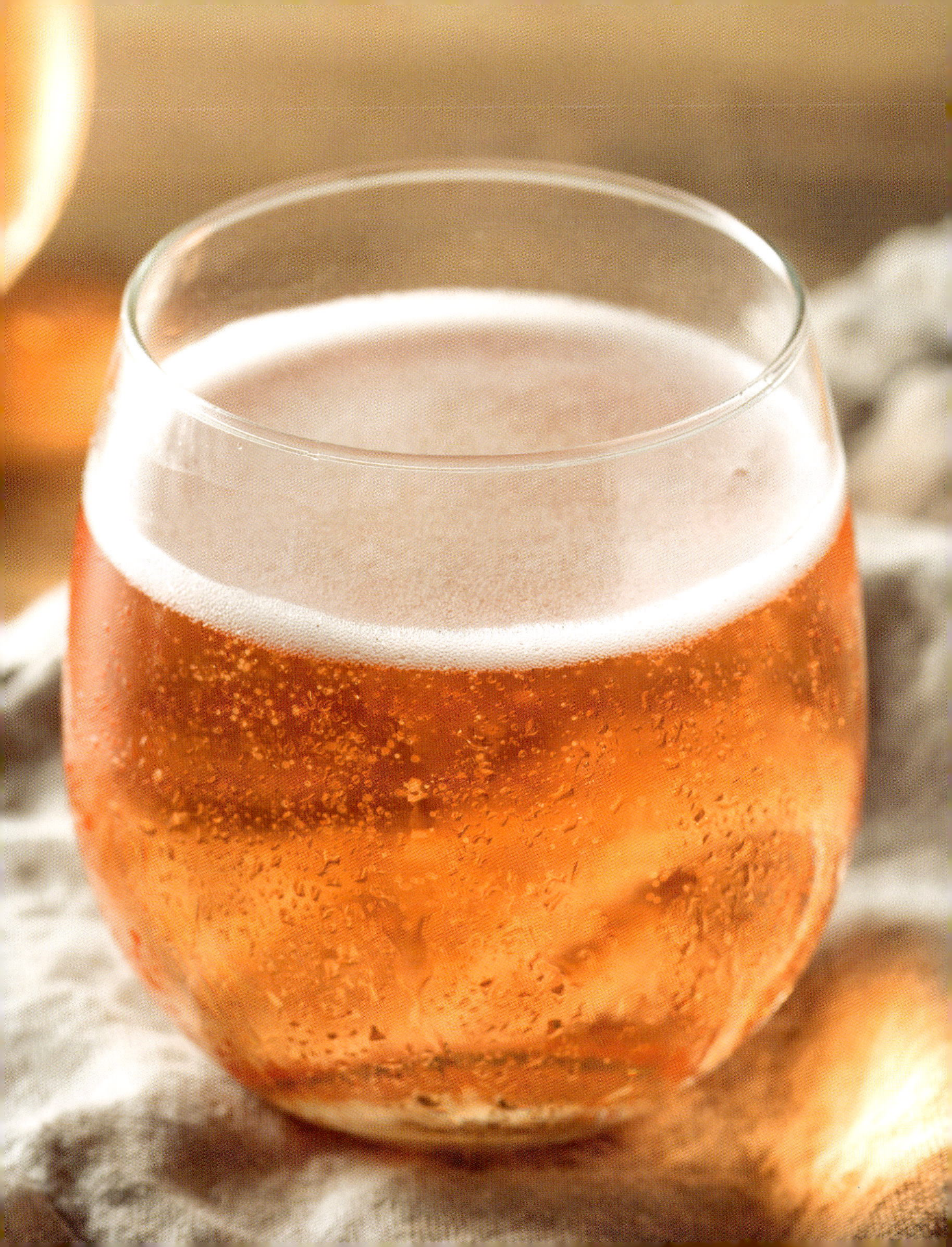

THAI BASIL & STRAWBERRY SHRUB

Place 2 lbs. strawberries, 8 cups sugar, 8 cups water, and 1 cup firmly packed Thai basil leaves in a large saucepan. Bring to a boil over medium-high heat and cook until the mixture has reduced by one-quarter, stirring to dissolve the sugar. Turn off the heat and let the mixture cool to room temperature. Strain through a fine sieve into a large bowl and stir in 2 cups of rice vinegar.

I'VE HIT MY HOLIDAY CHEER LIMIT

1 oz. Pimm's No. 1

¾ oz. pisco

¾ oz. Thai Basil & Strawberry Shrub (see sidebar)

¼ oz. fresh lemon juice

2 oz. sparkling wine

1 lemon twist, for garnish

Place the Pimm's, pisco, shrub, and lemon juice in a cocktail shaker, fill it two-thirds of the way with ice, and shake until chilled.

Strain over ice into a wine glass, top with the sparkling wine, and garnish with the lemon twist.

DON'T WINE ABOUT CHRISTMAS

3 oz. red wine

1 oz. Strawberry & Gin Reduction (see sidebar)

3 oz. Champagne

2 strawberries, for garnish

Place the wine and reduction in a wine glass and stir to combine.

Top with the Champagne, garnish with the strawberries, and enjoy.

STRAWBERRY & GIN REDUCTION

Place 2 oz. gin and 4 strawberries in a food processor and puree until smooth. Strain into a small saucepan and cook over medium heat until the mixture has reduced by half. Let cool completely before using.

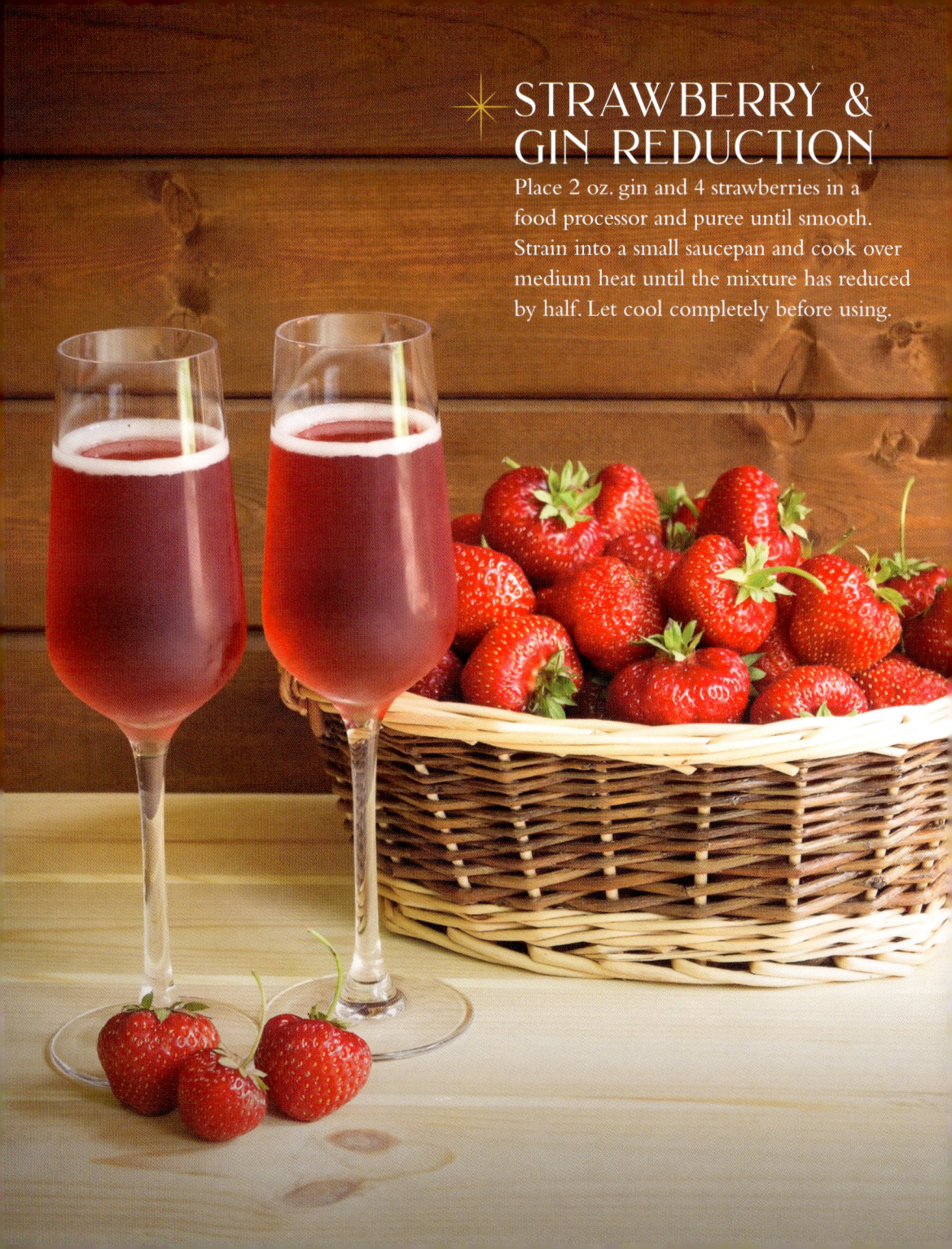

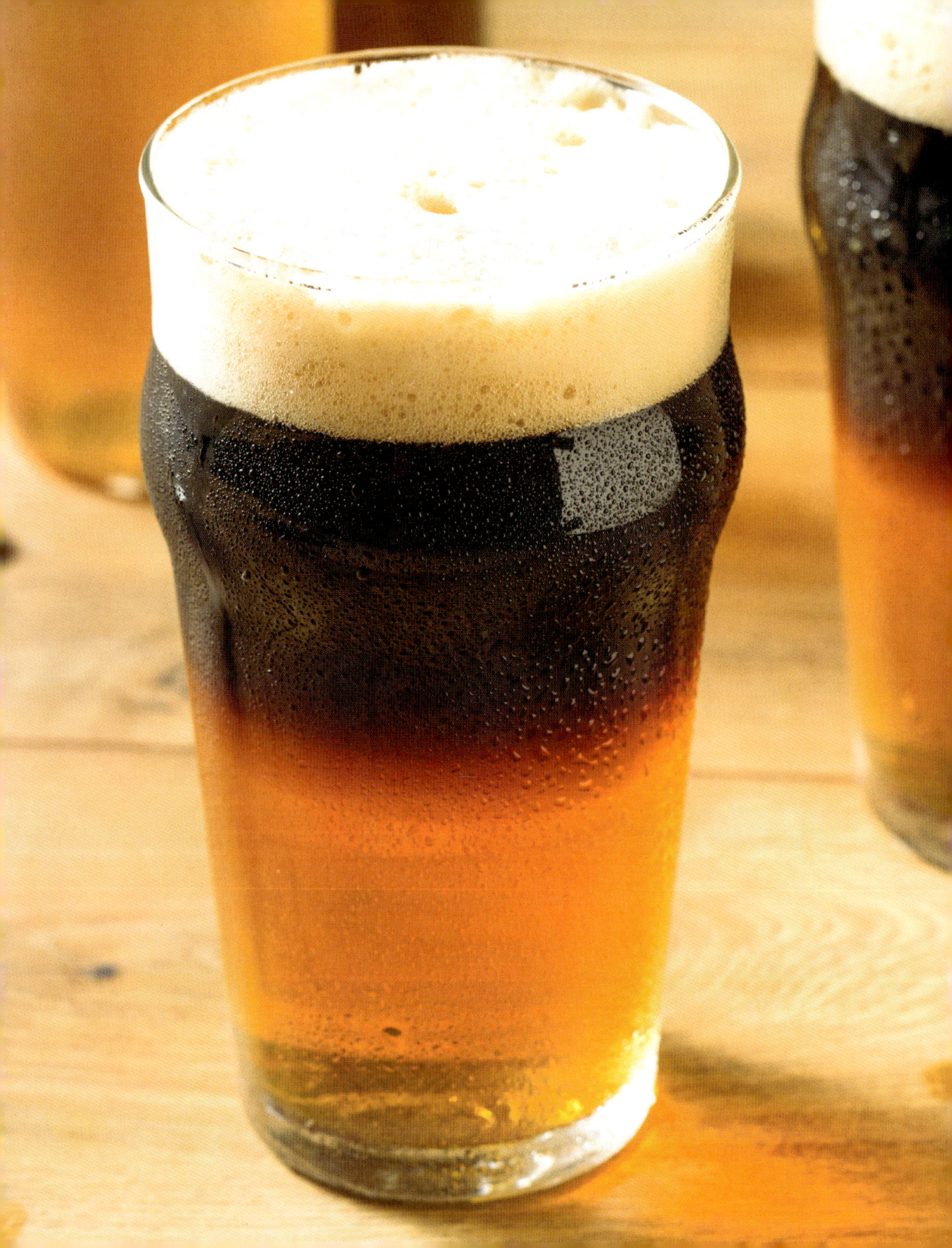

HO-HO-HOLD MY BEER

5 oz. Champagne

5 oz. stout

Pour the champagne into a mason jar or pint glass.

Carefully pour the stout over the back of a spoon to layer it on top of the Champagne.

All I Want for Christmas Is a Sparkly Drink

MS. CLAUS'S SIDE HUSTLE

1 oz. Cointreau

1 oz. brandy

3 oz. Champagne

Place the Cointreau and brandy in a cocktail shaker, fill it two-thirds of the way with ice, and shake until chilled.

Strain into a champagne flute and top with the Champagne.

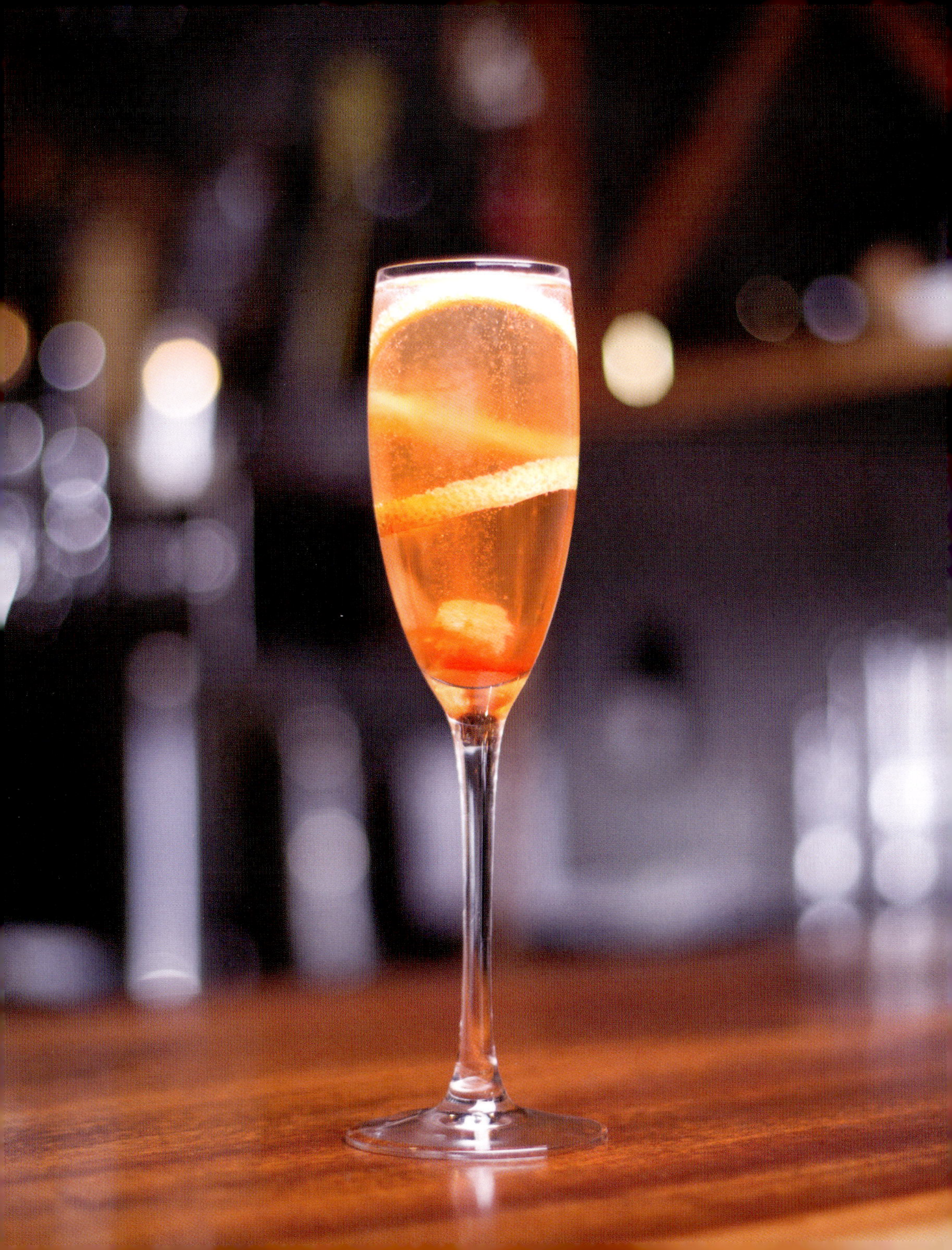

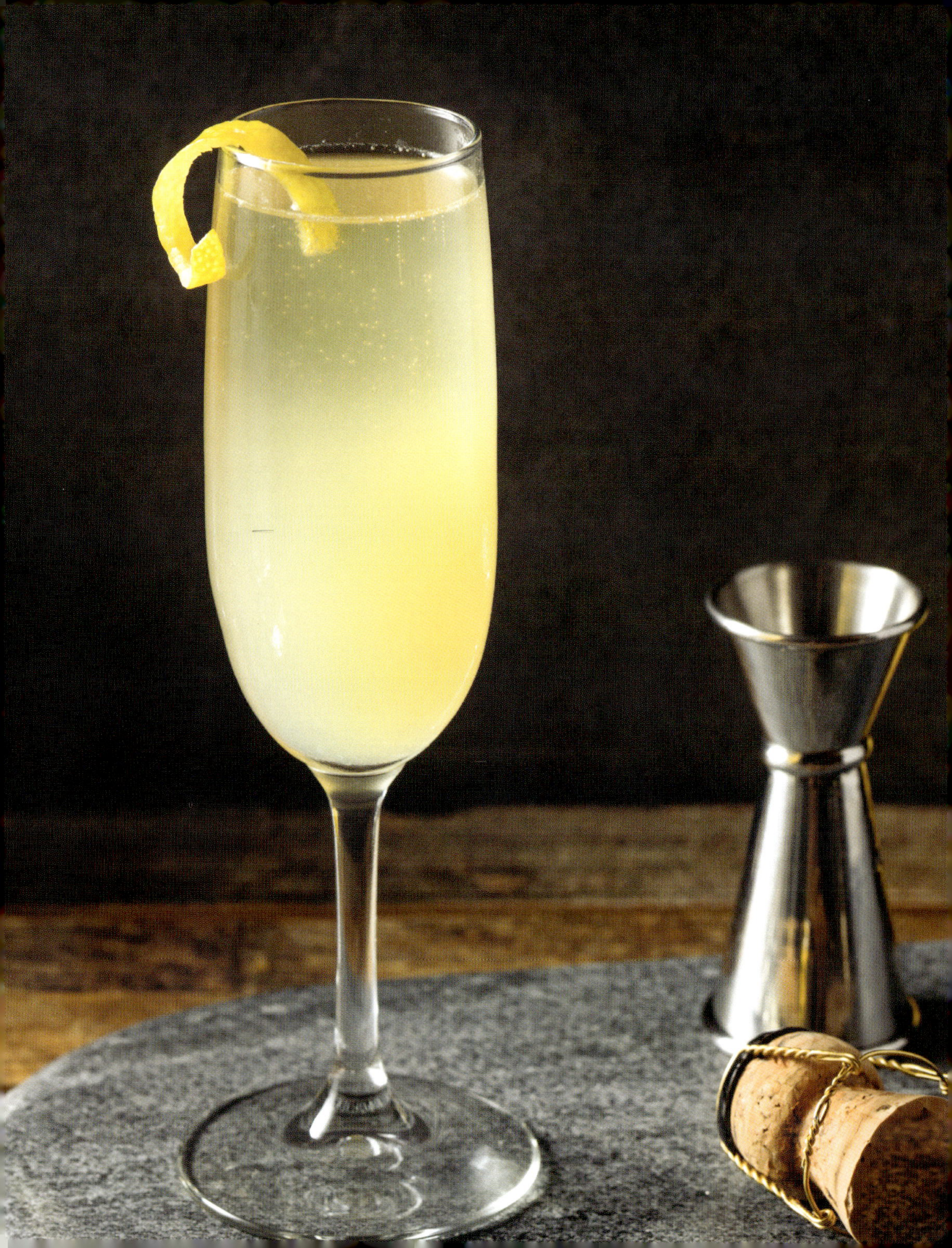

JINGLE ALL THE WAY . . . TO THERAPY

½ oz. gin

⅓ oz. fresh lemon juice

Pinch of caster sugar

3 oz. Champagne

1 lemon twist, for garnish

Place the gin, lemon juice, and caster sugar in a cocktail shaker, fill it two-thirds of the way with ice, and shake until chilled.

Strain into a champagne flute, top with the Champagne, and garnish with the lemon twist.

All I Want for Christmas Is a Sparkly Drink

'TIS THE SEASON TO KEEP SPIRITS BRIGHT

Life's too short to get through the holidays on eggnog alone, and this chapter is here to make sure your glass—and your spirits—stay as bright as your favorite Christmas lights. Whether you're sipping solo during your tenth rewatch of *Home Alone* (we don't judge), toasting mid–present opening chaos, or trying to endure a dinner where someone inevitably brings up politics, we've got you covered. These drinks are tailor-made for every festive moment, big or small. Because let's face it, the holidays can be a marathon, not a sprint—so you might as well drink like a pro.

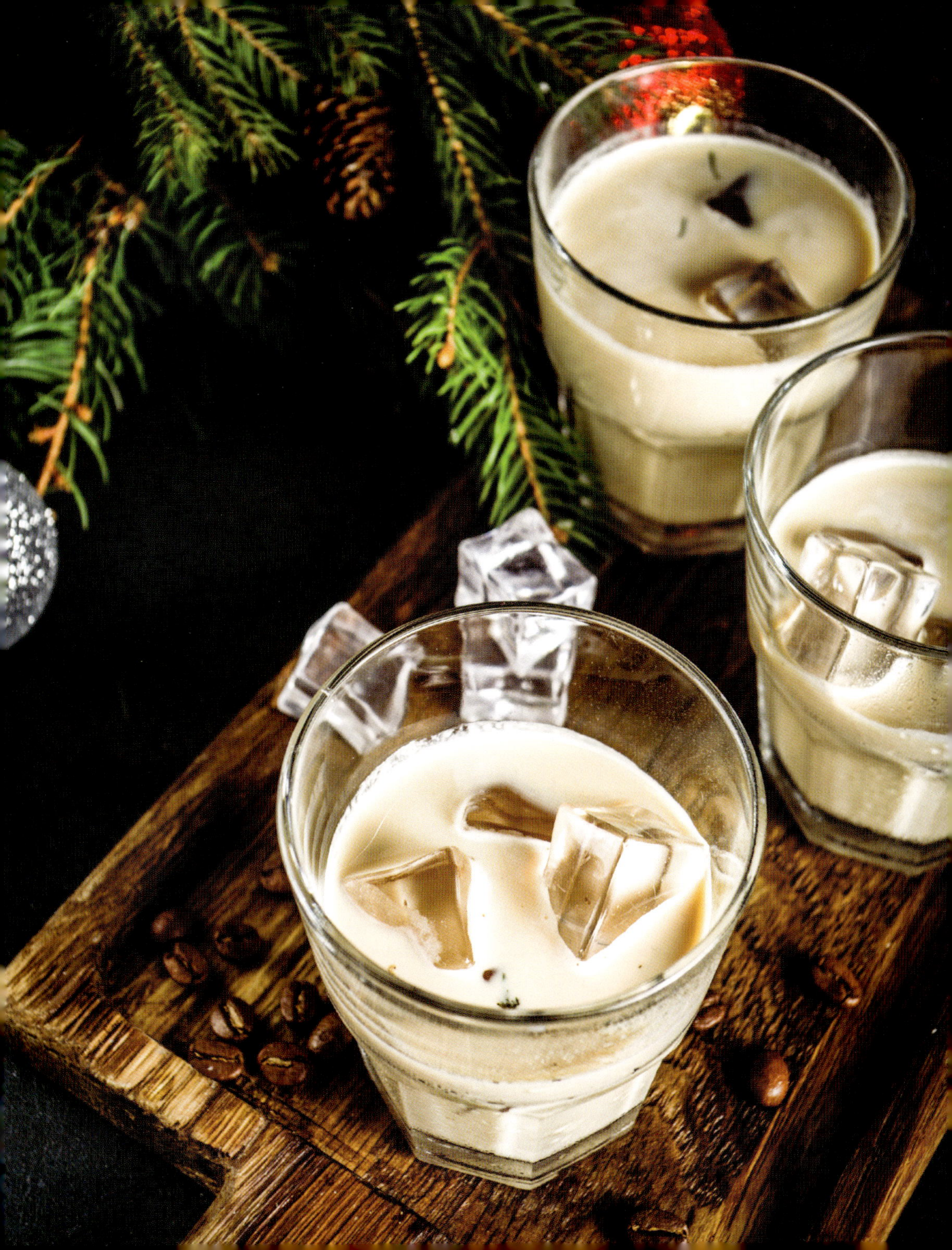

SLEIGH MY NAME, SLEIGH MY NAME

1½ oz. vodka

1 oz. St-Germain

1 oz. cranberry sauce

½ oz. fresh lime juice

2 dashes of fig bitters

Chill a cocktail glass in the freezer.

Place all of the ingredients in a cocktail shaker, fill it two-thirds of the way with ice, and shake until chilled.

Strain into the chilled glass.

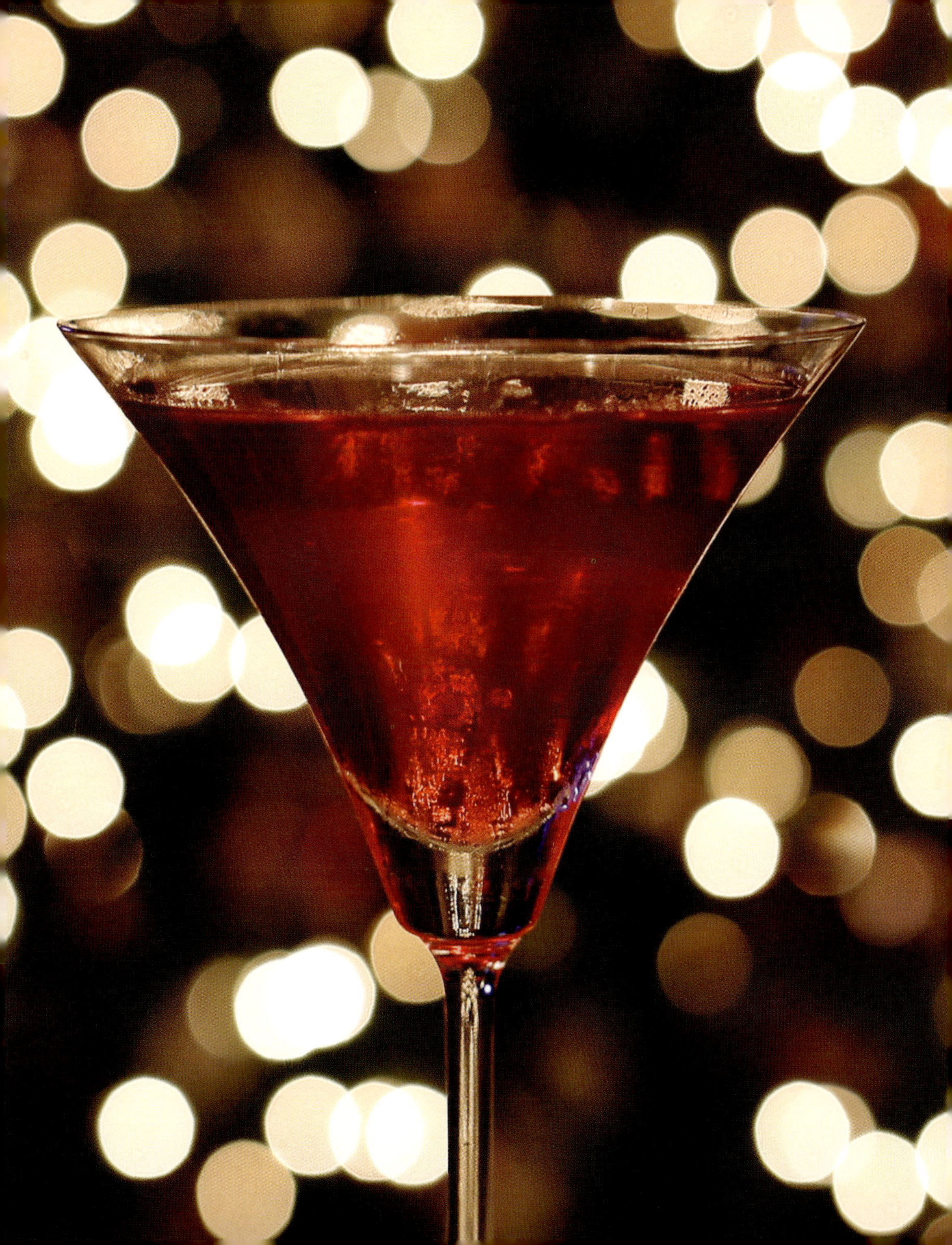

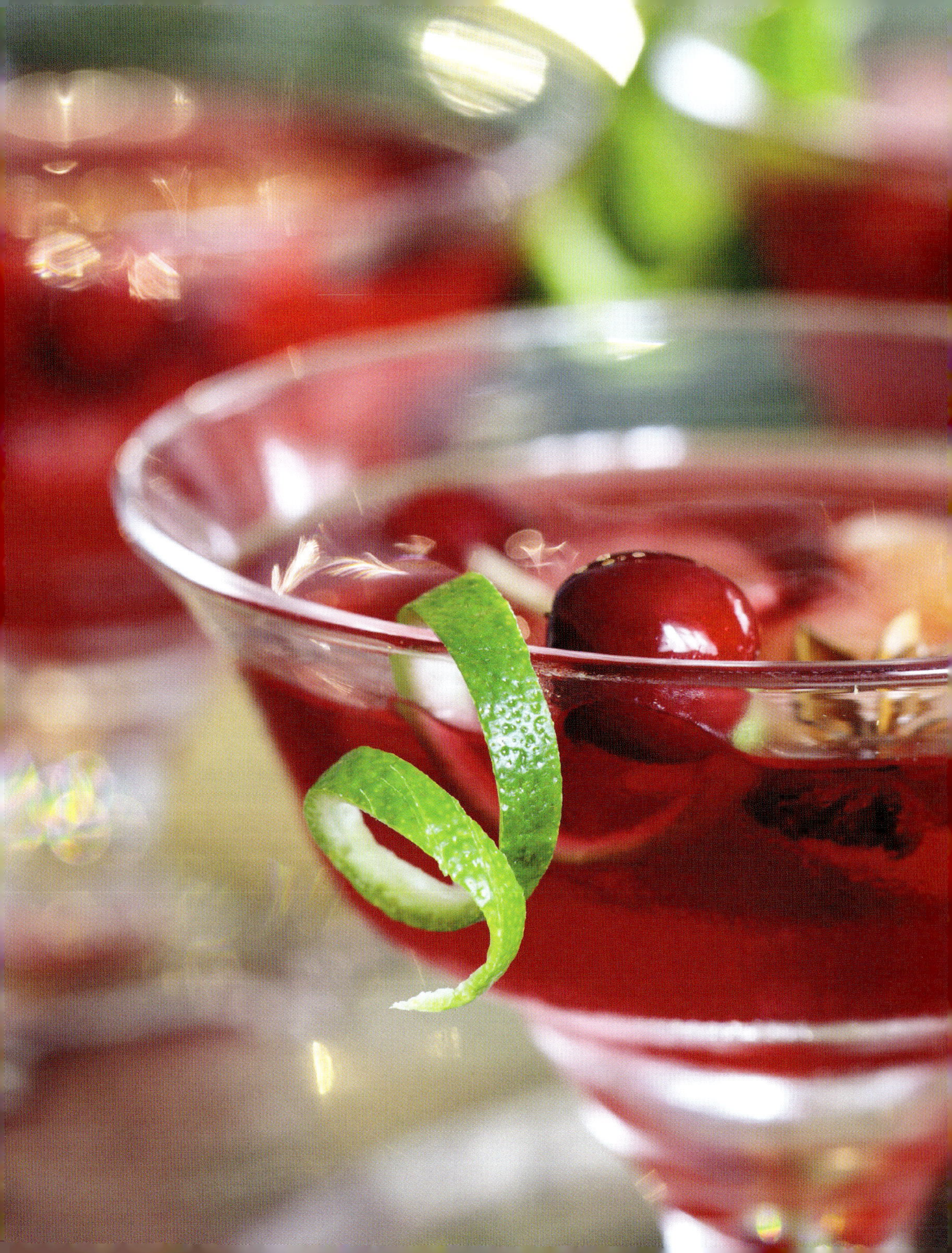

ON MY LAST NERVE

Salt, for the rim

1 oz. fresh lime juice

2 oz. tequila

1 oz. orange liqueur

2 oz. cranberry juice

1 lime twist, for garnish

Handful of cranberries, for garnish

Wet the rim of a coupe and coat it with the salt.

Place all of the remaining ingredients, except for the garnishes, in a cocktail shaker, fill it two-thirds of the way with ice, and shake until chilled.

Strain the cocktail into the rimmed coupe and garnish with the lime twist and handful of cranberries.

SIP ME BABY ONE MORE TIME

Candy cane crumbles, for the rim

2 oz. gin

⅔ oz. dry vermouth

⅔ oz. peppermint schnapps

1 peppermint, for garnish

Wet the rim of a cocktail glass and then dip it into the crumbled candy cane.

Place the gin, vermouth, and schnapps in a mixing glass, fill it two-thirds of the way with ice, and stir until chilled.

Strain into the cocktail glass and garnish with a peppermint.

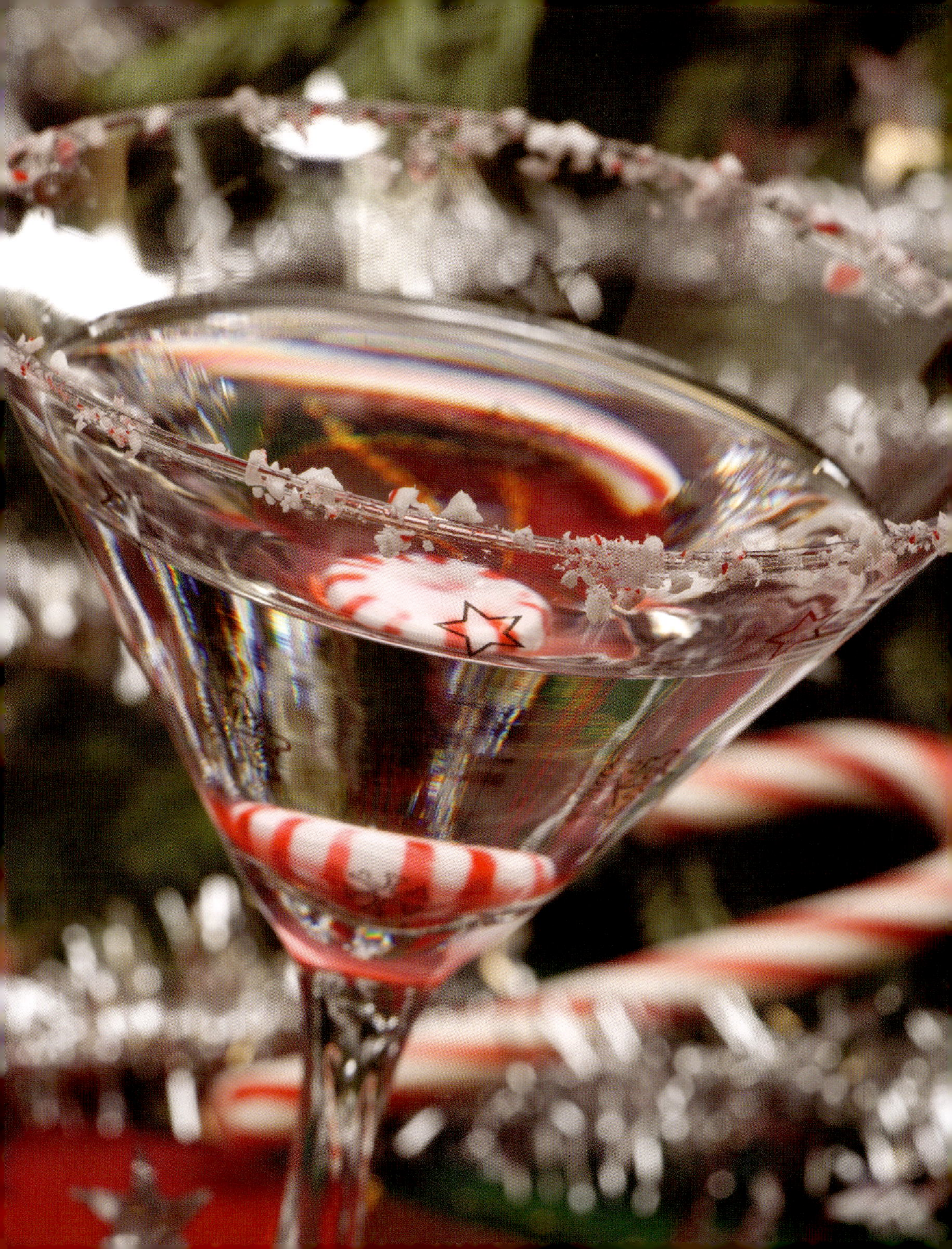

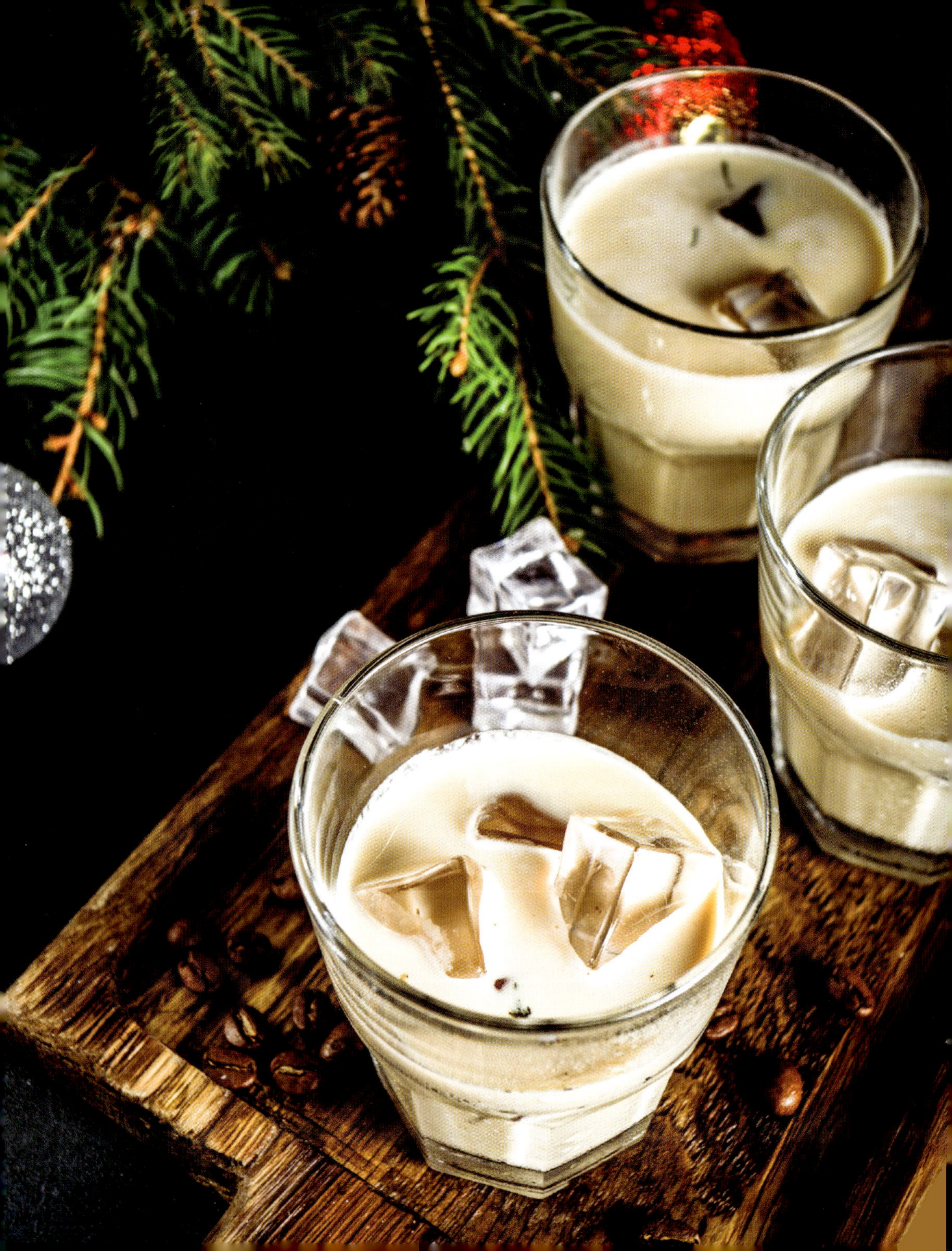

PASS THE LIQUEUR, NOT THE FIGGY PUDDING

2 oz. gin

2 oz. white chocolate liqueur

Splash of white crème de menthe

Freshly grated nutmeg, for garnish

Place the gin, liqueur, and crème de menthe in a cocktail shaker, fill it two-thirds of the way with ice, and shake until chilled.

Strain over ice into a rocks glass and garnish with a dusting of nutmeg.

SLEIGHING MY WILLPOWER

2 oz. tequila

1 oz. heavy cream

1 oz. crème de cacao

1 teaspoon Chambord

Chill a coupe in the freezer.

Place the ingredients in a cocktail shaker, fill it two-thirds of the way with ice, and shake until chilled.

Strain into the chilled coupe.

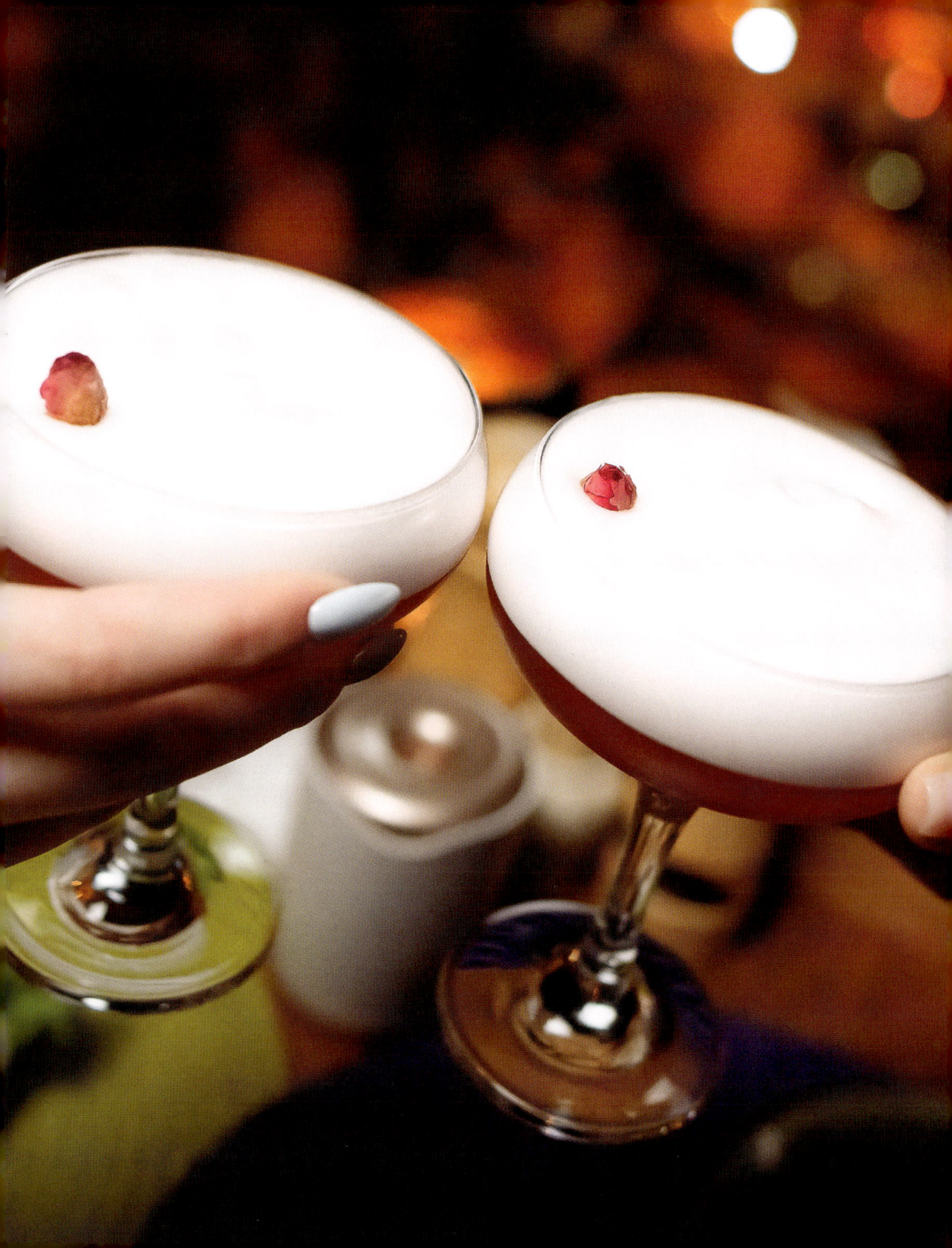

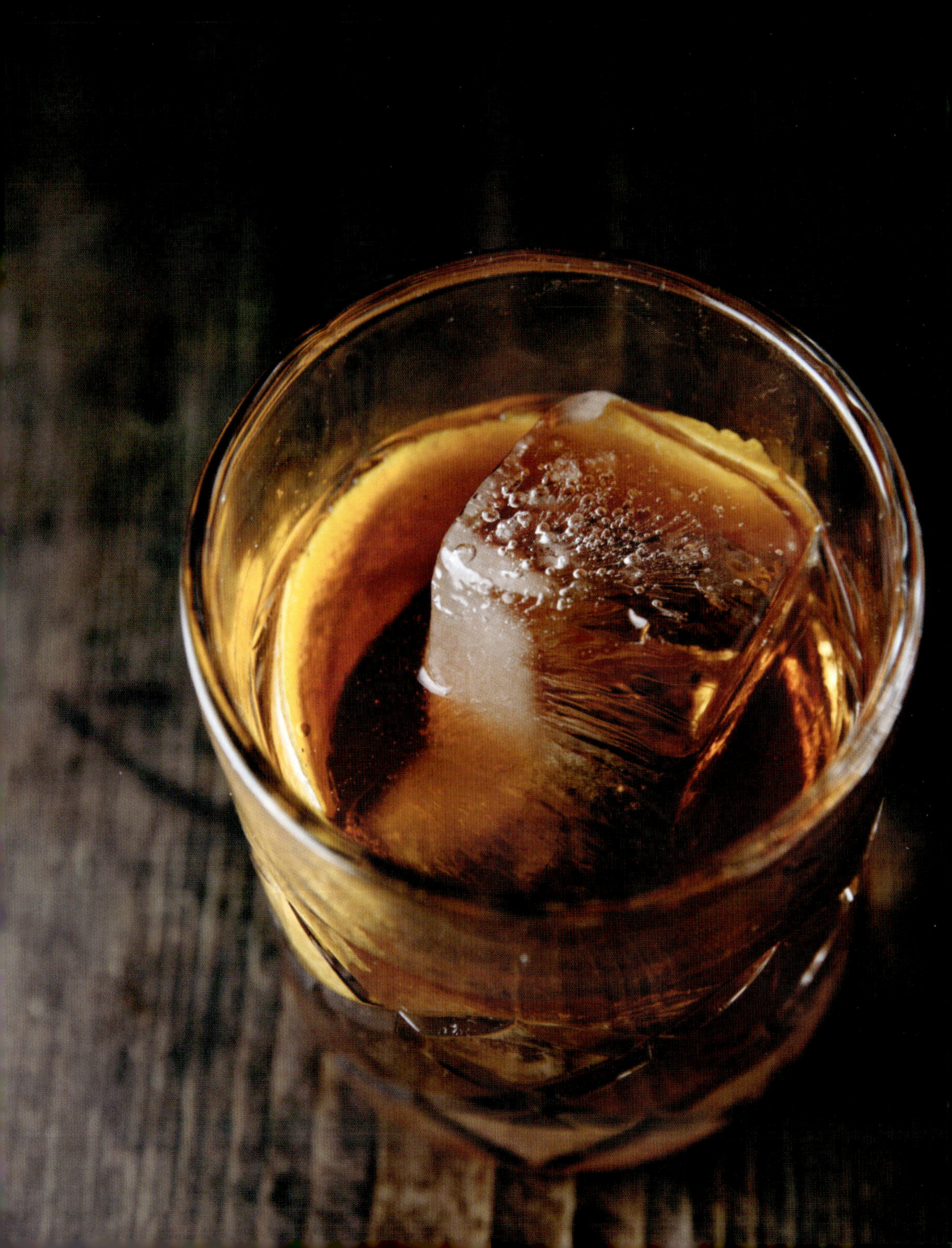

YULE REGRET THIS

1½ oz. bourbon

¾ oz. honey syrup

½ oz. fresh lemon juice

Dash of Tabasco

1 strip of lemon peel, for garnish

Add the bourbon, syrup, lemon juice, and Tabasco to a cocktail shaker, fill it two-thirds of the way with ice, and shake vigorously.

Strain over ice into a rocks glass and garnish with the strip of lemon peel.

SNOWED IN (AND TOTALLY OVER IT)

1½ oz. Jim Beam Vanilla

3 oz. half-and-half

1 oz. fresh lemon juice

1 oz. egg white

Splash of club soda

1 strip of orange peel, for garnish

Chill a Collins glass in the freezer.

Place all of the ingredients, except for the club soda and orange peel, in a cocktail shaker, fill it two-thirds of the way with ice, and shake until chilled.

Strain into the chilled glass, add the splash of club soda, and garnish with the strip of orange peel.

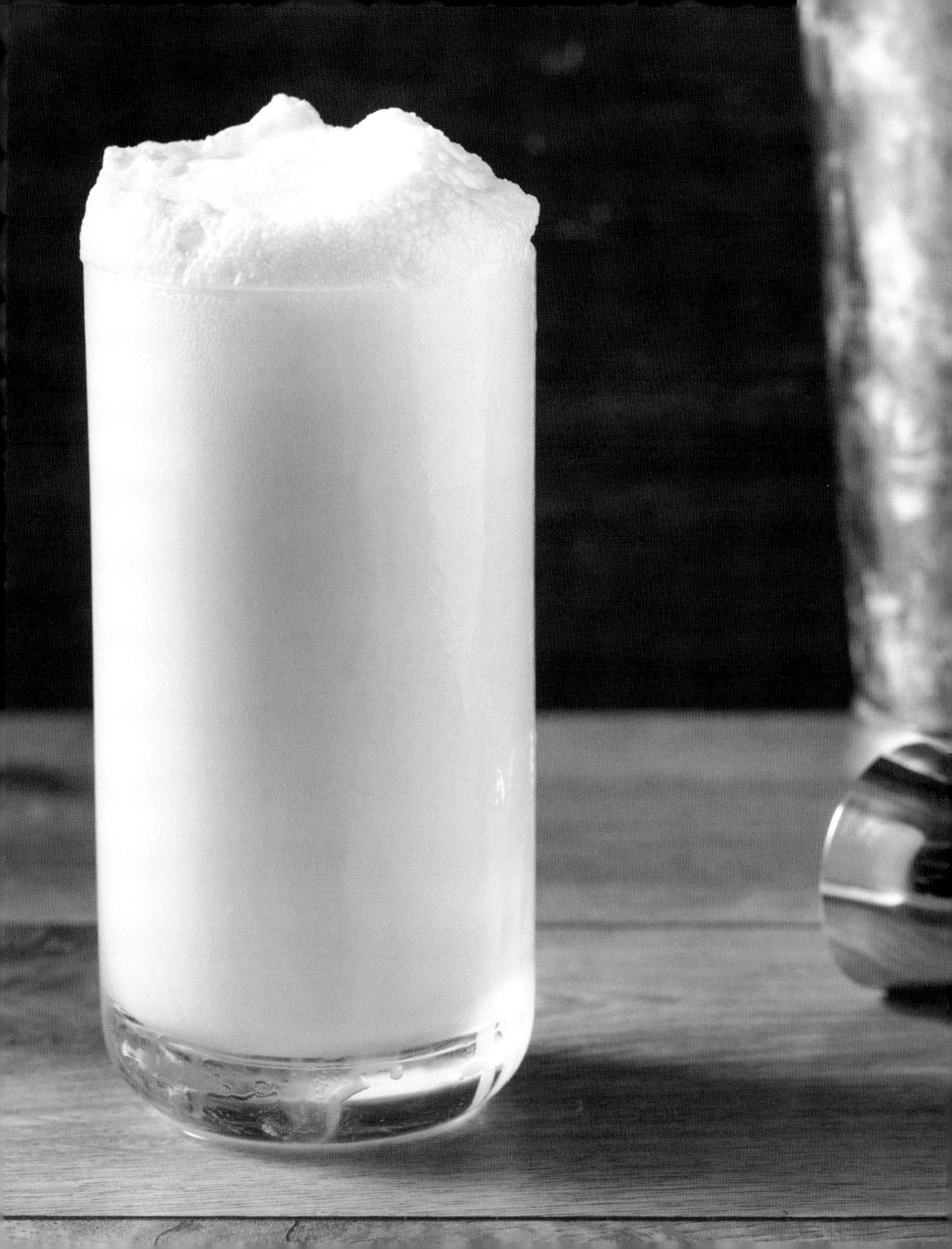

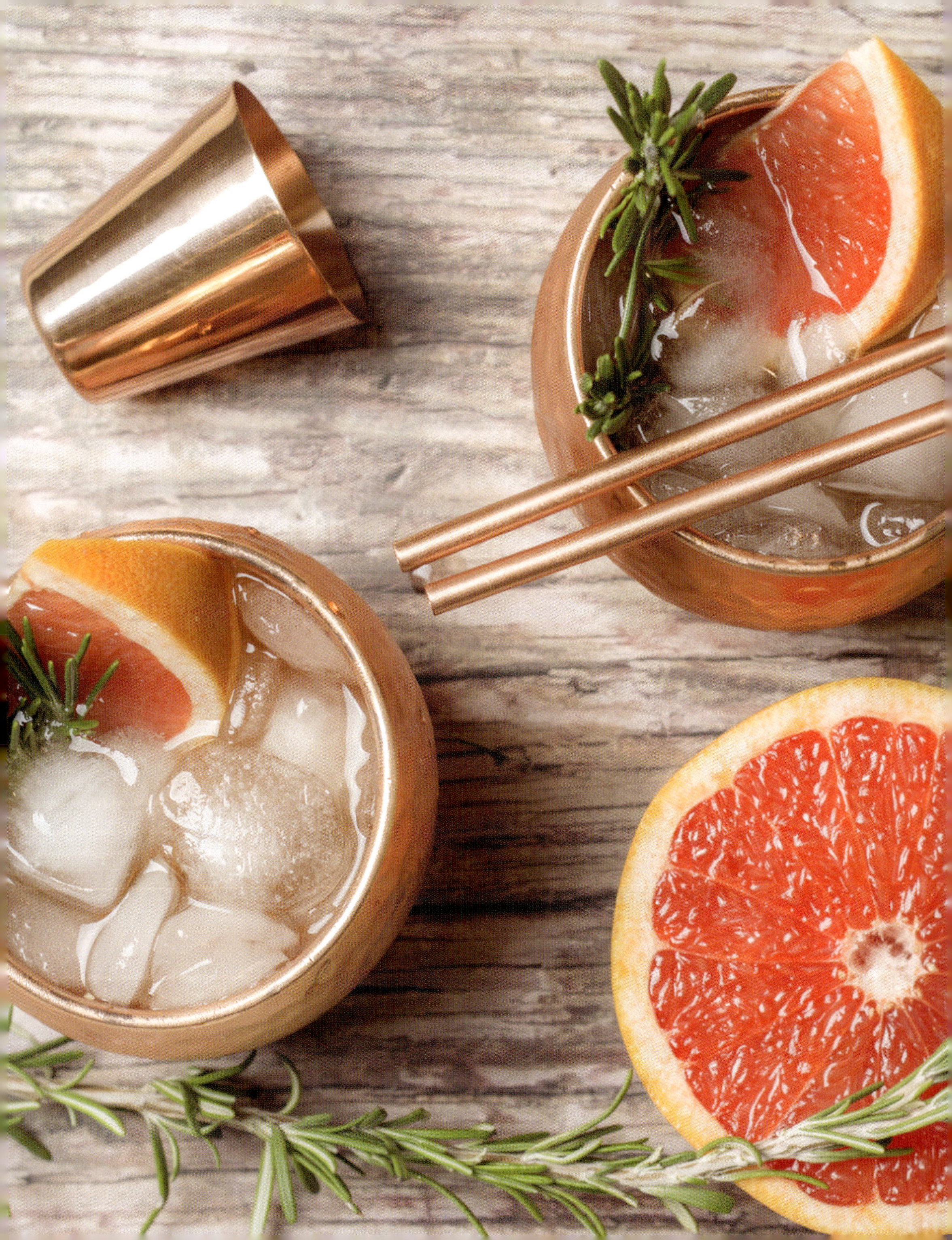

THE GHOST OF POOR CHRISTMAS CHOICES

2 oz. whiskey

¾ oz. Rosemary Syrup (see page 31)

Seltzer water, to top

1 sprig of fresh rosemary, for garnish

1 grapefruit wedge, for garnish

Place the whiskey and syrup in a tumbler filled with ice and stir until chilled.

Top with the seltzer and garnish with the sprig of rosemary and grapefruit wedge.

BLUE, BLUE, BLUE CHRISTMAS

Light corn syrup

Shredded coconut, for garnish

2 oz. pineapple juice

1 oz. blue curaçao

1 oz. coconut milk or cream of coconut

1 oz. white rum

Rim a coupe with the corn syrup, then roll the rim in coconut flakes.

Place the pineapple juice, blue curaçao, coconut milk, and white rum in a cocktail shaker, fill it two-thirds of the way with crushed ice, and shake until chilled.

Pour the contents of the shaker into the glass and garnish with more coconut flakes, if desired.

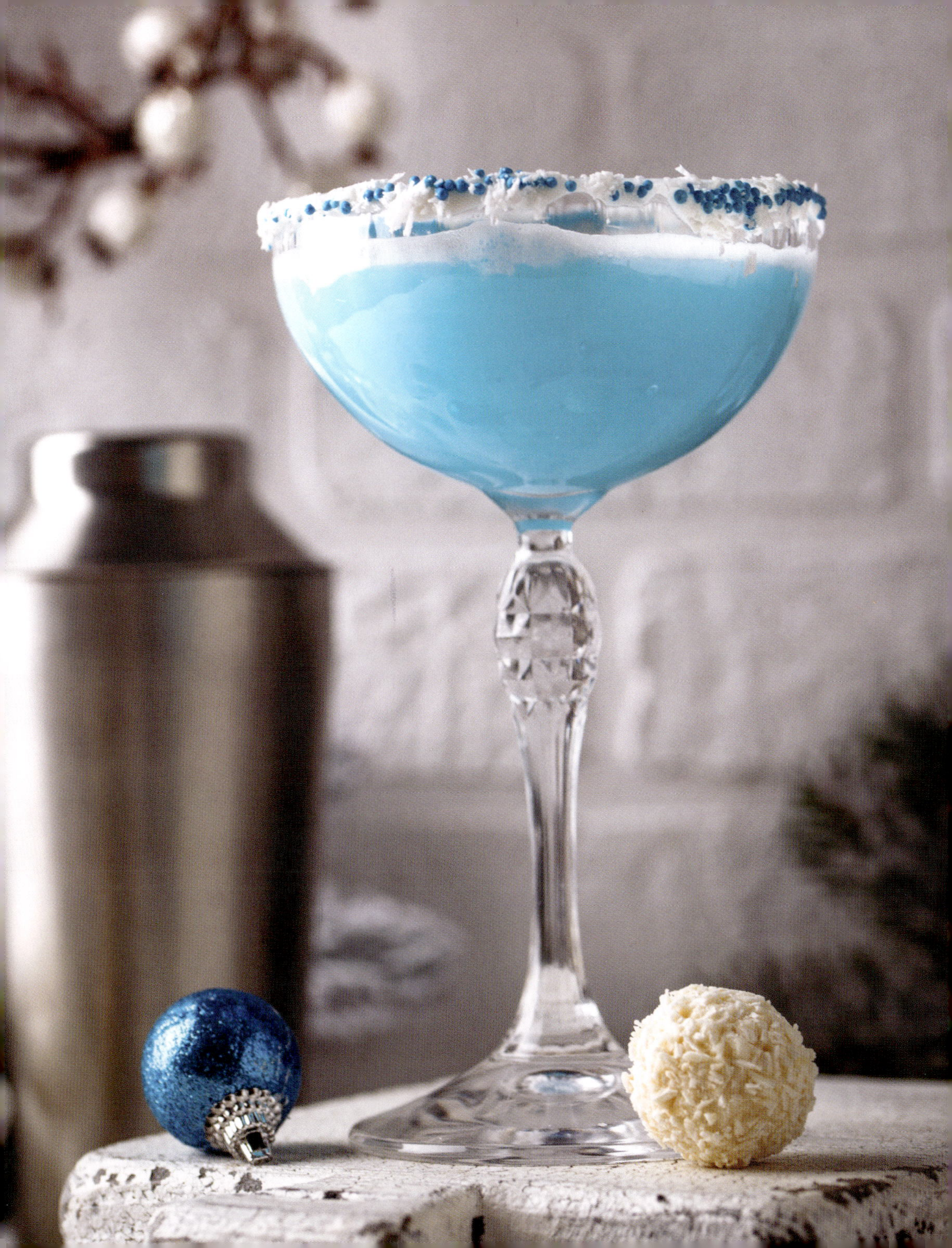

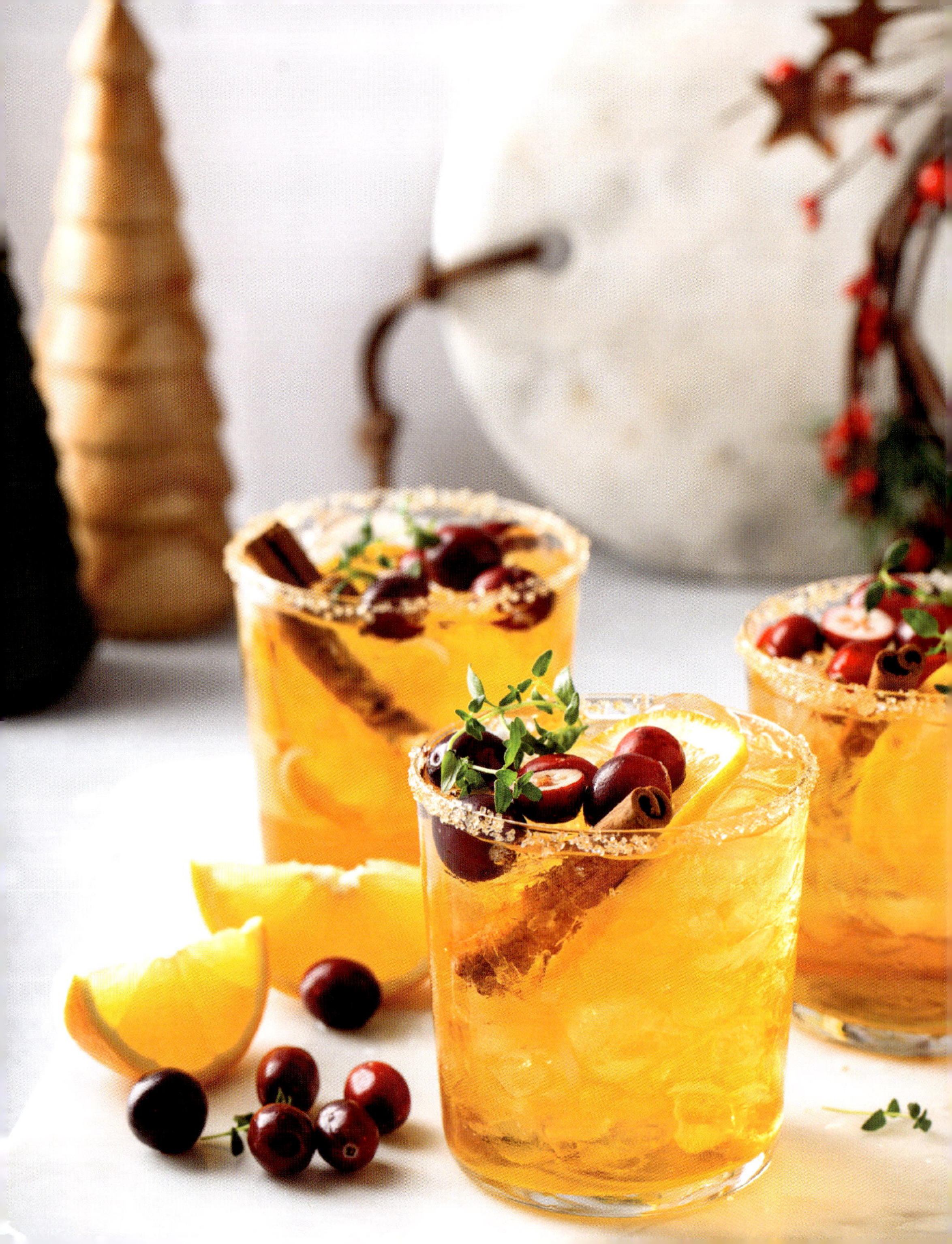

SON OF A NUTCRACKER

1 oz. fresh lime juice

Cinnamon-sugar mix, for rim

2 oz. reposado tequila

1 oz. orange liqueur

½ oz. Cinnamon Syrup (see page 110)

Orange slice, for garnish

Cinnamon stick, for garnish

Rim a glass with lime juice and dip into the cinnamon-sugar mixture.

Place all of the ingredients, except for the orange slice and cinnamon stick, in a cocktail shaker, fill it two–thirds of the way with ice, and shake until chilled.

Strain into a rocks glass and garnish with the orange slice and cinnamon stick.

RUM-PA-PUM-PUM

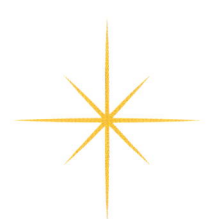

2 oz. Chipotle Rum (see sidebar)

1 oz. cream of coconut

1 oz. orange juice

4 oz. pineapple juice

Freshly grated nutmeg, for garnish

1 orange slice, for garnish

Place the rum, cream of coconut, orange juice, and pineapple juice in a cocktail shaker, fill it two-thirds of the way with crushed ice, and shake until chilled.

Pour the contents of the shaker into a mug or glass, grate nutmeg over the cocktail, and garnish with the orange slice.

CHIPOTLE RUM

Place 1 cup aged rum and 1 torn dried chipotle pepper in a mason jar and let the mixture steep at room temperature for 3 hours. Strain and use as desired.

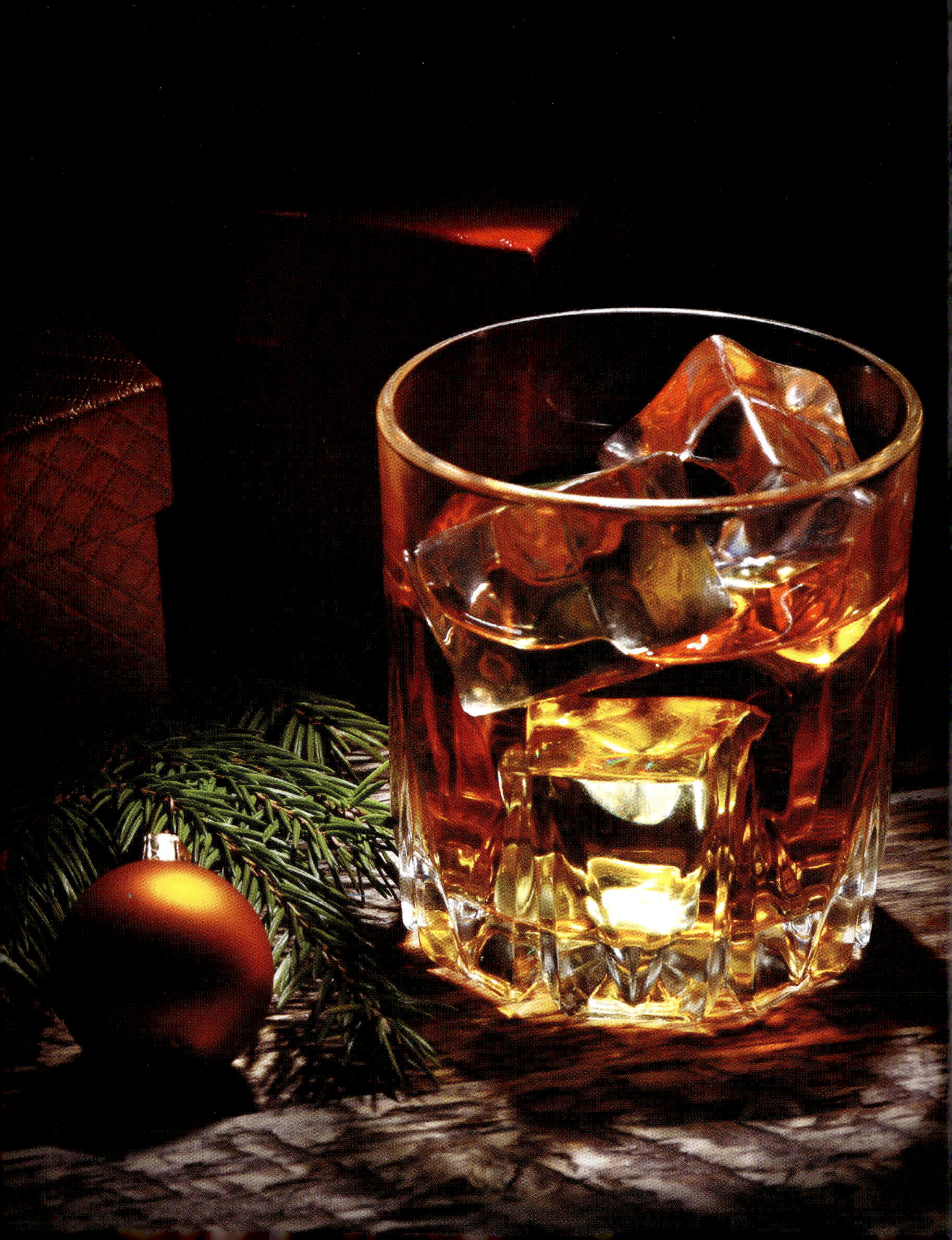

NO WISE MEN HERE

½ oz. Jim Beam bourbon

½ oz. Jack Daniel's Tennessee whiskey

½ oz. Johnnie Walker Scotch Whisky

Place the ingredients in a cocktail shaker, fill it two-thirds of the way with ice, and shake until chilled.

Strain over ice into a rocks glass and enjoy.

MERRY STRESSMAS!

Sugar, for the rim

½ oz. Cointreau

½ oz. Chambord

½ oz. cranberry juice

Place the ingredients in a mixing glass, fill it two-thirds of the way with ice, and stir until chilled.

Strain into a coupe and enjoy.

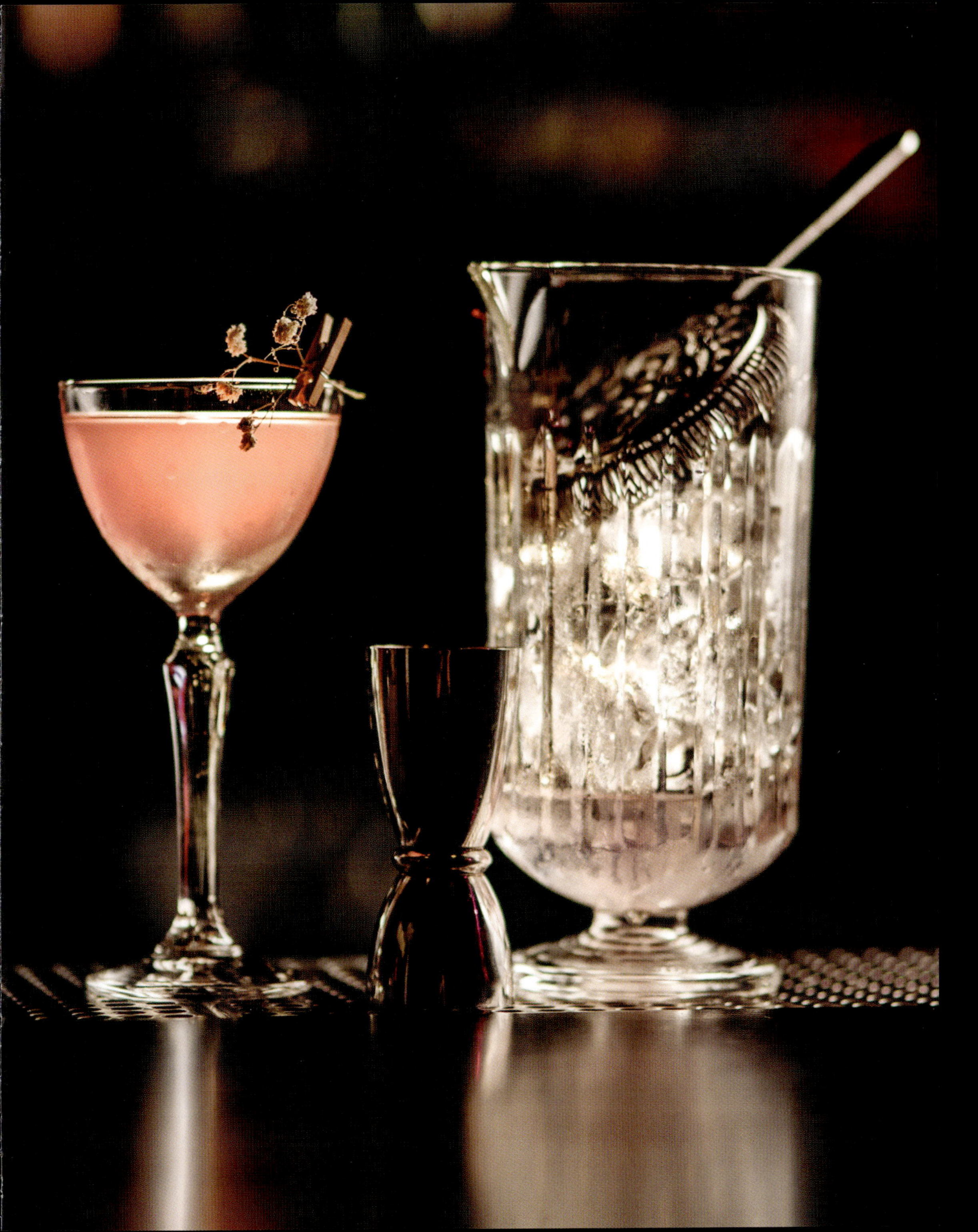

CINNAMON WATER

Combine a cinnamon stick, 1 teaspoon sugar, and 1 cup boiling water and steep for 30 minutes. Discard the cinnamon stick before using.

RESTING GRINCH FACE

1 teaspoon Cinnamon Water (see sidebar)

1½ oz. quality vodka

1 oz. fresh lime juice

1 oz. fresh orange juice

¼ oz. Grand Marnier

Cinnamon, for garnish (optional)

Place all of the ingredients, except for the cinnamon, in a cocktail shaker, fill it two-thirds of the way with ice, and shake until chilled.

Strain into a cocktail glass and garnish with a dusting of cinnamon, if desired.

METRIC CONVERSIONS

US Measurement	Approximate Metric Liquid Measurement	Approximate Metric Dry Measurement
1 TEASPOON	5 ML	5 G
1 TABLESPOON OR ½ OUNCE	15 ML	14 G
1 OUNCE OR ⅛ CUP	30 ML	29 G
¼ CUP OR 2 OUNCES	60 ML	57 G
⅓ CUP	80 ML	76 G
½ CUP OR 4 OUNCES	120 ML	113 G
⅔ CUP	160 ML	151 G
¾ CUP OR 6 OUNCES	180 ML	170 G
1 CUP OR 8 OUNCES OR ½ PINT	240 ML	227 G
1½ CUPS OR 12 OUNCES	350 ML	340 G
2 CUPS OR 1 PINT OR 16 OUNCES	475 ML	454 G
3 CUPS OR 1½ PINTS	700 ML	680 G
4 CUPS OR 2 PINTS OR 1 QUART	950 ML	908 G

INDEX

absinthe
  Baby, It's Way Too Cold Outside, 36
  Not Another Holiday Meltdown, 150
All Frost, No Chill, 64
All I Want for Christmas Is a Negroni, 125
allspice berries
  Spiced Hibiscus Syrup, 77
  Spiced Syrup, 67
amaretto
  I'm Stealing Santa's Rosy Glow, 188
Angostura Bitters
  Butter Late Than Sober, 91
  Love Actually Sucks Punch, 19
  New Year, New Nerves, 134
  Old-Fashioned Christmas Cheer, 118
  Royally Over the Holidays, 137
Aperol
  I'm Stealing Santa's Rosy Glow, 188
apple cider
  Apple-lujah, It's Boozy, 15
  Please, No Nightmares Before Christmas, 192
  Warm My Icy Heart, 103
  Yule Be Fine (Eventually), 44
apple juice
  Blitzen's Backup Plan, 60
apple schnapps
  Spice Spice Baby, 63
applejack
  Blitzen's Backup Plan, 60
  Clove Actually, 84
Apple-lujah, It's Boozy, 15
apples
  Jingle Juice Sangria, 39
  Yule Be Fine (Eventually), 44
Après This, I'm Done, 52
aromatic bitters
  Rye and Shine, It's Christmas-time, 130

Ask Me About My Job Again, I Dare You, 183
Averna Amaro
  Mariah Carey Is My Villain Origin Story, 175

Baby, It's Way Too Cold Outside, 36
Bah Humbug, 55
Baileys Original Irish Cream
  Irish You a Merry Hangover, 104
Basil & Strawberry Shrub, Thai, 194
Bénédictine
  Blitzen's Backup Plan, 60
  New Year, New Nerves, 134
blackberries
  More Cheer? Pass the Wine, 43
  Scrooge-Approved Sparkle, 51
Blitz the Halls, 35
Blitzen's Backup Plan, 60
blood orange bitters
  'Twas the Nightcap Before Christmas, 27
Bloody Merry, 126
Blue, Blue, Blue Christmas, 222
blueberries
  Après This, I'm Done, 52
bourbon
  Apple-lujah, It's Boozy, 15
  Butter Late Than Sober, 91
  Coal for the Soul, 141
  Dead After the Gift Rush, 28
  Family Fiasco Fixer, 24
  I'd Rather Be Home with My Dog, 20
  Is It Too Soon to Fake an Emergency? 32
  Mint Julep for the Jaded, 133
  No Wise Men Here, 229
  Old-Fashioned Christmas Cheer, 118

'Twas the Nightcap Before Christmas, 27
  Yule Regret This, 217
bourbon, vanilla
  Snowed In (And Totally Over It), 218
brandy
  Calories Don't Count at Christmastime, 161
  Eggnog's Overrated, 75
  Honk If You're Lit, 67
  Jingle Juice Sangria, 39
  Liquid Courage, 88
  Ms. Claus's Side Hustle, 200
  Peaked Last Christmas, 56
  When In-Laws Come A-Knocking, 23
brown sugar
  Butter Late Than Sober, 91
  Santa's Nightcap, 83
butter
  Butter Late Than Sober, 91
  Santa's Nightcap, 83
Buzz Off, Holiday Drama, 145

Calories Don't Count at Christmastime, 161
Campari
  All I Want for Christmas Is a Negroni, 125
  Coal for the Soul, 141
candy cane crumbles
  Sip Me Baby One More Time, 210
cardamom pods
  Pour Some Mulling on Me, 72
  Spiced Syrup, 67
caster sugar, about, 119
celery salt
  Bloody Merry, 126
chai tea
  Chai'll Be Tipsy for the Holidays, 100
  Dead After the Gift Rush, 28
Chambord
  Merry Stressmas! 230

Sleighing My Willpower, 214
Champagne
  Ask Me About My Job Again, I Dare You, 183
  Don't Wine About Christmas, 196
  Ho-Ho-Hold My Beer, 199
  I'd Rather Be Stuck in Traffic, 180
  I'll Carol After This One, 179
  I'm Classy, I Swear, 187
  It's 10 A.M. Somewhere, 172
  Jingle All the Way . . . to Therapy, 203
  Merry Mimosa-thon, 12
  Mittens Off, Spirits Up, 191
  Ms. Claus's Side Hustle, 200
  This Is My Emotional Support Drink, 176
  See also wine, sparkling
cherries
  More Cheer? Pass the Wine, 43
Chipotle Rum
  recipe, 227
  Rum-Pa-Pum-Pum, 226
chocolate
  Feliz Navi-done, 107
  Flake It Til You Make It, 87
  Mocha Me Forget My Family Drama, 16
chocolate liqueur, white
  Pass the Liqueur, Not the Figgy Pudding, 213
cider, hard sparkling
  Please, No Nightmares Before Christmas, 192
cinnamon
  Butter Late Than Sober, 91
  Santa's Nightcap, 83
  Yule Be Fine (Eventually), 44
cinnamon apple tea

Index 235

Clove Actually, 84
cinnamon schnapps
   Spice Spice Baby, 63
cinnamon sticks
   Apple-lujah, It's Boozy, 15
   Cinnamon Syrup, 110
   Cinnamon Water, 232
   Feliz Navi-done, 107
   Spiced Hibiscus Syrup, 77
   Spiced Syrup, 67
Cinnamon Syrup
   recipe, 110
   Shhh, It's Spiked, 111
   Son of a Nutcracker, 225
Cinnamon Water
   recipe, 232
   Resting Grinch Face, 233
Clove Actually, 84
cloves
   Apple-lujah, It's Boozy, 15
   Pour Some Mulling on Me, 72
   Spiced Hibiscus Syrup, 77
   Spiced Syrup, 67
club soda
   Blitzen's Backup Plan, 60
   Fizz the Season, 138
   Snowed In (And Totally Over It), 218
Coal for the Soul, 141
Cocchi Americano
   License to Chill, 157
coconut milk
   Blue, Blue, Blue Christmas, 222
coffee/espresso
   Espresso Yourself (or Don't, I Don't Care), 68
   Frothy the Snowman, 96
   How Do I "Irish Goodbye" This Shindig? 108
   I Just Want to Go to Bed, 158
   Irish You a Merry Hangover, 104
   Mocha Me Forget My Family Drama, 16
   Shhh, It's Spiked, 111
Cognac
   Calories Don't Count at Christmastime, 161
   Fa-La-La-La Lit, 76
   I'm Just Here for the Booze, 165
   New Year, New Nerves, 134
   Nipping at Your Nose, 59
   Nog Yourself Out, 71
   Pour Some Mulling on Me, 72
Cointreau

I'm Just Here for the Booze, 165
Merry Stressmas! 230
Ms. Claus's Side Hustle, 200
corn syrup
   Blue, Blue, Blue Christmas, 222
Cosmo Claus, 117
cranberries
   I'm Allergic to This Much Joy, 92
cranberry juice
   Cosmo Claus, 117
   The "I Can't Even," 184
   Merry Stressmas! 230
   On My Last Nerve, 209
cranberry juice, white
   All Frost, No Chill, 64
cranberry sauce
   Sleigh My Name, Sleigh My Name, 206
cream
   Baby, It's Way Too Cold Outside, 36
   Calories Don't Count at Christmastime, 161
   Eggnog's Overrated, 75
   Family Fiasco Fixer, 24
   Mocha Me Forget My Family Drama, 16
   My Face Hurts from Fake Smiling, 166
   Nog Yourself Out, 71
   Sleighing My Willpower, 214
   White Elephant, 153
cream of coconut
   Blue, Blue, Blue Christmas, 222
   Rum-Pa-Pum-Pum, 226
cream soda
   Why'd You Give Me a Partridge in a Pear Tree? 40
crème de cacao
   Calories Don't Count at Christmastime, 161
   Frothy the Snowman, 96
   Sleighing My Willpower, 214
crème de cacao, white
   My Face Hurts from Fake Smiling, 166
crème de menthe, green
   My Face Hurts from Fake Smiling, 166
crème de menthe, white
   Baby, It's Way Too Cold Outside, 36

Pass the Liqueur, Not the Figgy Pudding, 213
crème de pamplemousse rose
   Mittens Off, Spirits Up, 191
crème de violette
   Santa's Little Helper, 142
crème fraîche
   Frothy the Snowman, 96
curaçao, blue
   Blue, Blue, Blue Christmas, 222

Dead After the Gift Rush, 28
Dolin Blanc
   Blitzen's Backup Plan, 60
Domaine de Canton
   Is It Too Soon to Fake an Emergency? 32
Don't Make Me Eat Figgy Pudding, 47
Don't Wine About Christmas, 196

Earl Grey Syrup
   recipe, 102
   Warm My Icy Heart, 103
Earl Grey tea
   Earl Grey Syrup, 102
   Snow Way Out, 95
egg whites
   Baby, It's Way Too Cold Outside, 36
eggnog
   Liquid Courage, 88
Eggnog's Overrated, 75
eggs/egg whites
   Eggnog's Overrated, 75
   Espresso Yourself (or Don't, I Don't Care), 68
   Nog Yourself Out, 71
   Snowed In (And Totally Over It), 218
espresso/coffee
   Espresso Yourself (or Don't, I Don't Care), 68
   Frothy the Snowman, 96
   How Do I "Irish Goodbye" This Shindig? 108
   I Just Want to Go to Bed, 158
   Irish You a Merry Hangover, 104
   Mocha Me Forget My Family Drama, 16
   Shhh, It's Spiked, 111

Fa-La-La-La Lit, 76
Family Fiasco Fixer, 24
Feliz Navi-done, 107
fig bitters

Sleigh My Name, Sleigh My Name, 206
figs/fig juice
   Don't Make Me Eat Figgy Pudding, 47
Fizz the Season, 138
Flake It Til You Make It, 87
Frothy the Snowman, 96

Ghost of Poor Christmas Choices, The, 221
gin
   All I Want for Christmas Is a Negroni, 125
   Blitz the Halls, 35
   Buzz Off, Holiday Drama, 145
   Fizz the Season, 138
   Gin-gle All the Way, 122
   Hark! The Verbena Sings, 99
   I'll Carol After This One, 179
   I'm Allergic to This Much Joy, 92
   Jingle All the Way . . . to Therapy, 203
   License to Chill, 157
   Lime, Gin, and Zero Patience, 146
   Martini, Naughty and Stirred, 17
   Merry Christmas, Ya Filthy Animal, 149
   Not Another Holiday Meltdown, 150
   Pass the Liqueur, Not the Figgy Pudding, 213
   Santa's Little Helper, 142
   Scrooge-Approved Sparkle, 51
   Sip Me Baby One More Time, 210
   Snow Way Out, 95
   Strawberry & Gin Reduction, 197
   This Is My Emotional Support Drink, 176
ginger, fresh
   Pour Some Mulling on Me, 72
ginger beer
   Dead After the Gift Rush, 28
   Honk If You're Lit, 67
   If I Get Run Over by a Reindeer, Can I Bail? 154
   Is It Too Soon to Fake an Emergency? 32
ginger liqueur

Is It Too Soon to Fake an Emergency? 32
Ginger Syrup
   recipe, 49
   Sleigh My Sanity, 48
Gin-gle All the Way, 122
Grand Marnier
   Ask Me About My Job Again, I Dare You, 183
   Bah Humbug, 55
   Have a Pear-y Little Christmas, 31
   Merry Mimosa-thon, 12
   More Cheer? Pass the Wine, 43
   Resting Grinch Face, 233
grapefruit juice
   Blitz the Halls, 35
grapefruit soda
   I'd Rather Be Stuck in Traffic, 180
grapes
   Sleigh My Sanity, 48
   Why'd You Give Me a Partridge in a Pear Tree? 40
grenadine
   Love Actually Sucks Punch, 19
   When In-Laws Come A-Knocking, 23

half-and-half
   Espresso Yourself (or Don't, I Don't Care), 68
   Feliz Navi-done, 107
   Peaked Last Christmas, 56
   Snowed In (And Totally Over It), 218
Hark! The Verbena Sings, 99
Have a Pear-y Little Christmas, 31
Herbsaint
   Baby, It's Way Too Cold Outside, 36
   Ho-Ho-Holy Crap That's Strong, 169
hibiscus blossoms
   Spiced Hibiscus Syrup, 77
hibiscus tea
   I'm Allergic to This Much Joy, 92
Ho-Ho-Hold My Beer, 199
Ho-Ho-Holy Crap That's Strong, 169
honey
   Chai'll Be Tipsy for the Holidays, 100
   Pour Some Mulling on Me, 72
honey syrup

Buzz Off, Holiday Drama, 145
Yule Regret This, 217
Honk If You're Lit, 67
horseradish
   Bloody Merry, 126
How Do I "Irish Goodbye" This Shindig? 108

"I Can't Even," The, 184
I Just Want to Go to Bed, 158
I'd Rather Be Home with My Dog, 20
I'd Rather Be Stuck in Traffic, 180
If I Get Run Over by a Reindeer, Can I Bail? 154
I'll Carol After This One, 179
I'm Allergic to This Much Joy, 92
I'm Classy, I Swear, 187
I'm Just Here for the Booze, 165
I'm Stealing Santa's Rosy Glow, 188
Irish You a Merry Hangover, 104
Is It Too Soon to Fake an Emergency? 32
It's 10 A.M. Somewhere, 172
I've Hit My Holiday Cheer Limit, 195

Jingle All the Way . . . to Therapy, 203
Jingle Juice Sangria, 39

Kahlúa
   Espresso Yourself (or Don't, I Don't Care), 68
   Frothy the Snowman, 96
   I Just Want to Go to Bed, 158
   White Elephant, 153
key lime juice
   Hark! The Verbena Sings, 99

Lavender Syrup
   Après This, I'm Done, 52
   recipe, 52
lemon juice
   Bah Humbug, 55
   Bloody Merry, 126
   Buzz Off, Holiday Drama, 145
   Fizz the Season, 138
   Have a Pear-y Little Christmas, 31
   I'll Carol After This One, 179

I'm Allergic to This Much Joy, 92
I'm Classy, I Swear, 187
I'm Just Here for the Booze, 165
I'm Stealing Santa's Rosy Glow, 188
Is It Too Soon to Fake an Emergency? 32
I've Hit My Holiday Cheer Limit, 195
Jingle All the Way . . . to Therapy, 203
Nipping at Your Nose, 59
Santa's Little Helper, 142
Scrooge-Approved Sparkle, 51
Snowed In (And Totally Over It), 218
This Is My Emotional Support Drink, 176
Toddy Claus Is Comin' to Town, 80
'Twas the Nightcap Before Christmas, 27
Warm My Icy Heart, 103
Yule Regret This, 217
lemon peel/zest
   Oleo Saccharum, 33
   Pour Some Mulling on Me, 72
lemon verbena leaves
   Hark! The Verbena Sings, 99
lemon wheels
   Jingle Juice Sangria, 39
lemons
   Dead After the Gift Rush, 28
License to Chill, 157
Lillet Blanc
   License to Chill, 157
Lillet Rosé
   Blitz the Halls, 35
Lime, Gin, and Zero Patience, 146
lime juice
   All Frost, No Chill, 64
   Ask Me About My Job Again, I Dare You, 183
   Blitz the Halls, 35
   Bloody Merry, 126
   Cosmo Claus, 117
   Gin-gle All the Way, 122
   If I Get Run Over by a Reindeer, Can I Bail? 154
   Lime, Gin, and Zero Patience, 146
   Merry-rita, 114
   On My Last Nerve, 209

Resting Grinch Face, 233
Silent Night, Daiquiri Bright, 129
Sleigh My Name, Sleigh My Name, 206
Son of a Nutcracker, 225
"Too Much Family Time" Mojito, 162
lime wheels
   Jingle Juice Sangria, 39
Liquid Courage, 88
Love Actually Sucks Punch, 19

Madeira
   Nog Yourself Out, 71
maple syrup
   Clove Actually, 84
maraschino liqueur
   Santa's Little Helper, 142
Mariah Carey Is My Villain Origin Story, 175
marshmallows
   Flake It Til You Make It, 87
Martini, Naughty and Stirred, 121
Merry Christmas, Ya Filthy Animal, 149
Merry Mimosa-thon, 12
Merry Stressmas! 230
Merry-rita, 114
metric conversions, 234
Mexican hot chocolate
   Feliz Navi-done, 107
mezcal
   Shhh, It's Spiked, 111
   See also tequila
milk
   Chai'll Be Tipsy for the Holidays, 100
   Eggnog's Overrated, 75
   Espresso Yourself (or Don't, I Don't Care), 68
   Feliz Navi-done, 107
   Flake It Til You Make It, 87
   I'd Rather Be Home with My Dog, 20
   Mocha Me Forget My Family Drama, 16
   Nog Yourself Out, 71
   Peaked Last Christmas, 56
mint leaves
   If I Get Run Over by a Reindeer, Can I Bail? 154
   Mint Julep for the Jaded, 133
   "Too Much Family Time" Mojito, 162
Mittens Off, Spirits Up, 191

Index 237

Mocha Me Forget My Family Drama, 16
More Cheer? Pass the Wine, 43
Ms. Claus's Side Hustle, 200
My Face Hurts from Fake Smiling, 166

New Year, New Nerves, 134
Nipping at Your Nose, 59
No Wise Men Here, 229
Nog Yourself Out, 71
Not Another Holiday Meltdown, 150
nutmeg
    Butter Late Than Sober, 91
    Eggnog's Overrated, 75
    Feliz Navi-done, 107
    Santa's Nightcap, 83

Old-Fashioned Christmas Cheer, 118
Oleo Saccharum
    Is It Too Soon to Fake an Emergency? 32
    recipe, 33
olive brine
    Merry Christmas, Ya Filthy Animal, 149
On My Last Nerve, 209
orange blossom water
    Baby, It's Way Too Cold Outside, 36
orange juice
    It's 10 A.M. Somewhere, 172
    Jingle Juice Sangria, 39
    Love Actually Sucks Punch, 19
    Merry Mimosa-thon, 12
    Resting Grinch Face, 233
    Rum-Pa-Pum-Pum, 226
    'Twas the Nightcap Before Christmas, 27
    Why'd You Give Me a Partridge in a Pear Tree? 40
orange liqueur
    Blitz the Halls, 35
    Fa-La-La-La Lit, 76
    Merry-rita, 114
    On My Last Nerve, 209
    Nipping at Your Nose, 59
    Son of a Nutcracker, 225
orange peels/zest
    Apple-lujah, It's Boozy, 15
    Mocha Me Forget My Family Drama, 16
    Oleo Saccharum, 33

Pour Some Mulling on Me, 72
Santa's Nightcap, 83
oranges
    Bah Humbug, 55
    Jingle Juice Sangria, 39
    Yule Be Fine (Eventually), 44

Pass the Liqueur, Not the Figgy Pudding, 213
peach nectar
    I'm Classy, I Swear, 187
Peach Vodka
    The "I Can't Even," 184
    recipe, 185
Peaked Last Christmas, 56
pear cider
    Honk If You're Lit, 67
pears
    Have a Pear-y Little Christmas, 31
    Why'd You Give Me a Partridge in a Pear Tree? 40
pepper, black
    Bloody Merry, 126
peppermint schnapps
    Sip Me Baby One More Time, 210
peppers, chili
    Feliz Navi-done, 107
Peychaud's Bitters
    Fa-La-La-La Lit, 76
    Ho-Ho-Holy Crap That's Strong, 169
    Honk If You're Lit, 67
    New Year, New Nerves, 134
Pimm's No. 1
    I've Hit My Holiday Cheer Limit, 195
pineapple juice
    Blue, Blue, Blue Christmas, 222
    Love Actually Sucks Punch, 19
    Rum-Pa-Pum-Pum, 226
pisco
    I've Hit My Holiday Cheer Limit, 195
Please, No Nightmares Before Christmas, 192
plums
    More Cheer? Pass the Wine, 43
    Sleigh My Sanity, 48
pomegranate juice
    Don't Make Me Eat Figgy Pudding, 47
    Spiced Syrup, 67

Port wine
    Nipping at Your Nose, 59
Pour Some Mulling on Me, 72
Prosecco
    I'm Stealing Santa's Rosy Glow, 188

raspberries
    Après This, I'm Done, 52
    Bah Humbug, 55
    Don't Make Me Eat Figgy Pudding, 47
    Scrooge-Approved Sparkle, 51
Resting Grinch Face, 233
Rosemary Syrup
    The Ghost of Poor Christmas Choices, 221
    Have a Pear-y Little Christmas, 31
    recipe, 30
Royally Over the Holidays, 137
rum
    When In-Laws Come A-Knocking, 23
rum, aged
    Chipotle Rum, 227
    Fa-La-La-La Lit, 76
    Family Fiasco Fixer, 24
    Flake It Til You Make It, 87
    Honk If You're Lit, 67
    Mocha Me Forget My Family Drama, 16
    Rum-Pa-Pum-Pum, 226
    Santa's Nightcap, 83
rum, dark
    Eggnog's Overrated, 75
    Liquid Courage, 88
    Love Actually Sucks Punch, 19
    Nog Yourself Out, 71
rum, light
    Love Actually Sucks Punch, 19
rum, spiced
    Spice Spice Baby, 63
rum, white
    Blue, Blue, Blue Christmas, 222
    Silent Night, Daiquiri Bright, 129
    "Too Much Family Time" Mojito, 162
rye whiskey
    Ho-Ho-Holy Crap That's Strong, 169
    New Year, New Nerves, 134

Old-Fashioned Christmas Cheer, 118
Rye and Shine, It's Christmastime, 130

Saffron Syrup
    Hark! The Verbena Sings, 99
    recipe, 98
Santa's Little Helper, 142
Santa's Nightcap, 83
Scotch whiskey
    Chai'll Be Tipsy for the Holidays, 100
    Espresso Yourself (or Don't, I Don't Care), 68
    Frothy the Snowman, 96
    Have a Pear-y Little Christmas, 31
    No Wise Men Here, 229
    Royally Over the Holidays, 137
    Toddy Claus Is Comin' to Town, 80
Scrooge-Approved Sparkle, 51
seltzer water
    Don't Make Me Eat Figgy Pudding, 47
    The Ghost of Poor Christmas Choices, 221
    More Cheer? Pass the Wine, 43
    Sleigh My Sanity, 48
seltzer water, lemon-lime
    All Frost, No Chill, 64
    Spice Spice Baby, 63
sherry, Amontillado
    Is It Too Soon to Fake an Emergency? 32
sherry, Pedro Ximénez
    How Do I "Irish Goodbye" This Shindig? 108
Shhh, It's Spiked, 111
Silent Night, Daiquiri Bright, 129
Simple Syrup
    Baby, It's Way Too Cold Outside, 36
    Espresso Yourself (or Don't, I Don't Care), 68
    Family Fiasco Fixer, 24
    Fizz the Season, 138
    How Do I "Irish Goodbye" This Shindig? 108
    I'd Rather Be Home with My Dog, 20
    I'll Carol After This One, 179
    I'm Allergic to This Much Joy, 92
    Jingle Juice Sangria, 39

Liquid Courage, 88
Nipping at Your Nose, 59
Peaked Last Christmas, 56
  recipe, 21
Snow Way Out, 95
Son of a Nutcracker, 225
Toddy Claus Is Comin' to Town, 80
"Too Much Family Time" Mojito, 162
'Twas the Nightcap Before Christmas, 27
Sip Me Baby One More Time, 210
Sleigh My Name, Sleigh My Name, 206
Sleigh My Sanity, 48
Sleighing My Willpower, 214
Snow Way Out, 95
Snowed In (And Totally Over It), 218
Son of a Nutcracker, 225
Spice Spice Baby, 63
Spiced Hibiscus Syrup
  Fa-La-La-La Lit, 76
  recipe, 77
Spiced Syrup
  Honk If You're Lit, 67
  recipe, 67
star anise pods
  Pour Some Mulling on Me, 72
St-Germain
  Mittens Off, Spirits Up, 191
  Sleigh My Name, Sleigh My Name, 206
stout
  Ho-Ho-Hold My Beer, 199
strawberries
  Don't Wine About Christmas, 196
  Strawberry & Gin Reduction, 197
  Thai Basil & Strawberry Shrub, 194
sweetened condensed milk
  Feliz Navi-done, 107

Tabasco
  Yule Regret This, 217
tea, black
  Is It Too Soon to Fake an Emergency? 32
  Snow Way Out, 95
tea, chai
  Chai'll Be Tipsy for the Holidays, 100
  Dead After the Gift Rush, 28

tea, cinnamon apple
  Clove Actually, 84
tea, Earl Grey
  Earl Grey Syrup, 102
  Snow Way Out, 95
tea, hibiscus
  I'm Allergic to This Much Joy, 92
tequila
  Ask Me About My Job Again, I Dare You, 183
  Feliz Navi-done, 107
  I'd Rather Be Stuck in Traffic, 180
  Merry-rita, 114
  On My Last Nerve, 209
  Sleighing My Willpower, 214
  Son of a Nutcracker, 225
  See also mezcal
Thai Basil & Strawberry Shrub
  I've Hit My Holiday Cheer Limit, 195
  recipe, 194
This Is My Emotional Support Drink, 176
Toddy Claus Is Comin' to Town, 80
tomato juice
  Bloody Merry, 126
tonic water
  Gin-gle All the Way, 122
"Too Much Family Time" Mojito, 162
triple sec
  All Frost, No Chill, 64
  Cosmo Claus, 117
  Love Actually Sucks Punch, 19
  Not Another Holiday Meltdown, 150
  'Twas the Nightcap Before Christmas, 27

vanilla beans
  Spiced Hibiscus Syrup, 77
vanilla extract
  Eggnog's Overrated, 75
  Feliz Navi-done, 107
  I'd Rather Be Home with My Dog, 21
  Peaked Last Christmas, 56
  Santa's Nightcap, 83
vermouth, dry
  Martini, Naughty and Stirred, 121
  Merry Christmas, Ya Filthy Animal, 149
  Not Another Holiday Meltdown, 150

Sip Me Baby One More Time, 210
vermouth, sweet
  All I Want for Christmas Is a Negroni, 125
  Coal for the Soul, 141
  New Year, New Nerves, 134
  Royally Over the Holidays, 137
  Rye and Shine, It's Christmas-time, 130
vodka
  Bloody Merry, 126
  Cosmo Claus, 117
  The "I Can't Even," 184
  I Just Want to Go to Bed, 158
  If I Get Run Over by a Reindeer, Can I Bail? 154
  License to Chill, 157
  Peach Vodka, 185
  Resting Grinch Face, 233
  Sleigh My Name, Sleigh My Name, 206
  White Elephant, 153
vodka, apple
  Yule Be Fine (Eventually), 44
vodka, citron
  All Frost, No Chill, 64

Warm My Icy Heart, 103
When In-Laws Come A-Knocking, 23
whipped cream
  Snow Way Out, 95
  Warm My Icy Heart, 103
whiskey
  The Ghost of Poor Christmas Choices, 221
  How Do I "Irish Goodbye" This Shindig? 108
  Irish You a Merry Hangover, 104
  Mariah Carey Is My Villain Origin Story, 175
  No Wise Men Here, 229
  Please, No Nightmares Before Christmas, 192
  When In-Laws Come A-Knocking, 23
  See also bourbon; rye whiskey; Scotch whiskey
White Elephant, 153
Why'd You Give Me a Partridge in a Pear Tree? 40
wine, red
  Don't Make Me Eat Figgy Pudding, 47

Don't Wine About Christmas, 196
Jingle Juice Sangria, 39
More Cheer? Pass the Wine, 43
Pour Some Mulling on Me, 72
Sleigh My Sanity, 48
Why'd You Give Me a Partridge in a Pear Tree? 40
Yule Be Fine (Eventually), 44
wine, sparkling
  Ask Me About My Job Again, I Dare You, 183
  Bah Humbug, 55
  Don't Wine About Christmas, 196
  Fa-La-La-La Lit, 76
  Ho-Ho-Hold My Beer, 199
  The "I Can't Even," 184
  I'd Rather Be Stuck in Traffic, 180
  I'll Carol After This One, 179
  I'm Classy, I Swear, 187
  I'm Stealing Santa's Rosy Glow, 188
  It's 10 A.M. Somewhere, 172
  I've Hit My Holiday Cheer Limit, 195
  Jingle All the Way . . . to Therapy, 203
  Mariah Carey Is My Villain Origin Story, 175
  Merry Mimosathon, 12
  Mittens Off, Spirits Up, 191
  Ms. Claus's Side Hustle, 200
  Scrooge-Approved Sparkle, 51
  This Is My Emotional Support Drink, 176
  Warm My Icy Heart, 103
wine, white
  Après This, I'm Done, 52
Worcestershire sauce
  Bloody Merry, 126

Yule Be Fine (Eventually), 44
Yule Regret This, 217

Index 239

ABOUT CIDER MILL PRESS BOOK PUBLISHERS

Good ideas ripen with time. From seed to harvest, Cider Mill Press brings fine reading, information, and entertainment together between the covers of its creatively crafted books. Our Cider Mill bears fruit twice a year, publishing a new crop of titles each spring and fall.

"Where good books are ready for press"
501 Nelson Place
Nashville, Tennessee 37214

cidermillpress.com